SSSP

Springer Series in Social Psychology

SSSP

William N. Morris
In association with Paula P. Schnurr

Mood

The Frame of Mind

Springer-Verlag New York Berlin Heidelberg
London Paris Tokyo Hong Kong

William N. Morris
Department of Psychology
Dartmouth College
Hanover, New Hampshire 03755
USA

Library of Congress Cataloging-in-Publication Data
Morris, William N.
Mood : the frame of mind.
(Springer series in social psychology)
1. Mood (Psychology) 2. Affect (Psychology)
I. Title. II. Series. [DNLM: 1. Affect. BF 511 M877m]
BF521.M67 1989 152.4 89–21739
ISBN-13:978-1-4612-8190-0

Printed on acid-free paper.

Typeset by Impressions, Inc., Madison, Wisconsin.

9 8 7 6 5 4 3 2 1

ISBN-13:978-1-4612-8190-0 e-ISBN-13:978-1-4612-3648-1
DOI: 10.1007/978-1-4612-3648-1

For my mother and father.

Preface

This is a book about moods. Though I will define the term somewhat more carefully in Chapter 1, it might help to note here that I use the word "mood" to refer to affective states which do not stimulate the relatively specific response tendencies we associate with "emotions". Instead, moods are pervasive and global, having the capability of influencing a broad range of thought processes and behavior.

My interest in mood was provoked initially by the empirical and conceptual contributions of Alice Isen and her colleagues. What fascinated me most was the suggestion first made in a paper by Clark & Isen (1982) that mood seemed to affect behavior in two very different ways, i.e., mood could "automatically" influence the availability of mood-related cognitions and, thereby, behavior, or mood, especially of the "bad" variety, might capture our attention in that if it were sufficiently aversive we might consciously try to get rid of it, a "controlled" or "strategic" response.

Though stimulated by the automatic-controlled distinction as a way of making sense of the literature on the effects of mood on cognition and behavior, I no longer find it a fully satisfactory way of categorizing the full variety of processes associated with mood and, thus, in Chapter 1, I offer the classic "figure-ground"[1] distinction in its place. The inability of the automatic-controlled distinction to subsume all of the processes and phenomena associated with mood is not surprising when one considers that the literature reviews which spawned it (Clark & Isen, 1982; Isen, 1984) surveyed a rather limited subset from the domain of empirical studies of mood. Though laboratory and field experiments where mood was manipulated were included, two other literatures which purport to be concerned with mood states, namely the rather large literature which examines mood via self-report (e.g.,

[1] I am not the first to apply the figure-ground distinction to differentiate between affective phenomena. Ewert (1970) used it to distinguish between what he called "feelings" and "emotions", both of which differed from "moods" in his scheme. However his definitions of these terms were rather idiosyncratic, making the application of the figure-ground metaphor rather different in effect from that found here.

Nowlis, 1965; Watson & Tellegen, 1985; Wessman & Ricks, 1966) and the even larger body of information dealing with mood "disorders" (e.g., Depue, 1979; Whybrow, Akiskal, & McKinney, 1984), were left out.

Though Isen failed to discuss her reasons for omitting consideration of these literatures, there certainly are some good ones. As for the self-report literature, there is ample reason to be concerned about the ability of subjects to report their moods accurately. A great deal of evidence now exists attesting to the problematic nature of self-reports about internal processes (Nisbett & Wilson, 1977; Nisbett & Ross, 1980), some of it quite specifically addressed to self-reports of mood (Wilson, Laser, & Stone, 1982). As for the literature on mood disorders, the problem is that we do not yet know whether these reflect the same processes as "everyday" moods, differing only quantitatively on an intensity dimension, or whether they are fundamentally different occurrences with qualitatively different causes.

Whether or not these reasons or others prompted Isen's decision to truncate her review of the mood literature, it seems a good time to attempt a conceptualization of moods capable of encompassing more of the relevant data. Such an effort seems timely because the subject of moods is currently quite topical in the field of psychology. Isen's work appears to have stimulated a good deal of interest among cognitive psychologists, especially in the relationship between mood and memory. As for social psychology, no less a figure than Tomkins (1981) has predicted that the decade of the 80's will be the decade that belongs to affect, this after a preoccupation in the 70's with "cold" cognitive processes such as attribution and schema-driven processing. Tomkins' prediction is being borne out as we approach the end of the decade, especially with regard to mood. Finally, research activity by those interested in mood from a clinical perspective has reached a fever pitch, a fact which is probably due to the heuristic power of the theories currently vying as candidates for explaining mood disorders, especially depression (e.g., Abramson, Seligman, & Teasdale, 1978; Beck, 1967; Lewinsohn, 1974; Siever & Davis, 1985). The result of all this activity is a rapidly accumulating data base as well as a steady influx of conceptual advance.

I approach the task in Chapter 1 by seeking to establish the legitimacy of mood as a distinctive hypothetical construct, separable from emotion. Reviewing the writings of those psychologists who have attempted to preserve a distinctive status for the phenomenon of mood, namely Edith Jacobsen (1957), Vincent Nowlis (1965) and Alice Isen (1984), I discovered that despite enormous differences in theoretical persuasion (Jacobsen is a Freudian, Nowlis is of the behaviorist persuasion and Isen one of the current group of cognitively oriented social psychologists), they share broad areas of agreement about the nature of mood. This substantial area of overlap defines a core of meaning for the term "mood" which distinguishes it from emotion.

Chapter 2 acknowledges the variety of theories about affect that seem especially pertinent to understanding mood as it is defined in Chapter 1. More specifically, these theories are probed for their ability to explain the defining characteristic of mood, that it is global and pervasive in its effects. Interestingly, though the theories reflect sharply differing assumptions, rest on nonoverlapping data bases, and attribute the emergence of mood to different reasons, they appear to concur in identifying the conditions that favor the occurrence of mood as opposed to emotion, namely, that the affect arises in circumstances which interfere with labeling or attributional processes.

The next five chapters (3 through 7) are more empirically oriented. Chapters 3 and 4 discuss what is known about the relationship of mood onset to environmental events and endogenous processes. The knowledgable reader will no doubt detect in this partition a similarity to the various distinctions which have appeared in the clinical realm, e.g., exogenous-endogenous, psychotic-neurotic, autonomous-reactive (see Whybrow et al, 1984 for a discussion of these diagnostic categories). It is recognized that the distinction between external and internal "causes" of moods is an oversimplification of the truth; the hope is that it is a useful oversimplification.

Chapter 5 considers the large and steadily expanding literatures on the effects of everyday mood on cognition, perception, and social behavior. It more than establishes that the effects of mood are global and pervasive. In addition, the asymmetry between the effects of good and bad mood that led Clark and Isen (1982) to postulate the automatic-controlled distinction now appears to be more firmly established as an empirical phenomenon although there is still precious little data relevant to understanding the conditions that determine which sort of response is elicited. Finally, though associative network theories (Bower, 1981; Isen, 1984) still serve as the most common heuristic framework for generating studies and integrating results, a variety of findings stubbornly resist being explained this way leading me to consider an alternative account.

Chapter 6 surveys what is known about individual differences in moodiness. However, much of the chapter is given over to a discussion of various controversies surrounding the nature of the fundamental dimensions of the self-reported mood response. For example, are good and bad moods polar opposites and incompatible with each other or are they orthogonal and, thus, occasionally experienced simultaneously in the sense of ambivalence? Though there has been a sharp upswing in research activity here, probably as part of the general surge of interest in affect, I find too much uncritical acceptance of the validity of self-reports. This problem is particularly striking if one accepts the argument that mood is most often out of awareness. Until more of an effort is made to supplement self-report data with indirect "behavioral" mood measures we will be left with the nagging concern that we are getting half or less of the story and the part we're not getting has a different plot from the part we've got.

In Chapter 7, I move to the very edge of my competence (some will think I moved considerably beyond that) in order to consider the controversial proposition referred to as the Continuity Hypothesis. This hypothesis assumes that everyday variations in mood and the more extreme peaks and valleys we associate with clinically significant episodes of mania and depression can be explained in similar ways. The alternative view is that major affective disorders are largely the result of endogenous processes whereas everyday variations in mood are primarily the result of events. Most clinicians quickly write off the Continuity position though they acknowledge that some small proportion of clinically significant mood dysfunction may be purely reactive. In support of this position, they most commonly note that patients with a mood disorder present with a *syndrome* of symptoms, signifying a disease entity. The implication, of course, is that such syndromes do not characterize everyday elation and depression. Chapter 7 surveys the existing literature in an attempt to evaluate these claims.

Finally, in a brief Postscript I argue for a return to thinking about mood from a functional point of view. Early mood theorists, e.g., Jacobsen (1957) and Nowlis (Nowlis & Nowlis, 1956) saw mood as being part of a system designed to accomplish psychological self-regulation. Much of the data generated by more recent interests in the relationship between mood and cognitive processes are made more sensible when viewed from a self-regulatory perspective.

I hope readers will be stimulated by my attempt to unravel the very real mysteries about everyday affect. However, my most fundamental purpose is to continue the effort of my predecessors Vincent Nowlis, Edith Jacobsen, Alden Wessman, and Alice Isen, all of whom recognized that moods are distinctive affective states deserving of special attention. If there is value in this enterprise it is because a larger net more widely cast can catch a bigger fish.

Acknowledgments. The prospect of writing a book had always seemed dauntingly difficult. Two students, Ann Cianchette and Nora P. Reilly, provided me with the encouragement I needed to initiate the task. During the course of the actual writing, I was sustained by the joy brought to me by my wife, Shirley E. Napps, and my son, Michael, the intellectual companionship provided by my colleague, Paula Schnurr, and the patience of Bob Kidd at Springer-Verlag. Though they are not responsible for any shortcomings that remain, Jay Hull John Lanzetta, and Paula Schnurr made helpful criticisms of portions of the manuscript. Fran Perillo, Diane Tessier, Julie Ackerman, and George Wolford were there when I needed help, especially in those last desperate hours when every clerical task seemed monumental. And finally, thanks to Jim Kingsepp at Springer-Verlag, for calmly seeing me through the steps necessary to producing a finished product.

William N. Morris

Contents

Chapter 1
The Concept of Mood

One of the popular catchphrases associated with the "encounter-group" movement of the 1960s and the 1970s was "getting in touch with your feelings." The general idea seemed to be that we were so oversocialized, inhibited, and precariously tilted toward rationality that we were becoming alienated from the emotional side of our nature. As sensitivity to our most primitive and fundamental reactions deteriorated, we supposedly risked an existence driven by logic and social norms, a cold and robotic prospect. But as observers of the "touchy-feely" scene know, the *yin* to this *yang* was equally unpalatable. Ranging from self-absorption to mind-altering drugs and sexual experiment, the goal of augmenting the sensuous opportunities in life left little time (and patience) for the mundane problems of existence.

Ignoring feelings and celebrating feelings each have their place in a properly lived life, but a more precise prescription requires that we understand the *nature and function* of feelings. In large part, that is what this book is about.

Defining Mood

Any monograph about a specific construct or intervening variable must begin by carefully defining it, being certain to differentiate it from related constructs. This is particularly important when the construct label has been subjected to a history of casual use. This appears to be the case with "mood"; many emotion theorists seem to find no special purpose for the term "mood," using it interchangeably with other terms such as affect or emotion, for example, Bower (1981), Solomon (1980), Watson & Tellegen (1985).

However, there is a small group of theorists including the behaviorist Vincent Nowlis (1965), the neuropsychologist Karl Pribram (1970), the psychodynamicist Edith Jacobsen (1957), and the cognitivist Alice Isen (1984), who have attempted to preserve a distinctive meaning for the term *mood.* The significant degree of overlap in their descriptions of mood suggests a core of meaning; the diversity of their theoretical backgrounds encourages the belief that there is a reality to match the meaning.

The clearest consensus among these theorists concerns the breadth of influence that moods have. As compared with emotions, which are thought to instigate a relatively limited set of responses, moods are capable of altering our affective, cognitive, and behavioral responses to a wide array of objects and events. Jacobsen (1957), while describing a particular instance of a mood, put it this way:

> These changing moods found expression in particular qualities of his feelings as well as of his thought processes and his performances during the whole day, no matter what their object had been. They affected his emotional responses, his attitudes and his behavior, with regard not only to his girl friend but also to his work and to the whole surrounding object world, and influenced the choice and the course of all his activities. (p. 75)

Isen (1984) suggests similarly that the pervasiveness or lack of specificity of mood is its most defining characteristic, especially when one attempts to distinguish between mood and emotion:

> Compare, for example, anger with irritability. While the emotion of anger often has a particular referent or is directed at a particular object which caused the anger, and has sets of behaviors, such as glaring or shouting or hitting or insulting, associated with it, the feeling state [Isen uses "feeling" or "feeling state" interchangeably with "mood"] of irritability that may accompany the anger . . . is more global in its effects and indicators. This component of angry affect has neither specific targets nor specific behavioral impulses associated with it. (p. 186)

In addition to the consensus that the effects of mood are general and pervasive whereas those of emotion are relatively specific, mood theorists also agree that moods are *typically* less intense than emotions. Though this may be a valid way of differentiating modal moods from emotions, my own inclination is to reject intensity as a defining characteristic. This decision has the advantage of permitting full consideration in Chapter 7 of the "continuity" hypothesis (Blatt, D'Afflitti, & Quinlan, 1976; Depue, Slater, Wolfstetter-Kausch, Klein, Gopelrud, & Farr, 1981; Whybrow et al., 1984) which supposes that clinically significant mood disorders, which usually entail quite intense feelings, differ only quantitatively (rather than qualitatively) from everyday variations in moods.

A third area of agreement concerns the role or function played by moods. Nowlis, Pribram, and Jacobsen, explicitly concur that moods inform us about our general state of being.[1] Pribram (1970) describes them as "monitors" that reflect our appraisal of our life circumstances (pp. 51–52), Jacobsen (1957) called them "barometers of the ego" (p. 75), and Nowlis (1965, 1970; Nowlis & Nowlis, 1956), who has been most explicit on this point, defines moods as:

---

[1]This idea is implicit in Isen's position in that she acknowledges that moods can instigate behavior designed to maintain our good moods and "repair" our bad ones. In such instances, mood would appear to have cue value although it would be taking a liberty with Isen's position to suggest that moods are "informative" since that term implies conscious recognition.

> an intervening variable or predispositional factor that is a source of information or discriminable stimuli to the organism, about the current functioning characteristics of the organism. (Nowlis & Nowlis, 1956, p. 352)

In this capacity, moods are seen as facilitating self-regulation. Presumably the impulse to engage in some activity, as implied when someone says they are "in a mood" to do this or that, is the outcome of registration of a need of some sort.

More recently, Mandler (1975) has made a similar argument about the role of autonomic nervous system arousal in affective processes. He suggests that one function of such arousal is that it acts as a back-up alarm system, goading the individual to search the environment to find and appraise the meaning and significance of the events that apparently led to the arousal. Berscheid (1983) suggests that we should distinguish between such temporarily unexplained arousal and explained arousal, referring to the latter as "emotion" and the former as a "feeling state." Unfortunately, neither Mandler nor Berscheid explain the circumstances under which appraisals fail to occur; I will suggest in Chapter 2 that there are a variety of such circumstances and the most likely consequence of the experience of affect combined with the absence of appraisal is affect that is pervasive in its effects, that is, mood.

In summary, moods can be defined as affective states that are capable of influencing a broad array of potential responses, many of which seem quite unrelated to the mood-precipitating event. As compared with emotions, moods are typically less intense affective states and are thought to be involved in the instigation of self-regulatory processes.

The consensus on these various points is striking given the different theoretical backgrounds of the theorists. There is one further area of agreement which I have not mentioned to this point. It is that moods, though possessing enough unity to justify the existence of the construct, have manifestations that are sufficiently different so as to require a categorical differentiation.

Distinguishing the Major Types of Mood

Though they disagree on the category labels, Jacobsen, Nowlis, and Isen all suggest that mood has two different forms. The first such dichotomy was offered by Nowlis and Nowlis (1956), who suggested that moods might be "conscious" or "unconscious":

> Mood as an intervening variable may have a direct (unconscious) effect on the probabilities of occurrence of certain responses in certain situations. . . . Here mood is like Skinner's (1953) concept of predisposition, a state that directly changes the probabilities of certain acts in certain situations. . . . [W]e define conscious mood as the response to discriminative stimuli supplied by the hypothetical mood state. We . . . make the assumption . . . that these cues, which supply information about the current functioning of the

> organism, are involved in the self-monitoring and self-regulation of complex behavior. (pp. 352–353)

It was Nowlis' view that the most common manifestation of "conscious" mood was the verbal labeling of one's mood state. Indeed, applying the verbal label seemed to mark the transition between unconscious to conscious.

> To say "I feel angry" is a response one has learned to say when in an angry mood; its probability of occurrence is greater in that mood than in other moods. It is, as Ryle (1949) suggests, one of the many things one is disposed to do and which one sometimes finds oneself doing when in any angry mood. As the individual utters it, whether publicly or privately, its content and mode of expression may cause him for the first time to note that he is in an angry mood. (Nowlis, 1965, p. 354)

Though Nowlis was not explicit about this matter, it appears that he thought moods were conscious or unconscious as a function of crossing a simple sensory threshold. Recall that the purpose of mood was to inform the individual of his general state and needs. Presumably as the needs responsible for the mood state became more pressing, the mood would cross threshold and attract attention, making an instrumental response more likely and/or efficient. Similar models could presumably be applied to other self-regulatory systems such as those involved in the control of eating and drinking behavior.

Interestingly, after offering the unconscious-conscious distinction in 1956, Nowlis made no further mention of it in major presentations of his position (Nowlis, 1965, 1970). It is possible that he discontinued its use because such a distinction became generally disreputable during the 1960s. Another potential explanation is that Nowlis' research on mood relied almost exclusively on a self-report scale called the Mood Adjective Check List (MACL) which he and his colleagues developed during the late 1950s and early 1960s at the University of Rochester. Thus, Nowlis' operational definition of mood was of the conscious variety, precluding comments about unconscious mood.

For Edith Jacobsen (1957), the dichotomy was between "normal" and "pathological" moods, reflecting her clinical experience and outlook. Like Nowlis, Jacobsen based her differentiation between the two types of mood on the degree to which the person was aware of the true nature of his or her feelings. According to Jacobsen, though all moods involve some denial in the sense that the feelings produced by the affect-inducing event are generalized (i.e, transferred) rather than being attached to specific objects in the environment:

> the nature of this denial is quite different in normal and in pathologically motivated mood conditions.... [I]n normal moods the denial does not extend to the provocative external event or to its immediate emotional impact... [they] can be recognized as temporary ego states due to conscious reactions to realistic events. (p. 94)

Pathological moods, on the other hand, involve unconscious conflicts that interfere with reality testing and prolong the mood. In severe cases, the denial may even extend to lack of recognition of the mood itself, a problem Jacobsen referred to as the failure of "mood awareness."

Isen (Clark & Isen, 1982; Isen, 1984, 1985) has recently introduced a third distinction. She believes that mood phenomena result from the sorts of cognitive processes that are instigated by mood-inducing events. Following Posner & Snyder (1975), who first introduced the distinction, Clark and Isen (1982) suggested that the cognitive processes that occur during moods are of two types: "automatic" and "controlled." Automatic cognitive processes occur without intention or awareness and do not interfere with other ongoing cognitive processes, whereas controlled processes, being both effortful and conscious, occupy our limited capacity information processing system and thus can disrupt other cognitive activities. Notice that once again, the two types of mood differ at least in part in terms of how aware we are of them.

Clark and Isen (1982) attribute the bulk of mood effects to automatic processes. Subtly, and almost irresistibly, the hedonic tone associated with the mood-inducing event causes us to retrieve a string of similarly toned thoughts which influence our judgments, decisions, and behaviors. On some occasions, though, mood may affect us in a different way, via controlled cognitive processes. These are times when the presence of the mood becomes a factor in conscious decision-making or problem solving. The specific instances discussed by Clark and Isen (1982) are self-regulatory in nature, that is, people in good moods who make decisions designed to protect their mood from an impending negative event or people in bad moods who think or behave in ways designed to "repair" their moods.

Clark and Isen are not specific about the mechanism whereby the cognitive processes associated with a mood switch from the automatic to the controlled variety. However, as I did in the case of Nowlis' position, it seems one might offer a simple threshold explanation which can account for the phenomenon.

Although the mood dichotomies offered by these theorists are expressed in rather different ways, they all recognize what I regard as a fundamental fact about moods, namely, that they are capable of moving in or out of focal attention. Unfortunately, rather than following this elusive creature as it moved back and forth across threshold, each of the mood theorists largely restricted his or her interest to one part of the mood spectrum.

As mentioned previously, Nowlis' reliance on self-reports forced a concentration on conscious mood. Though one could hardly consider this work a deadend in view of the number of similar inventories it spawned, for example, Lubin (1965); McNair, Lorr, and Droppleman (1971); Zuckerman, Lubin, Vogel, & Valerius (1964); Nowlis, himself, appeared to lose faith in the mood construct at least partly because of the limited access verbal reports provided. In his last major statement on mood, Nowlis (1970) noted the inadequacy of the self-report methodology in that it not only reveals something of what a person feels but also "how he thinks he feels, thinks he ought to feel, or wants the investigator to believe he feels" (p. 268). In part, these comments may reflect the "crisis" that emerged in social psychology in the late 1960s in response to the threats to validity posed by the problems of expectancy effects (Rosenthal, 1966) and demand characteristics (Orne, 1962). Self-report methodologies surely are most vulnerable to these problems.

Isen also seems to have become trapped by her own methodological decisions. Recognizing the expectancy and demand problems associated with being transparent about what you are studying, Isen decided to employ a variety of relatively unobtrusive mood manipulations which were coupled with indirect measurement of their effects and carried out both in the laboratory and in the field. A typical experiment would use a mildly positive or negative event, for example, finding a dime in the coin return of a phone booth (Isen & Levin, 1972), combined with an indirect measure of mood such as helping. This strategy has been extremely successful in that it has shed a good deal of light on the processes, especially cognitive ones, associated with low levels of affect. Indeed, were it not for Isen's extensive empirical work, there would be little more than bald assertions in support of the view that mood can affect a broad range of behaviors unrelated to the mood-inducing event. However, Isen acknowledges that not all moods are mild:

> Feeling states can be produced not only by small things but also by major positive or negative events in our lives, and *can be intense* (italics added). (1984, p. 186)

Unfortunately, this realization has not manifested itself in research, possibly because of the ethical and moral issues involved in strong manipulations of affect, especially when they are negative. As a result, Isen's discussions of "controlled" processes, which one might expect to be relatively more likely when moods increase in strength and become intrusive, rely largely upon anecdotal evidence and *a posteriori* interpretations of results which are difficult to explain by way of "automatic" processes. Though it is understandable why Isen has gravitated away from studying stronger and negative moods, it is still frustrating that her rather elegant and ingenious conceptual and empirical approach to mood is restricted as it is.

Finally, though Edith Jacobsen (1957) draws upon observations of both "normal" and "pathological" moods, it should be noted that she is theorizing about moods that are at the other end of the intensity dimension from those considered by Nowlis and Isen. Indeed, the reason why there are deficits in awareness associated with moods according to Jacobsen is because the conflicts are so troubling that they must be repressed or denied. Given that Jacobsen sees moods as having this protective function, it must be supposed that she wouldn't regard finding a dime in a phone booth as a mood inducer. And yet, though the affective state described by Jacobsen is clearly more intense than the modal state depicted by Isen, they do share the similarities defining them as mood. Just as Isen's approach is weakened because it fails to actively consider mood that results from impactful events, Jacobsen's account is less than satisfactory because it cannot explain how very mild events alter our moods.

Each of the dichotomies discussed above has some weakness deriving principally from the fact that they were created by theorists who dealt with a truncated part of the mood domain. The conscious–unconscious distinction should probably be discarded because of its checkered past and the unwanted conceptual baggage it has acquired. The idea that moods can either be normal or pathological reflects clinical reality; some people are able to cope with the mood-inducing events in their lives whereas others are judged (or judge themselves) unable and are diagnosed as having a mood disorder. But this distinction assumes that every occurrence of mood reflects a coping or defensive process (which either succeeds or fails and, therefore, is of limited usefulness in understanding moods that result from relatively mild events. Finally, although the automatic-controlled distinction is a provocative way of describing the change in mood associated with crossing the threshold of awareness, it seems poorly suited for dealing with more intense manifestations of mood. For example, one of the phenomena associated with clinical levels of depression is "ruminative thinking" which is defined as "the tendency to dwell on the same thought or theme" (Nelson & Mazure, 1985, p. 41).This process seems quite involuntary and yet it occurs in full awareness, making it difficult to sort into either the automatic or controlled categories.

Full integration of what we currently know about the variety of mood processes and their effects on behavior requires a new and more comprehensive distinction. Such a distinction must: (1) be capable of application to the entire domain of mood states and (2) be compatible with the consensus which emerges from prior theorizing about mood, namely, that what distinguishes one category of mood from the other has something to do with level of awareness.

In addition, it would be desirable if the distinction were better suited to what is known or consensually supposed about the phenomenology of mood. Though moods may moderate our behavior via their influence on cognitive processes as argued by Isen and others (e.g., Bower, 1981), they are fundamentally "feelings." Traditionally it has been assumed that we come to "know" our feelings via processes that are relatively direct, that is, sensory or perceptual, rather than through "indirect" cognitive processes such as inference. Although this view has been challenged (Nisbett & Wilson, 1977; Wilson et al., 1982), there is still a widespread conviction that relatively primitive processes are involved in the registration of affect (Gazzaniga, 1985; Leventhal, 1980; Zajonc, 1980). Thus, a distinction applicable to perceptual and/or sensory processes would seem appropriate. The distinction I would propose is that of figure versus ground.

The Figure–Ground Distinction

The figure–ground distinction is considered a fundamental fact about the organization of perceptual fields (Hebb, 1949; Woodworth & Schlosberg, 1954). Usually employed to analyze visual perception, the distinction refers to the tendency for the perceptual field to break down into two "parts," the figure and the ground. According to Rubin (1915, 1921, as cited in Woodworth & Schlosberg, 1954) the phenomenal differences between the two include: (1) figure has form whereas the ground is formless, (2) the figure has the characteristic of a *thing*, whereas the ground seems like unformed *material* (italics in the original), (3) the ground seems to extend continuously behind the figure rather than being interrupted by the figure, (4) the figure is more impressive, better remembered, and more likely to suggest meaning.

Although manifested in the organization of the perceptual field, the figure–ground distinction is best understood as an attentional phenomenon. Because we have a limited capacity to take in information, it is necessary to concentrate our information-processing capability on part of the array of incoming data and ignore the rest. The part we attend to is figure; the rest becomes ground.

In most cases, the organization of a given field is relatively stable but its dynamic properties are easily shown. A good example is the "cocktail party" phenomenon. While participating in a conversation, we focus on what our interactant is saying. Other conversations, although within "earshot," are background noise. However, if your name is mentioned in one of those other conversations, attention can be rapidly deployed so as to tune in on what is being said. (Note, however, that the fact that your name intruded in the first place shows that some attention was already being allocated to the "ground.")

The same sort of thing happens in vision. The best known examples are "reversible" figure–ground displays. Switching back and forth between seeing the two possible "figures" occurs because the display was constructed in such a way so as to make each part rival the other for your attention. The trick is to draw them so that what is the ground in one of the two possible organizations can become the figure in the other and vice versa.

A central premise of this monograph is that the way in which mood affects us depends fundamentally on the degree to which it is in or out of focal attention. When not in focal attention, mood has the characteristics of ground; it is the formless backdrop against which we experience events. Although our moods may often escape our attention, the evidence reviewed in Chapter 5 suggests that they can nonetheless subtly insinuate themselves into our lives, influencing what we remember of the past, perceive in the present, and expect from the future. Thus, mood acts quite literally as the frame of mind. On the other hand, a given mood may enter focal attention, either because it intensifies, or because other demands on attention are relaxed, or because some event causes us to introspect. Upon entering focal attention, mood rapidly acquires the characteristics of a figure or thing. It takes on a specific form in that we may label the feeling and thereby partially understand or explain it. If negative, it may intrude upon our thoughts and behavior enough to motivate us to eliminate it, a goal that may be difficult to accomplish if the mood is permitted to continue operating as ground where it can influence our decisions in a dysfunctional way.

The difference between these two manifestations of mood can be quite dramatic. As Kagan (1984) has recently noted:

> The presence or absence of detection of internal changes is of extreme importance for the subsequent emotional state . . . [in that] the evaluation that follows detection often changes the affect experienced. (p. 41)

A similar though more general point of view may be found in recent proposals by Wilson (1985) and Gazzaniga (1985), who speculate that our experiences, including those of affect, are mediated by two very different systems, possibly localized in different regions or hemispheres of the brain. One is a rather basic and primitive system, widely shared among mammalian species. The other is a verbal-conceptual system or "interpreter" (Wilson, 1985) which superimposes a more specific character or imprint upon the output of the basic system.

To the extent that such different mechanisms are involved in the two basic manifestations of mood, it is easy to see why previous treatments of mood have concentrated on one manifestation of it to the relative exclusion of the other. This may also explain why some emotion theorists fail to award distinctive status to mood, namely, its two main meanings seemed to refer to qualitatively different phenomena. And yet, rather than discouraging a unitary approach, the fact that mood and its effects are altered as it crosses the threshold of awareness is perfectly consistent with the idea that mood plays the cuing role in a self-regulatory system.

There may be puzzles in what we will find as this book proceeds. Especially intriguing is the appearance of a design flaw in the operation of the self-regulatory system. Specifically, in a machine or organism that must perform multiple functions, many of which occasionally require the allocation of decision-making processes, one would presumably wish to preset parameter values to husband executive capacity. Thus, in the case of mood, it might be beneficial to have two sets of triggering values, one of which launches some "automatic" response. If this response fails to cause a return of the variable to the nominal range, one might expect the system to "signal" the need for executive attention as evidenced by the entry of the mood into awareness. The anomaly lies in the fact, revealed in Chapter 5, that the "automatic" responses triggered by mood seem to be anything but functional. It remains to be seen whether this apparent glitch can be accommodated within a self-regulatory framework.

Chapter 2

Theories of Mood

In Chapter 1, I argued that mood should be considered as a distinctive affective phenomenon, different from related constructs such as preferences, motives, and particularly emotions. Thus far, the prime basis for making this claim is definitional, that is, I have tried to indicate how mood differs from emotion, its nearest "neighbor" in the affect domain, by discussing the consensus about its diffuse and pervasive influence on thought and behavior. In this chapter I will add further substance to my claim by considering how one might account theoretically for the existence of such a state.

Of the psychologists described in Chapter 1 as having attempted to maintain a distinctive status for mood, Isen and Jacobsen have what might be called theories of mood. In addition to these theories, I will also describe the work of Zajonc (1980), who has offered a provocative set of ideas about the relationship between what he regards as two partly independent systems: cognitive and affective. It turns out that Zajonc's speculations yield a variety of insights about how moods might arise. Finally, I will consider the group of conceptions that might be labeled the "arousal plus cognition" theories of emotion including those of Berscheid (1983), Mandler (1975), Schachter and Singer (1962), and Zillman (1978). The ideas presented by this group may apply better to mood than to emotion. In each case my goal will be to describe how a particular theory accounts for the emergence of an affective state which has the distinctive diffuse and pervasive character that I and others attribute to mood.

I begin with Isen (1984), who might be said to have a cognitive theory of mood. It is her view that moods, like emotions, begin with an event of hedonic relevance. The importance of the event will determine whether the initial reaction is an emotion or a mood. Events of relatively great significance stimulate a strong reaction which interrupts our ongoing activity, attracting our attention and demanding some response. This sequence characterizes the typical emotion according to Isen. However, more mild events do not cause such an interruption. The affect they create:

> gently color(s) and redirect(s) ongoing thoughts and actions, influencing what will happen next but almost without notice and certainly without ostensibly changing the context or basic activity. (Isen, 1984, pp. 186–187)

However, recall from Chapter 1 that Isen also hedges her bet in the sense that she refuses to accept low intensity as a defining characteristic of moods.

Mild events, she says, are the most *frequent* antecedents of mood, not the only antecedents. Indeed, Clark and Isen (1982) earlier made the observation that mood and emotion can be instigated by the very same event because the two processes can operate in parallel. However, in this case one may not be able to detect the presence of the mood because the emotion has the more powerful and dramatic effects. As the emotion wanes, the influence of the mood may appear. In this way, Isen is able to account for what some, for example, Ruckmick (1936), have said is the most common way in which mood arises, namely as an aftermath of emotion.

The processes responsible for redirection of thought processes are "automatic" associative-type cognitive processes which Isen thinks are triggered by the affect-inducing event. More specifically, Isen (1975, 1984; Isen, Shalker, Clark, & Karp, 1978) has suggested that the affect produced by the event can "prime," that is, make more accessible from memory, similarly toned thoughts or recollections (see also Bower, 1981, who has proposed a similar idea). According to Isen (Clark & Isen, 1982; Isen, 1984), such an idea follows from a number of currently popular views of the organization and dynamics of memory. For example, according to a network and spreading activation model such as that of Anderson and Bower (1973), similarly toned events might be stored near each other in memory. When a given event occurs it might activate an affect "node" that is connected to a set of events associated with that affective state. Nearby memories would tend to be activated since excitation is assumed to spread to adjacent regions. According to Isen, it is this flow of hedonically toned ideas which *is* the mood.

Perhaps the most illustrative study supporting this theorizing about moods is a field experiment reported by Isen et al. (1978). Shoppers at a mall were stopped and offered a small promotional gift. Further down the mall, they were stopped and asked to participate in a brief consumer survey that required that they answer questions about the performance of their cars and TV sets. As compared to control subjects who did not receive a gift, these shoppers reported greater satisfaction with their cars and TVs. Isen's argument is that the gift creates positive feelings that cue positive material in memory. When asked about their possessions, the greater availability of the positive material biases the answers one gives. A great deal of evidence has now accumulated in response to the general prediction that memory will be biased in such a way that when items in memory and current mood share the same hedonic tone, these items will be favored in recall. We will consider that evidence in a later chapter on the effects of mood on cognitive processes and behavior; suffice it to say now that Isen's position receives reasonably good support (though her predictions and the data are more complicated than I have yet indicated).

By now it should be apparent that Isen's explanation for the diffuse effect of mood is that it quite literally is a "frame of mind." It therefore affects whatever happens to be in focal attention or "figural" at the moment. Moreover, because the feeling state arises as a result of automatic cognitive processes, we may not even be aware that we are in a mood. Thus, it can operate as a context or, in my terms, a ground, subtly influencing our responses to events.

A rather different set of answers as to how moods might arise can be derived from recent theorizing by Zajonc (1980, 1984). Though Zajonc does not distinguish between mood and emotion, his speculations about the relationship between cognitive affective systems can be used to predict three different ways in which diffuse and global affect might arise.

Zajonc's major contentions are that cognitive and affective systems are at least partially independent of each other and that the affective system has primacy in that it is the more sensitive of the two systems, able to respond to lower stimulus intensities. The implication of all this according to Zajonc is that:

> it is entirely possible that the very first stage of the organism's reaction to stimuli and the very first elements in retrieval are affective. It is further possible that we can like something or be afraid of it before we know precisely what is and perhaps even *without* (italics in the original) knowing what it is. (1980, p. 154)

These comments suggest how Zajonc might account for an affective state with mood-like characteristics. Given the greater sensitivity of the affective system, events of minor hedonic relevance might activate the affective system without triggering the cognitive system. The result would be a change in feeling without an appraisal to go with it. Without the appraisals that connect feelings backward to ostensible causes and forward to potential responses, the affect would remain diffuse and pervasive, literally unattached to specific objects or particular responses.

But the possibilities don't stop there. Other speculations and assumptions made by Zajonc permit inferences about alternative ways in which moods may arise. One possibility results from two assumptions that Zajonc makes: (1) that consciousness or awareness, which operates within the cognitive system, has a limited capacity and (2) that the cognitive and affective systems can operate in parallel. It follows that an event could engage affective processes while consciousness was occupied to capacity by on-going cognitive demands. The result would be affect of which one would be at least temporarily unaware. (This case differs from the previous one in that here the affect-inducing stimulus could be above the "normal" threshold for activating the cognitive system but fails to do so because the cognitive system is heavily involved elsewhere.) When the demand on focal attention or consciousness was relaxed, awareness of affect could result but because of the temporal lag between instigation and detection, one might be unable to identify the cause of the affect. Once again, to the extent that affect acquires specificity, that is, becomes an emotion, as a function of recognition of its cause, affect arising in this fashion would be experienced as diffuse and pervasive.

I am reminded of the feeling I sometimes have after completing a lecture to a large class, a sense that it went particularly well or particularly badly, but I cannot determine why I feel that way. I suspect that the expressions of students, which are detected during the perfunctory scanning of audience faces which we are all taught to do, directly engage affective responses in me. However, because of the heavy demands that lecturing places on focal attention, the appraisal process fails to occur and I am left to speculate about my post-class reaction.

Finally, mood-like affect might occur because, according to Zajonc, the affective system can control access to consciousness in accordance with its own "motives." So, for example, when the affective system encounters disturbing or threatening stimuli, it may prevent our becoming aware of them. This idea has a familiar ring, having originated with Freud (1927) and, indeed Zajonc explicitly invokes Freud and mentions perceptual defense and vigilance as phenomena that can be accounted for within his model of cognitive and affective system interaction. In view of the running battle between Zajonc and Lazarus over the relationship between cognition and emotion (Lazarus, 1982, 1984; Zajonc, 1984), it is no small irony that for evidence of defense and vigilance, Zajonc cites the classic work of Lazarus and McCleary (1951).

The main evidence for these various claims is data accumulated by Zajonc and others (Kunst-Wilson & Zajonc, 1980; Seamon, Brody, & Kauff, 1983a, 1983b; and Wilson, 1979) which show that the affective response of liking of initially neutral stimuli can be enhanced through repeated exposures even when stimulus presentations are sufficiently degraded to prevent recognition that the exposure occurred. Other relevant data come from studies in which words that had been previously associated with shock alter psychophysiological responding (GSR) even though presented in ways that prevent recognition, for example, backward masking in a tachistoscopic viewing procedure (Tassinary, Orr, Wolford, Napps, & Lanzetta, 1984) or to the unattended ear in a dichotic listening procedure (Dawson & Schell, 1982). Zajonc (1980, 1984) cites a number of other arguments and findings that are consistent with his view. He refers to literature reviewed by Moore (1973) which appears to establish that direct pathways exist between the retina and the hypothalamus. Because the hypothalamus plays a central role in the arousal and expression of emotion, such pathways suggest the possibility that purely sensory inputs can activate an emotional reaction.

Because Zajonc's speculations permit the derivation of so many ways in which diffuse and global affect might arise, it seems as if he might have had moods specifically in mind while generating his position. In fact, in a recent analysis of Zajonc's thesis, Russell and Woudzia (1986) have suggested that the appeal of his arguments lies in their relevance to mood. However, Zajonc does not systematically distinguish between mood and emotion.

Whereas Zajonc dabbles in Freudian notions, Jacobsen (1957) offers a full-blown psychoanalytic theory of mood. Despite the great difference between her theoretical predilections and those of the other theorists I draw from, Jacobsen defines mood similarly, emphasizing the central aspect of diffuseness:

> moods seem to represent . . . a cross-section through the entire state of the ego lending a particular, uniform coloring to all its manifestations . . . they do not relate to a specific content or object but find expression in specific qualities attached to all feelings, thoughts, and actions. (p. 75)

Jacobsen's view of mood, like that of Nowlis, was a functional one. However, where Nowlis saw mood as leading to responding of a self-regulatory nature, Jacobsen regarded the mood state itself as being self-regulatory. Her analysis supposed that various experiences generate unusually high energetic tensions which cannot be safely and adequately relieved by the focal discharge process characteristic of emotions. Moods served an economic function in that they permitted:

> a repetitive affective discharge on a great number and variety of objects. . . . This gradual discharge certainly tends to protect the ego from the dangers of too explosive, overwhelming discharge. (p. 81)

Jacobsen's claim is that the ego is capable of inhibiting an emotional response targeted at the instigating stimulus. It does so by diffusing or spreading the cathectic energy about.

Though we are left with a homunculus rather than a specific mechanism, a common problem in psychoanalytic theory, Jacobsen's ideas about mood complement the other views I present. In fact, she is the only theorist who has proposed an account of "normal" moods where the felt affect would be relatively strong. Recall, for example, that although Isen (1984) admits that moods can be intense, her explanation as to how they arise seems limited to the mild case.

Unfortunately, the evidence that Jacobsen presents on behalf of her explanation of moods is anecdotal, deriving from case studies. However, there are some data in the experimental literature that can be adduced to Jacobsen's point of view. Since these data are relevant specifically to the idea that mood results from the inhibition of emotional responding, I will review them in the next chapter when I consider what we know about the antecedents of mood.

Finally, we arrive at the arousal plus cognition theories of emotion, variants of which have been proposed by Schachter and Singer (1962, 1979), Mandler (1975, 1984), Zillman (1978), and Berscheid (1983). Although none of these theories have been specifically applied to mood, they are capable of providing an account of the circumstances that should produce states that are mood-like as opposed to emotion-like.

All the theories argue that for a full-blown emotional experience to occur, there must be both the self-perception of a non-normal level of autonomic nervous system arousal and an explanation of that level of arousal in terms of the identification of some emotion-instigating environmental event. It is this identification or emotion "label" which, according to these theories, gives the relatively diffuse and general arousal state its specific character. The various experiments that have been done to test these theories use paradigms in which individuals are aroused through concealed administrations of epinephrine (Schachter & Singer, 1962; Zimbardo & Marshall, 1979) or hypnosis (Maslach, 1979), and plausible "causes" are scattered about the laboratory environment to see if the individual who is both aroused and supplied with a plausible "emotional" cause will experience the specific emotion suggested by that cause.

Since these theories specify that perception of arousal and identification of an emotional cause in the environment are both necessary for the experience of emotion, it follows that arousal plus a failure to isolate the environmental event would produce some state other than emotion. Indeed, Berscheid (1983) specifically says that "feeling" states, rather than emotions, will result "if there is actual physiological arousal as well as the perception of that arousal, but these are unaccompanied by a cognitive 'emotional' appraisal" (p. 124).

But under what circumstances might this occur? One possibility would be instances where arousal arose as the result of a process that was substantially endogenous in nature. Though most of the experimental literature on mood appears to assume that mood is the result of actual, remembered, or imagined events of hedonic relevance, clinical approaches to mood disorders, for example, Depue, Monroe, and Shackman (1979); Whybrow et al. (1984) typically assume that hormones and brain chemistry play a key role in the production of affective states. Though these processes may be instigated by environmental events such as the amount of available sunlight (Rosenthal, Sack, Carpenter, Parry, Mendelson, & Wehr, 1985), or the concentration of negative ions in the air (Baron, Russell, & Arms, 1985), if those affected fail to perceive the relevant environmental event then, effectively, the source of the arousal might as well be endogenous.

Whether or not substantially endogenous arousal will result in emotion through misattribution as appears to have occurred in Schachter and Singer's (1962) classic experiment should depend upon the availability of a plausible environmental cause which bears a proper temporal relationship to the detection of the arousal. If one cannot be discerned, then one might label the state as an approaching illness or fatigue. Another possible explanation may be simply that you're "in a mood," that is, this is just one of those "good" or "bad" days.

Though we may occasionally seem to settle for this default explanation of our arousal, it rather obviously begs the question. Indeed, there is some evidence suggesting that people are aware that mood states often entail some degree of ambiguity as to their source. In an interview study, Rippere (1977) asked people what they did when they found themselves feeling depressed. The most popular answer was to seek out social contact but the second most frequent, mentioned by over a third of the subjects, was to "think of the reason for it," a finding that clearly implies that when depressed mood is detected it is often initially regarded as having an unknown origin.

Although these arousal plus cognition theories of emotion, especially that of Schachter and Singer, dominated the scene in experimental psychology for a good 15 years, they were thriving more on their heuristic ability than anything else. In the late 1970s and early 1980s, vigorous attacks were leveled both at the theory (Leventhal, 1980; Shaver & Klinnert, 1982; Zillman, 1978) and its supporting data (Marshall & Zimbardo, 1979; Maslach, 1979; see Reisenzein, 1983, for a review).

Particularly damaging was the charge that the theory explained the rare casc but seemed ill-suited to the vast majority of cases involving instigation of emotion where no ambiguity is involved. As Zillman (1978) put it:

> The proposal must appear awkward and in violation of parsimony of explanation, however, when applied to response conditions devoid of ambiguity. Whey should one, for example, assume that a person who has just been blatantly insulted must consciously go through the motion of causally attributing his arousal to the assaultant's action and that only after that does he know what he feels? (pp. 353–354)

However, because it is characteristic of mood that its sources are obscure (Nowlis, 1965), a theory that supposes that detection of some internal change of state without a suitable explanation leads to attributional activity provides a useful framework. Moreover, it should be noted that the predicted and sometimes confirmed result (Schachter and Singer, 1962; Zillman, 1978) that the effect of arousal is *general*, that is, capable of energizing a wide variety of behavior, is similar to the view I have advanced about mood in that its effects are diffuse.

The various theories reviewed herein are not mutually exclusive. Affective states that are diffuse and pervasive may arise under the circumstances specified by all these theories. But, if so, it would be hoped that the various circumstances converge on a common or superordinate cause. The most likely candidate at this point would seem to be the lack of a label or appraisal of the affective state. In the case of Isen's account, the typical cause of mood is an event of modest hedonic relevance, sufficient to prime thoughts sharing the same hedonic tone but insufficient to interrupt ongoing behavior and attract focal attention, occurrences Isen associates with emotion. Labeling does not occur because the event initially engages only automatic associative or retrieval processes; conducting an appraisal or "meaning" analysis would require the involvement of higher level cognitive processes which are ordinarily reserved for events of more importance. The three sets of conditions that promote mood according to my adaptation of Zajonc's theorizing also entail a lack of labeling. This is because the cognitive system is required for labeling and Zajonc's speculations suggest a variety of ways in which affect may arise without engaging the cognitive system. According to Jacobsen's theory, nonpathological mood states are initially labeled in the sense that the person knows perfectly well why he is experiencing the affect.

However, it would seem that this awareness must necessarily be quickly lost for moods to be functional. That is because the mood does entail a distortion of sorts in that feelings become attached to all objects encountered even though they played no part in the emergence of the affect. It is generally assumed that self-deception cannot be successful if one is aware of it (e.g., Lazarus & Folkman, 1984; Sackheim, 1983). Thus, as the cathectic energy diffuses it would seem that the individual should "forget" the source of the feelings. Finally, in the case of the arousal plus cognition theories, I simply supposed that labeling is sometimes problematic, especially when the "arousal" is primarily produced endogenously.

Thus, to summarize, Isen and Zajonc suggest how affect-relevant events might occur without producing an appraisal (though a more primitive process does activate "memories" sufficient to produce the affective response I refer to as mood) whereas in the case of Jacobsen, the appraisal occurs initially but is subsequently lost. Arousal plus cognition theories posit unlabeled or unappraised affect, i.e., mood, in cases where changes in arousal cannot be connected with antecedent environmental events either because there isn't one, as in cases of endogenously triggered arousal, or because the event that did produce the arousal is not viewed as a plausible cause. In addition to bridging mood theories, the suggestion that the *lack* of an appraisal is necessary for mood serves also to clearly distinguish mood from emotion in that for many emotion theorists, the *activation* of such appraisal processes is necessary for emotion.

The focus of discussion in this chapter has been on the proximal "causes" of mood, the intrapsychic processes that give mood its distinctive character of being diffuse and pervasive. The more distal sources of mood are antecedent events, both environmental and endogenous. It is time to consider what we know about these sources of mood.

Chapter 3

Sources of Mood: Events of Affective Significance

In spite of the apparent tendency of moods to appear from "out of the blue," they do have causes. In this chapter, I will consider the speculations that have been offered about the environmental antecedents of mood and, where it exists, the relevant evidence regarding these supposed sources of mood.

Just as we found that a large number of rather diverse theoretical statements were pertinent to mood, there is an equally large set of proposed antecedents to consider. Before doing so, however, it will be necessary to establish what we are willing to consider as evidence that a mood exists.

Mood Measurement Issues

Mood is a hypothetical construct. Since a hypothetical construct cannot be measured directly we must settle upon indirect indications of its presence. Commercially available products such as "mood rings" and "magic mood pencils" have yet to be validated so we must rely upon more mundane measures of which there are two major types: self-reports and the so-called "behavioral" measures.[1]

Self-reports of mood are widely used in both laboratory and field studies. They are typically the measure of choice when investigators wish to "check" the effectiveness of a mood manipulation. Sometimes a single "good-bad" scale is used, for example, Johnson and Tversky (1983); Wilson et al. (1982). Often, some *ad hoc* set of scales is used, for example, Isen and Gorgoglione (1983); Wessman and Ricks (1966). Alternately, one can choose from among the large number of mood scales which have been developed including the Mood Adjective Check List (Nowlis, 1965), the Profile of Mood States (McNair, Lorr, & Droppleman, 1971), the Depression Adjective Check List (Lubin, 1965) and the Multiple Affect Adjective Check List (Zuckerman et al., 1964).

Unfortunately there are a number of potential problems with self-reports, some of which were alluded to in Chapter 1. The first is that of respondent

[1]It is possible that physiological measures of mood may ultimately be validated but the fact that mood states are typically low-level discourages such an approach. Nonetheless, a number of investigators, for example, Cacioppo, Petty, Losch, and Kim, 1986, and Schwartz, Fair, Salt, Mandel, and Klerman, 1974, have reported success using electromyographic measures of the facial musculature in connection with various imagining and remembering instructions that ought to be mood-inducers.

"sincerity" (Nowlis, 1965), that is, to what extent does an individual report what he actually feels? Though Nowlis was optimistic in 1965 that sincerity could be achieved, he later (1970) became somewhat disillusioned. There is little doubt that subjects sometimes shape their behavior so as to accord with others' expectations (Rosenthal, 1966) or to achieve a favorable self-presentation (Schlenker, 1980) and self-reports seem the kind of behavior most vulnerable to these problems.

Let us assume, however, that we know how to motivate our subjects to be honest with us. Can we trust that the reports we receive under these circumstances are an accurate reflection of their underlying mood states? Here again, Nowlis (1965) did not see this as a significant issue but due to the seminal work of Bem (1965) and Nisbett and Wilson (1977), many doubts now exist about our ability to accurately report on covert internal processes (e.g., Katkin, 1985; Laird & Crosby, 1974; Nisbett & Ross, 1980; Skelton & Pennebaker, 1982; Wilson, 1985) including mood (Wilson et al., 1982).

However, the problem here is not really one of accuracy. To say that a self-report of some internal state is "inaccurate" suggests that there is some objective standard against which the report might be assessed. For example, one *can* measure the accuracy with which people judge internal physiological processes such as heart rate (e.g., Katkin, 1985). However, moods seem largely subjective and, therefore, unverifiable. If someone complained of feeling "jittery," it would be foolish of you to tell them they were wrong . . . that they didn't really feel that way (though you might try to explain to them why they *shouldn't* feel that way).

And yet, self-reports of mood may be in error in a different sense than that which implies comparison to an objective standard. Such a possibility exists because mood reports may arise from a "constructive" process of the sort mentioned in connection with the "arousal plus cognition theories" discussed in Chapter 2, that is, an individual introspectively detects some internal "feeling" *and then labels it in terms of what seems its most likely antecedent.* In this case, the inferential process can go awry because the scheme applied to explain the feeling state might be an incorrect one and yet it would be wrong to say that the individual did not feel what he claimed to feel.[2]

Notice, however, that according to this analysis, the individual has *two* "feelings," one of which is detected through introspection with the other being "constructed." Which of these two is the mood? The answer, as suggested in Chapter 1, is that they both are! The first reflects mood in its more

[2]This problem is not distinctively associated with self-reports of mood but is a general problem long recognized by students of sensation and psychophysics. Titchener (1909) called it the "object error" (p. 267) but it is more generally referred to as the "stimulus error" (Woodworth & Schlosberg, 1954, p. 293). It refers to the tendency to attend to and report about the object which gives rise to the sensation rather than to the sensation itself.

typical manifestation . . . as ground, that is, the relatively formless context which frames and colors what it "surrounds," namely our ongoing focal experience. Bringing it into focal attention, as we must do to report on it, transforms it into figure, that is, it acquires form giving it the characteristic of a thing including meaning.

But where does this analysis leave us in terms of the question with which we began as to the validity of self-reports of mood? If there are two fundamentally different manifestations of mood, then there are two different answers to this question. With respect to mood as it occurs in focal attention, I agree with Nowlis (1965) who argued, in effect, that no validation of self-reports of mood is necessary (unless there is reason to suspect subject "sincerity"). Validation is unnecessary because the use of self-descriptive mood labels is a *direct* measure of mood when one conceives of it as Nowlis did, namely as a source of information to the organism about its current state. According to this view, it is in the nature of mood states that they give rise to such labels (and the self-regulatory behavior that follows application of the label).

However, if one wishes to use self-reports of mood as an index of the presence of mood in its "ground" manifestation, validation is necessary. The reason is that some unknown amount of violence is associated with the transformation from ground to figure. Presumably it is for reasons such as these that Isen, the only one of the mood theorists who has empirically studied mood primarily in its manifestation as ground, has opted for a "converging operations" solution to the problem of demonstrating that her experimental manipulations have influenced mood (see Isen, 1984, for a discussion of this methodological decision).

This brings us to the topic of "behavioral" measures of mood. Two different approaches have been taken to establish that a given behavior reflects the presence of mood. One is the above-mentioned converging operations approach wherein one employs a variety of different mood inductions and determines the extent to which they similarly affect a given behavior which, itself, is measured in different ways. The procedure begins with a relatively high degree of uncertainty both about the validity of the construct and the behaviors which reflect it. With each case of "convergence," confidence in both the independent and dependent variable operations increases as does one's faith in the validity and explanatory power of the construct itself.

The drawback of this technique is that it is relatively slow and risky as a way of validating a particular behavioral measure of mood; the use of different realizations of the measure may add strength to the claim of construct validity when the results replicate previous findings, but when they do not the confidence in the measure drops. Unfortunately, for all three of the most heavily researched dependent measures: helping, memory retrieval, and perceptual judgments, a similar pattern of results has been found in a subset of the studies and it is not one which encourages the use of these behaviors as "checks" on the presence of mood.

The pattern, first noted by Clark and Isen (1982), is one of asymmetry in that good and bad moods, seemingly "opposites" of each other (but see Watson & Tellegen, 1985), do not produce "opposite" results on helping and memory measures. In the case of memory, though positive mood inductions seem to facilitate recall of positive memories, bad mood does not always have the opposite (or symmetrical) effect of making recall of negative memories more likely (see Blaney, 1986 and Isen, 1984 for reviews of this literature). Similarly, in a recent review of the helping literature, Dovidio (1984) summarizes the good mood findings as follows:

> The results of many experiments involving a variety of subject populations, research settings, ways of inducing feelings, and types of helping situations have found that people who feel good, successful, happy, and fortunate are more likely to help someone else than are people who are not in a positive state. (p. 390)

On the other hand, Dovidio describes the outcomes with bad mood as "mixed": sometimes bad mood depresses helping behavior but on other occasions, it leads to more helping.

Finally, though it looked for a while as though evaluative judgments and perceptions were sufficiently exempt from this asymmetry that one could advocate their use as a check on the presence of good and bad mood, for example, see Isen and Shalker (1982), results recently published by Forgas and Moylan (1987) found the familiar lack of an effect on the negative mood side while good mood manipulations resulted in robust effects. In addition to this one asymmetry, there are a few claims that mood manipulations have resulted in actual mood-*in*congruent effects on perception, for example, Dermer, Cohen, Jacobsen, and Andersen (1979), S. Thayer (1980a, 1980b), and Manstead, Wagner, and MacDonald (1983).

Discovery of the asymmetry has been far from a total loss in that it has led to interesting theorizing (Clark & Isen, 1982; Isen, 1984) and some data collection (Manucia, Baumann, & Cialdini, 1984) concerning this difference between good and bad moods. Less attention has been devoted to explaining when mood-congruent versus mood-incongruent (contrast) effects will occur. I intend to discuss these matters at some length in Chapter 5 but for the time being one thing is clear, namely, that it is premature to use such behaviors as mood measures.

The other approach that has been taken as a way of validating behavioral measures of mood is to use a consensually accepted manipulation of mood followed by a battery of behavioral measures. The closest thing to a consensually-accepted manipulation of mood has been the Velten (1968) procedure which relies upon an autosuggestion technique. Subjects are instructed to read a series of self-referent statements which are either neutral, increasingly positive, or increasingly negative (e.g., "Every now and then I feel so tired and gloomy that I'd rather just sit than do anything.") and are urged to "try to feel the mood suggested by the statements" (Velten, 1968, p. 474.)

A variety of researchers have taken this tack and their findings suggest that measures of psychomotor speed or activation are positively associated with mood as it is induced by the Velten procedure. As compared with good or neutral mood, bad mood is associated with: longer latencies to speak, slower speech rate, more pauses in an interview situation (Natale, 1977), slower writing speed (Hale & Strickland, 1976; Velten, 1968), longer decision times in a weight-judging task (Velten, 1968), longer word association latencies (Velten, 1968), less spontaneous verbalization during the experimental session (Velten, 1968), fewer hand movements while speaking (Natale & Bolan, 1980), less expansive doodling (Strickland, Hale & Anderson, 1975; Hale & Strickland, 1976), and poorer performance on a digit-symbol substitution task (Hale & Strickland, 1976).

Impressive as this list may seem, it is offset by serious problems associated with the Velten procedure. The one which has received the greatest attention is that of role demand (Buchwald, Strack, & Coyne, 1981; Kenealy, 1986; Polivy & Doyle, 1980; Velten, 1968). Because the procedure is transparent as to its purpose, concern has been expressed that differences in the behavior of subjects is due to their motivation to comply with what they perceive to be the expectations or desires of the experimenter. Attempts to solve this problem through the use of various demand control groups (Polivy & Doyle, 1980; Velten, 1968) have not been completely successful in my judgment or that of others (Kenealy, 1986, but see Berkowitz & Troccoli, 1986, who disagree).

Another charge against the procedure is that it is weak (Blaney, 1986) and that its effects are very time-limited (Frost & Green, 1982; Isen & Gorgoglione, 1983). Perhaps it is for these reasons that Teasdale and his colleagues, who had until recently relied exclusively upon the Velten procedure, decided to employ a preestablished mood change criterion for retaining subjects (Teasdale & Forgarty, 1979; Teasdale & Russell, 1983; Teasdale & Taylor, 1981; Teasdale, Taylor, & Fogarty, 1980). Though this may solve the problem of the strength of the manipulation, it obviously introduces a serious subject selection bias as Teasdale and collaborators were forced to eliminate an average 50% of their subjects in the above-cited studies for failing to meet the criterion.

A more serious problem which has not been much discussed is that the Velten procedure seems to be ineffective when used on male subjects (Strickland, Hale, & Anderson, 1975). The result is that the very large majority of studies using the procedure limit themselves to female subjects (e.g., Alloy, Abramson, & Viscusi, 1981; Berkowitz, 1987; Brown & Taylor, 1986; Coleman, 1975; Frost & Green, 1982; Nagata & Trierweiler, 1988; Hale & Strickland, 1976; Natale, 1977; Natale & Bolan, 1980; Polivy & Doyle, 1980; Ranieri & Zeiss, 1984; Rogers, Miller, Mayer, & Duval, 1982; Snyder & White, 1982; Teasdale & Taylor, 1981; Teasdale, Taylor, & Fogarty, 1980) with Velten (1968), himself, being no exception. This naturally raises the question as to whether the consistent findings on psychomotor speed and activation apply sufficiently well to males so as to justify the use of these measures as indications of the presence of good and bad mood.

Fortunately, a recent study by Mayer and Bremer (1985) provides some reassurance with respect to these various misgivings. Rather than manipulating mood, Mayer and Bremer simply measured subjects' moods upon arrival at the laboratory using scales developed by Russell (1979). Moreover, Mayer and Bremer used both males (N=72) and females (N=34) and report no sex differences. Their findings replicate the typical results found with the Velten procedure, that is, they obtained a positive relationship between scores on a "pleasant arousal versus unpleasant tiredness" dimension (Velten considers his treatments to be manipulations of "elation" and "depression") and a composite measure of speed in tasks such as letter cancellation, letter search, and writing a list of numbers (but only in the forward direction). In addition, they also found a relationship between mood and estimates of the probability of occurrence of pleasant and unpleasant life events where the worse the mood the more pessimistic were prognostications for the future. This finding replicates those obtained by Johnson and Tversky (1983) who manipulated mood. Results such as these are consistent with the findings I reviewed earlier where it was found that mood influences evaluative rating and judgments. Taken together, both sets of results are compatible with the view that mood influences the positivity or negativity of one's general outlook of life.

My conclusion, then, is that if "behavioral" indices are used to establish the presence of mood in its manifestation as a ground, dependent variables of psychomotor speed or activation are suitable choices. Given the various problems with self-report measures, these behavioral measures should be the method of choice when trying to establish that a given event is a mood-inducer.

Unfortunately, the literature has only recently evolved to the point where such recommendations could emerge. Up to this point, most researchers who have tried to establish whether or not a given environmental event produced good or bad mood did so through the use of some form of self-report. Consequently, we must be cautious in accepting their claims if it is mood in the form of "ground" which they had intended to induce.

Events Which Produce Mood: Speculations

Four general categories of events have been implicated as antecedents of moods. They are: (1) the onset of a mildly positive or negative event, (2) the offset of an emotion-inducing event, (3) the recollection or imagining of emotional experience, and (4) the inhibition of emotional responding in the presence of an emotion-inducing event.

The idea that pleasant or unpleasant experiences can produce a mood has been around for a long time. For example, Ruckmick (1936), one of the first psychologists to award mood a role distinct from emotion, supposed that:

> many moods are occasioned through circumstances which have occurred in experience—a series of mishaps during the day, a stroke of luck in many enterprises, a gay evening with many pleasures. (pp. 72–73)

The second candidate as an antecedent to mood is the offset of an arousing or emotion-inducing stimulus. This has been the most provocative of the supposed antecedents of mood in that there are four distinctive accounts (Isen, 1984; Ruckmick, 1936; Solomon, 1980; Zillman, 1978) of the manner in which emotion gives way so as to leave a mood-like state.

Three of the four theorists base their account upon the idea that emotional arousal decays when the emotion-producing stimulus disappears. Ruckmick (1936) actually equated decaying emotion with mood, that is, as the intensity of the emotion dissipates the emotion *becomes* a mood. Isen (1984) argues that emotion and mood can operate in parallel, each being instigated by the same emotion-inducing event. Though she does not specifically mention a decay process, she does describe mood as the "residual" (p. 186) state. The implication is that initially, the more intense and targeted emotion holds sway but with time it weakens and the more subtle mood, which had actually been there in the background all the time, manifests itself.

Zillman's (1978) analysis is of a phenomenon he refers to as "excitation transfer." Though he does not refer to mood at any point, he employs a paradigm one might select if one wished to show that moods followed in the wake of emotional arousal. According to Zillman (1978), when arousal-inducing events (many of which produce emotions) terminate, excitation remains and slowly decays. To the extent that a new, emotion-inducing stimulus occurs before the residual excitation is gone, it is possible that the excitation will "transfer" and invigorate response to the new stimulus. Since Zillman presumes that the decaying arousal predisposes intensified responding *in general*, it seems fair to say that its influence is pervasive like that of mood.

The final argument about how the offset of an emotion-inducing event affects the organism is that of Solomon (1980; Solomon & Corbit, 1974). It is distinctive in two ways. First, Solomon does not believe that emotion decays. Rather, it is actively eroded by what he calls an "opponent process" designed to bring the organism back toward an affective baseline. Second, the affective consequence of offset is dramatically different in Solomon's theory. According to Ruckmick (1936) and Isen (1984), the general hedonic tone of the mood is of the same valence as the emotion which preceded it. Zillman's position (1978) is that there is no necessary relationship between the hedonic tone of the initial emotional arousal and the valence of the affective response amplified by the residual arousal. However, Solomon asserts that the typical affective consequence of offset is a state which is *opposite in quality* to the original, for example, the disappearance of a fear-inducing stimulus leads to calm or relief whereas the loss of a pleasure-producer instigates distress or depression.

The third proposed antecedent to mood is the remembrance or imagining of an emotional experience. Clark and Isen (1982) speculate that recall of positive or negative experiences may represent a special attentuated case of mood induction. What would seem to set this antecedent of mood apart from the others is that no event of hedonic relevance need occur.

That we can vicariously experience affect without direct exposure to a positive or negative event would not surprise the average moviegoer or recreational reader. Images and symbols have been used by artists and writers for centuries as a way to stir up feelings in those exposed to their work. Recall, though a different "medium" than perception, presents the same possibilities. Indeed, it may be that the evocative potential of vicariously experienced events depends upon the similarity of the observed circumstance to one previously experienced and stored in memory (Bandura, 1977).

Not only is there little doubt that affect can be generated through recall as well as other thought processes such as imagining but, in addition, there is good reason to suppose that the most likely result would be a mood-like state. Because a remembered event is temporally remote, the intensity of the state should be less than that originally experienced and low intensity is characteristic of mood. Also, it is relatively unlikely that the recollection or imagining of an emotional experience would be accompanied by a specific response tendency. Thus, the affect associated with these cognitive processes should be relatively diffuse.

The last speculation as to sources of mood is that of Jacobsen (1957) who proposed that mood is the result of inhibition of responding in the face of highly charged events. As I noted in Chapter 2, Jacobsen thought that when some event threatens to overwhelm a person because of the conflict it engenders, a primitive (but normal) protective device used by the ego is the spreading about of the cathectic energy. This prevents an explosive emotional reaction directed at the source of the conflict and creates the generalized affective state Jacobsen called mood.

All in all, these speculations, if confirmed, suggest that the claimed ubiquity of mood (Clark & Isen, 1982) may be due to the varied ways in which it can come about. (And remember that we have not yet considered possible endogenous sources of mood which are to be discussed in the next chapter.) I turn now to a consideration of the relevant evidence.

Events Which Produce Mood: Evidence

Mildly Pleasant and Unpleasant Occurrences. The evidence on behalf of this category of mood antecedent is strong, largely because of the efforts of Alice Isen. Because she alone among current researchers investigating "mood" has been concerned with demonstrating the utility of mood as a hypothetical construct with an identity independent of emotion, it has been necessary for her to establish that lawful relationships exist between mood as a conceptual variable and a variety of independent and dependent variable realizations, that is, a converging operations analysis. Though such programmatic research was designed to establish construct validity, incidentally it has affirmed that pleasant and unpleasant events are causes of mood.[3] For example, Isen has successfully employed the following manipulations to produce a positive feeling state: success on a perceptual-motor task (Isen, 1970) or at a computer game (Isen et al., 1978, Study 2), the offer of refreshments to students studying in the library (Isen & Levin, 1972), finding a dime in the coin-return slot of a telephone (Isen & Levin, 1972), and providing a free sample (Isen, Clark, & Schwartz, 1976). Other investigators have added to this list, for example, Fried and Berkowitz (1979) and Clark and Teasdale (1985) used pleasant music, and Cunningham (1979), nice weather. A similar list, though less extensive, exists in the case of bad mood. Included here are failure experiences (e.g., Isen et al., 1978), hot and crowded conditions (Griffitt, 1970), rainy weather (Schwarz & Clore, 1983), hearing bad news (Veitch & Griffitt, 1976), and depressing music (Clark & Teasdale, 1985). The most recent addition is odors. Ehrlichman and Halpern (1985) have shown that pleasant and unpleasant odors influence memory in mood-congruent ways just as other mood manipulations do (see Chapter 5 for a review of these studies).

One can see, in this catalog of mood manipulations, the influence of the distinctions between mood and emotion that were discussed in Chapter 1. Clearly, an effort was made to select events which, though hedonically relevant and therefore productive of affect, are of sufficiently low intensity that they would not produce the "interruptive" effects (Mandler, 1975; Simon, 1982) and specific responses (Epstein, 1983) characteristic of emotion.

The dependent variables in these studies have included self-reports as well as a variety of the cognitive and behavioral measures discussed above (the results will be discussed in more detail in Chapter 5 which is devoted to reviewing the effects of mood), thereby establishing that the influence of pleasant and unpleasant events is, indeed, pervasive. On the other hand, it bears repeating that the scorecard on the bad mood side of the ledger is considerably less convincing than it is on the good mood side, a result which Isen (Clark & Isen, 1982; Isen, 1984, 1985) and others (Blaney, 1986; Morris & Reilly, 1987) attribute partly to the tendency to take action designed to protect against the influence of bad mood manipulations. We will consider this possibility in some detail in Chapter 5.

---

[3]Also relevant is the literature on "minor" life events (see Zautra, Guarnaccia, Reich, & Dohrenwend, 1988, and Reich & Zautra, 1988, respectively, for discussions of negative and positive events). It is clear that such events are correlated with concurrent mood but the causal relationships are less clear in this literature.

The Offset of an Emotion-Inducing Event. Even though this category of mood antecedent has spawned a variety of suggestions as to the nature of the transition between emotion and mood, and is claimed by some (e.g., Ruckmick, 1936) to be the most common source of mood, there is very little solid evidence to show that mood actually appears subsequent to emotion.

No tests exist of Isen's (1984) parallel process account. Such a test might be difficult to conduct. It would require an affect-inducing event sufficient to produce both mood and emotion. Following this, distinct measures of mood and emotion would be required so that it could be shown that as emotion reached a premanipulation level, mood effects emerged. Such repeated measures pose a dangerous threat to validity in that they are likely to create reactivity (Nagata & Trierweiler, 1988). It would also be necessary to find a way to show that the automatic cognitive processes which constitute the mood were ongoing during the period of time when the emotion held focal attention. Moreover, unless emotional decay rates were relatively constant from subject to subject, a condition which seems difficult to satisfy (Zillman, Johnson, & Day, 1974), it would be hard to decide where to place the measurement points.

The other three arguments are simpler to test in that they presume that at any given moment in time, one is either in an emotional state or a mood state. They would only require that emotion be induced and that measurements of mood and emotion follow. As emotion dissipated, mood should appear. Unfortunately, Ruckmick's view did not stimulate such research and although a few studies have been done as tests of the ability of Solomon's "opponent process" theory to account for human affective responses (e.g., Ranieri & Zeiss, 1984; Sandvik, Diener, & Larsen, 1985), none satisfy the design requirements spelled out above. This leaves tests of excitation transfer as the sole source of relevant evidence.

The general paradigm employed by Zillman certainly fits the prescription. Initially, Zillman arouses his subjects. Though he sometimes uses exercise (e.g., Zillman and Bryant, 1974; Cantor, Zillman, and Bryant, 1975), emotion inductions such as disgust have been used as well (e.g., Cantor and Zillman, 1973; Cantor, Bryant, and Zillman, 1974). Then, after varying delays, new affect or arousal-instigating stimuli are produced, for example, humorous stimuli (Cantor et al., 1974), targets provocative of anger (Zillman, Katcher, & Milavsky, 1972), or sexually arousing stimuli (Cantor et al., 1975). The delays are introduced because Zillman believes (1978) that excitation transfer will not occur unless one permits the initial arousal to decay to the point where it is no longer salient. If the second arousal-instigating event occurs when the symptoms of the original arousal are still strong, the individual will supposedly recognize that his response might be affected and he will adjust his reaction accordingly, hence no transfer will be observed.

The results of the studies done by Zillman and his colleagues generally support Zillman's ideas about the conditions necessary for excitation transfer to occur. Transfer, as indicated by an invigorated response to the second instigating event, only occurs following a delay sufficient to permit the symptoms of excitation to fall below threshold but where measurable arousal still exists. No transfer is found if the second instigating event occurs while symptoms are still noticeable or if measurable arousal is gone (e.g., Cantor et al., 1975). Such studies show, as a group, that residual arousal left over from an initially arousing event can energize a variety of responses which are unrelated to the nature of the original arousal. Though Zillman is certainly entitled to refer to this as excitation transfer, I would note that it also corresponds to the idea that emotional arousal will, after a period of time, lose its specificity at which point its influence becomes more general and pervasive . . . like that of mood. Indeed, Zillman and I even agree as to the critical determinant of pervasiveness, that is, that it lies in the capacity of the state to exist apart from attributional labels or construals.

The major difference between a mood and an arousal interpretation of such data is that arousal is even more general in its influence than mood in that it is presumed capable of invigorating any kind of behavior be it positive, negative, or neutral. Thus, the findings indicating that residues of a negative emotion such as disgust can facilitate positive responses to music (Cantor & Zillman, 1973) and cartoons (Cantor et al., 1974) seem to favor an arousal over a mood interpretation. Also, Zillman explicitly assumes that the relevant state involves residual sympathetic excitation reflected in indices such as heart rate and blood pressure. Whether or not moods are necessarily associated with varying levels of physiological arousal is unclear. Though there is evidence that techniques such as the Velten (1968) mood induction procedure produce effects on psychomotor speed and vigor suggesting an activation component, more mild manipulations such as those typically employed by Isen may not.

Recollection or Imagining of Emotional Events. Attempting to induce mood by asking subjects to try to imagine themselves as being in the mood was popularized by Velten (1968). As compared to procedures of the sort used by Isen, the Velten procedure is considerably more efficient and can be mechanized. Unfortunately, as I noted earlier the procedure has been plagued with problems such as role demand and ineffectiveness with male subjects.

Closely related to the Velten procedure is a technique which relies on subjects to supply their own positive and negative thoughts by recalling happy or sad occasions. Though originally developed for use with children, (e.g., Moore, Underwood, & Rosenhan, 1973; Masters & Furman, 1976; Nasby & Yando, 1982), the procedure has been successfully applied to adults as well (e.g., Baumann, Cialdini, & Kenrick, 1981; Brewer, Doughtie, & Lubin, 1980; Manucia et al., 1984). Bower and his colleagues (e.g., Bower and Cohen, 1982; Bower, Gilligan & Monteiro, 1981; Bower, Monteiro, & Gilligan, 1978) use this same procedure but amplify it through the use of hypnotic suggestion.

The recollection technique seems superior to the Velten procedure in that it produces equivalent effects on both sexes and seems likely to be less subject to demand problems (except when used in conjunction with hypnosis) though this remains to be empirically established. It also has the advantage of being suitable for use by both children and adults, permitting comparative studies of mood effects though no such studies appear to have been done as yet.

Finally, it would seem appropriate to include in this category those studies which employ presentations of affect-inducing stories either in written form (e.g., Diener & Iran-Nejad, 1986), on audiotape (e.g., Schiffenbauer, 1974), or via film or videotape (e.g., Gouaux, 1971). These procedures have the advantage of permitting greater standardization than can be achieved using recollection.

It is clear from this kind of work that mood states can be directly induced via the activation of cognitive processes and without the participation of consequences that are of direct hedonic relevance. Such data provide a desirable methodological option to researchers and, at the same time, demand continuing attention to the way in which cognitive processes, especially memory, are related to affect.

The Inhibition of Emotional Responding. Unfortunately, the evidence which Jacobsen presents on behalf of her explanation of moods is anecdotal and selective, deriving principally from case studies. Given some latitude of interpretation, however, there are data in the experimental literature on emotion which seem consistent with Jacobsen's claim. The most pertinent data come from a study conducted by Berkowitz, Lepinski, and Angulo (1969). Subjects were provoked by a confederate of the experimenter and then given false feedback about their anger level via a "rigged" psychophysiological recording device. After this, subjects were given an opportunity to retaliate against the confederate and, finally, had their mood measured using Nowlis' (1965) Mood Adjective Check List (MACL). Findings showed that as compared with subjects who were led to believe that their anger level was either low or medium, subjects who were led to believe that their anger level was high were less aggressive and showed an elevated level of fatigue on the MACL, a classic symptom of bad mood.

Berkowitz et al. argued that these results occurred because the realization that one is very angry threatens loss of self-control which leads to anxiety. It is the anxiety which supposedly produces the two cited outcomes: fatigue because the anxiety is of the neurasthenic sort which manifests itself as tiredness and low aggression because the individual can reestablish self-control by carefully inhibiting himself.

Following Jacobsen, a different interpretation is possible. Here, the negative mood, as indicated by the elevated level of fatigue, would be the *result rather than the cause* of the reduced level of aggressiveness. More specifically, the hypothetical sequence of events would be that realization of a high anger level both threatens and embarrasses the subject who inhibits his aggressive behavior to convince both himself and the experimenter that he's not the hothead he seems. The inhibition of the emotional response of aggression produces negative mood as indicated by the MACL results. Given the order in which the dependent measures were collected, that is, the MACL results were obtained *after* the aggression measure, this explanation seems more likely to be correct than that of Berkowitz et al. since, according to their account, one might expect that the anxiety would diminish subsequent to the subject's inhibition of aggressive responding in that such inhibition is "proof" of the maintenance of self-control.

Other potentially relevant data might be found in studies that test the "facial feedback" hypothesis (Darwin, 1872; Izard, 1971, 1977; Tomkins, 1962, 1979) which suggests that facial expressive behavior influences the subjective experience of affect either because of sensory feedback from the facial musculature (Izard, 1971, 1977) or skin (Tomkins, 1979) or because of self-perception processes (Laird, 1974). One derivation from this hypothesis is that exaggeration of facial displays expressive of emotion should heighten emotional reactions whereas suppression should dampen them. The latter prediction also follows from Jacobsen's theory.

Data relevant to this prediction have been gathered in a series of studies by Lanzetta and Kleck and their colleagues (Colby, Lanzetta, & Kleck, 1977; Kleck, Vaughan, Cartwright-Smith, Vaughan, Colby, & Lanzetta, 1976; Lanzetta, Cartwright-Smith, & Kleck, 1976). The general procedure involved exposing subjects to electric shock under conditions leading to inhibition or exaggeration of facial displays of pain. For example, Kleck et al. (1976) led subjects to believe that they were being observed by an introductory psychology student while being shocked. This led to inhibition of facial displays of pain which, in turn, produced lower physiological responding and reports of decreased pain. The significance of these data for the facial feedback hypothesis has been questioned on the grounds that the "pain system" is argued to be a separate system, distinct from emotion (Tourangeau & Ellsworth, 1979; Winton, 1986). However, similar results have been obtained by Zuckerman, Klorman, Larrance, and Spiegel (1981) using videotaped scenes designed to produce affective responses.

Though these data are consistent with Jacobsen's view, they do not test the distinctive prediction that, in addition to dampening the response to affect-inducing stimuli, inhibition should also produce a more diffuse and pervasive response. Unfortunately, only one of the studies (Tourangeau & Ellsworth, 1979) that tried to test the suppression prediction gathered data that might permit an inference as to whether inhibition led to a more global affective response.

Tourangeau and Ellsworth (1979) showed subjects one of three different short films designed to produce fear, sadness, or be neutral. While watching the films, subjects were induced to arrange their facial muscles so as to produce expressions of fear, sadness, a nonemotional expression, or no instructions were given. The data relevant to Jacobsen's theory are the self-reports of feelings of fear and sadness collected from subjects immediately after the films were over. If suppression of expressive behavior makes the affect more global and less specific, then subjects who were induced to adopt a nonemotional expression while watching either the sad or frightening film should show a more *generally negative reaction* than subjects who were unmanipulated or subjects who were induced to adopt the expressive behavior which corresponded to the affective quality of the film. That is, when watching a sad film, subjects who inhibit their expressive behavior should report more fear than subjects who pose a sad expression or subjects who do not pose, and similarly, subjects who suppress while watching the fear-inducing film should show the most sadness.

Of the four relevant comparisons, three are in the direction I have deduced on behalf of Jacobsen with the other being a washout. Subjects who watched the fear-inducing film while suppressing their expressive behavior produced a mean sadness rating of 4.7; subjects who posed fearful expressions or who were unmanipulated rated their sadness at 4.1 and 3.5, respectively (the scales ranged form 0 to 16 with higher numbers indicating greater affect). Subjects who adopted a non-emotional expression while watching the sad film rated their fear at 3.9 whereas subjects who adopted a sad expression rated their fear at 3.2. In the only comparison that fails to support Jacobsen's prediction, subjects who watched the sad film without having their expression manipulated also rated their fear at 3.9.

It must be admitted that the data from Berkowitz et al. (1969) and Tourangeau and Ellsworth (1979) provide only modest support for Jacobsen's ideas. On the other hand, it is difficult to find support for a theory that is not subjected to test. Hopefully, more such tests will be conducted in the future although realism demands the recognition that experimentalists generally do not take psychoanalytic positions very seriously.

Evaluation of the Evidence on Proposed Sources of Mood

It seems clear that mildly pleasant and unpleasant events and the recollection or imagining of emotional occasions (whether involving self or not), both qualify as categorical antecedents of mood as I have defined it. In each case, a relatively large number of studies performed in different laboratories, using different indices of mood ranging from self-report to measures of memory and cognition, psychomotor activation, and other overt behaviors thought to be indicative of mood such as evaluative judgments and helping behavior seem to establish clearly that such antecedents produce rather general and pervasive effects.

On the other hand, little evidence was found to support various versions of the idea that mood follows the offset of emotion-inducing events and the same might be said of the suggestion that the inhibition of emotional response in the face of an instigating event produces mood. However, it should be observed that neither of these notions was put to a direct test by an investigator interested in mood, *per se.* Consequently, the designs and operations used in the few relevant studies I found were not optimal for the purpose of evaluating mood hypotheses.

The other assessment I might make at this point pertains to the degree to which these data tend to support or refute the various theoretical approaches to mood which were described in the last chapter. The theories which fare the best are that of Isen (1975, 1984; Isen et al., 1978) and the related theory proposed by Bower (1981). However, the findings which best support Isen are not those she contributed that show that mildly pleasant and unpleasant events cause mood since these data are also consistent with other views, such as Zajonc (1980). Rather, it is the data showing that imagination and recollection of pleasant and unpleasant occasions produce mood that her account best explains. That is because Isen assumes that the essence of mood lies in the tendency to think thoughts that share a similar hedonic tone. It is such thoughts that are responsible for the manner in which people describe themselves (including their feelings), the decisions they make, and the behaviors in which they engage. Any manipulation that causes a person to access such thoughts should be an effective mood inducer. None of the other theoretical positions would make this prediction.

As for the other theories considered in Chapter 2, I have already noted that support for Jacobsen's view (1957) is minimal in that few relevant data exist though what little evidence there is seems mildly encouraging. The evidence on antecedents of mood does not seem pertinent to evaluating the relevance of Zajonc's speculations specifically to mood; the evidence reviewed in the previous chapter, though consistent with the idea that cognitive and affective systems are at least partially independent, cannot be readily generalized to mood because the dependent measures used, that is, preference ratings and physiological indices, are not clearly indicators of mood. As to the arousal plus cognition theories, I would withhold judgment at this point. Though Zillman's (1978) theory, which belongs to this group, is supported by data I reviewed in this chapter, the general idea that unexplained arousal states function like moods can be better assessed after data on endogenous sources of mood are reviewed in the next chapter. It is time to turn in that direction.

Chapter 4

Endogenous Factors Associated With Mood

Paula P. Schnurr, Dartmouth Medical School

Moods commonly arise as the result of perceiving, recalling, or imagining hedonically-toned environmental events, but also may appear without any obvious precipitating occurrence. Although one might argue that these latter instances simply reflect a failure to identify the mood-inducing event, it is possible that, at least in some cases, the mood is attributable to circumstances that are substantially endogenous and nonpsychological in nature. Consider the case of 48-hour cycles in bipolar disorder, a rare form in which episodes of mania and depression occur on alternate days (Wehr, Goodwin, Wirz-Justice, Craig, & Breitmeier, 1982). It is hard to imagine how environmental events could be responsible for eliciting profound states of mania and depression in such a regular pattern. Moreover, from a purely reductionistic point of view, moods cannot arise from anything other than an endogenous source given the unarguable fact that affective experiences, like all others, must emerge from the biological substrate. Because this is so, it follows that direct (i.e., not psychologically mediated) perturbations of the substrate can mimic effects normally instigated by hedonically relevant environmental events. From a less reductionistic perspective, however, it is legitimate to question whether endogenous factors function autonomously to induce mood.[1]

In the present chapter, I consider this possibility by reviewing the evidence on endogenous events associated with mood. The review will be biased toward mood states of relatively long duration, as most of the research on endogenous factors has centered around mood disorders such as depression and mania, rather than on everyday moods. However, findings related to everyday moods will be presented in somewhat greater detail than the clinical evidence to provide a basis for the discussion of continuity between normal and pathological moods in Chapter 7.

---

[1]However, for those still wondering how mood can be anything other than a reaction to environmental events I offer an analogy based on two genetic disorders: dwarfism and phenylketonuria (PKU). In dwarfism, biological processes unfold according to an endogenous maturational timetable, not in response to the environment (although growth certainly can be affected by the environment). In PKU, there is an inherited inability to metabolize the amino acid phenylalanine, the ingestion of which can result in toxic accumulations that damage the central nervous system. Unlike in dwarfism, the biological abnormality in PKU does not lead to disorder without exogenous precipitation.

A note on continuity: Over 10 years ago, Blatt, D'Afflitti, and Quinlan (1976) stated that there had "been relatively little investigation of depression as a normal affective state that may have continuity with various types of clinical depression" (p. 384). Today, the extent of similarity between normal and pathological states, and the extent to which one yields information about the other still are not known. The appropriateness of discussing both types of states in the present chapter thus may be questioned, but the question may be addressed empirically by comparing the presence of endogenous factors in everyday and disordered moods.

Let me begin by defining an endogenous event as any of the nonperceptible physical concomitants of the cognitive and affective changes that occur during mood states. For example, I would not consider as an endogenous event the increase in heart rate experienced by subjects who received an injection of adrenalin in Schachter and Singer's (1962) experiment. Instead, I would consider the increase in available epinephrine to be an endogenous event. Given this definition, endogenous events can only be detected with sophisticated biomedical techniques, although these events may produce clearly perceptible physical changes. Therefore, the discussion of endogenous events will center around processes such as neurotransmitter synthesis and neuroendocrine function.

The idea that unexplainable moods result from endogenous factors goes back at least as far as the ancient Greeks, who believed an imbalance of the bodily representations of the four basic elements (fire, water, earth, and air) could lead to states they described as "melancholia" and "mania" (see Jackson, 1986, for an excellent discussion of this subject). Many modern conceptualizations of mood disorder have neglected the role of organic factors in favor of psychosocial events (e.g., Freud, 1986, and early object loss), but the hypothesis of endogenous malfunction is intuitively compelling and far from dead. For example, in two current undergraduate textbooks of abnormal psychology (Sarason & Sarason, 1984; Schumer, 1983), it is stated that "many depressive disorders do not arise as a result of external stressors or life events" (Schumer, p. 251, citing Akiskal & McKinney, 1975[2]) and "depression may have an organic cause: problems in neural transmission caused by the unavailability of a sufficient amount of the chemical transmitters called catecholamines" (Sarason & Sarason, 1984, p. 242).

The quote from Schumer (1983) illustrates the kind of thinking that has helped to maintain the viability of endogenous explanations of mood disorder: If an external cause cannot be identified, the disorder must be internally caused. In statistical terms this is accepting the null hypothesis as

[2]This is an inaccurate citation of Akiskal and McKinney (1975), who actually said that "depressive phenomena are neither inherently psychological (reactive) nor organic (endogenous)" (p. 288), and when discussing other theories presuming that a neurobiological defect is primary in mood disorder, went on to "propose that such a defect, if indeed it does exist, can also be secondary to developmental and interpersonal events" (p. 298).

true because the alternative could not be proven, a logically-flawed, but sometimes acceptable practice if one has demonstrated sufficient power to prove the alternative.[3] In specific terms, satisfying the latter condition means that one has carefully looked for precipitating psychosocial events in cases of disorder where there seem to be none. Unfortunately, this is difficult to do. Leff, Roatch, and Bunney (1970) reported that repeated interviewing with so-called endogenously depressed patients—those who shared features such as early morning awakening and feeling at their worst in the morning, and whose depressed episodes seemed to have occurred without any precipitating stress—uncovered evidence of psychosocial stress that had not been obtained from early interviews. They also reported that repeated interviewing revealed all patients to have experienced more than one stressor, and endogenously and nonendogenously depressed patients to have experienced a similar number of stressors. However, no statistical comparisons were performed so the study is best interpreted as demonstrating that stressors known to precipitate depression occurred in all depressions defined by having endogenous features. This has been shown by others (e.g., Thompson & Hendrie, 1972); hence, I will use the term "endogenous" only to imply "from within" without making a causal assumption.

After summarizing the state of current knowledge on neurobiologic correlates of disordered mood, I will discuss two cases in which mood covaries with known endogenous changes, and one in which the mechanism of change is presumed to operate at an endogenous level: premenstrual syndrome, postpartum depression, and seasonal affective disorder. I also will summarize what is known about the neurobiologic correlates of everyday mood and then end by reviewing several theories of mood in which endogenous factors are incorporated along with nonendogenously-triggered factors to explain the origin and maintenance of disordered mood.

Neurobiologic Aspects of Disordered Mood

Depression and Mania

According to the American Psychiatric Association's (1987) *Diagnostic and Statistical Manual (DSM-III-R)*, the distinguishing feature of affective disorders is "a disturbance of mood, accompanied by a full or partial Manic or Depressive Syndrome, that is not due to any other physical or mental disorder" (p. 213). Mood, in turn, is described as "a prolonged emotion that colors the whole psychic life" (p. 213), involving either depression or elation. Affective disorders are classified in terms of symptom severity and duration. I concern myself here with the Major Affective Disorders, in which symp-

[3]Cohen (1977) describes this as "functionally" accepting the null hypothesis.

toms are most severe and prolonged: Major Depression and Bipolar Disorder.

Major Depression is diagnosed for individuals who are experiencing or have experienced a Major Depressive Episode that cannot be attributed to either an organic factor or normal bereavement, but who do not report symptoms of mania. A Major Depressive Episode is characterized by dysphoric mood (e.g., depression, irritability, or hopelessness) or a loss of interest or pleasure in usual activities. The mood disturbance must persist most of the day for two weeks, and it must be a change from a person's typical level of functioning. In addition to dysphoric mood or loss of interest, at least four of the following symptoms must be present: increased or decreased appetite, or unintended weight gain or loss; insomnia or hypersomnia; psychomotor agitation or retardation; decreased sexual drive; fatigue or loss of energy, feelings of worthlessness or inappropriate guilt; complaints or evidence of a decrease in the ability to think clearly; and recurrent thoughts of death or a suicide attempt. Depression with melancholia[4] is a subclassification of Major Depression in which there are at least five of the following symptoms: a loss of pleasure in almost all activities; an inability to feel pleasure even when something good happens; depression at its worst in the morning; awakening at least two hours before usual; prominent psychomotor retardation or agitation; significant decrease in appetite or weight loss; no history of significant personality disorder before the first Major Depressive Episode; one or more previous episodes from which there had been good recovery; and previous improvement in response to a somatic therapy such as a tricyclic antidepressant.

Bipolar Disorder is diagnosed whenever there has been a full Manic Episode because future depressive episodes are likely for those who experience mania; as in Major Depressive Disorder, the diagnosis cannot be made if an organic cause is likely. In a Manic Episode, mood is elevated, often to the point of having an infectious quality, expansive, or, less often, irritable. At least three of the following symptoms (four if mood is irritable only) must be present during the mood disturbance: increased activity (social, occupational, sexual); increased talkativeness; racing thoughts, inflated self-esteem; decreased need for sleep; distractibility; and an increase in hedonically-relevant activities that may have negative consequences. Mania thus seems to be a positive, energized mood, but it differs from everyday positive mood in that it usually involves inappropriate behavior (e.g., a sudden and unusual increase in religiosity or sexual activity), and sometimes involves irritability, especially when concerned others attempt to constrain the manic individual's expansivity.

A great variety of drugs and illnesses are capable of inducing profound and disruptive mood states, even in individuals who do not have a mood

[4]Melancholic depression is also described as "endogenous depression," but was labeled as the former in *DSM-III-R* to avoid the erroneous implication that precipitating stress does not occur in this syndrome.

disorder. For example, depression can result from medical problems as diverse as infection, endocrine dysfunction, cerebrovascular accident, and nutritional deficiency (Griest & Griest, 1979). Depression also can result from taking non-mood-altering drugs as common as antihypertensives (Klerman & Hirshfeld, 1979), and mania can result from taking steroids and thyroid hormones (Krauthamer & Klerman, 1978). Although a psychological component may be invoked as a plausible cause of depression in cases of debilitating illness such as stroke, it is unlikely that psychological factors play a causal role in many other instances. Thus, even though one cannot make a *DSM-III-R* diagnosis of affective disorder if an organic cause is likely (a different label is applied instead), the findings on the affective side effects of drugs and illness strongly suggest that there is a biologic component of mood.

Biogenic Amine Disturbance. Observations of depression occurring in 5 to 15% of individuals taking the antihypertensive drug reserpine in the 1950s (e.g., Fries, 1954) set in motion much of the current research on neurobiology and mood. These reports stimulated interest in this relationship because one action of reserpine is to deplete brain levels of neurotransmitters known as biogenic amines: the indoleamine, serotonin, and the catecholamines, dopamine and norepinephrine. Heightening this interest was the fact that the action of the antidepressant drugs in use at that time was to increase the availability of biogenic amines at post-synaptic receptors in the brain (Cole, 1964).

Therefore, by the mid-1960s, several investigators had proposed theories of mood disorder based on levels of brain amines (see Schildkraut, 1965, for a review). According to these theories, which came to be known collectively as the "catecholamine hypothesis" of mood disorder, depression was associated with the depletion of brain amines and mania was associated with an excess. The lines of evidence offered in support of this hypothesis were of two types: first, that from studies in which the consequences of manipulating brain amines were observed (e.g., Schildkraut, Klerman, Hammond, & Friend, 1964), and second, that from studies in which amine metabolism was observed in groups known to differ in their mood (e.g., Strom-Olsen & Weil-Malherbe, 1958).

The principal data collected in investigations of brain amine metabolism are measures of neurotransmitter metabolites in urine, cerebrospinal fluid (CSF), and plasma. Low metabolite levels indicate low neurotransmitter activity. It is unfortunate that these measures are contaminated to an unknown degree by the presence of peripheral amines. Moreover, error due to variables such as illness, age, gender, and measurement technique is rarely controlled, but potentially substantial; for example, Potter and Linnoila (1989) cite a mean difference of 20% in separate assays taken from the *same* patients in the *same* lab. Nevertheless, increasing evidence points toward a degree of complexity in the association between brain amines and mood beyond that posited by the catecholamine hypothesis.

First of all, subgroups of depressed individuals differ in amine metabolism, although the pattern of differences is disputed. Some data suggest that the catecholamine hypothesis is most true of bipolar, rather than unipolar, depressives. As predicted, bipolar depressives have been shown to excrete low levels of the norepinephrine metabolite, 3-methoxy-4-hydroxyphenylethyleneglycol (MHPG), during the depressed phases and high levels of MHPG during the manic phases of their illness (Greenspan et al., 1970). In contrast, not all unipolar depressives have been shown to excrete low levels of MHPG, relative to controls (Schatzberg et al., 1982), and some have been shown to excrete higher levels than normals (Garfinkel, Warsh, & Stancer, 1979). Some recent data even suggest that differences between depressives and normals in amine function are due mostly to the unipolar subtype. Maas et al. (1987), who claim that absolute levels of catecholamines and catecholamine metabolites are less informative than are ratios of synthesis to excretion, found that only unipolar, and not bipolar, depressives differed markedly from normals in excretion ratios; the lack of differences between bipolars and controls may have been due in part to diagnostic heterogeneity in Maas et al.'s bipolar group, but the pattern of means and standard errors suggests that this was not the case. Similar complexity exists for investigations of serotonin and dopamine (Gerner & Bunney, 1986). Although the precise nature of differences between bipolar and unipolar depressives remain to be elucidated, depression is not always accompanied by decreased serotonin or catecholamine metabolism and there appear to be biologic subtypes of depression.

Second, there is variability in responses to drugs that relieve symptoms of depression by increasing the availability of biogenic amines, such as tricyclic antidepressants and monoamine oxidase (MAO) inhibitors. For example, these drugs induce mania in many bipolar depressives during a depressed phase (Krauthamer & Klerman, 1978) but do so in only a small percentage of unipolar depressives (Wehr & Goodwin, 1987); note that the induction of mania cannot be due to high pretreatment levels of norepinephrine, as bipolar types have lower MHPG levels than do unipolar types during a depressive episode (Schatzberg et al., 1982). Also, for a time it was thought that there were low norepinephrine and low serotonin subtypes of depression because unipolar depressives who excrete low levels of the serotonin metabolite, 5-hydroxyindolacetic acid (5-HIAA), were shown to benefit most from tricyclic antidepressants thought to selectively increase serotonin availability, such as amitryptiline; those who excreted low levels of MHPG were shown to benefit most from tricyclics thought to selectively increase norepinephrine availability, such as imipramine (Maas, 1975; Schildkraut, 1973). The reason that Maas and Schildkraut observed selective responding is unclear because both drugs have relatively greater effects on norepinephrine than serotonin (Richelson & Pfennig, 1984), and even the existence of the subtypes has recently been questioned (Davis et al., 1988). However, the fact that there is heterogeneity in response to drugs that influence the metabolism of biogenic amines is unquestionable.

Taken together, the evidence suggests that biogenic amine levels are neither uniformly low in depression nor high in mania. Instead, there appear to be biological subtypes of affective disorder (Schatzberg et al., 1982, 1989), with unique patterns of deficiency and excess. Maas and his colleagues (1987) argue that "[s]ubsequent analyses, research and second-generation amine-depression hypothesis formulations will need to take into account variables such as drug response type, clinical subtype, and clinical characteristics of the history of the illness as they relate to amine and metabolite measures if we are to understand the complexities of altered amine neuron function in depression" (p. 343). However, the "first-generation" catecholamine hypothesis was known to be too simplistic even when proposed (Schildkraut, 1965). It should not be dismissed in its entirety but rather evaluated for its heuristic value, which seems reasonably high.

Neuroendocrine Disturbance: Cortisol. The adrenal cortex releases cortisol in response to stress, illness, and changes in metabolism. Cortisol regulation is mediated through the hypothalamic-pituitary-adrenal (HPA) axis, with the hypothalamic stimulation occurring via several neurotransmitter pathways (see Pepper & Krieger, 1984, for a brief review). Besides varying in response to environmental and endogenous challenges, cortisol levels follow a circadian pattern, with release peaking in the early morning around awakening, then falling off toward evening, and finally hitting a low around midnight (e.g., Fibiger, Singer, Miller, Armstrong, & Datar, 1984; Halbreich, Asnis, Shindledecker, Zumoff, & Nathan, 1985a).

In some depressed individuals, cortisol secretion follows abnormal patterns. Basal cortisol production is increased in individuals who experience anxiety and psychotic disorganization along with their depression (Sachar, Hellman, Fukushima, & Gallagher, 1970). Cortisol production is increased also in melancholic depression; however, basal cortisol levels in melancholia are highly variable and are often not outside the normal range (Halbreich, Asnis, Shindledecker, Zumoff, & Nathan, 1985b). In almost 50% of melancholic depressives, cortisol production quickly escapes suppression by the steroid dexamethasone, which signals the hypothalamus to reduce the production of corticotropin-releasing factor (CRF), a vital link in cortisol's release (Carroll et al., 1981). Therefore, this kind of response to what is known as a dexamethasone suppression test (DST) is often used as an index of melancholia. Note that although a negative DST result does not provide conclusive information, a positive test result does, as less than 10% of nonmelancholic depressives fail to show suppression (Carroll et al., 1981).

Neuroendocrine Disturbance: Thyroid Hormone. Another widely researched relationship between mood and neuroendocrine function involves thyroid hormone. Dysregulation of the hypothalamic-pituitary-thyroid (HPT) axis, resulting in decreased circulating thyroid hormone, is seen in approximately 30% of depressed individuals (Whybrow, Akiskal, & McKinney, 1984). Yet thyroid hormone by itself is an ineffective treatment for depression (Feldmacher-Reiss, 1958), although it can induce mania in persons predisposed to bipolar illness (Josephson & MacKenzie, 1979). Instead, recovery from depression is facilitated by the addition of thyroid hormone to treatment with a tricyclic antidepressant like imipramine (Prange, Wilson, Rabon, & Lipton, 1969).

About one-third of depressed individuals show a blunted response to an infusion of thyrotropin-releasing hormone (TRH), a substance that in normals, and especially in hypothyroid individuals, increases thyroid hormone levels (Prange, Wilson, Lara, Alltop, & Breese, 1972). In fact, the TRH test has been used like the DST in the diagnosis of depression, and when the two tests were used together, at least one abnormal result was seen in almost 90% of melancholic depressions, as compared to 0% in depressions without melancholic features (Levy & Stern, 1987). As in biogenic amine metabolism, bipolar and unipolar depressives differ in response to TRH, with bipolar depressives showing a less blunted response (Extein, Pottash, Gold, & Cowdry, 1984).

What do these types of findings tell us about the nature of the relationship between thyroid function and mood? Whybrow and Prange (1981) have proposed that thyroid hormone modulates the action of catecholamines, particularly norepinephrine, and thereby functions as an adjustment mechanism in times of stress-induced demand. According to their account, in individuals with normal thyroid function, thyroid hormone facilitates the use of norepinephrine by enhancing receptor sensitivity, and thus serves to regulate transmission along norepinephrine pathways. It appears that this regulatory mechanism is not powerful enough to maintain homeostasis in the face of unusual demand, as norepinephrine levels are low in some depressed individuals and thyroid hormone is incapable of restoring these levels to normal values. Rather it seems that a substance that increases the availability of norepinephrine, such as imipramine, is needed combined with thyroid hormone's sensitizing function to facilitate recovery. However, Whybrow and Prange (1981) propose that in individuals predisposed to bipolar illness, the rising amount of norepinephrine may overshoot a desirable level and lead to mania.

The key concept of Whybrow and Prange's (1981) hypothesis is that of regulation; depression and mania result when the demand on neurotransmitter pathways is so great that thyroid hormone cannot play its regulatory function. These authors have highlighted the need to think in complex terms about the complex interactions that occur between neurobiological systems.

Neuroendocrine Disturbance: Endogenous Opiates. Because opiate compounds like heroin and morphine induce such profound euphoria in addition to their analgesic effects, it is little wonder that endogenously-produced opiates have been included in the study of the neurobiological aspects of mood. First of all, animal research has suggested that endogenous opiates are produced in response to stress and pain (Amir, Brown, & Amit, 1980; Madden, Akil, Patrick, & Barchas, 1977), with the increase resulting in what is known as stress-induced analgesia. This analgesic property has been invoked as a component of "runner's high," as running increases beta-endorphin levels (Colt, Wardlaw, & Frantz, 1981) and naloxone, an opiate antagonist, increases pain perception from normal post-run levels (Haier, Quaid, & Mills, 1981). Secondly, there may be a direct link between mood and the endogenous opiate system, which includes substances such as beta-endorphin and the enkephalins. Endogenous opiate receptors are found in areas of the central nervous system thought to be involved in emotional behavior (Kuhar, Pert, & Snyder, 1973).

It has been proposed that depression results from a deficit in endogenous opiate activity and that mania results from an excess (Byck, 1976). Clinical evidence bearing on the hypothesis is mixed. Of the studies on naturally occurring opiate activity, few associations with mood have been observed. Increased endogenous opiate activity has been reported in depression (Terenius, Wahlstrom, & Agren, 1977) and mania (Lindstrom, Widerlov, Gunne, Wahlstrom, & Terenius, 1978), but the increase is observed only in some patients. Post and his colleagues (Post, Pickar, Ballenger, Naber, & Rubinow, 1984) found no differences in total opiate activity or beta-endorphin levels between any of the five groups in their study: normals, unipolar depressives, bipolar depressives, manics, and recovered affectively ill. Correlations between opiate activity and mood were negative for self-reports of state anxiety in normals, and positive for observer reports of anxiety in depressives (bipolar and unipolar combined). There were no significant correlations between opiate activity and other measures of positive and negative mood for the normals and the depressed group, and no significant correlations between any variables for the other groups. Of the studies in which opiate activity has been manipulated (see Cohen & Pickar, 1981, for a review), a double-blind, placebo-controlled format has rarely been used. However, there is a report of an improvement in depression after injections of beta-endorphin (Gerner, Catlin, Gorelick, Hui, & Lui, 1980). Also, naloxone has been reported to improve mania (Judd, Janowsky, Segal, & Huey, 1979), although the finding is not consistent (Pickar, Vartanian et al., 1982). These results are intriguing, but the variability in both the correlational and experimental findings casts serious doubt on the likelihood that aberrations in endogenous opiate levels are a cause of either depression or mania.

Neurophysiologic Function. In their review of the neurophysiologic correlates of mood, Whybrow and Mendels (1969) proposed that depression, and possibly mania, are disorganized and highly aroused states of the central nervous system. This proposal was determined on the basis of evidence taken from electrolyte, electromyographic (EMG), electroencephalographic (EEG), and sleep behaviors. Of these areas, it is sleep that has received the greatest attention, so I will only briefly mention the other subjects.

Intracellular sodium concentration is increased in states of mania and depression and it tends toward normal levels after recovery (Coppen & Shaw, 1963; Coppen, Shaw, Malleson, & Costain, 1966). Shaw (1966) proposed that this increase would lower the resting potential of the cell, and thereby result in neural hyperexcitability. The consequence of the hyperexcitability would be above-normal arousal. In 1969 Whybrow and Mendels noted that this hypothesis needed further testing, but according to Whybrow et al. (1984), the earlier paper is still current, which implies that this testing has not taken place or has not yielded fruitful information.

However, other evidence supports the proposition that depression, at least, is a state of extreme arousal. For example, depressives have higher muscle tension and greater EMG responsiveness to noise than do normals (Goldstein, 1965). Also, depressives show a prolonged EEG arousal response (blocking of the EEG alpha wave rhythm) to external stimulation relative to the responsiveness they show after recovery (Paulson & Gottlieb, 1961). Similar findings of prolonged arousal have been observed for cortical evoked potentials (Shagass & Schwartz, 1966), although this may be true only for psychotic depressives (Whybrow & Mendels, 1969).

The sleep patterns of depressed individuals also suggest a state of hyperarousal. In fact, self-reported sleep disturbance is a component of the diagnosis of Major Depressive Disorder (American Psychiatric Association, 1987). Using EEG recording techniques, researchers have found that depressives, relative to normals, have a harder time falling asleep, experience shallower sleep, have a shorter latency to rapid eye movement (REM) sleep onset, and have lower sleep efficiency (time in bed/time asleep); depressives with the diagnosis of melancholia also experience a type of insomnia known as "early morning awakening," a tendency to wake up several hours earlier than usual (see Gillin et al., 1984, for a review). Of these problems, shortened REM latency has been considered most diagnostic of depression. Kupfer and Foster (1972) have actually proposed that shortened REM latency may be taken as a state marker of depression. Although REM latency (as well as density) may distinguish some subtypes of depression from each other (Feinberg & Carroll, 1984), short REM latency is found in many other affective and medical conditions and in normals (Gillin et al., 1984). Also, many depressed individuals do not differ from normals in REM latency. For example, Gillin and his colleagues (1984) present histograms of REM latency data from an earlier study (Gillin, Duncan, Pettigrew, Frankel, & Snyder, 1979) in which it can be seen that 70% of the REM latency values for a group of depressed patients fell within the range observed for normals, despite a statistically significant mean difference between groups. Therefore, the utility of REM latency as a state marker for depression is questionable, although the aroused character of depressive sleep is clear, if nonspecific to depression.

The early morning awakening typical of melancholic depression, along with the therapeutic effect of sleep deprivation in the second half of the night (Schilgen & Tolle, 1980) and the short REM latency observed in many depressives, have been interpreted as suggesting that depression is associated with a disturbance in the body's circadian (24 hour) rhythms. An excellent review of the literature on human biological rhythms and their relevance to mood may be found in a chapter by Wehr and Goodwin (1981). In this review, Wehr and Goodwin state that findings across a variety of aspects of biological function are consistent with the hypothesis that in depression, many circadian biological cycles are advanced relative to the sleep/wake cycle; this is known as the "phase-advance" hypothesis of depression. For example, short REM latency may be the advance of the REM cycle relative to sleeping and waking.

The therapeutic effect of sleep deprivation in the second half of the night led Wehr and Wirz-Justice (1982) to propose a variant of the phase-advance hypothesis. These authors suggested that it is necessary to be awake during a certain part of the day to avoid becoming depressed. This time period is determined by circadian rhythms, which in normals, are synchronized so that waking occurs before the necessary period. Depressives, in whom most circadian cycles are advanced, are presumably asleep during the time when they need to be awake; hence, being awakened early improves depression. Although Wehr and Wirz-Justice's suggestion is consistent with the results of sleep deprivation experiments, I am left wondering why individuals with early morning awakening, who, one might argue, are self-administering sleep deprivation, are among the most seriously depressed. Perhaps the early awakening does not occur early enough.

A recent proposal is that depressed individuals with early morning awakening, who are phase-advanced, need to avoid bright light in the morning and then be exposed to bright light in the evening to force their other circadian cycles back into phase with their sleep/wake cycle (Lewy, Sack, & Singer, 1984, 1985); Lewy et al. also propose that individuals with recurring winter depression, who typically have morning hypersomnia, are phase-*delayed*, and thus, should be treated with bright light in the early morning hours. It is important to note that Kripke (1981) has suggested that the exposure to light correlated with sleep deprivation, rather than the deprivation itself, is the causal factor in the improvement that results from this treatment. I will consider the possibility that light produces endogenous effects that lead to mood change in a later part of this chapter.

Summary. Cases of disordered mood are characterized by both neurobiologic abnormality and diversity: abnormality, in the sense that many aspects of neurobiologic function are observed to deviate from normal levels in depression and mania (with only some returning to normal upon recovery);

and diversity, in the sense that there appear to be biological subtypes of affective disorder. The latter feature is especially important, as it adds complexity to the investigation of etiological factors by reducing the probability of a single cause of disorder. I will review theories in which the issues of abnormality and diversity are considered, but first, I discuss several mood disorders in which endogenous mechanisms are strongly implicated.

Premenstrual Syndrome

Most women report systematic changes in their physical and emotional state during the course of the menstrual cycle, with negative affect and uncomfortable physical symptoms predominating in the luteal phase before menstruation and then subsiding with the onset of menstruation. The moderate to severe manifestations of this pattern, affecting approximately 40% of all women (Reid, 1985) are known as premenstrual syndrome (PMS) or tension (PMT). The most commonly reported symptoms of PMS include depression, anxiety, irritability, fatigue, headache, breast tenderness, and water retention (Bancroft & Bäckström, 1985; Logue & Moos, 1986; Reid & Yen, 1981), with negative mood being reported by virtually all sufferers (Halbreich & Endicott, 1985; Rubinow, Roy-Byrne, Hoban, Gold, & Post, 1984).

Given the co-occurrence of premenstrual symptoms and the biologically-caused events of the menstrual cycle, it is easy to see why an endogenous cause for PMS might seem likely. Yet our understanding of the etiology of PMS has been hampered by methodologic problems, making both cross-study comparisons and negative results difficult to interpret (see Rubinow & Roy-Byrne, 1984, for a review). Most notable among these problems is the use by some investigators of retrospective accounts of PMS symptoms, as such accounts do not correspond to prospective daily symptom records (DeJong et al., 1985; Schnurr, 1988); for example, 42% of DeJong et al.'s subjects, who retrospectively reported themselves as having PMS, did not show cycle-related changes in daily symptom levels. Fortunately, most of the research published in the past several years has been based on prospectively validated diagnoses. Another serious problem has been a lack of agreement about the degree of premenstrual symptom change required for a diagnosis of PMS; what is PMS in one study may not be so in another (Schnurr, in press).

Estrogen and progesterone are two gonadal hormones that increase and decrease systematically in the course of the menstrual cycle. Estrogen is low during menstruation, peaks at ovulation, and then drops to rise again before falling to low levels in the week before menstruation. Progesterone is low until estrogen reaches its second peak, and then reaches higher levels than estrogen before dropping off in the week before menstruation. Because the symptoms of PMS are coincident with these changes, various hypotheses about the etiological role of progesterone and estrogen have been explored.

One of the most prominent hypotheses is that a low level of post-ovulatory (luteal phase) progesterone leads to PMS. A related hypothesis holds that

PMS is caused by high luteal phase estrogen, relative to progesterone. Both Reid (1985) and Bancroft & Bäckström (1985) note that the apparent excitatory effect of estrogen and inhibitory effect of progesterone on the central nervous system have been used to support these hypotheses. However, the possibility that unopposed estrogen leads to a state of overarousal is challenged on logical and empirical grounds. Unopposed estrogen cannot account for PMS because the estrogen : progesterone ratio is highest at ovulation, when many women experience a sense of well-being. Also, symptoms of PMS often appear before abnormal changes in levels of these hormones are observed (Reid, 1985). Moreover, evidence suggests that PMS is not associated with either absolutely or relatively low levels of progesterone in the luteal phase (Bäckström et al., 1983; O'Brien, Selby, & Symonds, 1980; Taylor, 1979; but see Munday, Brush, & Taylor, 1981). Finally, controlled trials of progesterone therapy show it to be ineffective in relieving symptoms of PMS (e.g., Maddocks, Hahn, Moller, & Reid, 1986).

All in all, it would seem that the observed covariance between premenstrual symptoms and gonadal hormone levels is nothing more than spurious, yet additional data cast doubt on such a sweeping conclusion. Halbreich, Endicott, Goldstein, and Nee (1986) reported that the rate of progesterone decrease from peak luteal phase levels, and less strongly, the rate of estrogen decrease and the relationship between the rates, were positively related to symptom severity; neither daily estrogen and progesterone levels, daily ratios, nor luteal phase levels—in other words, the static factors previously investigated—were associated with symptoms. Also, inhibition of ovulation, which prevents profound changes in estrogen and progesterone levels, is an effective treatment for PMS (Hammarbäck & Bäckström, 1988; Muse, Cetel, Futterman, & Yen, 1984). Thus, the role of gonadal hormones in the etiology of PMS cannot be dismissed. I will return to this issue after discussing several other proposed causes of the disorder.

An excess of the hormone prolactin, which peaks during ovulation and then again during the mid- and late luteal phases, has been suggested as a cause of PMS (e.g., Horrobin, 1973), although abnormal prolactin secretion is rarely found in this disorder (e.g., Roy-Byrne, Rubinow, Hoban, Grover, & Blank, 1987; Steiner, Haskett, Carroll, Hays, & Rubin, 1984; but see Halbreich, Assael, Bendavid, & Borsten, 1976). Also, treatment with bromocriptine, which inhibits prolactin release, only improves premenstrual symptoms of breast tenderness and not negative mood (Steiner et al., 1983). Thus, prolactin levels appear unrelated to the affective components of PMS. Recently, Horrobin (1983) has addressed the number of studies in which prolactin was not found to be elevated by proposing that hypersensitivity to this hormone, rather than a high absolute level, leads to PMS, but I was unable to find any data that directly support his hypothesis.

Like prolactin, cortisol does not appear to be associated with PMS. In normal women, cortisol does not vary with menstrual cycle phase, and if anything, is lower premenstrually than postmenstrually (Abplanalp, Livingston, Rose, & Sandwisch, 1977). Even in women with severe PMS, Haskett, Steiner and Carroll (1984) found no relationship between mood and cortisol in either postmenstrual or premenstrual phases; these authors also observed a low rate of nonsuppression to dexamethasone, which suggests that the depression in PMS is biologically dissimilar to that observed in severe clinical depression.

However, the results of a recent study (Roy-Byrne et al., 1987) contradict this statement. As noted earlier in this chapter, some depressed individuals show a blunted response of thyroid stimulating hormone (TSH) to an infusion of thyrotrophin-releasing hormone (TRH; Prange et al., 1972) whereas others show an augmented response (Gold, Pottash, & Extein, 1981). Roy-Byrne and his colleagues measured basal thyroid hormone levels and did TRH tests on women whose PMS had been prospectively confirmed. Relative to controls, women with PMS did not differ in basal TSH levels at either follicular or luteal phases, but were more likely to show either an augmented or a blunted response to TRH. None of the controls responded abnormally, whereas 7 of the 10 PMS patients who were symptomatic in the cycle in which they were tested did. Also, four other PMS patients whose prospective records did not show evidence of PMS during the cycle in which the TRH was administered responded normally to the test. That the abnormal response to TRH infusion may be a trait marker for consistent PMS is suggested by the following: 1) of the seven women who responded abnormally, all did so during the follicular phase, when they were asymptomatic, and only four had abnormal responses during their symptomatic luteal phase; and 2) none of the four women with inconsistent PMS responded abnormally at either time. This suggests that abnormal thyroid function is not a primary cause of PMS, although it may predict the consistency of symptom recurrence.

Another hypothesis of PMS is that excessive release of or hypersensitivity to endogenous opiates during the luteal phase, followed by acute withdrawal in the late luteal and menstrual phases leads to other neuroendocrine changes capable of producing the symptoms of PMS (Reid & Yen, 1981). Rein and Yen make the hypothesis attractive by suggesting examples of how this change in endogenous opiate activity could trigger the variety of symptoms associated with PMS. However, a serious point of contention regarding the hypothesis is whether endogenous opiate levels change as proposed during the menstrual cycle. One study on humans found no increase in endogenous opiates during the luteal phase (Hamilton, Aloi, Mucciardi, & Murphy, 1983). In contrast, one study (Vrbicky et al., 1982) found a preovulatory peak and a postovulatory trough in beta-endorphin, although the difference is ambiguous in an absolute sense because the data were collected for only approximately one week before and one week after ovulation, that is, there are no data on menstrual or late luteal phase levels. Another study found that, in nonhuman primates, endogenous opiates were highest during the luteal phase, lowest during the menstrual phase, and moderate before ovulation, as proposed by Reid and Yen (Weherenberg, Wardlaw, Frantz, & Ferin, 1982).

More relevant to Reid and Yen's (1981) hypothesis are data from three recent studies. In one, Giannini, Price, and Loiselle (1984) measured beta-endorphin levels on menstrual cycle days 7 and 24 (post- and premenstrual, respectively) among women classified as experiencing either mild, moderate, or severe PMS. After computing the amount of change between measurement periods for each subject, the authors cross-tabulated those above and below the overall median amount of decrease as a function of symptom severity and found that women with moderate or severe symptoms tended to score above the median decrease, while none of the women with mild symptoms did so. My own reanalysis of these data, treating cycle day and symptom severity as factors in a mixed design analysis of variance, showed a main effect of each factor and a highly statistically significant interaction ($p = .006$). The nature of the interaction was that beta-endorphin levels did not differ between days 7 and 24 for women who experienced mild or moderate symptoms, but decreased dramatically for women with severe symptoms; the symptom groups did not differ in day 24 levels. Choung and his associates (Choung, Coulam, Kao, Bergstralh, & Go, 1985) measured beta-endorphin levels on days 7 and 25 in women with PMS and asymptomatic controls. In contrast to Giannini et al., these authors found no difference between groups on day 7, but that the control group had higher levels than the PMS group on day 25. Although one cannot tell from the analyses performed, a graph of the data suggests that this difference probably was due to both an increase in the controls and a decrease in the women with PMS. It is difficult to reconcile these seemingly disparate findings but it should be noted that in both studies, women with PMS showed a significant decrease from post- to premenstrual phases, whereas women without PMS did not. Given this interpretation, the data from both studies are consistent with the withdrawal hypothesis. Further support is provided by data showing that the opiate antagonist naltrexone given at midcycle is superior to placebo in relieving premenstrual symptoms (Choung, Coulam, Bergstralh, O'Fallon, & Steinmetz, 1988).

Several possible associations between abnormalities in brain amines and mood in PMS have been explored. The activity of MAO enzymes varies with the menstrual cycle, peaking at ovulation and reaching a low 5 to 11 days later (Belmaker, Murphy, Wyatt, & Loriaux, 1974). On one hand, this pattern is inconsistent with the hypothesis of a relationship between MAO and PMS, as high MAO activity, which decreases available norepinephrine, is associated with depression (see the section on brain amines above). On the other hand, this low MAO activity may reflect low norepinephrine release, as MHPG, the main metabolite of norepinephrine, reaches a high level at ovulation and then drops to a low in the premenstrual phase

(DeLeon-Jones, Steinberg, Dekirmejian, & Garner, 1978). In any case, mood variability has been found to be unrelated to MAO activity throughout the menstrual cycle in normal women (Belmaker et al., 1974). This may not be true in women with PMS. A recent study (Ashby, Carr, Cook, Steptoe, & Franks, 1988) reported higher MAO activity premenstrually than postmenstrually in women with PMS and no difference between phases in controls. These data are consistent with expectations based on the observed relationship between MAO activity and depression, but are inconclusive because the study's authors failed to report on the correlation between MAO activity and mood.

Alterations in serotonin metabolism have been explored as a cause of PMS by looking at uptake of 5-hydroxytryptamine (5-HT, or serotonin) in blood platelets, which is decreased in some patients with major clinical depression (Tuomisto & Tukiainen, 1976). Overall, the data suggest that serotonin metabolism may be decreased in PMS. One study found no relationship between mood and platelet uptake of 5-HT in normals, even during a premenstrual increase in negative affect (Tam, Chan, & Lee, 1985). In contrast, a study on women with PMS (Taylor, Matthew, Ho, & Weinman, 1984) reported that premenstrual uptake was inversely related to premenstrual increases in several symptoms, including negative affect and concentration difficulty. Also, in the study by Ashby et al. (1988), premenstrual uptake was lower in patients than in controls, but postmenstrual means did not differ.

Other biologically-based hypotheses of PMS have received partial support, presenting a picture of etiology that is difficult to interpret. It is sensible to ask how so many hypotheses could be simultaneously valid. A likely reason for some of the apparent confusion is that the variables involved interact with each other in positive and negative feedback loops, making it difficult to isolate initial causes. Halbreich, Alt, and Paul (1988) have attempted to address this complexity by proposing a stress-diathesis account of PMS that rests on the concept of homeostasis, with special emphasis on temporal dynamics. According to their account, the normal state of affairs is for gonadal hormones and other factors to change harmoniously in terms of rate and magnitude. Disruption of the harmony, which would occur if one of these factors increased at an abnormally rapid rate, for example, would not necessarily produce symptoms. Typically, a woman would be able to cope with the disruption and the limiting factor would be her own vulnerability, subject to individual and environmental influences. Halbreich et al. describe vulnerability as "dynamically evolving" and suggest that repeated exposure to destabilization may engage a "sensitizing 'kindling' " process (p. 186; emphasis in original) which exacerbates future vulnerability. They do not specify whether the coping occurs primarily by biologic or psychologic mechanisms, but they clearly allow psychological factors a role by noting that a positive event like a vacation could prevent symptoms in a vulnerable woman in whom disruption had taken place. Symptoms are only predicted to occur when temporal parameters of biological variables change asynchronously and the individual is unable to adapt to the desynchronization. The symptoms themselves may be determined by the nature of the biological disruption.

Overall, Halbreich et al.'s (1988) model is appealing because its generality allows it to account for the diversity of both biological correlates and symptoms in PMS. The model itself is virtually untested. The best data supporting the temporal component are his lab's findings that premenstrual symptoms were correlated with increased, but dissimilar rates of postovulatory decline in estrogen and progesterone (Halbreich et al., 1986). Data clearly supporting the vulnerability component are lacking. Nevertheless, I mention the model here for its heuristic value because it foreshadows a discussion of more general accounts of mood disorder in a later part of the chapter.

At the time of this writing, consistent endogenous correlates of premenstrual syndrome have not been identified. Methodological problems with most of the research in this area may have limited our understanding, but the contribution of psychological factors to the report of symptoms cannot be overlooked. Marked placebo effects have been observed for most treatments tested in a controlled trial (Bancroft & Bäckström, 1985; Reid, 1985). Moreover, cognitive factors can bias even prospective or current symptom reports (AuBuchon & Calhoun, 1985; Ruble, 1977). The experiment by AuBuchon and Calhoun is especially provocative. These authors studied variations in physiological, cognitive, and affective measures over time in men and in women who did not complain of PMS. Half of the women were told that the purpose of the study was to examine changes in psychological and physiological variables over the course of the menstrual cycle. The remaining women and the men were told that the study's purpose was to examine changes in these variables over time. Only women who knew that the study was investigating the menstrual cycle reported premenstrual increases in negative affect and physical complaints; the unaware women were very similar to the men in their self-reports and showed no evidence of premenstrual worsening. These data cause one to wonder if women who complain of PMS are imposing a negative interpretation in the premenstrum on symptoms that they would fail to notice during other phases of the menstrual cycle. An alternative explanation, however, is that attention to the fact that one is premenstrual produces negative symptoms by causing stress and anxiety about whatever subtle variations in symptoms actually do occur.

Negative Affect in the Postpartum Period

Most women experience some degree of negative affect after giving birth to a child. For about 50 to 80% of puerperal women, the severity and the duration of the disturbance is minimal (Pitt, 1973; Yalom, Lunde, Moos, & Hamburg, 1968). This mild form includes depressed mood, crying, fatigue, confusion, headache, and anxiety as prominent symptoms, and last no longer than two weeks. For a smaller percentage of women, the disturbance is similar in character to the mild form, but is more disruptive and lasts up to several months or longer. A distinction between these two extremes of mood change is made by labeling the mild form as "postpartum blues," and the severe form as "postpartum depression," although the distinction is not always preserved. For example, several recent reviews of the literature on postpartum *depression* (Affonso & Domino, 1984; Hopkins, Marcus, & Campbell, 1984; Steiner, 1979) include many studies of postpartum *blues.* Whether the two states are qualitatively similar is the same question one faces in the comparison of everyday bad mood with depression. Fortunately, I am spared from having to provide an answer, as virtually all of the research in this area involves postpartum blues.

Given the profound physiologic and endocrinologic changes that occur after delivery, there have been many attempts to determine the extent to which these changes are sources of negative postpartum affect. However, research on postpartum mood change has been hampered by several factors. The first of these is a lack of agreement about how the components of change should be used to determine that change has, in fact, occurred. Despite general agreement on component features, for example, crying, fatigue, and confusion, studies vary in terms of how much of each component, or how many components, are necessary to assign an individual to a "blues" group. There is also a related lack of agreement about which instruments should be used for assessment. Moreover, some studies lack antenatal measurements, thereby making it impossible to determine if postnatally measured effects are actually continuations of preexisting conditions. Finally, the statistical analysis is often inappropriate, for example, multiple t-tests have been used when factorial analysis of variance is indicated. Space considerations prevent me from detailing the extent to which each of these problems may qualify the interpretation of every study I review, but I would like to suggest that all of the research in this area should be interpreted cautiously.

Several authors have proposed biologic accounts of the etiology of negative affect in the postpartum period. According to one such account, the negative affect is triggered by abnormal changes in progesterone levels, which like estrogen levels, are high before delivery and then decrease rapidly (Yalom et al., 1968). However, a test of this hypothesis failed to provide evidence that postpartum blues is associated with either higher antenatal progesterone, an unusually steep postnatal decline in progesterone, or an abnormal estrogen/progesterone ratio (Nott, Franklin, Armitage, & Gelder, 1976). Similar to Nott's findings are those of Kuevi and his associates (1983) who found no relationship between postpartum blues and estrogen and progesterone levels; however, both studies had low statistical power. In contrast, Feski, Harris, Walker, Riad-Fahney, & Newcombe (1984) found postpartum progesterone and estrogen to be higher in a severe postpartum blues group, relative to a no-blues group. It thus seems that mean progesterone and estrogen levels are not associated consistently with negative postpartum affect.

Prolactin is the hormone that causes lactation to begin after delivery. Based on findings of high prolactin levels in depression (Sachar, Frantz, Altman, & Sassin, 1973) and in premenstrual syndrome (Halbreich et al., 1976), Steiner (1979) discusses the hypothesis that elevated prolactin is a cause of negative postpartum mood change. Although intriguing, there is no other empirical support for this hypothesis. Kuevi et al. (1983) found no association between serum prolactin and postpartum blues for either a blues-no blues comparison, or a pre-post comparison for individuals who experienced only one peak bad day. Again, low power may be obscuring effects in this study, but even the means observed by Kuevi et al. are not ordered as would be expected from Steiner's hypothesis.

The known association between neurotransmitter metabolism and affective illness has led some investigators to measure the association between postpartum mood change and several of the biogenic amines. Evidence bearing on this association is somewhat confusing. Kuevi et al. (1983) found no differences between blues and no blues groups in norepinephrine and epinephrine levels in the postpartum but did observe a significant drop in these neurotransmitters on a peak bad day; norepinephrine appeared to return to pre-peak levels after the peak. Instead of observing a decrease in norepinephrine, another study found low norepinephrine levels among blues subjects both before and after delivery (Treadway, Kane, Jarrahi-Zadeh, & Lipton, 1969).

Other studies have explored the role of tryptophan, the amino-acid base of serotonin, in the production of postpartum negative affect because tryptophan levels may be associated with affective illness (Coppen, Whybrow, Noguera, Maggs, & Prange, 1972). Results suggest that tryptophan may be low in women who develop postpartum blues (Stein, Milton, Bebbington, Wood, & Coppen, 1976), although in one study this was found only during the months January to April, when tryptophan levels were high among both blues and no-blues subjects (Handley, Dunn, Waldron, & Baker, 1980). Handley et al. also found the absence of a peak in tryptophan after delivery both in women who developed postpartum blues and postpartum depression.

The role of cortisol in negative postpartum affect has been explored in several studies with mixed results. Handley et al. (1980) found high cortisol levels in women who later developed postpartum blues both before delivery and on postpartum day 5 but not on postpartum days 1 through 4 and not on a six-month follow-up. Treadway et al. (1969) reported a nonsignificant association between high cortisol and postpartum blues, and Kuevi et al. (1983) and Feski et al. (1984) found no association between cortisol and postpartum blues.

There are at least two important similarities between PMS and postpartum blues/depression. First of all, these are disorders that, by definition, affect only women. Secondly, the disorders covary with a number of biological changes, particularly with changes in sex hormones. In light of these changes, along with the fact that being female is generally accepted as a risk factor for depression (Weissman & Klerman, 1977), it is not surprising that a common biological etiology has been proposed. Halbreich et al. (1988) have suggested that disrupted temporal dynamics of gonadal hormone activity may occur in both disorders, as well as other conditions associated with abnormal mood changes, like menopause. Unfortunately, data do not exist to prove that there are common biological causes (or even correlates) in PMS and PPD. Both disorders have been investigated from the same perspectives—the changes in sex hormones known to occur in pregnancy and menstruation, and the abnormalities known to be present in mood disorder—but so far a distinctive link has not been identified. Yet the hypothesis of common biological factors is compelling in its simplicity, as PMS and PPD differ greatly in terms of the extent to which each involves lifestyle change; it is easy to imagine how having even a much-wanted baby could be temporarily distressing, whereas it is difficult to imagine why the anticipation of menstruation would be equally so (see Bernsted, Luggin, & Peterson, 1984).

When taken together, the findings on the neurobiological correlates of negative postpartum affect present a confusing picture. Of all the endogenous changes that occur as a function of pregnancy and delivery, not one has been clearly linked to the development of either postpartum blues or postpartum depression. Two current reviews of the literature in this area (Affonso & Domino, 1984; Hopkins et al., 1984) have suggested that psychosocial variables such as the quality of the marital relationship are more consistently associated with negative postpartum affect than are biological variables, although the research on which these reviews are based is flawed in a number of ways (Arizmendi & Affonso, 1984).

Seasonal Affective Disorder

For some affectively ill individuals, mood change follows a seasonal pattern, with depression occurring in the fall and winter, and then remitting or turning into mania during the spring and summer (Rosenthal et al., 1984). This pattern of recurring winter depression has been termed Seasonal Affective Disorder (SAD). In Rosenthal's study (N = 29), 86% of the patients were women, 93% had a diagnosis of manic-depressive disorder, and the average age of onset was 27 years. The behavioral symptoms of these patients included decreased activity (100%), increased appetite (66%), carbohydrate craving (79%), weight gain (76%), morning hypersomnia (76%), and increased sleep time (97%), in addition to the affective symptoms of sadness (100%), anxiety (72%), and irritability (90%).

Little is known about the endogenous correlates of SAD. Rosenthal et al. (1984) compared summer (nondepressed) and winter (depressed) responses to dexamethasone suppression and thyrotropin releasing hormone tests in a subset of seven patients from their larger study. The authors found no evidence of abnormal responses to these tests, and no difference between summer and winter responses in any patient. Summer-winter comparisons of sleep behavior in eight SAD patients from the same study revealed winter increases in total sleep time and sleep latency, and a decrease in delta sleep (the "deepest" type of sleep); no change was observed in REM latency during the winter depressive phase. One study of responses to pharmacological challenge in SAD patients and normals (Jacobsen, Sack, Wehr, Rogers, & Rosenthal, 1987) is difficult to interpret given its lack of a depressed comparison group without a seasonal pattern of recurrence. However, when compared with normal controls at baseline, patients with SAD had similar melatonin, higher prolactin, and nonsignificantly higher cortisol levels; the groups did not differ in the response of these hormones to the administration of the serotonin precursor, 5-hydroxytryptophan.

Of the climatic variables that distinguish the fall and winter from the spring and summer, day length, or the photoperiod, has received the most attention as an influence on the SAD pattern. The interest in day length emerged after the finding that the human circadian system, like that of other species, is affected by light. Melatonin is a hormone secreted by the pineal gland, almost exclusively during the night. This hormone is an excellent index of the human circadian rhythm, as its release is not subject to influence by extraneous factors such as stress and locomotor activity (Lewy, 1984). It has been found that nocturnal melatonin secretion may be suppressed artificially in affectively normal individuals by exposure to bright (1,500–2,500 lux) light during the hours of darkness (Lewy, Wehr, Goodwin, Newsome, & Markey, 1980). There is also evidence that manic-depressives are especially sensitive to light, as suppression may be achieved at lower intensities (500 lux) in these patients (Lewy, Wehr, Goodwin, Newsome, & Rosenthal, 1981). In fact, supersensitivity of the melatonin response to light has been suggested as a trait marker of manic-depressive illness (Lewy, Nurnberger, et al., 1985).

Artificial light that extends the photoperiod has been used in several studies as a treatment for winter depression (Hellekson, Kline, & Rosenthal, 1986; Rosenthal et al., 1984, 1985). Rosenthal and his colleagues have found that exposure to bright light (2500 lux Vitalite) before dawn and after dusk has antidepressant effects on patients with winter depressions, although similar exposure to dim ($\leq$300 lux) light does not. Bright light, relative to dim red light, also has been observed to have antidepressant effects in nonseasonally-depressed patients (Kripke, Risch, & Janowsky, 1983). In addition, evening exposure to bright light may be as effective as a morning-evening regimen (Hellekson et al., 1986; James, Wehr, Sack, Parry, & Rosenthal, 1985) or morning light only (Hellekson et al., 1986) for SAD patients.

The effectiveness of evening exposure contradicts Kripke's (1981) hypothesis that early morning sleep deprivation improves depression by exposing an individual to light during a critical morning period. It also contradicts the proposal of Lewy et al. (1984; 1985) that winter depression, because it is indicative of phase delay, should be treated with early morning light only; a problem with their proposal is that evening light should exacerbate symptoms of winter depression (remember that these authors thought that evening light should be used for melancholic depressives, whose symptoms are in many ways opposite to those reported by winter depressives). Thus it appears that any explanation for the effectiveness of light therapy based on its ability to resynchronize circadian rhythms is flawed.

How is it then, that light therapy improves depression? Kripke et al. (1983) suggest that light works by altering the timing of the circadian melatonin rhythm, a possibility that I think is refuted by the similar effectiveness of markedly different schedules of light. Alternatively, James et al. (1985) discuss the possibility that the antidepressant effect of light is due merely to the suppression of melatonin secretion, the consequence of which would seem to be an increase in arousal. Relatively little is known about the behavioral effects of melatonin in humans, although it has been observed to induce sleepiness. In one study, affectively normal subjects who were given melatonin during the daylight hours reported decreased vigor, and increased fatigue and confusion (Lieberman, Waldhauser, Garfield, Lynch, & Wurtman, 1984). If patients with SAD were observed to have elevated melatonin levels, the effectiveness of bright light therapy for treating their symptoms of low energy would be explained.

One problem with this suggestion is that there is no documentation of abnormal melatonin secretion in patients with SAD (Jacobsen et al., 1987). Another problem is that elevated levels would not be expected if the finding of increased sensitivity to light in manic-depressives (Lewy et al., 1981; Lewy, Nurnberger, et al., 1985) is true of those with a seasonal pattern to their disorder; if so, manic-depressives might have especially low melatonin levels because suppression could be brought on so easily. Another problem is that there is no evidence linking high endogenous melatonin and any type of depression; on the contrary, melatonin levels appear to be low in depression (Claustrat, Chazot, Brun, Jordan, & Sassolas, 1984), even when the depression has remitted (Beck-Friis, von Rosen, Kjellman, Ljunggren, & Wetterberg, 1984). Finally, the most serious problem is that the results of two recent studies show that neither suppression of melatonin, nor the extension of the photoperiod is necessary to the effectiveness of bright light therapy. In one (Wehr et al., 1986), the sham treatment was bright light exposure during daylight hours, when melatonin production is virtually undetectable and the actual treatment was bright light of the same intensity before dawn and after dusk, when melatonin is produced. The sham treatment led to as much improvement as the actual treatment in depression ratings, and melatonin production was unaffected even in those subjects who showed the clearest response to the sham treatment. In the other study (Isaacs, Stainer, Sensky, Moor, & Thompson, 1988), bright light during daylight hours was actually superior in its antidepressant effects to either dim light or bright light before dawn and after dusk.

Although all of the data are not in on the question of why bright light therapy improves winter depression in SAD, it appears that the mechanism by which improvement occurs is neither resynchronization of internal circadian rhythms nor the suppression of melatonin secretion. James and his colleagues (1985) have suggested that the increased number of photons received in light therapy could be responsible for the improvement, although if so, then Isaacs et al. (1988) should not have observed a difference between bright light therapies as a function of time of day. Further speculation about other possible mechanisms is impeded by our lack of knowledge about the endogenous correlates of the disorder. However, some insight into the problem may be derived from a reexamination of studies that have found antidepressant effects of bright light. Specifically, in all of the studies on patients with SAD (except those of Wehr et al., 1986, and Isaacs et al., 1988), the actual light treatment has differed noticeably in brightness from the sham treatment, which has not differed from ordinary room light. Subjects in these crossover-type studies who received bright light first could clearly distinguish the treatments from each other, but even those who received the dim light first might have guessed that the dim light was not expected to improve their symptoms. Thus it is entirely possible that bright light has appeared to "work" because of subjects' expectations about its effectiveness. Consistent with this hypothesis is the fact that up to 30% of subjects respond to dim light therapy, and some even respond better to dim lights than to bright lights (James et al., 1985; Rosenthal et al., 1984, 1985).[5] Even stronger evidence of an expectancy effect comes from the clever study of Wehr et al. (1986), although it does not allow one to rule out the possibility that bright light improves seasonal depression by affecting variables other than circadian rhythmicity and melatonin secretion. Also, in yet another study, Wehr and his colleagues (Wehr, Skwerer, Jacobsen, Sack, & Rosenthal, 1987) attempted to get around the problem posed by subject's expectancies by comparing, in a crossover design, phototherapy applied only to eyes with a sham treatment of phototherapy only applied to skin. They reasoned that "powerful emotional associations" (p. 753) regarding the effect of light on skin as well as eyes would make both treatments equally plausible. They found eye phototherapy to be superior to skin phototherapy, but also found that subjects' expectations about the effectiveness of the two treatments predicted outcome in seven of the eight cases for whom expectation data were available (a pattern for which I compute the binomial probability of chance occurrence to be .07).

Thus, although it is clear that some individuals experience a seasonally recurring pattern of affective disorder, the reason why they do is not yet known, and the explanations that have been offered based on the apparent effectiveness of phototherapy are inadequate for encompassing the range of findings. Further complicating the picture is a subgroup of patients with

[5]Of course, I am assuming that a response to dim light is a placebo response.

SAD who experience summer depression and often winter hypomania, and who report that temperature change is the variable that triggers their mood shifts (Wehr, Sack, & Rosenthal, 1987). None of the previous explanations of SAD can account for this pattern. An interesting hypothesis is that climatic factors may act as conditioned stimuli to trigger affective episodes (Isaacs et al., 1988). The two patterns of SAD heretofore identified might simply represent cases in which depression is the conditioned response to annually-recurring social or climatic events (e.g., Christmas, increased day length) initially coinciding with an episode of mood disturbance precipitated by other causes. If so, one might expect the same heterogeneity of endogenous factors observed in depression, rather than a distinct homogeneity, to be present in SAD. Moreover, one would not need to invoke endogenous factors as causes when explaining seasonal recurrence.

Neurobiologic Aspects of Everyday Mood

As suggested at the beginning of this chapter, everyday moods that seem to occur for no reason may stem from a failure to identify their environmental source, but also may arise from endogenous changes. For example, Thayer (1987b) has reported that everyday mood worsens from morning to late afternoon. His measures of mood included scales of energy (energetic, lively, active, vigorous, full of pep) and tension (tense, clutched-up, fearful, jittery, intense), and a single happiness item.[6] Subjects rated themselves as less energetic in the afternoon than in the morning, but comparably tense and happy at both times. These findings beg the question of whether an endogenous factor capable of producing mood change follows a circadian pattern and thus produces the mood shift. Of course, an alternative explanation is that the shift is due to fatigue, which seems especially likely given the lack of concomitant change in tension and happiness. Nevertheless, findings like this suggest the need to consider endogenous factors as possible mechanisms of action.

Studies of the endogenous correlates of everyday mood have involved the same variables known to be associated with disordered mood, primarily neurotransmitters and neuroendocrine substances. As previously mentioned, mood variability has been found to be unrelated to either MAO activity (Belmaker et al., 1974) or serotonin uptake (Tam et al., 1985) in normal women. Of two additional studies, neither showed conclusive re-

[6]Although the labels of these scales do not represent what we typically mean by good and bad moods, the energy scale is in fact similar to Watson and Tellegen's (1985) description of positive affect (except for the absence of terms indicating elation and enthusiasm) and the tension scale is similar to their description of negative affect (except for the absence of terms indicating hostility and scorn). See Chapter 6 for a more extensive discussion of the relationship of "good" and "bad" moods with more specific affects.

lationships. Ballenger, Post, Jimerson, Lake, and Zuckerman (1984) measured amine metabolites in 21 normal volunteers who had been screened for psychopathology before testing. These authors found a negative correlation between scores on the Minnesota Multiphasic Personality Inventory (MMPI) depression scale, a trait measure, and plasma MHPG, as would be expected on the basis of findings in clinical depression. They also found a negative correlation between plasma MHPG and two MMPI scales thought to tap some of the somatic components of depression, the Hypochondriasis and the Psychasthenia scales. However, none of these measures correlated with urinary and CSF MHPG, although the sign of all of these nonsignificant correlations was negative. It is difficult to tell whether this lack of correlation reflects the true state of affairs or resulted from either low statistical power or the contamination of metabolite measures from peripheral sources.

Murphy and his colleagues (Murphy et al., 1977) looked at the correlation of three measures of biogenic amine-related enzyme activity and MMPI scores in 30 males and 65 females who had been screened for psychopathology. There were few significant correlations, although one measure correlated positively with Hypochondriasis and Psychasthenia scores in females. Note that Ballenger et al. (1984) had observed these correlations to be negative in their study. Thus, the data on the relationship between enduring subclinical levels of mood and biogenic amine metabolism are inconclusive. An observation by Ballenger et al. of nonsignificant negative correlations between depression scores on the Multiple Affective Adjective Checklist (MAACL) and measures of norepinephrine metabolism is the only hint that brain amine levels may be related to everyday mood states.

There is weak evidence of a relationship between mood and cortisol production in normal individuals. Ballenger et al. (1984) observed a positive correlation between scores on the trait depression scale of the MAACL and urinary cortisol levels, even after partialling out the effects of variables known to affect cortisol production (age, height, and weight). However, because neither plasma cortisol or CSF cortisol correlated with trait depression, and none of the three cortisol measures correlated with four other measures of depression, including the state scale of the MAACL, it is possible that the single correlation observed was due to chance. Similarly, these authors' observation of an inconsistent pattern of negative relationships between cortisol levels and indices of manic behavior also demands that some attention be given to the Type I error problem. This seems especially important in light of the fact that Fibiger et al. (1984) observed a positive relationship between reports of mental arousal (on a "sluggish-alert" continuum) and cortisol secretion in a sample of normals. Their additional finding of a marginally significant positive relationship between cortisol and restedness suggests that this arousal was experienced as a positive state. It should be clear that depressed mood is not uniformly associated with abnormal cortisol secretion, and that this is especially true for subclinical levels of depression.

In the previous discussion of the endogenous opiate system, it was noted that analgesia is often experienced after running. However, another, and perhaps the defining attribute of "runner's high" is positive affect. People report an improvement in mood after running (Janal, Colt, Clark, & Glusman, 1984; Markoff, Ryan, & Young, 1982). That this effect does not merely result from a sense of satisfaction and pride comes from the fact that the increase in positive affect is naloxone-reversible; runners do not experience the same increase if they are given naloxone after running (Janal et al., 1984), although naloxone appears to have no such effect on immediate post-run ratings (Janal et al., 1984; Markoff et al., 1982).

The effects of naloxone on everyday mood in individuals who have not recently completed sustained aerobic exercise are generally disruptive. One study found decreases in self-reports of elation and observer reports of subjects' well-being after naloxone administration (Judd et al., 1980). Another study found the negative mood state induced by naloxone to be irritability, with increases in measures of tension-anxiety and anger-hostility dimensions (Pickar, Cohen, Naber, & Cohen, 1982). A more recent study found no effect of naloxone when administered alone, but a pronounced effect on mood when naloxone was given in conjunction with yohimbine, a presynaptic adrenergic receptor antagonist that by itself increases norepinephrine activity (Charney & Heninger, 1986). The mood state that resulted from this combination of drugs was one of nervousness and anxiety, but also included a paradoxical state of sexual arousal in male subjects (no increased drive, but full penile erection lasting at least 60 minutes).

Thus, there appears to be an association between mood and endogenous opiate activity, even though endogenous opiates are questionably implicated in mood disorders. The fact that the association is stronger for mild and transient mood states, rather than for serious and longer-lasting disorders, is interesting. Virtually all other relationships between mood and neurobiological variables are clearer for mood disorder, so it may be the case that the endogenous opiate system is relatively short-acting and capable of restoring itself to normal function in times of prolonged demand. It also may be the case that there is a qualitative, rather than a quantitative difference between normal and disordered moods, with opiates involved in the regulation of the former and substances like biogenic amines involved in the regulation of the latter.[7]

Several researchers have proposed that weather affects mood (Cunningham, 1979; Howarth & Hoffman, 1984; Schwartz & Clore, 1983). This might seem obvious: we have positive associations to good weather, such as the brilliant blue of a clear sky on a sunny day, and feel good; we have negative associations to bad weather, such as the gloomy gray of an overcast sky, and feel bad. One reason for these associations may be that the hedonic relevance of weather variables results from repeated pairing with hedoni-

[7]I would like to thank Matthew Friedman for suggesting this possibility to me.

cally-relevant stimuli. For example, warmth and sunshine enable us to engage in desired activities outdoors, although such an answer does not account for why those who prefer indoor activities also would feel good when the sun is shining.

Another possible answer is that weather variables produce endogenous changes that directly influence mood, as has been proposed in SAD. Support for this hypothesis comes from the observation of seasonal variation in levels of endogenous substances implicated in mood disorder, such as serotonin (Arora, Kregel, & Meltzer, 1984) and tryptophan (Swade & Coppen, 1980). However, it is difficult to control for cognitive factors when assessing the hypothesis of mood being influenced by endogenous changes associated with easily detectable weather variables like temperature, precipitation, and sunshine. The only case in which control may be achieved is in the study of a variable whose presence cannot be detected, and thus, whose effects on mood must be assumed to be endogenous. One such variable is atmospheric ionization.[8] Positive and negative ions are always present in the atmosphere. The concentration of both types increases with weather changes such as the coming of a storm (Muecher & Ungeheuer, 1961) and desert winds like the Sharav in Israel (Sulman et al., 1974). Such increases have been linked to behavioral changes. Muecher and Ungeheuer (1961) reported that in the period around the beginning of a storm, simple behaviors like reaction time are slowed and job-related accidents are more likely. When manipulated in the laboratory (unaccompanied by naturally-occurring atmospheric correlates), increased negative ionization has been shown to lead to decreased choice reaction time but have no effect on more complex behaviors (Wofford, 1966); it is difficult to draw a conclusion about the influence of positive ion concentration on behavior in the laboratory (but see Frey, 1961 for a review).

The effects of ionization on mood have been explored in two recent studies. Charry and Hawkinshire (1981) exposed subjects to moderate or high levels of positive ions and measured their mood, reaction time, and physiological arousal. Among individuals low in the ability to adapt to environmental stress, the high ion level induced negative mood, slower performance on the reaction time task, and decreased arousal; environmentally-adaptive individuals also experienced negative mood when under high ion exposure, but showed an increase in arousal and no slowing of reaction time. Similarly, Baron, Russell, and Arms (1985) showed that negative ion levels affect mood. The authors exposed subjects to low, moderate, or high negative ion levels and found that the high level reduced depression and fatigue, but only among those who had not been angered by an experimental

[8]Although Frey (1961) cites some older data as indicating that changes in ionization may be detectable under certain conditions, he mentions no evidence that people are capable of identifying the nature of the changes. Because most people are unfamiliar with the concept of atmospheric ionization, it is unlikely that even a small minority would be able to label a change in ion levels as such.

confederate; angry subjects' ratings of negative affect were increased in the high level condition.

Baron et al. (1985) suggested that the mechanism behind the contextual specificity of their results was increased arousal, a position which seems in line with Schachter and Singer's (1962) arousal-plus-cognition theory of emotion. This suggestion implies that the endogenous changes produced by ions are necessary, but not sufficient to determine the resultant mood. Baron (1987) went on to explore the arousal-inducing properties of ionization in two experiments. In one, female subjects were led to believe either that a female confederate had evaluated them positively and shared similar interests, or that she had evaluated them negatively and had dissimilar interests. These manipulations took place under either high or low negative ion levels. Subjects' ratings of the confederate were intensified under high ambient ionization: more positive for the similar confederate and more negative for the dissimilar confederate. These findings are much like those obtained by Schachter and Singer (1962) with their use of epinephrine to induce arousal. In a second experiment, blood pressure and pulse[9] were measured in female subjects engaged in letter and digit copying tasks under either high or low negative ion conditions. Those working in the high ion condition had higher systolic and diastolic blood pressure, made more letter copying errors, and rated their arousal as higher, relative to those in the low ion condition.

It seems that negative ionization increases arousal, and that this arousal can intensify both one's interpretation of a situation and mood. In contrast, positive ionization leads to negative mood, but increases arousal in some individuals and decreases it in others. Taken together, these data do not support either Schachter and Singer's (1962) position that unexplained arousal is explained in terms of plausible environmental causes, or Maslach's (1979) and Marshall and Zimbardo's (1979) position that unexplained arousal is aversive and induces negative mood. However, the data are consistent with the hypothesis that weather can influence everyday mood by producing endogenous changes.

Overall, relatively weak associations have been observed between endogenous factors and everyday mood. This weakness may be due to a lack of sensitivity in physiological measurement technique; physiological changes should be proportional to the degree of mood change, which is relatively mild in everyday mood. It also may be due to the fact that everyday moods often result from nonendogenous sources. In either case, the data are not consistent enough to say whether the pattern of association between endogenous factors and everyday mood is similar to that observed for disordered mood states. Thus, the question of whether endogenous factors play a role in everyday moods remains unanswered.

[9]Note that changes in heart rate and blood pressure fall outside of my definition of endogenous events.

Neurobiologic Theories of Mood Disorder

It is a mistake to think of any of the preceding areas of function—neurotransmitter, neuroendocrine, and neurophysiological—independently of the others. The complex interactions within and between all of these systems make it difficult to conduct research and develop theory. As an example of this complexity, Whybrow, Akiskal, and McKinney (1984) discuss the neurosecretory cells of the hypothalamus. These cells look like neural cells and respond to neurotransmitters like norepinephrine and serotonin, but they also respond to and are capable of producing neuroendocrine substances. These neuroendocrine substances, known as pituitary releasing factors, link the hypothalamus to the pituitary gland. Because production of cortisol and thyroid hormone is regulated through the pituitary, these hormone systems are also affected by neurotransmitter function.

The largest stumbling block for any neurobiologic account of mood is thus the issue of complexity. In particular, such an account must explain the diversity in both the precursors of mood and its neurobiological correlates. One is the model described by Akiskal and McKinney (1973) and then expanded by Whybrow et al. (1984). According to this model, mood disorder is the state resulting from a final common pathway of interaction between endogenous and exogenous factors. Whybrow et al. view the individual and his or her environment as a general system and the mood state as "a function of the dynamic behavior of the system itself rather than the product of a single external variable" (p. 178). Within this model, predisposing factors to disorder are genetic vulnerability, temperament and character, age, gender, physical illness, drugs, and loss of attachment in childhood. Precipitating factors include psychosocial variables such as loss of attachment and a high number of life events occurring in a short time span, and physiological variables such as drugs and illness. Intermediary mechanisms, which can hinder an individual's ability to respond to the challenge put forth by precipitating factors, include neurotransmitter, neuroendocrine, and neurophysiological functions. These mechanisms are coordinated through the limbic-diencephalic structures of the brain, especially the hypothalamus. This is the area of the brain thought to be involved in emotional responding, and, at least in nonhuman animals, in reinforcement. Impairment of this region can result in abnormalities of the sleep-wake cycle, biogenic amine metabolism, cortisol metabolism, and thyroid function.

Whybrow et al. (1984) propose that stress (a precipitating factor) beyond the coping ability of an individual (determined by predisposing factors), along with its neurobiological and psychic correlates, leads to heightened arousal. This arousal, in turn, leads to a dysregulation of the reinforcement system in the diencephalon that impairs the individual's response to reinforcers and results in a sense of losing control. The sense of losing control can serve as a further source of stress, thereby engaging the system again, producing even further dysregulation. Essentially, this model assumes that everyone has a breaking point, that is, a point beyond which regulatory mechanisms fail. It also assumes that the perceived consequences of this failure escalate the dysregulation, and can engage a "[v]icious cycle of more turmoil, arousal, and hopelessness" (p. 199). Unfortunately, the model does not specify how to determine an individual's breaking point. Even though the lack of specificity is understandable given the complexity of the genetic, historical, and situational interactions likely to be involved, we are left wanting to know when biological regulation will no longer allow coping.

Nevertheless, by proposing that various predisposing and precipitating factors interact via the final common pathway of the limbic-diencephalic structures of the brain, Whybrow et al. (1984) are able to account for both the diversity in antecedents and the similarity in the symptoms of mood disorder. Indeed, this is their goal, for while they view brief depressive experiences as "ubiquitous," they acknowledge that the real task for any theory of mood disorder is to explain why most people do not become depressed[10] despite constant exposure to the stressors encountered in daily living. In doing so, Whybrow and his colleagues seem to be making a distinction between depressed affect and the state of depression, although at times they use the word "depression" in an unqualified way to refer to the former state. Yet they also seem to be suggesting continuity by likening the difficulty in separating mood *change* from mood *disorder* (emphasis in the original) to that of deciding when normal variations in blood pressure are extreme enough to indicate the onset of hypertensive illness. Given the lack of a clear statement, I am not sure whether the states Whybrow et al. are trying to explain are more extreme versions of everyday moods, and thus, whether their account can be extended to the experience of everyday mood.

An important feature of Whybrow et al.'s model is the concept of biological dysregulation, which is seen as the intermediary mechanism leading to a maladaptive reaction to stress. This concept has been elucidated more clearly by Siever and Davis (1985), who proposed a dysregulation hypothesis of depression in response to the inadequacy of theories that posit either an excess or a deficiency of some neurochemical substance to account for the inconsistency of data relevant to those theories. Siever and Davis propose, "the functional abnormalities of central neurotransmitter systems such as the biogenic amines may be reconsidered in terms of a failure of regulation or buffering of these systems, not as simply too much or too little activity" (p. 1017). Thus, like Whybrow et al. (1984), they rely on a disturbance of regulatory mechanisms as a key feature of their model, but unlike the former authors, they provide criteria for testing it. Whybrow et al., although they suggest that dysregulation must be localized in the limbic and diencephalic structures of the brain, are less specific about how to determine the presence of dysregulation.

---

[10]Whybrow and his colleagues are most likely referring to depression rather than disorder here because virtually all manifestations of mood disorder involve depression at one time or another.

According to Siever and Davis (1985), the first criterion for a dysregulated neurotransmitter system is that regulatory or homeostatic mechanisms must be impaired. As an example of one such system, they cite the relationship between norepinephrine and tyrosine hydroxylase, which is the catalyst that acts in the first step of norepinephrine synthesis from the amino acid tyrosine. Normally, tyrosine hydroxylase activity increases in response to prolonged stress so that increased norepinephrine may be produced to meet the needs of the system. However, in the case of dysregulation, one would predict from Siever and Davis's model that tyrosine hydroxylase activity would not increase under stress and the rate of norepinephrine production would be insufficient.

The second criterion of Siever and Davis's model is that the basal output of a dysregulated neurotransmitter system must be more erratic in both short-term (hourly) and long-term (daily) variance when compared with a normal system, which should change only in response to environmental stimulation. The third criterion is that normal periodicities such as circadian rhythms in cortisol release and body temperature must be altered. Siever and Davis state that this should be so because these and other rhythms are coordinated by neurons whose activity is influenced by neurotransmitters. If neurotransmitter levels are altered, as they should be in a dysregulated system, it is easy to see how periodicities could thus be altered. However dysrhythmia may be more than a marker for dysregulation; it may be an endogenous bridge between life events and depression. The loss of routine due to event-induced change may affect the stability of biological rhythms and result in somatic symptoms that are likely to produce depression in vulnerable individuals (Ehlers, Frank, & Kupfer, 1988). These symptoms also may be experienced as so unusual that they elicit contextually-appropriate reactions characteristic of an episode of depression—for example, guilt and loss of self-esteem over one's seemingly unexplainable thoughts and feelings—even in otherwise nonvulnerable individuals (Healy & Williams, 1988).

Siever and Davis's fourth criterion is that a dysregulated system responds less selectively to external stimulation. They describe the decrease of selectivity as a reduction of the signal-to-noise ratio, which when coupled with the production of erratic basal output (increased "noise") according to criterion 2 suggests that it should be manifested as a problem in determining the factor(s) precipitating a response to an environmental stimulus in the context of increased "background" responding. However, it is difficult to known what Siever and Davis actually mean because they cite data in support of this criterion that only show either increased or decreased responsiveness to environmental challenge, which, strictly speaking, are not evidence of decreased selectivity. It seems that they mean to say that a dysregulated system is inappropriately responsive to the environment, a hypothesis consistent with the data they review. The fifth criterion is that a dysregulated system is slower to return to baseline following stimulation, and the sixth is that effective pharmacological treatments must work specifically by regulating the dysregulated neurotransmitter system.

Siever and Davis's model is compelling for several reasons. First, existing data, if sparse at points, are generally consistent with each criterion; the data they cite involve the noradrenergic system only, although Siever and Davis note that this choice should not imply the centrality of noradrenergic disturbance in the etiology of depression. Second, as mentioned above, the criteria are stated in terms that make it possible to specifically test components of the model. Third, a dysregulation hypothesis acknowledges the dynamic interplay that static excess or deficiency models (e.g., Byck, 1976; Schildkraut, 1965) do not.

The model is less satisfactory regarding how it informs us about the instigation of dysregulation. Siever and Davis say that susceptibility to mood disorder is genetically determined, and that "environmental factors such as stress or loss may play a role in the onset of depression" (p. 1019), but do not elucidate the mechanism by which the environment operates. Presumably, not all individuals with the genetic permission for mood disorder experience episodes of disordered mood; among those who do, it is not in response to every environmental stressor. Like Whybrow et al.'s (1984) model, Siever and Davis's needs to be able to predict when biological homeostatic mechanisms fail, which may be difficult if Halbreich et al. (1988) are correct in claiming that vulnerability is "dynamically evolving."

No existing theory of mood disorder has been successful in predicting the evolution of vulnerability, but one model (Post, Rubinow, & Ballenger, 1984) has attempted to explain vulnerability in biological terms. The model is based on the concept of sensitization, which was mentioned previously in the discussion of Halbreich et al.'s (1988) account of PMS.[11] Post et al. define behavioral sensitization as the progressive effects on behavioral responsivity that result from low dose administration of psychomotor stimulants and dopamine agonists, or in response to stressors; in other words, it can be thought of as the opposite of habituation or tolerance. The authors have proposed that affect-inducing stressors can enhance responses to future stressors, so that eventually mild stressors and even anticipation of a stressor can elicit an episode of mood disorder. This physiologically-based explanation of the concept of vulnerability is appealing because if substantiated, it can account for how reactions to exogenous stress-inducing events can take on the character of autonomy and be endogenously-produced. Another advantage is that it could explain how early loss could put a person at risk for affective disorder later in life, that is, by causing biological stress-response systems to overreact to affect-inducing stimuli. The model's primary drawback is that relatively little is known about behavioral sensitization in hu-

[11]Halbreich et al. (1988) actually mention sensitization and kindling together but Post et al. (1984) distinguish these phenomena is such terms as their duration and parallels with symptoms of affective disorder.

mans, and although Post and his colleagues make a good case based on mostly animal data, the role of behavioral sensitization in affective disorders needs to be experimentally tested.

Summary and Conclusions

Whybrow, Akiskal, and McKinney (1984) see everyday moods as normal responses to external events and disordered moods as the failure of the system to respond to external events. The transition between these states is determined by the ability of an individual to cope with the stress of those events. The authors do not see the neurobiological features associated with disordered mood as sources of mood, but rather, as permissions for inappropriate response to other sources.

The complex and inconsistent findings reviewed in this chapter seem to support their position by default. The effectiveness of pharmacological interventions in treating mood disorder is clear evidence that endogenous factors *can* cause mood change, but data do not exist to prove whether neurobiological abnormality is typically a cause in and of itself or secondary to a reaction to an exogenous event. Of course, it is extremely difficult to establish causal relationships in the context of complex dynamic systems. Even if one can identify a cause-effect relationship, it is usually part of a longer sequence in which effects become causes for later-occurring effects that often are part of a feedback loop with the initial cause. It would seem that greater efforts in the area of animal research, where it is possible to use manipulations that are not ethical to administer to humans (e.g., random assignment to prolonged stress), would be highly desirable.

With respect to the question of correlation, even the picture of associations between mood and endogenous factors is confusing. No single endogenous factor has been implicated in all cases of mood disorder. The variation in terms of patterns of excess and deficiency makes it easy to see why Siever and Davis (1985), along with Whybrow et al. (1984) now invoke the concept of dysregulation to describe the endogenous correlates of mood disorder. Biogenic amine disturbance is seen in many, but not all cases, although the exact pattern of the disturbance is variable. For example, MHPG profiles suggest biological subtypes of unipolar depression (Schatzberg et al., 1982). Other disturbances seen in some depressions include increased cortisol production, reduced thyroid function, increased endogenous opiate levels (also high in mania), and decreased REM latency. The key word for interpreting these data is "some": some disturbances have been observed in some people. None of the disturbances is necessary to produce mood disorder, and none is sufficient because disturbance, such as hypothyroidism, can occur without a concomitant alteration of mood. The inconsistency of findings is interpretable within a framework that acknowledges the existence of distinct biological subtypes (Schatzberg et al., 1982, 1989). If biological subtypes exist, and especially if they are not distinguishable in terms of demographics or clinical features (Gibbons & Davis, 1986) so that even careful diagnosis would not delineate them, comparisons of samples consisting of different "mixes" of the underlying types might lead to different conclusions.

The picture becomes even more complex when specific mood disorders that share many overlapping features with depression and mania are considered. Neurobiologic function may be altered in PMS, but the data are too inconsistent to be precise about either the nature of the alteration and whether it is causal: does PMS arise from endogenous opiate withdrawal (Reid & Yen, 1981), decreased neurotransmitter metabolism (Ashby et al., 1988; Taylor et al., 1984), or accelerated rate of decrease in gonadal hormones during the luteal phase (Halbreich et al., 1988)? The observed associations suggest multiple potential causes for negative postpartum affect as well, such as increased cortisol function and decreased neurotransmitter metabolism. It is unclear whether any abnormal endogenous factors are present in SAD, beyond what would be expected for a mostly bipolar population.

Research on everyday mood has borrowed hypotheses from research on disordered mood, but relatively little is known about the biological correlates of the former. Inconclusive data exist regarding the relationship between subclinical depression and brain amines, and the data regarding cortisol are sparse. The best evidence of a relationship between an endogenous factor and mood involves endogenous opiates. An increase in endogenous opiates occurring after aerobic activity is accompanied by an improvement in mood that may be reversed if opiate levels are artificially suppressed by naloxone. Also, naloxone by itself or in combination with other drugs induces an aroused-anxious type of negative mood. (These findings strongly suggest the desirability of testing whether endogenous opiate activity tends to be low on days that are experienced as "grouchy.") Other evidence suggesting a relationship between an endogenous factor and everyday mood is that the arousal induced by high concentrations of atmospheric electricity is associated with negative mood, or at least with the intensification of emotional responses to a situation.

In general, the data do not allow a formal assessment of biological similarity between everyday and disordered mood. Even the case of endogenous opiate activity is difficult to judge because the data from patients with mood disorders are inconsistent at best. On the one hand, increasing beta-endorphin levels can improve depression and decreasing them can improve mania, but on the other, increased endogenous opiate activity has been observed in both depression and mania; and, as mentioned above, these relationships have not always been observed. How do we attempt to compare data on everyday mood with this varied set of findings? The answer is that we cannot. Until we know which set of findings represents the true (or probable) state of affairs, we must avoid drawing a conclusion. More and better research is required.

However, this lack of information should not be taken as evidence that everyday and disordered mood states are biologically dissimilar. Several methodological problems could have inflated the chance of type II error. One problem involves the precision of measurement. For example, peripheral amine levels have been used to make inferences about central levels, although the peripheral levels are contaminated by peripheral sources of these substances. Also, there is not complete agreement about which assay procedures are most accurate. A second, and related problem, involves power and sample size. It is often the case that the expense of running subjects limits a given study to be able to detect only the largest of true effects, despite the fact that it is not at all obvious that the effects being investigated are always large.

Returning to the question of whether moods arise from endogenous sources, I would like to conclude that endogenous abnormalities clearly are present but that their role in instigating episodes of disorder has not been established. Instead, the abnormalities seem to permit maladaptive responses to environmental events. I must refrain from drawing a conclusion about the presence of the same endogenous factors in everyday mood states for lack of information. At the present time, we cannot reject the hypothesis that everyday moods that seem to "come out of the blue," whether extreme or mild, arise from unidentified environmental sources.

Acknowledgements. William N. Morris provided invaluable assistance during the preparation of this chapter by engaging in hours of discussion and commenting on all earlier versions of the manuscript. Matthew J. Friedman also made many helpful comments. It has been greatly improved through their efforts.

Chapter 5

The Influence of Mood on Thought and Behavior

I have identified moods in terms of (1) the breadth of their influence on thought and behavior, and (2) their capacity to cross the threshold of awareness such that they change from a ground-like context into an object in focal attention, that is, a figure. The claim of breadth pertains principally to the effects of mood in its manifestation as context or ground. Because mood in this form does not come to attention or interrupt ongoing behavior, theoretically it can influence whatever is happening at the time. On the other hand, when mood enters focal attention it must be dealt with so that we can get on with our lives. Thus, actions taken as a result of mood in its figural manifestation are most often self-regulatory and are therefore targeted or goal-directed.

If these assertions about mood are to be found credible, it will be because of the evidence I will review in this chapter. I am confident that the case on behalf of the pervasiveness of mood is good. Mood, manipulated in a myriad of ways, or measured through the use of various standardized instruments or face-valid rating scales, will be seen to be associated with (1) automatic cognitive processes,[1] especially memory, (2) perceptual and judgmental or evaluative processes and, (3) many kinds of overt behavior such as helpfulness, sociability, self-indulgence, alcohol use, and general activity preferences.

The case in behalf of the idea that some of these consequences of mood reflect self-regulatory responding is more circumstantial and therefore somewhat suspect. And yet, there seems to be no other good way to make sense of all the data. But, that's my conclusion . . . it's time to see if I can persuade you of its validity.

The Effects of Mood on Memory

The most fundamental way in which mood might have its effects is by altering what "comes to mind," that is, memory. Indeed, many of the other effects that mood has on perception, judgment, and behavior may be

[1]A small number of studies by Isen and her colleagues have examined the relationship between mood and other cognitive processes such as categorization (Isen & Daubman, 1984), decision-making (Isen & Means, 1983), and word association (Isen, Johnson, Mertz, & Robinson, 1985) but as yet, the results are too scattered and few to be coherent.

mediated by the effect moods can have on memory. Because of the importance of this possibility, the mood-memory link has attracted a great deal of empirical and theoretical attention.

One possibility is that moods might influence the ease and success with which material is encoded into, or retrieved from, memory. For example, it seems reasonable to speculate that bad moods might interfere with the capacity to engage in any task, including remembering, especially when the task demands are relatively great. Ellis and colleagues have proved this both on the input side in terms of elaborative encoding and semantic processing (Ellis, Thomas, & Rodriguez, 1984) and on the output or retrieval side (Ellis, Thomas, McFarland & Lane, 1985).

Another possibility, one that has received much more attention, is that mood affects memory by making it *selective* or *biased.* This literature has recently been surveyed by Blaney (1986). There are two similar hypotheses as to how mood might play a role in affecting what comes to mind: one derives from the concept of *state dependence* and the other from the notion of *mood congruence.* State dependence refers to a phenomenon wherein events experienced in a given psychological state are better remembered on occasions when in that same state. For example, the idea of state dependence helps explain why people who drink too much wake up the next morning without a clue as to what happened the night before. The notion of state dependence suggests that this dissociation is due to the difference between the person's current state and the state that prevailed the previous evening. According to state dependence, memory for events of the previous evening would be facilitated by drinking enough alcohol so as to reenter the same psychological state. Evidence supporting the idea of state dependence is considerable for drug induced states, for example, for nicotine (Peters & McGee, 1982), marijuana (Eich, 1980), and alcohol (Parker, Birnbaum, & Noble, 1976).

The second way in which mood might affect memory is through what Blaney (1986) has referred to as "mood congruence." Mood congruence refers to cases in which memory for hedonically toned material is facilitated as a result of a match between *its* valence and that of the mood state the person is in either while learning the material or trying to remember it. Simply put, mood congruence effects consist of the tendency of people in a bad mood to better store or retrieve distressing events whereas happy people perform better when the to-be-remembered occurrences are pleasant.

The differences between the two phenomena are that (1) the similarity between mood at encoding and mood at retrieval which is critical for state dependency, is irrelevant for mood congruence, and (2) state dependency predictions can be made for memory for neutral material (as well as for material which is of hedonic significance) whereas mood congruence is relevant only to the extent that the material is, itself, affectively toned. Though the two phenomena are, thus, conceptually distinguishable, in practice it is virtually impossible to tell which one might be accounting for any given set of results (Blaney, 1986). The problem is due to the fact that there is a reciprocal relationship between the valence of moods and stimulus events such that (1) moods alter our evaluation of events so that the perceived valence of the event tends toward the valence of the mood (see below for a more extended discussion of this phenomenon), especially when the event is neutral (Schiffenbauer, 1974; Isen & Shalker, 1982), and (2) exposure to hedonically toned events alters mood although, again, this may be more likely when mood is neutral (Barden, Garber, Duncan & Masters, 1981). Thus, the ideal circumstance for testing state dependent effects of mood, which is that we learn and remember neutral material in moods that either match or do not match each other, is hard to achieve since the material will tend to pick up the coloration of the encoding mood. A similar problem occurs if one wishes to argue that a given effect is unambiguously due to congruence effects since the introduction of affectively colored material, necessary if one wishes to control for exposure to the to-be-remembered material, will tend to eliminate the neutral mood during encoding which would distinguish congruence from state dependence. Despite the difficulty in distinguishing state dependence from mood congruence effects, I shall discuss the research literatures separately because there is some distinctiveness associated with the paradigms that have been employed by researchers whose interest has been aroused by one phenomenon versus the other.

Bower (1981; Bower & Cohen, 1982; Gilligan & Bower, 1984) has been the main proponent of the idea that mood may produce state dependent effects upon memory. According to Bower, the prediction of state dependency, whether for mood or any other psychological or physiological state, follows from network theories (for example, Anderson & Bower, 1973) which regard memory as an associative network of nodes representing items such as concepts, schemata, and events. Bower (1981) has argued that affective states are represented by such nodes and that associative links can form between them and other units with which they are related.

A key assumption in such a model is that activation of a memory unit spreads to neighboring, that is, associated, nodes. Thus, if material is learned while in a given mood, the material and the mood become associated in memory. Consequently, if one later experiences the same mood, the associated memory should be more accessible as compared to the case when one's mood is disparate from the original mood. Notice that the very same theorizing can explain instances of congruence associated with retrieval mood.

Supporting evidence that such a process can occur with regard to mood states was uncovered by Bower, Monteiro, and Gilligan (1978, Study 3). Subjects learned two lists of words, one while happy and the other while sad with the affective states being hypnotically induced. Twenty minutes later, subjects were induced once again to be either sad or happy and asked to recall the first list they had learned. If moods produce state dependent effects on memory it should be the case that the best memory for the first list should be shown by subjects whose recall mood matched the mood in which they learned the list, whereas the worst memory should occur when learning and recall moods were discordant. The results clearly conformed to this pattern.

However, other research suggests that the state dependency effect of mood on memory is a fragile phenomenon. It appears that the possibility of interference (produced by having subjects learn two separate lists in Bower et al., 1978, Study 3) is important since designs which fail to introduce it (Bower et al., 1978, Studies 1 and 2; Brown & Taylor, 1986; Isen at al., 1978, Study 2; Bower, Gilligan, & Monteiro, 1981, Study 3; Leight & Ellis, 1981, Study 2; Schare, Lisman, & Spear, 1984, Studies 1 and 2) fail, for the most part, to produce results suggesting state dependency. One exception is Mecklenbräuker and Hager (1984) who replicated Bower et al. (1981, Study 3) but used a different mood manipulation and found state dependence. However, even with interference the results are mixed with Schare et al. (1984, Study 3) and Gage and Safer (1985) replicating Bower et al. (1978, Study 3) whereas Bower and Mayer (1985) and Wetzler (1985) did not.

The situation is similar with respect to research done with child subjects. State dependent effects have been reported by Bartlett and Santrock (1977) and Bartlett, Burleson, and Santrock (1982, Study 2) but they have failed to obtain in other cases (Bartlett et al., 1982, Study 1 and Nasby & Yando, 1982, Studies 1 and 2). Clearly, more research is needed to untangle the current situation.

Studies looking for mood congruence effects in memory are a more heterogenous lot. Blaney (1986) breaks the mood congruence studies into two types: those that rely upon relatively enduring individual differences between people as a source of affective state during recall, and those that use some mood manipulation. Studies relying on individual differences, where subject assignments are based either upon a clinical diagnosis or a score on a self-report inventory of depression, are generally harder to interpret than those using mood inductions because of the likelihood that the individual differences are connected with variations in life experiences, associative histories, or response biases that might account for observed effects otherwise attributable to mood congruence. For example, Lloyd and Lishman (1975) report an association between existing depression and the speed of recall of pleasant and unpleasant memories. Similar findings have been reported by others, such as Fogarty and Hemsley (1983), Mayo (1983), Stone (1981), and Williams and Broadbent (1986). Though such data might indicate the presence of a mood congruence effect, it might just as well reflect differential experience. To avoid such interpretive problems when performing studies where individual differences in depression constitute the independent variable, it is generally necessary to provide subjects with the to-be-remembered material. I will restrict my reporting to such studies except as otherwise noted.

In addition, like Blaney (1986), I omitted studies reporting congruence when it appears that subjects were permitted to control the length of exposure to the to-be-remembered material (Derry & Kuiper, 1981; Forgas & Bower, 1987; Frith, Stevens, Johnstone, Deakin, Lawler, & Crow, 1983; Hammen & Zupan, 1984; Lishman, 1972; Slife, Miura, Thompson, Shapiro, & Gallagher, 1984; Zuroff, 1980; Zuroff, Colussy, & Wielgus, 1983). Such findings are excluded because they may be due to differences in attention rather than memory processes. Indeed, Mischel, Ebbesen, and Zeiss (1973) have shown that success, presumably an inducer of good mood, caused subjects to spend more time examining materials describing their personality assets and less on those describing their liabilities than did control subjects. Forgas and Bower (1987) found similar effects for the time taken to read sentences describing positive and negative characteristics of others. Complementary to these results are those of Roth and Rehm (1980) who found that depressed inpatients were more interested in examining instances of their failures than psychiatric controls.

One way of introducing hedonically toned material has been to ask subjects to engage in tasks and then provide them with feedback indicative of success or failure. Subsequent to performance, subjects are asked to recall how they did. In general, depressed subjects clearly underestimate their frequency or proportion of success compared to controls (Buchwald, 1977; DeMonbreun & Craighead, 1977; Dobson & Shaw, 1981; Wener & Rehm, 1975). Johnson, Petzel, Hartney, and Morgan (1983) have added to these results by showing that the congruence effect extends to memory for the task *content* associated with successful and unsuccessful performances.

A limitation on the generality of mood congruence within this paradigm is indicated by the results reported by Craighead and his colleagues (that is, Craighead, Hickey, & DeMonbreun, 1979; DeMonbreun & Craighead, 1977; and Nelson & Craighead, 1977). As a group, these studies showed that mood congruence effects did not appear when overall success rates were low but did when subjects were led to believe their general performance was positive (but see Dennard and Hokanson, 1986, for an exception). Such results, which we will encounter repeatedly as this review proceeds, suggest the possibility that when depressed affect produces mood congruence it does so by interfering with positive memories rather than facilitating negative ones.

Another way in which investigators have introduced to-be-remembered material with affective valence is through the use of semantic material such as words and phrases normatively regarded as pleasant or unpleasant. A rather large number of such studies have been performed by now, some using patient groups diagnosed as depressed (Bradley & Mathews, 1983; Breslow, Kocsis, & Belkin, 1981; Dunbar & Lishman, 1984; McDowall, 1984, Study 1; Post, Lobitz, & Gasparikova-Krasnec, 1980), whereas others relied upon self-reports of depressive affect (Buchwald, 1977; Finkel, Glass, & Merluzzi, 1982; Gotlib & McCann, 1984, Study 1; Hammen, Miklowitz, & Dyck, 1986; Hasher, Rose, Zacks, Sanft, & Doren, 1985; Ingram, Smith, & Brehm, 1983; Kuiper & Derry, 1982; Kuiper, Olinger, Derry, & Shaw, 1985; Mathews & Bradley, 1983; Pietromonaco & Markus, 1985). The large majority of these studies found evidence of poorer memory for positive material and/or superior memory for negative material among self-reported or clinically diagnosed depressed individuals. One again there was a report showing that congruence did not appear among self-reported depressives when the material was predominantly negative but did when most stimuli were positive (Finkel et al., 1982).

The studies that did not find evidence for congruence are Gotlib and McCann (1984, Study 1), Hasher et al. (1985), and Pietromonaco and Markus (1985). Various explanations have been offered to account for these failures to find congruence. Blaney (1986), for example, suggests that because Gotlib and McCann (1984, Study 1) used the Stroop color-naming procedure, the tendency subjects might have to regard the stimuli (words associated with happiness or sadness, printed in different colors) in a self-referent sort of way was interfered with. And indeed, a number of studies which have incorporated manipulations of self-reference set during exposure have found that congruence effects do not occur without it (Bradley & Mathews, 1983; Ingram et al., 1983; Kuiper & Derry, 1982; McDowall, 1984, Study 1).

A different tack has been taken by Ellis (1985) who has argued that Hasher et al. (1985) may not have found congruence effects because the material they used was narrative. Being more meaningful (than words or phrases), narrative material might be less dependent on mood cues for recall. Consistent with this interpretation are results reported by Mecklenbräuker and Hager (1984) who induced mood using the Velten procedure and also failed to find congruence with narrative materials (though they did obtain a state dependent effect).

Finally, all of these studies used the Beck Depression Inventory (Beck, Ward, Mendelsohn, Mock, & Erbaugh, 1961) as a basis for assigning their college student subjects to conditions.[2] Ellis (1985) and Mayer and Bower (1985) wondered if such differences in mood are really strong enough to produce significant effects. This explanation seems less persuasive than the others in view of the fact that a number of other studies using self-reported depression did find congruence effects.

Isen's (Clark & Isen, 1982; 1984; 1985) reaction to failures to find congruence is completely different. Rather than looking for specific variables which might explain these "exceptions," she suggests that processes associated with negative affect (such as memory bias) are inherently unstable and unpredictable (relative to positive affect) because of the tendency for people to use "mood repair" strategies designed to control unpleasant feelings. Unfortunately, the idea of "mood repair," unless elaborated in some way, suffers as did the intensity explanation (Mayer & Bower, 1985; Ellis, 1985) discussed above in that it cannot account for the times when con-

[2]Hasher et al. (1985) also used the Multiple Adjective Affect List (Zuckerman et al., 1965) and got comparable results.

gruence *does* obtain. I will have much more to say about this later in the chapter when self-regulation of mood is discussed.

In conclusion, it would be a mistake to concentrate too much on the failures to find congruence. Though it is tempting to focus attention on the exceptions and the richly provocative array of explanations proposed to account for them, the general pattern of results from studies of individual differences in existing depressive affect rather clearly supports the notion of congruence. As Blaney (1986) says:

> The mood-congruence findings ... involving naturally occurring mood-relevant states are numerous and have been obtained across varied tasks, indices of memory access, stimuli, and subject samples. At present it appears most reasonable to treat mood congruence as a demonstrated correlate of noninduced differences in depression. (p. 233)

Though the evidence from these studies seems relatively firm, they still suffer from a number of problems that interfere with their ability to provide clear support for mood congruent memory. Principal among these is the "third variable" problem which plagues all correlational research. That is, the observed results may be the product of some characteristic of people who display relatively enduring depressive affect other than their mood. One candidate is negative self-concept. Such an explanation of mood congruence results is particularly appealing in view of the consistent evidence cited above that self-referent exposure set seems to mediate congruence effects. Also, it is generally hard to tell in studies which use individual differences as the independent variable and find evidence of mood congruence whether the effect is due to mood during exposure, mood during recall, or both because subjects would typically be in the same mood at both times.[3] Finally, studies in this literature have restricted their attention almost exclusively to the relation between memory and depressive affect. An exception is a study by Weingartner, Miller, and Murphy (1977) which used patients with bipolar disorder as subjects. They found that the ability of subjects to recall associated responses made four days before test day was a function of the degree of mood change during the period; the greater the change, the less recall. Though these findings are consistent with either a state dependent or mood congruent effect, the possibility that there are distinctive biological concomitants associated with this disorder clouds the meaning of the results.

Studies that manipulate mood avoid the shortcomings associated with the use of individual differences. Though any given manipulative study may have its own individual problem due to the particular mood induction

[3]One study seems to avoid this problem. Clark and Teasdale (1982) capitalized on the well-established (see Healy & Williams, 1988) finding of diurnal variation in the mood of clinically depressed patients. This permitted them to sample recall of happy and unhappy memories on two closely spaced occasions in a within design. Findings showed clearly that variations in mood during recall affected retrieval in a congruent way.

selected by the investigator, the literature as a whole benefits because different researchers select different manipulations. In addition, because this literature is less dominated by researchers interested in clinical depression, there has been a more evenhanded treatment of positive and negative moods.

My review is selective. Unpublished studies are not included. In addition, I avoid studies that use dependent measures that are not clearly memory measures. The largest such group involve studies which ask subjects for some rating or judgment that may or may not be based upon remembered events, for example, Isen et al. (1978, Study 1), Kavanaugh and Bower (1985), Madigan and Bollenbach (1982, Studies 1a and b) Procidano and Heller (1983, Study 2). One cannot tell in these studies whether mood is affecting memory, judgment, or both. A more controversial omission, at least to some, is studies that investigate the effect of mood on thresholds for word recognition (Gerrig & Bower, 1982; Postman & Brown, 1952; Small, 1986). Since such results are often interpreted in terms of the ability of mood to differentially prime mood-congruent memory, it is not unreasonable to include them—Blaney (1986) does in his review. However, I have decided to consider these studies in the section on perception and judgment instead where the interested reader will also find discussion of some of the above-mentioned rating studies. Finally, I exclude recall data presented by Clark, Teasdale, Broadbent, and Martin (1983) because mood during exposure and retrieval appear to be confounded.

Examination of the literature reveals that six different mood manipulations have been utilized: (1) the Velten procedure (or a modification thereof) used either alone or in combination with another manipulation (Brown & Taylor, 1986; Coleman, 1975; Gotlib & McCann, 1985, Study 2; Madigan & Bollenbach, 1982; Mathews & Bradley, 1983; Mecklenbräuker & Hager, 1984; Natale & Hantas, 1982; Rholes, Riskind, & Lane, 1987; Riskind, Rholes, & Eggers, 1982; Siegel, Johnson, & Sarason, 1979; Snyder & White, 1982; Teasdale & Fogarty, 1979; Teasdale & Russell, 1983; Teasdale & Taylor, 1981; and Teasdale, Taylor, & Fogarty, 1980), (2) hypnosis (Bower et al., 1981; Bower & Mayer, 1985; Bower et al., 1978; Forgas, Bower, & Krantz, 1984; Natale & Hantas, 1982), (3) memory elicitation, where the individual is instructed to recall and concentrate on either positive or negative experiences (Gage & Safer, 1985; Nasby & Yando, 1982; Wright & Mischel, 1982, Study 1), (4) depression or elation-producing music combined with instructions to engender mood in oneself (Clark & Teasdale, 1985, Study 1; Clark et al., 1983; Mathews & Bradley, 1983; Teasdale & Spencer, 1984), (5) success and failure (Derryberry, 1988; Isen et al., 1978, Study 2; Mischel, Ebbesen, & Zeiss, 1976), (6) posturing, wherein the subject's face and/or body are positioned so as to mimic the usual expressive accompaniments of happiness, sadness, anger, or fear (Laird, Wagener, Halal, & Szegda, 1982, Studies 1 and 2; Riskind, 1983, Studies 1 and 2), and (7) cues signaling a trial where one stood either to gain or lose points in a laboratory game (Derryberry, 1988). The large majority of these manipulations were intended to produce moods of elation or depression but a small number induced other affects, such as fear (Derryberry, 1988; Laird et al., 1982, Study 2), anger (Laird et al., 1982, Studies 1 and 2; Nasby & Yando, 1982, Study 2), and loss, frustration, relief, and joy (Derryberry, 1988).

As noted above, many of these manipulations have drawbacks. I have already discussed the problems with the Velten procedure, the most popular manipulation of mood, in Chapter 3. The use of that procedure in connection with studies of memory has an additional defect in that it allows for an alternative interpretation of results that appear to support mood congruence, namely cognitive priming (Blaney, 1986). That is, the verbal contents of the statements used in the technique may directly influence what subjects remember without regard to the mood change produced by the procedure. Some evidence consistent with this concern has recently been provided by Rholes et al. (1987). These investigators showed that the mood congruence effects produced by positive and negative self-referential statements of the sort found in the Velten procedure are independent of the degree of mood change produced by the statements. Such findings suggest that the mood congruence effect that is produced by such statements is mediated by the specific content of the statements rather than their capacity to induce affect. Hypnosis has also come in for its share of criticism (for example, Isen, 1984; Nasby & Yando, 1982). Its most obvious failing is that only a small proportion of the population meets the hypnotic-suggestibility criterion, thereby limiting the generality of results achieved but it is also susceptible to the problem of cognitive priming discussed above.

I considered two ways of breaking down the studies for the sake of presentation and retained one. The discarded distinction is between studies using recall measures, which represents the bulk of research cited above, and those employing other measures of memory such as recognition (Gage & Safer, 1985; Mischel et al., 1976; Siegel et al., 1979; Snyder & White, 1982, Study 2), association (Coleman, 1975; Madigan & Bollenbach, 1982, Study 2), and lexical decisions (Derryberry, 1988; Clark et al., 1983). Because memory measures other than recall require the presentation of cues of some sort to subjects, it could be argued (e.g., see Forgas et al., 1984) that they provide relatively insensitive tests of the mood congruence hypothesis in that the influence of the mood "cue" is relatively reduced. However, the pattern of results for these studies is similar to that arising in those using recall measures so there seems no reason to cull them out.

The distinction I retained is between reports of mood congruence associated with a matching of the hedonic valence of the to-be-remembered material with that of the *exposure* mood versus those that are associated with a match between the valence of the material and mood during *retrieval*. As noted earlier, effects associated with exposure mood, usually referred to as mood-congruent learning, are difficult to interpret because of the possibility that mood may affect attention to the material and the way in which it is encoded. Blaney (1986) points out that this problem is exacerbated when exposure duration is subject-controlled as it is in a number of the studies reporting congruence effects due to exposure mood. Because of these interpretive problems, it seems wise to briefly report the box-score on exposure effects before moving on to look at retrieval.

I was able to find 11 tests of the congruence hypothesis for exposure, eight of which (Bower et al., 1981, Studies 1, 3, and 5; Bower and Mayer, 1985; Brown & Taylor, 1986; Nasby & Yando, 1982, Studies 1 and 2; Wright & Mischel, 1982) found full or partial evidence of congruence whereas the other three (Gotlib & McCann, 1984, Study 2; Isen et al., 1978, Study 2; Mecklenbräuker and Hager, 1984) did not. Unfortunately, the experiments reported by Bower et al. (1981, Studies 1, 3 and 5) and Mecklenbräuker and Hager (1984) suffer from the subject-controlled exposure duration problem mentioned above. If one were to take the conservative path and eliminate these latter findings from consideration, the remaining results, though suggestive, seem insufficient to support a strong conclusion.

The body of evidence assessing congruence due to retrieval mood is more substantial. Twenty-eight original research papers report 42 tests of the congruence hypothesis. Of these tests, six (Isen et al., 1978, Study 2; Mischel et al., 1976, the no-expectancy control condition results; Nasby & Yando, Study 1; Natale & Hantas, 1982; Teasdale & Fogarty, 1979; Teasdale et al., 1980) produced an asymmetry in that good mood appeared to enhance memory for positive materials but negative memories were not facilitated by bad mood. In addition, in one of the four tests reported by Derryberry (1988, Study 2 "cross trial" effects), a significant mood-*in*congruent result was found. Using a lexical decision task that required subjects to press a button indicating whether a trait term was "positive," "negative," or "neutral," Derryberry found that reaction times were faster to "positive" than "negative" terms when the preceding trail led to a negative outcome (i.e., feedback indicating an error or a failure to respond fast enough). Findings indicating that mood congruence cannot be reliably obtained on the negative side have attracted a good deal of attention recently (Blaney, 1986; Isen, 1985; Morris & Reilly, 1987) and I shall consider their meaning later on in this chapter. For the time being, however, I shall concentrate on the remaining 35 tests, 21 of which fully support congruence and 14 which do not.

Though this could hardly be described as overwhelming confirmation, closer examination of these findings reveals that they can be sorted with great success into supportive and non-supportive columns as a function of the type of design they used. More specifically, among studies that manipulated mood during *retrieval only*, namely: Clark & Teasdale (1985, Study 1),[4] Clark et al. (1983, the lexical decision data only); Coleman (1975),

---

[4]Though Clark and Teasdale's overall analysis supported congruence, they also report an interaction with gender such that females show congruence but males do not. This finding reinstigates the concern, first brought up in Chapter 3 in connection with the Velten procedure, that there are important sex differences in the causes and

Derryberry (1988, Studies 1 and 2 each with two separate tests), Forgas et al. (1984), Laird et al. (1982, Studies 1 and 2), Madigan and Bollenbach (1982, Study 2), Mathews and Bradley (1983), Riskind (1983, Studies 1 and 2), Riskind et al. (1982; 1987), Siegel et al., (1979), Snyder and White (1982, Studies 1 and 2), Teasdale and Russell (1983), Teasdale and Spencer (1984), and Teasdale and Taylor (1981), 18 of the 21 tests of the congruence hypothesis were supportive and in one of the exceptions, namely Siegel et al. (1979), the data were consistent with mood congruence but the results were not significant. Only the findings of Clark et al. (1983, the lexical decision data) and one of the four tests reported by Derryberry (1988) were clearly nonsupportive.

The remaining studies, where mood was manipulated (orthogonally) during both exposure and retrieval, produced 14 tests of the congruence hypothesis for retrieval mood (Bower et al., 1981, Studies 2, 3, and 4; Bower & Mayer, 1985; Bower et al., 1978, Studies 1, 2, and 3; Brown & Taylor, 1986; Gage & Safer, 1985; Mecklenbräuker & Hager, 1984; Nasby & Yando, 1982, Study 2) and only three of these (Bower et al., 1981, Study 3, estimates of positive versus negative story elements; Bower et al., 1978, order effects in Studies 1 and 2) were supportive.

Such patterning in the results seems to hold out the promise of discovering what mediates the appearance of congruence effects associated with retrieval mood. Seemingly, manipulations of mood during initial exposure prevent such effects. Unfortunately, however, this inference is tenuous because the decision to manipulate mood during exposure turns out to be correlated (and thus, confounded) with (1) how mood was induced and (2) the nature of the to-be-remembered material.

Specifically, of the 14 findings generated by studies that manipulated exposure and retrieval mood, 10 (7 of which were non-supportive of congruence) were produced by Bower and associates who use hypnosis as their sole means of inducing mood. Hypnosis may produce different results because of subject selection (subjects low in suggestibility are eliminated), role demand, or differences in the intensity of the mood produced by hypnosis as compared to other mood induction procedures. On the other hand, even if one eliminated all tests coming from studies using hypnosis, one is left with four studies: Brown & Taylor (1986), Gage and Safer (1985), Mecklenbräuker and Hager (1984), and Nasby and Yando (1982, Study 2), none of which found congruence. Though the number is small, the pattern is obviously completely divergent from studies which manipulate mood only during retrieval.

The second possibility of a "confound" arises because in 13 of the 14 studies that manipulated mood during exposure and retrieval, the material

---

consequences of mood which are going unnoticed because studies in the experimental literature typically use subjects of one sex, mostly females, or fail to consider sex as a factor in their analyses when both sexes are included. This is especially unfortunate in view of the substantial difference between the sexes in their apparent vulnerability to clinical depression (Weissman and Klerman, 1977).

to be remembered (unfamiliar faces, stories, positive and negative words) was not self-relevant to subjects. Though studies that manipulated mood only during retrieval found congruence effects whether the material was personally meaningful (11 out of 12) or not (7 out of 9), suggesting that this variable is not accounting for the result, it is possible that some aspect of studies that manipulated mood during both exposure and retrieval is interacting with the nature of the materials. Unless and until studies are done that orthogonally manipulate mood during exposure and retrieval *and* use personally meaningful material, we cannot be sure.

Fortunately, a study recently published by Brown and Taylor (1986; the exception or 14th study from above) did just that. Brown and Taylor manipulated happy and sad mood and then presented all subjects with the same set of 40 trait adjectives (20 positive and 20 negative) but manipulated (on a within basis) whether or not they were self-relevant by varying processing instructions. More specifically, subjects were asked to react (yes/no) to words either in terms of whether they were self-descriptive or rhymed with another word (e.g., "Does phony rhyme with pony?"). After a 10-minute distractor task, subjects were asked to recall as many of the 40 trait adjectives as they could.

As I indicated earlier when discussing effects associated with encoding mood, Brown and Taylor regard their results as indicating a congruence effect with respect to encoding mood although the effect was limited (as they had predicted) to terms that were processed in a self-referent way and that were judged to be self-descriptive. Under these circumstances, subjects who were in a happy mood during encoding recalled more positive than negative traits. However, no difference was found for sad objects, a result that Brown and Taylor assimilate to other studies finding asymmetries between the effects of good and bad mood, a result that I shall discuss further below.

Brown and Taylor do not report finding any significant effects involving retrieval mood and this was equally true regardless of whether the material was processed in a self-referent fashion or not. They argue that memory is more susceptible to mood during encoding than retrieval because it is during initial registration that the stimulus information is organized. Once organized, the information resists realignments that might occur due to retrieval mood. To the extent that this seemingly plausible explanation is supported by future research, it tends to explain why the boxscore for congruence effects due to retrieval mood is so sharply affected by whether or not mood was manipulated during encoding.

Even if congruence due to manipulated retrieval mood is ultimately shown to be hard to produce when encoding mood is manipulated in close temporal proximity to the occasion for recall, it is obvious from my review as well as that of Blaney (1986) that it is a highly replicable phenomenon. When added to the results from studies reviewed earlier that use an individual difference approach to studying congruence, the robustness of the phenomenon is underscored. These findings have theoretical and practical implications.

On the theoretical side, the data showing congruence with retrieval mood are consistent with associative network theories of the relationship between mood and memory (Bower, 1981; Clark & Isen, 1982). According to these theories, one's current mood makes any thoughts that have been associated with it in the past more accessible. For most people (sadists and masochists excepted), the valence of thoughts and mood match, thus producing congruence. The tendency for congruence results to be more likely to occur when the material to be retrieved is considered from a self-referent point of view (Bradley & Mathews, 1983; Ingram et al., 1983; Kuiper & Derry, 1982; McDowall, 1984, Study 1) and when it is personally meaningful (but remember that the latter assertion is clouded because of the "confound" between meaningfulness of the material and whether mood was manipulated during exposure and retrieval) is also consistent with such theories. Other things being equal, affect is more likely to be created by self-relevant events than it is by stimuli which are merely hedonically toned. Hence, associations between affect and the former stimuli will be stronger.

The practical implications of congruence due to retrieval mood have to do with the fate of moods, most especially the possibility that mood congruence may contribute to the maintenance of bad moods and even the onset of clinically significant depression. The idea that there might be a reciprocal relationship between depressive mood and negative cognitions producing a vicious cycle capable of inducing, maintaining, or worsening dysphoric affect is most closely associated with Beck's cognitive theory of depression (1967, 1976), but this theme is being increasingly endorsed by others (e.g., Ingram, 1984; Teasdale, 1983, Wenzlaff, Wegner, & Roper, 1988) as the data demonstrating congruence have accumulated.

On the other hand, as Blaney (1986) has suggested, the notion that bad moods, once initiated, lead inexorably toward depression is obviously inconsistent with the fact that most of us spend the great majority of our time in relatively neutral moods. Relevant data come from studies looking at the duration of moods. Moods produced by experimental manipulations fade quickly (Frost & Green, 1982; Isen et al., 1976; Isen & Gorglione, 1983; Ranieri & Zeiss, 1984), but even the declines in mood produced by relatively "severe" events occurring in the real world such as the illness of one's child, arguments with one's spouse, and the death of friends or neighbors, do not appear to survive beyond the day on which they occur (Stone & Neale 1984; Neale, Hooley, Jandorf, & Stone, 1987). Furthermore, some studies (Lewinsohn & Graf, 1973; Lewinsohn & Libet, 1972; Rehm, 1978) have found that although same-day correlations between mood and self-reports of positive and negative behavior are substantial, if one correlates mood with behaviors lagged by one day, the relationship disappears. These data are consistent with the suggestion that mood effects do not typically extend beyond one day.

In order to account for the clear evidence of mood-induced congruence of recall and the findings showing that moods are of limited duration, one might suppose that after a brief period in which moods produce congruent memories that maintain or even strengthen them, moods either decay spontaneously (Ingram, 1984), are interfered with, or destroyed by some "opponent" process that is instigated either automatically (Solomon & Corbit, 1974) or purposely as a means of self-regulation (Clark & Isen, 1982; Morris & Reilly, 1987). If so, only those individuals with some special vulnerability, such as a poor self-concept (Ingram, 1984), "depressogenic" attributional style (Abramson et al., 1978; Abramson, Metalsky, & Alloy, 1989), or an inability to control their thought process (Wenzlaff et al., 1988), would be expected to display vicious cycling.

Of the three hypotheses meant to account for the disappearance of moods: decay, automatic "opponent" processes, and instrumental self-regulatory responding, the latter has excited the most interest and attention. Though the idea that moods might simply decay is attractive because it seems to fit the phenomenology of mood, decay notions are very difficult to test in that we are active organisms psychophysiologically, cognitively, and behaviorally. With so many processes ongoing, it is virtually impossible to rule them all out as being responsible for the subsidence of mood and yet that is what is necessary if a decay process is to be supported. Solomon's idea (1980; Solomon & Corbit, 1974) that the arousal of any strong affect triggers an "opponent" process designed to return the organism to an affective "baseline" is intriguing but so far, laboratory tests of the theory have failed to support it when applied to mood (Ranieri & Zeiss, 1984; Sandvik et al., 1985). An exception can be found in research recently reported by Mauro (1988), but because Mauro employs hypnotic inductions that require serious subject selection bias, the generalizability of his results are in doubt.

The idea that individuals would engage in self-regulatory acts hardly seems surprising. Indeed, it had been regarded more or less as an article of faith by social learning theorists (Mischel, 1973; Bandura, 1977) and has more recently become a popular subject for theorizing in its own right (e.g., Carver & Scheier, 1981; Kanfer & Karoly, 1982). I intend to consider most of the evidence that such self-regulatory activity is engaged in as a way of maintaining good moods and reducing or eliminating bad moods later in this chapter. The exception that needs to be considered now is the loose end remaining to be tied up from studies of mood-memory congruence, namely the findings of asymmetry alluded to earlier. Such findings have been argued to reflect differences in the desirability of good and bad moods which causes individuals to attempt to rid themselves of the latter (Isen, 1984, 1985).

Studies claiming to find an asymmetry or cited by others as producing one include: (1) Isen et al. (1978, Study 2) who found that subjects who succeeded in a computer game before recall remembered more positive trait words than did subjects who had failed but the opposite effect did not occur with negative trait words; (2) Mischel et al. (1976) who also used a success-failure manipulation after having given subjects (false) feedback about personality assets and liabilities. They found that the successful subjects remembered more of the assets than did the unsuccessful subjects but there was no effect on memory for the liabilities; (3) Nasby and Yando (1982, Study 1) who used a memory elicitation procedure to manipulate mood and found that subjects who were made to feel elated subsequent to exposure to a list of adjectives containing happy, sad, and neutral members remembered more of the happy ones than did subjects in a neutral mood during retrieval but that sad mood subjects did not differ from those in a neutral mood; also, no significant effects were found for sad adjectives; and (4 & 5) Teasdale and Fogarty (1979) and Teasdale et al. (1980) who manipulated elated and depressed mood using the Velten procedure and found that subjects had shorter latencies for retrieving positive memories when elated than when depressed but there was no comparable (i.e., significant) difference with regard to the retrieval of negative memories.[5]

Examination of these results reveals that in each case, mood affected the recollection of positive items but not negative ones. This is exactly the sort of asymmetry (some examples of which were cited earlier) found in studies of mood-memory congruence among depressed individuals, for example, Bousfield (1950), Breslow et al. (1981), DeMonbreun and Craighead (1977), Finkel et al. (1982), and Williams and Broadbent (1986).

How are these results to be interpreted? Isen (Clark & Isen, 1982; 1984; 1985) has offered two rather different speculations. One has to do with the degree of interconnectedness of positive and negative material in memory. Life is generally on the positive side for most people (Diener, 1984). Perhaps for that reason, there is more positive material in memory and it is better interconnected than is negative material (e.g., Cramer, 1968; Matlin & Stang, 1979). This could explain why bad moods are less effective as retrieval cues for negative material than good moods are for positive items.

The other possibility is one I mentioned earlier, namely, that asymmetries arise because of a tendency people have to self-regulate their affect. According to this view, people might actively interfere with the tendency to think congruent thoughts when that tendency would have the effect of maintaining or exacerbating negative feeling states. The inclination to self-reg-

[5]I have decided not to include Natale and Hantas (1982) though they report an asymmetry. This study used standard hypnotic trance instructions followed by the Velten procedure to induce mood and then asked subjects to recall happy, sad, and neutral personal memories. Natale and Hantas reported that elated subjects recalled more positive memories and fewer negative memories than neutral mood control subjects whereas depressed subjects recalled fewer positive memories (compared to neutral mood controls) but not more negative ones. However, their measures of positive and negative memories were not independent . . . subjects were asked to report happy, sad, and "ordinary" memories during one 5 minute period. Indeed, it is hard to know what to make of their data since they were improperly analyzed with Anova followed by *t*-tests when Chi-Square was in order. Consequently, they will not be mentioned further.

ulate might, itself be responsible for the fact that negative items are less well-interconnected in memory in that one means of self-regulation is to distract oneself to terminate unpleasant thoughts (Hull, 1981; Morris & Reilly, 1987; Strack, Blaney, Ganellen, & Coyne, 1985; Wegner, 1988). If negative thoughts are banished relatively quickly, they should be retained less well.

No matter how plausible a self-regulation argument may seem, it is embarrassed in two ways. First, as noted by Blaney (1986), the notion of mood repair would seem to predict more than a failure to obtain mood congruence with negative moods and negative memories . . . we also should be finding *in*congruence such that bad mood enhances the recall of positive items because such memories should interfere with the aversive bad mood. Only one such finding has appeared in the literature[6] thus far, namely the results reported by Derryberry (1988, Study 2, the "cross trial" effects) that I described earlier. But it should be noted that Study 2 was a close replication of Study 1 which failed to find this effect.

The other problem with the self-regulation explanation is its *post hoc* nature. No explanation has been offered as to why asymmetries appear in some studies but not in the majority. (This criticism would also apply to the explanation based upon differences in interconnectedness.) On the basis of the conceptual and theoretical analyses of mood made in earlier chapters, my first guess would have to do with mood salience. That is, studies finding asymmetries would be those that, in some way, caused subjects' moods to remain figural in focal attention whereas in those producing congruence, mood assumed its more common status of a background or contextual state. But this discussion is clearly premature. If self-regulation of mood depends upon this or other factors, it will be better revealed in a systematic examination of the full variety of ways in which people are likely to self-regulate. Thus, I shall postpone any further discussion of this issue until the relationship between mood and behavior has been more fully reviewed.

The Effects of Mood on Perception and Judgment

Many people will tell you that the world simply looks different to them in their different moods. The possibility that mood alters the very appearance of things is suggested by metaphors involving color. Bad mood is often referred to as the "blues" and the idea of "Blue Monday" persists even though the evidence fails to support the idea that Monday moods are worse than those of the other weekdays (Stone, Hedges, Neale, & Satin, 1985).

[6]Blaney (1986) claims that such an effect was found by Clark et al. (1983) with their recall data. However, mood incongruence results were found for *both* positive and negative mood inductions and were actually stronger in the former condition. Thus, one could hardly argue for a self-regulation interpretation.

Conversely, the cheerful person is said to view the world through rose-colored glasses.

There is a modest-sized literature comprised of studies where moods are either induced or existing affect is measured and the effect on some perception or judgment is assessed. The evidence from these studies tends to confirm popular wisdom; mood does influence how things look to us and, in general, that influence is mood-congruent. Moods, both good and bad, have been shown to influence our perception and evaluation of words and other symbolic stimuli, events, nonsocial objects, other persons, self, our attitudes about social issues, and our expectations of the future.

The idea that the state one is in can influence what is perceived was popularized by advocates of the so-called "new look" in perception, for example, Bruner and Postman (1947). Clearly relevant are studies indicating a projection-like phenomenon whereby a perceiver's specific emotional state, such as fear, anger, or disgust, causes him to judge others as having more of that particular emotion[7] (e.g., Feshbach & Feshbach, 1963; Feshbach & Singer, 1957; Hornberger, 1960; Izard, Wehmer, Livsey, and Jennings, 1965; Schiffenbauer, 1974). Such findings have often been interpreted as evidence of motivated perception in that attributing or projecting negative affects to others may mitigate the significance of the reaction; if others feel as negatively as you do then your own feelings are more likely to be perceived as appropriate.

A very different perspective is offered by Byrne (1971) whose analysis was associationist. Though his principal interest was in the reinforcing effect of attitudinal similarity on interpersonal attraction, he took the more general position that "Any stimulus that elicits an affective response can determine evaluative responses toward other stimuli through association with them" (p. 281).

More recently, analyses of mood-induced perception and judgment have focused on the mediating influence of cognitive processes. The prevailing view derives from the network models of the relationship between mood and memory (Bower, 1981; Isen et al., 1978) that we considered earlier. According to such models, affective states prime or make more available concepts and memories related by association to the states. The biased sample of items available in memory could influence what we perceive and how we categorize and evaluate it.

---

[7]Given the effort to maintain a distinction between mood and emotion in Chapter 1, the reader may well wonder why I now blithely include studies apparently of emotion in my review of mood's effects. The reason is that studies of mood are not the only studies that manipulate mood. Some studies which attempt to manipulate emotion probably produce mood and fail to induce emotion. Unfortunately, it is rare to find a researcher on either the mood or emotion "side" who checks to see whether he has produced a mood, an emotion, or both. Consequently, I have decided to take a conservative path and err on the side of inclusiveness; if the manipulation in a study seems to be a mood-inducer, I have included it.

An alternative view of much of the evidence is based upon the possibility of misattribution (Schwarz & Clore, 1983; 1988). More specifically, because moods are often out of awareness, the coloration they produce may not be associated with their source leading to the possibility that it (the coloration or feeling) might be misattributed to the object being perceived or judged. Though spruced up with references to cognitive processing, the view offered by Schwarz and Clore is really quite similar to that of Byrne (1971); Nowlis and Nowlis (1956) had also speculated along these lines. I will consider the relative merit of these explanations after reviewing the empirical literature.

The Influence of Mood on the Perception of Symbolic Stimuli

If mood influences perception by acting as a retrieval cue for associated items, one might predict that the perception of words that are semantically associated with the affective state one is in would be facilitated. One of the earliest tests of this hypothesis was carried out by Postman and Brown (1952). These investigators manipulated success and failure and then presented subjects with words that were either success- or failure-related. They found that recognition thresholds were lower for words that were congruent with their previous task outcome. Using the Velten procedure to produce elation and depression, Small (1986) demonstrated similar effects on word recognition. However, Gerrig and Bower (1982) used hypnosis to manipulate happy and angry moods and uncovered no evidence of an advantage in recognizing mood-congruent words. The results in this general area would not have improved (i.e., become more consistent) if I had included in this section the studies examining the influence of mood on lexical decisions (Clark et al., 1983; Derryberry, 1988; both reviewed in the preceding Mood and Memory section) because they also produced mixed results. Clearly, more systematic research will be required to elucidate the conditions in which mood influences the near-threshold perception of mood-congruent symbolic stimuli.

The Influence of Mood on the Perception of Objects and Events

Much of the current research in this area has been stimulated by the work of Alice Isen and her collaborators. In one of their most frequently cited studies (Isen et al., 1978, Study 1), people in a shopping mall were given a small free promotional gift. These subjects, along with a control sample that did not receive the gift, were stopped further on down the mall and asked to respond to a brief consumer survey inquiring about their experience with their automobiles and televisions. Subjects who had received the free gift reported more favorable experiences with their cars and televisions than did control subjects.

In a subsequent study, Isen and Shalker (1982) manipulated good and bad mood and asked subjects to rate the pleasantness of slides depicting local scenes. Planned comparisons indicated that the effect of mood was significant only for ambiguous scenes, that is, those that an independent group of judge-subjects had rated as neither clearly pleasant or unpleasant. Isen and Shalker had predicted this effect, arguing that the accessibility of mood-related material in memory accounts for judgment effects by altering the interpretations made of the stimuli. They suggested that it is only when stimuli are complex, ambiguous, or neutral that they need to be "interpreted" (see Forgas et al., 1984, for a similar argument).

However, there appear to be no other studies where such stimuli were compared with simple, nonambiguous, or nonneutral ones in terms of their susceptibility to mood effects where the pattern of results supports the Isen and Shalker prediction.[8] This is especially troublesome because Isen and Shalker, to protect the effect of their mood manipulations from the influence of the slides, presented the ambiguous slides before the pleasant and unpleasant ones. Consequently, their data are open to the rather plausible interpretation that the weaker results for pleasant and unpleasant stimuli are due to their greater distance in time from the mood manipulation, a point they acknowledge. Moreover, as will be evident as this review proceeds, there are a number of studies finding significant effects of mood on judgments of stimuli that are clearly positive and negative. Thus, even if Isen and Shalker are correct in their explanation of how mood influences the judgment of ambiguous stimuli, some other account would be necessary to explain the effect of mood on positive and negative stimuli.

A variety of studies, all of which used the Velten procedure, indicate that mood influences the evaluation of both anticipated and actually experienced events. Carson and Adams (1980) interposed their mood manipulation between two separate measurements of ratings of the pleasantness of a large number of everyday activities and found significant changes in mood congruent directions for both the elation and depression manipulations.[9] Cunningham (1988) has recently replicated and extended these findings. Hawkins, French, Crawford, and Enzle (1988) followed their mood manipulation with a manual sorting task after which subjects provided ratings of the enjoyability of the task and how slowly time seemed to pass while performing the task. Depressed subjects rated the task less enjoyable and said time

[8]Isen and Shalker (1982) cite Schiffenbauer's (1974) data (see below) as supportive of their argument in that his mood manipulations did not affect judgments of happy and angry faces while they did alter judgments of "ambiguous" fear/surprise blends. But they fail to note that Schiffenbauer reports significant effects of mood on disgust expressions which are as unambiguous as happy and angry ones.

[9]It should be noted, however, that Carson and Adams failed to find differences between depressed and nondepressed students (as measured by the Beck Depression Inventory) in pretest ratings of the activities. Given that other investigators have found such differences (MacPhillamy & Lewinsohn, 1974), the most likely explanation here is that the difference between the Beck scores of Carson and Adams' two groups was rather small (Depressed M=4.11; Nondepressed M=.94), and in fact, a score of 4 on the Beck is well within what is usually considered to be the normal range of 0 to 9 (e.g., see Martin, Abramson, & Alloy, 1984).

passed more slowly while doing it than did neutral and elated subjects who did not differ.

Not only does mood influence the evaluation of objects and events, but it would appear that it similarly governs the expectations that positive and negative events will come to pass, that is, good mood seems to produce optimism and bad mood, pessimism. The association between mood and expectation has been found repeatedly both for measured and manipulated mood. Bower and Cohen (1982) and Johnson and Tversky (1983) manipulated mood and found perceptions of risk were congruent with induced mood whereas Mayer and Bremer (1985) and Mayer and Volanth (1985) measured existing moods and found them to be congruently correlated with the perception of the probabilities of desirable and undesirable future events.

Though such results should hardly seem surprising considering the earlier results I have reviewed showing mood-congruent memory and perception, there was a surprising aspect to those reported by Johnson and Tversky (1983). Johnson and Tversky used newspaper stories to manipulate mood. In their initial study (Experiment 1), all subjects, except for controls, read about a death but for some it was caused by leukemia, for others it was homicide, and yet another group read about a death by fire. The dependent measures consisted of completion of a "Perception of Risk Questionnaire" that asked subjects to indicate their level of concern for each of 18 causes of death. The risks had previously been scaled for similarity so that it was possible to determine for each of the various experimental groups the degree to which reading the newspaper story had affected their worry about the "target" risk, that is, the risk they read about, near-target risks, that is, its two closest neighbors, and nontarget risks.

Johnson and Tversky found that the stories about deaths did have a depressing effect on subjects as compared to the control group and also that the experimental subjects showed an increased "global" concern about dying from the entire set of causes of death. However, there was no greater concern shown either about the target cause or causes related to it (referred to as "local" concerns) than was shown for the remainder of the causes of death. In subsequent studies, Johnson and Tversky first replicated these results (Experiment 2) and then extended them by using a story that was depressing but unrelated to death and adding a new set of nonfatal risks, for example, alcoholism, divorce, unemployment (Experiment 3). In Experiment 4, Johnson and Tversky used a good-mood inducing story and were able to demonstrate reductions in perceived concerns about the expanded set of risks.

The most interesting aspect of these results is the consistent failure (In Experiments 1 to 3) to find a so-called "local" effect of mood manipulation. According to Johnson and Tversky:

> The pervasive global effect of mood and the absence of a local effect pose a serious problem to memory-based models . . . such as spreading activation within a semantic network. In such models, the impact of an experience is largely determined by the strength of an association between the input (e.g., the story) and the target (e.g., the risks). Risks that are closely linked to the

story should be influenced more than unrelated risks, contrary to the present findings. (p. 30)

But if spreading activation within semantic networks cannot explain the effect of mood on perception of risk, what does? Johnson and Tversky did not offer an alternative account but the misattribution notion (Schwarz & Clore, 1983) referred to earlier was waiting in the wings.

According to Schwarz and Clore (1983), evaluative judgments may be mistakenly based on the affective state one is in while considering the object to be judged, an idea that can be traced back to Byrne (1971) and, even further, to Nowlis (e.g., Nowlis & Nowlis, 1956) Thus, if one considers the possibility of death by heart disease while in a bad mood, the negative affect may be "read" as fear or concern and inflate the perception of risk.

Schwarz and Clore conducted two studies to test their view. The general design of each involved manipulations of mood followed by treatments designed to make a possible mood-altering factor salient (or not). The dependent measure in both studies was a rating of life satisfaction. The reasoning was that making possible causes of mood salient would cause subjects to discount their mood when making judgments; when not salient, however, moods will influence judgments in a mood-congruent direction.

In the first study, Schwarz and Clore used a recollection procedure to induce happy and sad moods. Before collecting the ratings of general happiness and life satisfaction, some subjects were led to believe that the experimental cubicle they were in, which was "an odd-looking soundproofed room," might make them feel "tense" and "depressed."[10] As predicted, when no mention was made about the potential influence of the room, life-satisfaction judgments were mood congruent but no such effects occurred when possible effects of the room were noted. In the second study, subjects were called on the telephone on Spring days which were either rainy or bright and sunny and asked to respond to the same questions about happiness and satisfaction. A manipulation check established that moods did differ as a function of the weather, a finding that replicates results reported by Cunningham (1979). As in the first study, for some subjects, an explanation for their current mood was made salient before measuring their perceived well-being by having the interviewer either inquire about the weather or specifically state that his interest was in the influence of weather on mood. A comparison group of subjects was run with no mention made of the weather. Once again it was found that mood, induced by differences in the weather, influenced subjects' appraisals of their current life circumstances unless the cause of their mood was made salient.

[10]Schwarz and Clore also attempted to manipulate the expectation that the room might, in itself, make subjects elated. However, the results in this condition are weak at best and Schwarz and Clore acknowledge that "subjects may have found it less credible that the soundproof room could produce elation than that it would produce tension." (p. 518)

Implicit in the Schwarz and Clore position is the premise that subjects are generally unaware of their moods. This is precisely the position I have taken in Chapter 1. The ability of mood to influence perception and judgment, and possibly memory as well, exists because moods, in their typical manifestation as "ground" or context, are not focused upon; we cannot discount something of which we are unaware. From this perspective, what is critical in the procedures employed by Schwarz and Clore is that they brought mood into focal attention. The fact that this was done by alerting subjects to possible causes of their moods is irrelevant in my view. But, setting aside the fine tuning on this point, it should be clear that the Schwarz and Clore data, like those of Johnson and Tversky (1983), are difficult to explain in terms of the influence of mood on memory. We shall encounter more results embarrassing to network models in findings reported later in this chapter.

The theoretical importance of the Schwarz and Clore results should not divert attention from the fact that in conditions where mood was not made salient, mood congruent judgments, here of life satisfaction, were obtained once again. Before moving on to consider other effects of mood on perception and judgment, however, it should be noted that *exactly opposite* effects of mood on life satisfaction judgments have been reported by Dermer et al. (1979, Study 2). Arguing from adaptation level (Helson, 1964) and comparison level (Thibaut & Kelley, 1959) perspectives, these investigators predicted and obtained a contrast effect such that instructions to imagine a series of negative life experiences (e.g., being severely burned and permanently disfigured), actually led to significantly more positive judgments of current life satisfaction than were obtained from subjects asked to imagine positive life events, (e.g., winning an all-expenses-paid vacation). A mood check administered after the series of imagined events indicated that appropriately good and bad moods had been induced. Complicating the situation even more, Dermer et al. used a pre-post design in which they measured life satisfaction at the beginning of the semester during which the study was conducted. The data indicate that imagining positive events actually led to a marginally significant *increase* in a composite measure of satisfaction (the average of satisfaction with one's personal appearance, health, and general life circumstances), i.e., a weak assimilation effect was obtained within the positive mood condition.

The results of Schwarz and Clore (1983) and Dermer et al. (1979) are rather difficult to reconcile. It would seem that because Dermer and coworkers measured mood immediately after the manipulation and just before measuring life satisfaction, their results should be compared to the Schwarz and Clore conditions where mood was made salient, conditions where mood did not influence life satisfaction judgments. Thus, the specific disparity that must be reconciled is that Dermer et al. appeared to obtain a contrast effect with bad mood and an assimilation effect (mood-congruent) with good mood in a condition where Schwarz and Clore twice observed no effect of mood. The most obvious way to reconcile these results is to suppose that even though Dermer et al. apparently affected mood, the life-satisfaction judgments were influenced not by mood but rather a change in frame of reference caused by requiring a *series* of hedonically significant events to be imagined. Schwarz and Clore, on the other hand, manipulated mood by asking subjects to recall a *single* event or gathering judgments on sunny versus rainy days, treatments sufficient to influence mood but not to alter one's frame of reference.

What evidence do I have to substantiate my speculation? First, the fact that Dermer et al. (1979) obtained both a contrast and an assimilation effect (though the latter was quite weak) is consistent with what one would predict from adaptation-level theory. More specifically, assimilation effects are expected when the object to be judged and the preceding stimuli are relatively close or similar to each other; contrast effects would be expected when they are far apart or unlike (e.g., see Petty & Cacioppo, 1981). Given that the subjects used by Dermer et al. (1979) were generally satisfied with their lives before the manipulation, the observed pattern of results is exactly what would be predicted.

The other evidence that makes me believe that mood was irrelevant to obtaining the Dermer et al. effects is that in the majority of other studies where subjects were presented a *series* of hedonically-relevant stimuli in a homogeneous grouping, such as happy or sad faces (S. Thayer, 1980a), clips from comedy or horror films (Manstead et al., 1983), and positive or negative newspaper stories (Reilly, 1985), a contrast effect was obtained on judgments of a stimulus unlike those in the adaptation series. The lone exception, by Sandvik et al. (1985, Study 2), used slides of happy or disturbing scenes and found no effect of repeated presentation of the disturbing slides on reactions to a single positive slide but did obtain an assimilation (mood-congruent) effect when the adaptation series was positive and the judged slide was negative, that is, the latter was rated as *less* negative when rated after the adaptation series as compared to when it was rated before the series had been presented.

Though these various data are relatively supportive of my proposed reconciliation of the divergent results obtained by Schwarz and Clore (1983) versus those of Dermer et al. (1979), they do not answer the question as to why mood is ineffectual in altering judgments in cases where an adapting series of stimuli are used. Though one could argue that the stimuli used by Thayer (1980a), Manstead et al. (1983), and Sandvik et al. (1985) might not have influenced mood due to the brevity or repetitiousness of their presentation, the same cannot be said of the stimuli used by Dermer et al. (1979) and Reilly (1985) since mood checks in the latter two studies indicated that mood had been successfully induced.

The Influence of Mood on Judgments of Other People

Given that mood influences our reactions to objects and events, it would seem likely that similar effects could be obtained with regard to perceptions of people. Izard et al. (1965) studied this phenomenon by manipulating mood and examining the way it influenced resolutions of binocularly rivalrous stimuli. Positive and negative affect were created by having the experimenter be pleasant and unpleasant. The pleasant experimenter praised the subject's performance and attempted to create a warm and supportive relationship. The unpleasant experimenter was critical of the subject's performance and questioned his abilities. Throughout the process, he was curt and irritating. The dependent measure was the way in which subjects subsequently resolved stereoscopic rivalries created by displaying pairs of photographs in a stereoscope that contained either a happy and angry expression (of the same person) or two pictures of an interpersonal scene involving the same two people with one scene showing a friendly interaction, and the other a hostile interaction. Subjects were asked to report what they saw. Significant differences were obtained for both kinds of stimuli with subjects exposed to an unpleasant experimenter seeing more hostile faces and interactions than subjects exposed to a warm experimenter. Similarly, Schiffenbauer (1974), using audiotapes that produced positive and negative affect, showed that mood congruently affected perceptions of slides showing surprise/fear blends and those depicting disgust expressions.

Judgments such as these may be due to the influence of affect on attention. Bower (1981), for example, has suggested that mood-congruent stimuli should be more salient and "pop out" at perceivers. Ritchie (1986) has recently reported data consistent with this prediction. Ritchie manipulated mood by having subjects repeatedly make wagers that were won or lost. Subsequent to receiving win-lose feedback, subjects had to detect the presence of features in a computer-controlled display. Reaction times were faster when the feature to be detected was displayed near a schematic face (happy or unhappy) that was congruent with the gambling outcome (won or lost).

A number of studies indicate that mood congruently affects how attractive we find other people to be. For example, Gouaux (1971) manipulated elation and depression using films and then had subjects rate an anonymous stranger whose attitudes varied in their similarity to those of the subject. The ratings were made on the Interpersonal Judgment Scale (IJS) (Byrne & Nelson, 1965), a six-item scale requiring evaluations of intelligence, how likable the person is, etc. Attitudinal similarity and mood both affected reactions on the IJS. In other studies, mood manipulated by room temperature (uncomfortably hot and humid or normal; Griffitt, 1970), population density (Griffitt & Veitch, 1971), and good versus bad news heard over the radio (Veitch & Griffitt, 1976) have all been shown to have similar effects on reactions to strangers using the IJS. Forgas and Bower (1987) have recently shown that mood-altering feedback indicating that one's personality is problematic or strong affects the positivity of judgments about hypothetical individuals.

Finally, Cunningham (1988a) induced both positive and negative moods using either a self-relevant manipulation (good versus bad performance on a task that was supposedly correlated with general intelligence and social skills), or depressing versus upbeat films. Both sorts of mood manipulations affected the degree to which subjects conversed with a confederate and the intimacy level of their disclosures; happy subjects broached subjects at a medium or high level of disclosure (and talking more overall) while depressed subjects preferred topics low in intimacy. Though perceptions of the confederate were not assessed, it is quite possible that the observed differences in disclosure could have been mediated by more favorable reactions to the confederates in the positive mood conditions.

Taken together, these studies have produced consistent evidence in support of the idea that bad mood can lead to a misanthropic attitude just as good moods can foster an outgoing or positive orientation toward others. Such findings lead to the question of the influence of mood on the way one sees oneself.

The Influence of Mood on Self-Perception

Undoubtedly because of the influence of theory (Abramson et al., 1978; Beck, 1967, 1976) relating clinically significant depressive affect to negative thoughts about self (see Chapter 7 for a discussion of these cognitive theories of depression), a relatively large number of studies have been conducted that have related being "down" to being "down on oneself." Recent reviews of this literature (Alloy & Abramson, 1988; Miller & Moretti, 1988; Ruehlman West, & Pasahow, 1985; Sweeney, Anderson, & Bailey, 1986) document an impressive range of different kinds of judgments and perceptions about self that have been shown to be reliably and congruently associated with depressive affect. The main categories of these effects include causal attributions (depressed individuals, relative to nondepressed, make internal, stable, and global attributions for failures and external, unstable, and specific attributions for successes), self-evaluations (depressives' self-perceptions tend to be balanced between positive and negative whereas nondepressed persons are more positive), expectancy of future success and failure, and judgments of control.

However, rather than forming a firm base of support for the theories of Beck and Seligman that were responsible for generating most of the studies and predict that it is the depressed who are irrationally negative about self, these various results have been interpreted as evidence of "depressive realism," that is, a tendency for depressives' judgments to be *less* biased and distorted than those of normals who, it is argued, display egotistical bias. This conclusion was first suggested by data reported by Alloy and Abramson (1979, Experiments 1 through 4) who presented depressed and nondepressed college students with varying contingencies between a button-pressing response and an experimental outcome. These effects have, by now, been replicated many times and extended across the response domains mentioned above.

Such data have been taken by some, for example, Pyszczynski and Greenberg (1985) and Sackeim (1983), to indicate that the problem of depressives may not be a tendency to distort events in a negative direction as suggested by Beck (1967) but, rather, the *failure to distort in a positive, self-enhancing direction* as is typical among the nondepressed (see Zuckerman, 1979, for a review of data documenting the egotistical bias among normals). As intriguing as this possibility is, both Alloy and Abramson (1988) and Miller and Moretti (1988) caution that we are a long way from fully understanding the role of cognitive, motivational, and situational factors that are responsible for the differences that have been found. Especially important at this point is research on expectancies of depressed and nondepressed individuals and the way in which these expectancies are related to differential experiences of each group.

Though fascinating and practically important, the debate over depressive realism tends to skirt the fundamental issue of the causal role of mood in these effects. Most of the research has compared depressed and nondepressed individuals and is, thus, correlational in nature, leaving open the possibility that mood is only epiphenomenally involved. Various "third variable" explanations have been proposed including low self-esteem (Alloy & Abramson, 1988), differences in cognitive schemata (Miller & Moretti, 1988), and even physiological or biochemical processes (Miller & Moretti, 1988). Clearly, the case in behalf of mood would be strengthened if one could show judgmental bias to result from mood manipulations with normal subjects.

A small number of such studies exist. Wright and Mischel (1982) manipulated mood by asking subjects to imagine happy, sad, or neutral situations and try to feel the reactions such situations would produce. Subsequently, all subjects engaged in a "mental rotation" task were given bogus success or failure feedback and were asked to evaluate their performance in terms of self-satisfaction. There was no effect of mood within the success condition, however, subjects who received failure feedback produced a significant mood-congruent effect with self-satisfaction being lowest among negative-mood subjects and highest among positive-mood subjects. Stronger evidence of mood-congruent judgments of self derived from a different dependent measure. After the mood manipulation but before task performance, Wright and Mischel asked subjects to assess themselves using 11 pairs of trait-levels descriptors such as "intelligent", "self-confident", "socially skilled", etc. Significant or near-significant mood-congruent effects were found for 11 of the 12 with "trustworthy" the lone exception.

Baumgardner and Arkin (1988) manipulated the same variables of mood and task outcome but rather than measuring how subjects *felt* about the outcome, they asked subjects to make *atttributions* about the outcome. Their results were very different from those obtained by Wright and Mischel. Baumgardner and Arkin found that mood affected attributions only among subjects who had succeeded. And, though good mood subjects displayed what might be considered a mood-congruent judgmental bias in that they were more likely than neutral mood subjects to attribute their good performance to self, bad mood subjects showed the very same bias. Baumgardner and Arkin interpreted these results in terms of self-regulation. They argued that people in a bad mood use self-serving attributions about success to help themselves out of the doldrums and people in a good mood use them to maintain how they are feeling whereas people in a neutral mood have neither motivation and so are less biased.

It is difficult to compare the Wright and Mischel and Baumgardner and Arkin studies because they used different mood manipulations (personal recollections versus brief movies), different performance tasks (a novel perceptual judgment task versus a test of general knowledge), and, most importantly, very different dependent measures. Wright and Mischel asked subjects how they *felt* about how they had done whereas Baumgardner and Arkin asked subjects to offer an *explanation.* The latter judgment may induce a very different sort of set.

Two other relevant studies (Forgas et al., 1984, and Kavanagh & Bower, 1985) manipulated mood through hypnotic induction and found mood-congruent judgments of, respectively, social skills and self-efficacy. Forgas et al. (1984) videotaped the interview behavior of subject pairs in unmanipulated moods and, on a subsequent occasion, hypnotized them so as to produce positive and negative moods. This was done by asking subjects to recall "a specific experience from the past in which they either (a) felt unhappy, depressed, disappointed, let down, unsuccessful, and rejected by others or (b) felt happy, successful, liked, and accepted by others" (p. 502). While in these moods, subjects viewed the videotapes and, for each 5 second segment of tape, noted a positive or negative behavior. Subjects had been trained to identify such behaviors, defined as "any behavior, act or communication, including both verbal and nonverbal cues, which indicates interest, positive behavior, poise and social skills, or the opposite, lack of skill and poise" (p. 503). The results showed that self-perceptions were clearly congruent with induced mood.[11]

Unfortunately, the Forgas et al. results appear to be open to an alternative interpretation that has nothing to do with mood. In a prepublication airing of the data,[12] Gordon Bower (1981) was more specific about the particular sort of event that the Forgas et al. subjects were instructed to recall under hypnosis. According to Bower, subjects were told to "relive the feelings of, either an occasion when they succeeded gloriously by acting in a socially adept manner or an occasion when they failed and were rejected and embarrassed by acting in a socially inept, awkward manner" (p. 140). As noted by Blaney (1986) and as I mentioned earlier while discussing the various mood manipulations used in mood and memory experiments, procedures that bring specific cognitions to mind are susceptible to priming explanations that have nothing to do with affect. The instructions used by Forgas et al.

[11]Forgas et al. (1984) also report effects of mood on ratings of the co-interviewees behavior. However, the effects are considerably weaker than those associated with the self-ratings and their significance unclear because the *F*-tests Forgas et al. used to analyze their data were inappropriate given that their four "different" dependent measures were not independent of each other.

[12]Forgas has confirmed in a personal communication that the data described by Bower (1981) are, in fact, the same as those reported in Forgas et al. (1984).

(1984), as described by Bower (1981), appear to be a particularly extreme example of this sort of problem in that the memories that subjects were instructed to retrieve to create good and bad mood are obviously very closely related to the sort of judgment used as a dependent measure.

Kavanagh and Bower (1985) hypnotized subjects and, in a within design, asked them to enter happy, sad, and neutral moods by recalling, respectively, occasions of romantic success, failure, and sitting on a sofa at home and reading a textbook. After achieving each desired mood state, subjects responded to one of three equivalent forms of an efficacy questionnaire that asked them to rate the extent to which they felt capable of performing acts across a range of performance areas including romantic, social skills, athletic, and academic. As predicted, the linear contrast testing the effect of the three levels of mood on the combined efficacy judgments was clearly significant. No differences were observed as a function of the performance area, that is, even though mood was manipulated via recall of romantic successes and failures, self-efficacy effects were no stronger in the romantic realm than they were for other realms of endeavor. These findings, and the results of Wright and Mischel (1982) showing that mood manipulations influence judgments of the possession of a wide range of positive and negative traits, are reminiscent of the lack of "local" effects in the data reported by Johnson and Tversky (1983). Though Kavanagh and Bower dismiss the idea that such results contradict Bower's (1981) network model, I believe that they do and will discuss an alternative explanation below.

These four studies provide modest support for the idea that mood congruently influences judgments about self. The only result that clearly deviates from this generalization is the Baumgardner and Arkin (1988) finding showing that saddened subjects are more likely to take credit for success than neutral mood subjects. Though such a result is consistent with the idea that event attributions can be used to improve mood, it is not clear why such self-regulatory actions would not also occur in the case of failure on the test.

Mood and Perception: A Summary

It is clear that mood has an important influence on our perception and judgment of a wide range of social and nonsocial objects. However, though the empirical effect cannot be questioned, the available theoretical accounts have yet to be adequately tested against each other.

The idea that mood can influence the perception and judgment of objects and events by being mistaken as part of the reaction to the stimulus appears capable of explaining most of the findings of mood-congruent perception including those of Johnson and Tversky (1983), Schwarz and Clore (1983), and Kavanagh and Bower (1985), all of which appear to contradict a memory explanation. Moreover, unlike the network and spreading activation account, this explanation is not embarrassed by the results indicating that mood generally fails to influence the detection of mood congruent words presented at or near recognition threshold (Clark et al., 1983; Gerrig & Bower, 1982, Studies 1 and 2) because the misattribution or mood salience explanation predicts effects only for evaluative judgments.

Does this mean that memory is irrelevant to such effects? In some cases it probably is. For instance, some studies, such as Isen and Shalker (1982) and Forgas et al. (1984), require judgments that rely minimally on memory because the stimulus to be judged is directly available to the subject while judging. In cases such as these, predictions based upon memory are likely to do poorly. On the other hand, memory could play a role in studies such as Isen et al. (1978, Study 1), Carson and Adams (1980), and Kavanagh and Bower (1985). Though it seemed not to in Schwarz and Clore (1983) and Johnson and Tversky (1983) where it might well have, it must be remembered that I have considered but a single memory model. It is possible that some other model of memory such as that recently offered by Wyer and Srull (1986) might be able to do better.

Finally, at the risk of further confusing the issue I would note that the existing results could also be explained by postulating that mood produces a tendency to make mood-congruent *responses*. Kavanagh and Bower (1985) considered such an explanation for their findings showing that mood influences self-efficacy judgments but rejected it. However, the particular sort of response bias considered by Kavanagh and Bower was a narrow and easily dismissed one relating to the possibility that subjects in good and bad moods use numbers differently. A more likely possibility is that mood simply predisposes one to make responses that are positive or negative quite independent of any effects the mood might have on their perceptions or memories. Consider the following "thought" experiment. What if one induced subjects into a mood and then asked them to view tachistoscopically presented slides after which they would indicate from an array of options which one they thought they had seen. If exposure durations were brief enough, one could present blank slides but keep subjects ignorant of the fact that nothing had been presented. If told to guess, subjects might display a mood-congruent bias that would have nothing to do with perception or memory.

If the theoretical situation is still somewhat murky, the practical consequences of mood congruent biases in perception and judgment seem less so. Like the similar effects found for memory, these are compatible with the idea that moods have the capacity to feed upon themselves and intensify. If the mood in question is a good one that seems acceptable assuming that the result stops short of mania but if your bad moods cause you to: (a) feel less attracted to other people (Griffitt, 1970), (b) negatively construe interpersonal feedback (Gotlib, 1983), (c) perceive yourself as more vulnerable to all sorts of unpleasant occurrences (Johnson & Tversky, 1983), (d) see various everyday activities as relatively unenjoyable (Carson & Adams, 1980), and (e), regard your own behavior as relatively inept (Kavanagh & Bower, 1985), it is difficult to see how you could ever dispel the gloom.

However, the likely fate of good and bad moods is probably even more responsive to the last category of effects I have yet to consider, namely, the effects of mood on overt behavior.

The Effects of Mood on Behavior

Given that (a) mood generally influences in a congruent way what we remember of the past, especially about ourselves, and the way we perceive and judge presently available objects, and that (b) behavior is often determined by how we remember the past and perceive the present, it would be reasonable to expect that (c) mood would alter behavior in mood congruent or consistent ways. So, for example, while considering whether to accept the invitation of an acquaintance to have dinner, the literature I have reviewed to this point suggests that my mood would tend to determine (1) whether I remembered more pleasant or unpleasant occasions of that sort from my personal history, (2) the degree to which the acquaintance would seem an appealing dinner partner, and, therefore, (3) my likelihood of accepting the invitation.

As will become evident, these expectations are often confirmed but there are enough exceptions as to require a search beyond the influence of mood on memory and perception for an explanation.

Positive Mood and Behavior

The most frequently studied behavioral correlate of moods, both good and bad, has been helping behavior. Dovidio (1984), in his review of this rather large literature, found that the effects of good mood were remarkably consistent:

> The results of many experiments involving a variety of subject populations, research settings, ways of inducing feelings, and types of helping situations have found that people who feel good, successful, happy, and fortunate are more likely to help someone else than are people who are not in a positive state. (p. 390)

Though the effect of positive mood on helping is quite predictable (but see below for a discussion of the exceptions), no consensus has developed around a particular explanation. Carlson, Charlin, and Miller (1988) have recently identified what they regard as six separate hypotheses that have been advanced to explain one or more of the findings relating good mood to helping behavior. They attempted to assess their validity using a novel procedure. Judges read the Method section for each of 61 positive affect conditions in which it was possible to generate an effect-size estimate for the good-mood manipulation. Their task was to assess the operative level of each variable specified as relevant by the various hypotheses. Higher-order partial correlations were used to identify the independent contribution of each of these theoretically relevant variables. Carlson et al. concluded that four of these hypotheses were best supported: focus of attention, separate process, social outlook, and mood maintenance.

Though Carlson and coworkers developed an interesting and innovative technique to evaluate the success of the various hypotheses, their choice of hypotheses was puzzling at best. Two of the so-called hypotheses do not offer independent explanations of good-mood induced helping at all; rather, they propose boundary conditions for the effect. For example, the focus of attention results (Rosenhan, Salovey, & Hargis, 1981) show that good mood created by outcomes positive to oneself promote helping whereas the good mood created by observing outcomes positive to friends do not. The lack of increased helping in the latter instance is attributed to jealousy that interferes with any influence that positive affect might have. Of course, it is not clear that jealousy and positive affect can coexist (see Chapter 6 for a discussion of the compatibility of positive and negative mood states). In any case, focus of attention is not an explanation of why good mood does promote helping when it does.

Similarly, the "separate process" explanation (Cunningham, Steinberg, & Grev, 1980) sets out to show that the mediating links between mood and helping are different in the case of good and bad mood but offers no explanation of its own for either type of effect. Finally, the "social outlook" explanation (Holloway, Tucker, & Hornstein, 1977) specifically denies the influence of mood, *per se*. It assumes that certain kinds of events alter one's view of the social community in a favorable direction, making the individual more helpful. In fact, Holloway et al. (1977) conducted a check and found that the event that increased helpfulness, overhearing a story about a person who risked his life and successfully rescued a family from a fire, *failed to improve mood*. Under these circumstances, it is difficult to see why this hypothesis and its supporting studies were included.

Also curious was the decision by Carlson et al. (1988) to exclude priming, that is, the idea that the good mood state temporarily increases the availability of generally positive thoughts, as a specific explanation of good mood induced helping. Instead they briefly discussed it at the outset, noting that it "is pertinent to each of the hypotheses" (p. 211). Indeed it is, making it the most satisfactory general account in my view.

Not only is priming able to explain why good mood increases helping, it is also able to account for the variety of results showing that good mood increases positive behavior generally. For example, Isen (1970) reported that as compared to control subjects, those who had experienced success on a laboratory task indicated a greater desire to work with someone rather than alone on a subsequent task. Mayer and Volanth (1985) found that the better the mood of their subjects, the more likely they were to give social advice that was positive in nature. And, finally, Mischel, Coates, and Raskoff (1968) and Underwood, Moore, and Rosenhan (1973) have demonstrated that good mood induced either by success or the "imagine-remember" technique, caused their child subjects to reward themselves more in terms of taking freely available tokens or pennies.

But, the priming explanation is unable to explain findings showing that good mood sometimes results in *less* helping (Forest, Clark, Mills, & Isen, 1979; Harada, 1983; Isen & Levin, 1972; Isen & Simmonds, 1978). For example, Isen and Levin (1972) found that good mood subjects were *less* likely to agree to help the experimenter by becoming an accomplice if their task as a confederate was to annoy another subject. These results led Isen to introduce the notion of "mood-maintenance" that assumes that good moods promote helping only if the helping act is not a threat to the continuation of the good mood. In each of the above-mentioned studies, the helping act could be construed as distasteful and, therefore, capable of reducing or eliminating good mood.

Various findings from studies investigating behaviors other than helping are also consistent with the idea of mood maintenance. For example, Bell (1978) showed that elated subjects were more negative than depressed subjects in their ratings of someone as a potential work partner when that person described himself/herself as being sad. Avoiding a sad partner while happy can be considered mood maintaining behavior because other results (e.g., Coyne, 1976a) show that interacting with depressed individuals induces dysphoric mood. Also predictable from a mood-maintenance position, Mischel et al. (1973) have shown that good-mood subjects avoid unfavorable self-relevant information more than controls.

Finally, the same kind of mood maintenance process has been postulated by Isen and her colleagues (Isen, Nygren, & Ashby, 1988; Isen & Patrick, 1983) as an explanation for data they collected regarding the relationship between positive affect and risk-taking. On the basis of the results I discussed earlier showing that optimism about the future covaries with mood, one might expect that good mood would lead to greater risk-taking. However, Isen and Patrick (1983) found that subjects induced into a good mood before playing a laboratory roulette game gambled more than control subjects *only when the bet available to them was a low-risk one.* In fact, the results were significant in the opposite direction on high-risk bets with controls gambling more than good mood subjects. Further data (Isen et al., 1988) suggest that this sort of conservatism is due to good mood subjects showing an enhanced sensitivity to what they might lose in a failed gamble. Even though they are optimistic in the sense that they estimate the probability of winning to be higher and that of losing to be lower, they are risk averse, perhaps because losing not only costs them whatever was gambled but their good mood as well.

Applied in combination, the priming and mood maintenance explanations appear capable of explaining most of the data in the literature relating good mood to behavior. The main problem is that priming is supposedly an automatic cognitive process whereas mood maintenance is strategic in nature and the hypothetical crossing of the awareness threshold that is implied has not been directly measured or manipulated. The same weakness exists in the application of the idea of mood repair to the asymmetry in the mood and memory literature discussed earlier; it will arise again in connection with the findings showing that negative mood can increase various positive behaviors including helping. I will discuss that literature now.

Negative Mood and Behavior

The literature on negative feeling states and their influence on behavior is much larger than that exploring the role of positive affect. The major reason for this is the lure associated with applying the results of studies of bad mood to the phenomenon of clinically significant depression.

My review of this literature is predicated on the assumption that the observed effects of bad mood reflect one or the other of its two faces ... the bad mood may either lurk in the background influencing behavior by predisposing congruent memories, perceptions, and overlearned or habitual responses or it may come to attention and promote self-regulatory attempts to mitigate or terminate the state. Though it might seem to be easy to distinguish which of these two processes is responsible for any given example of behavior induced by bad mood, that is not the case. One of the major problems with this literature is the general failure of investigators to make efforts to track down and measure the specific processes mediating observed behaviors.

Alternatively, one could attempt to diagnose which of the two processes is occurring by determining what sort of effect the mood-induced behavior is having on the mood. Generally speaking, self-regulatory efforts should mitigate negative moods whereas the automatic effects of mood would be expected to produce mood-congruent behavior and vicious cycling. Unfortunately, virtually all the studies I have found that purport to examine the self-regulation of mood or can be interpreted in that way, fail to obtain a post-measure of mood; the same is true of studies that consider their results to be suggestive of vicious cycling. As will become evident, this state of affairs will force conclusions that are quite speculative.

Because the review[13] that follows covers a great many studies, it seemed useful to take advantage of an available typology for the purposes of organization. The typology, offered by Pearlin and Schooler (1978), is borrowed from the literature on coping with stress[14] and, as such, is clearly more appropriate for categorizing behaviors deemed to be attempts at self-regulation. Nonetheless, it turns out that examples of memory or perception-

---

[13]Much of the material in this review is drawn from Morris and Reilly (1987).

[14]Use of a coping with stress typology prompts a question as to the degree of overlap between self-regulation of bad mood and coping with stress. Though it is difficult to maintain a firm line separating one phenomenon from the other, I would observe that the most commonly considered antecedents of stress are the so-called "major life events," for example, losing your job, the death of a spouse, major illnesses, etc. (Holmes & Rahe, 1967; Dohrenwend & Dohrenwend, 1974). These occurrences almost certainly arouse strong emotions at first rather than moods as I have defined them. On the other hand, stress researchers are becoming increasingly interested in the role of familiar daily stresses and strains referred to as "microstressors" (McLean, 1976; Pancheri, DeMartino, Spiombi, Biondi, & Mosticone, 1979) or "hassles" (DeLongis, Coyne, Dakof, Folkman, & Lazarus, 1982; Lazarus, 1984). These events may well produce mood.

mediated mood-congruent behavior can be conveniently included as I proceed in that they generally consist of an opposite tendency with respect to behaviors thought to be self-regulatory. For example, some people in a bad mood might try to distract themselves but others would find themselves involuntarily dwelling on the negative feelings, perhaps making themselves feel even worse.

The typology posits three major ways in which one might cope with bad mood (stress): one can attempt to manage the negative affect itself, one can redefine the significance of the inducing event so that it becomes less bothersome, and one can take direct action designed to eliminate whatever is instigating the affect. These categories comfortably subsume the sorts of actions that have been proposed as means of self-regulating mood with one exception, that being affiliation. Affiliation is troublesome because it may be sought for any of the three "reasons" suggested by the typology, that is, (1) social interaction may be sought because it is fun or distracting and thereby eliminates or reduces bad mood, or, (2) because others, especially friends, may provide consensual validation for some cognition that greatly reduces the apparent significance of the problem, and finally, (3) other people may be approached because they can help eliminate the apparent source of the problem through direct action. Consequently, affiliation will be considered apart from the typology though it should be evident that each instance of it could be classified if it were only known on a given occasion to what particular use the social interaction were being put.

Managing the Mood. Survey data (Folkman, Lazarus, Dunkel-Schetter, DeLongis, & Gruen, 1986; Parker & Brown, 1982; Rippere, 1977) indicate that when people are asked how they deal with bad moods, they readily nominate a bewildering array of different techniques. Though research ultimately may be able to document many of these self-management processes, there is good reason to be suspicious of the accuracy of self-reports about the relationship between mood and behavior (Wilson et al., 1982), especially when the accounts are retrospective (Nisbett & Wilson, 1977) as they are in the case of these survey data. Therefore, though I do not exclude self-report data, I will rely more heavily upon studies that attempt to directly measure mood, behavior, or both. To this point, there is evidence suggesting the use of four different types of activity as ways of managing mood: self-reward, the use of alcohol, distraction, and the management of expressive behavior.

The notion that one might relieve a bad mood through exposure to reinforcing events has occurred to a variety of researchers. One of the most persistent advocates of this view is Lewinsohn (1974) who has made the connection between reward and mood the centerpiece of his theory of depression. According to Lewinsohn, depression results from a low rate of positive reinforcement (and a high rate of punishment). Such a view implies that one might rid himself of negative mood by increasing the rate of activities which one finds rewarding.

The first direct test of this idea was conducted by Hammen and Glass (1975). In two separate studies, these investigators selected college subjects with depressed mood using the Depression Scale of the MMPI and instructed them to increase the number of "pleasant" events they engaged in each day for a two week period. The pleasant events were identified by giving subjects the Pleasant Events Schedule (MacPhillamy & Lewinsohn, 1971), which consists of a checklist of 320 commonly enjoyed events or activities, and asking them to generate a list of the 160 most pleasant activities they had experienced in the last month. Members from this set of 160 were the activities subjects were supposed to do more often. Upon their return two weeks later, subjects in both studies reported that they had indeed engaged in significantly more of these pleasurable activities than had various control groups but, contrary to prediction, these increases in pleasurable activity were not associated with mood improvement. In fact, the evidence from both studies showed that increased pleasurable activities were associated with an *increase* in depressive affect.

Because of the potential clinical significance of these results, a number of investigations have subsequently appeared attempting to assess the replicability of the results obtained by Hammen and Glass (1975). Perhaps it will come as no surprise to find that the issue is still unresolved. Both Fuchs and Rehm (1977) and Zeiss, Lewinsohn, and Munoz (1979) have reported reduced depression in patients who were instructed to increase rewarding activities but, in the case of Fuchs and Rehm, the instruction was part of an omnibus therapy procedure, other aspects of which might have been responsible for improvement and Zeiss et al. found that *all* of their treatments reduced depression; there was nothing distinctive about increases in positive activities. On the other hand, Reich and Zautra (1981) report that inducing subjects to undertake pleasurable activities provided no general benefit in terms of psychiatric distress or depression although they did find that subjects assigned to engage in a large number of such activities (12) were less distressed if they also experienced a large number of negative life events during the monthly reporting period studied. These findings suggest a buffering role for positive events, rather than a direct role, on negative mood. Finally, Biglan and Craker (1982), in what appears to be the closest to an exact replication of Hammen and Glass (1975), found much the same results; four clinically depressed women increased pleasant activities in response to instruction but each reported slightly more depression.

Though quite interesting, these data are of limited relevance in terms of self-regulation because subjects changed their behavior (according to their self-report, that is) in response to an experimenter's or clinician's instructions rather than initiating the change themselves. Indeed, according to a recently introduced model (Reich and Zautra, 1988) designed to explain the impact of positive events on positive and negative feelings, one might expect *instructed* self-reward to have either no positive effect or a negative effect because such instructions might reduce a subject's sense of mastery or control.

More pertinent perhaps are studies in which subjects' moods are measured and correlated with freely occurring behavior. Two such studies have been conducted by Lewinsohn and his colleagues (Lewinsohn & Libet, 1972; Lewinsohn & Graf, 1973). Each study used equal numbers of normals, depressed, and psychiatric controls. (No differences were found among these three groups in either study.) Both studies measured mood using the Depression Adjective Check List (Lubin, 1965) and activity using the Pleasant Events Schedule (MacPhillamy & Lewinsohn, 1971). Lewinsohn and Libet's subjects were asked to fill out each for 30 consecutive days. Lewinsohn and Libet calculated three different kinds of correlations between mood and activity: (1) synchronous correlations, (2) correlations between activity on day t and mood on days $t+1$ and $t+2$, and (3) correlations between activity on day t and mood on days $t-1$ and $t-2$. The synchronous correlations were substantial and positive. Though such results are consistent with Lewinsohn's theory if they are interpreted as evidence of an effect of activities on mood, the direction of causation is unclear from these data. More suggestive of regulation through self-reward would be findings showing that bad mood on a given day predicted an increase in reinforcing activities on a subsequent day but the average of these lagged correlations was near 0. Lewinsohn and Graf (1973) computed similar cross-lag correlations but do not report them. However, I assume that they were similarly small in that Lewinsohn and Graf say in their discussion that their data provided no clarification on questions of the direction of causation. The only (scant) evidence of self-regulation in these studies was noted by Lewinsohn and Libet who suggested that a self-regulatory pattern emerged among a small number of their subjects leading them to suggest that future research might address itself to individual difference variables that might be moderating reactions to mood.

More recently, Rehm (1978) conducted a similar study but expanded it by including a consideration of the relationship between negative events and mood. Thirty undergraduate subjects maintained logs for roughly two weeks. The logs, which were to be filled out at the end of the day, asked for an assessment of mood that day and also asked subjects to record all pleasant and unpleasant events. Once again, none of the cross-lagged correlations were significant although the synchronous correlations for both positive and negative events were highly significant.

There is no reliable evidence from these three studies that depressed mood leads to self-regulatory behavior in the form of increased self-reward. However, the minimal measurement lag in each of the studies was one day. It seems likely that if self-regulatory activity is to be triggered by an unacceptable level of mood, the optimal measurement lag would be much shorter especially when one considers that moods, even when induced by events of real significance, do not typically survive the day (Stone & Neale, 1984).

If self-regulatory behavior is more likely to be detected when measurement attempts are made relatively close in time to mood induction, then laboratory studies may be more successful in revealing self-regulation since there one can tightly control the temporal relationship between mood onset and the opportunity to regulate it. A variety of such studies have been done with positive results. The most comprehensive program of research studying self-regulation of mood through self-reward is that of Cialdini and his colleagues. In 1973, Cialdini, Darby, and Vincent offered what they referred to as the "negative state relief" model which stated that one can relieve negative affective states by exposing oneself to "any positive, reinforcing state of affairs" (p. 505). Though it seems presumptuous to refer to the mere idea of self-regulation through self-reward as if it were a model, the program of research that Cialdini and his colleagues have conducted over the years (Baumann et al., 1981; Cialdini, Baumann & Kenrick, 1981; Cialdini et al., 1973; Cialdini & Kenrick, 1976; Cialdini, Schaller, Houlihan, Arps, Fultz, & Beaman, 1987; Kenrick, Baumann, & Cialdini, 1979; Manucia et al., 1984; Schaller & Cialdini, 1988) provides the most systematic and persuasive evidence of self-regulation of bad mood in the literature.

In the first published report in this series, Cialdini et al. (1973) showed that subjects who were induced into a bad mood were more likely to help a fellow student in response to a request than were control subjects *unless* either of two positive mood-inducing experiences (unexpected monetary reward or approval for task performance) intervened between the bad mood induction and the helping opportunity. In both of these cases, helping was not facilitated. Cialdini et al. had predicted these results based upon the idea of negative state relief. Their argument was that helping a fellow student is expected to produce positive affect (Harris, 1977) and that because of this, the opportunity to help will be particularly attractive to people who are in a bad mood since it is a way of relieving that mood. However, if some other event which is a positive mood inducer occurs before the helping opportunity, the individual will have his mood relieved by that event and will not need to help.

The Cialdini et al. account assumes that the helping act is instrumental in nature in that it is motivated by the subject's desire to rid himself of a bad mood through self-reward. Though this may be plausible, it is also possible that the mood-helping relationship results from the "automatic" effect of mood on cognitive processes. For example, perhaps people in bad moods are more likely to help because they imagine that if they turn down the request for help, something bad will happen to them. I have already considered evidence that bad mood makes such negative or pessimistic thoughts more likely (e.g., Johnson and Tversky, 1983).

Fortunately, in a recent study in this series (Manucia et al., 1984), this ambiguity appears to have been removed. Subjects were first exposed to a mood manipulation designed to produce either sad, neutral, or happy affect and then were given a drug which supposedly had the side-effect of fixing their mood at current levels for roughly 30 minutes. Control subjects were not led to expect such a side-effect. Finally, all subjects were asked for help by a confederate. Manucia and coworkers reasoned that if the act of helping were intended to regulate mood, it would be less likely if subjects thought their mood could not be altered.

Subjects in the happy mood conditions helped more than neutral mood controls but the side-effect manipulation had no effect. Manucia et al. interpret these results as indicating that good-mood-induced helping is not self-regulatory but, rather, a result of what they term a "concomitant" effect of mood. (Clark and Isen [1982] would have called it an automatic effect of mood.) However, within the sad mood condition the pattern of results was consistent with the idea of helping being a self-regulatory tactic in that helping was decreased by the side-effect manipulation.

This result (which has since been replicated and extended in Cialdini et al., 1987) appears difficult to explain in terms of automatic effects of mood. If, as we suggested earlier, bad mood simply predisposed you to be more susceptible to a request for help because you anticipated some unpleasant consequence for refusing, it is not obvious why the side-effect manipulation would have an effect.

The ingenious research of Cialdini and his colleagues, especially this most recent study, makes a convincing case for the idea that people in a bad mood will sometimes help as a way of making themselves feel better. Confirmation that helping may be undertaken for this reason provides a sensible explanation for the very large number of studies that have demonstrated increased helping following various sorts of negative affect inducing events, especially ones where the individual has caused or witnessed harm to another person (see Carlson & Miller, 1987, for a review of this literature). However, negative affect does not invariably lead to increased helping (Isen, 1970) and, in fact, a number of studies have found the opposite result (e.g., McMillen, Sanders, & Solomon, 1977, and Underwood, Froming, & Moore, 1977). Determined on the basis of currently available findings, it would appear that the influence of mood on helping depends on other variables such as the ratio of benefits to costs associated with the helping act and the focus of attention. Specifically, Weyant (1978) found that bad mood facilitated helping only when the potential benefits were high and the cost of helping was low; when the cost-benefit ratio was reversed, bad mood subjects were marginally less likely to help than controls. As for focus of attention, it appears that when people are preoccupied with self, as they often are when sad or anxious, helping others is less likely but if the other's plight is attended to, helping is increased (Dovidio & Morris, 1975; McMillen et al., 1977; Thompson, Cowan, & Rosenhan, 1980).

However, a problem with helping as a means of managing one's own mood is that the right sort of occasion does not always present itself. A more generally accessible option might be self-indulgence. Indeed, right around the time that Cialdini et al. (1973) put forth the negative state relief model, Underwood et al. (1973) presented the similar notion that negative affect should lead to "self-therapeutic" efforts to eliminate it through "maximization of pleasurable resources" (p. 212). Though their data were rather weak, *post hoc* analyses showed that third-grade females (but not males) helped themselves to more freely available pennies when in a bad mood than did controls. Similar results were reported by Rosenhan, Underwood, & Moore (1974).

These results have been extended in a series of studies examining the role of affect in the ability to delay gratification. Findings have consistently shown that depressed affect leads to a preference for immediate smaller rewards over more distant but larger rewards (Moore, Clyburn, & Underwood, 1976; Rehm & Plakosh, 1975; Schwarz & Pollack, 1977; Seeman & Schwarz, 1974). One could argue, as have some of these authors, that the preference for immediate gratification reflects a self-regulatory strategy; being in a bad mood, subjects are willing to forego a larger but more distant reward so as to ameliorate their current feelings.

However, once again there is an explanation of these results that does not invoke the idea that subjects are strategically self-regulating their mood but depends instead on the propensity of bad mood to produce pessimism. Subjects who are pessimistic about the future may take the currently available reward based upon "bird in the hand" thinking. Hence, the smaller reward is chosen not because it can reduce your bad mood but because, if you don't take the smaller reward, you might get nothing at all!

If bad mood increases the tendency to self-gratify, might it also make people postpone unpleasant activities? Wertheim and Schwarz (1983) wondered if depressed affect would cause people to choose to delay unpleasant tasks versus getting them over with. College student volunteers were used as subjects. They were told that the study would require that they complete six different tasks, three at each of two sessions separated by a week. The tasks were then described to them and they were permitted to choose the three that they would do immediately with the remainder left for the next session. In a pretest, three of the tasks had been judged to be neutral whereas the other three had been judged unpleasant, for example, an electroshock pain threshold test. Rather than manipulating mood, Wertheim and Schwarz chose to measure existing negative affect by using the Beck Depression Inventory (Beck et al., 1961). They then correlated a subjects's score on the Beck with a score reflecting the proportion of unpleasant tasks that subjects decided to delay until the next session. The results were significant only for males and showed that the more depressed the subject, the more likely he was to delay the unpleasant tasks until the next session. Wertheim and Schwarz regard this as evidence of attempted self-management of affect though they argue it is dysfunctional in that delaying the unpleasant tasks adds the unpleasantness of anticipating them for a week on top of the aversiveness of having to do them.

Whether or not such choices are functional in the sense of minimizing total aversiveness, they do appear to be self-regulatory in nature in that there is no obvious explanation of these results in terms of automatic mood processes. These results require that we extend our conception of self-regulation of mood. Not only might people take action directed at reducing or eliminating negative states as Cialdini et al. (1973) and Underwood et al.

(1973) supposed but, in addition, they may take action designed to prevent a further deterioration of an already bad mood.

My last example of mood management through self-reward involves a common form of indulgence, namely, eating. Frost, Goolkasian, Ely, and Blanchard (1982) induced elated, neutral, and bad moods using the Velten (1968) procedure and made M & M candies freely available during the remainder of the experimental session. Frost et al. found that among subjects who scored high on a self-report measure of weight fluctuation, those in a bad mood ate significantly more candy than those in neutral or good moods. Such findings were not obtained among subjects whose weight tended to be stable. Interestingly, Frost et al. (1982) interpret their findings as indicative of a *failure* of self-regulation. They argue that individuals whose weight fluctuates a good deal are people whose self-regulation of *eating behavior* is disrupted by negative affect. Though possible, we would note the obvious alternative explanation, namely, that people whose weight fluctuates are people who use the self-reward of food to extricate themselves from bad moods. Making this explanation more plausible are data recently reported by Thayer (1987a). He found that sugar snacks such as candy bars provide a quick lift in the sense of increasing feelings of pep and energy in the short term (i.e., 20 minutes). However, Thayer's subjects ate candy in response to experimental instructions. As noted by Thayer, what is needed at this point are studies that show the mood-lifting effect in subjects who voluntarily seek out sugar snacks.

In sum, when provided with opportunities in the laboratory to engage in putatively rewarding activities such as low-cost helping acts or various forms of self-indulgence, subjects who are in a bad mood often avail themselves of them. To varying degrees, depending upon the viability of alternative explanations, such studies suggest that individuals sometimes take pleasure-producing action intended to improve mood. On the other hand, it bears repeating that field studies have failed to find similar evidence. Though we suggested earlier that the time lags used in the field studies may not have been appropriate for finding a relationship between mood and self-rewarding activity, it is also possible that self-regulation through self-reward is a relatively unusual event and hard to find unless one creates optimal circumstances of the sort which have been arranged in laboratory settings.

Though of a self-report nature and therefore suspect, we (Morris, Reilly, & Englis, 1984) have data encouraging this speculation. We asked a sample of undergraduates questions about 52 everyday activities such as doing their laundry, getting together with friends, jogging, etc. Specifically, they were asked to indicate the degree to which the activities were made more or less likely by good and bad moods and, also, the extent to which engaging in the activity was liable to improve or worsen their mood. Though seemingly rewarding activities such as getting together with friends, dancing, sports, and sex were judged as having the biggest potential for producing mood improvement, these very same activities were reported to be much less likely to occur during bad moods. Corroborating evidence has recently been reported by Cunningham (1988b). Similarly, Rehm (1977) has noted that depressives are particularly unlikely to engage in self-gratifying behavior. Perhaps the problem is that the person in a bad mood simply doesn't feel like initiating such activities, either because the rewards seem less attractive (Carson & Adams, 1980) or attainable (Seligman, 1975; Wright & Mischel, 1982) than usual. Or perhaps, as Clark and Isen (1982) have suggested, bad mood simply makes you too tired to put out the effort. If so, one important consequence of being in a supportive social network might be that friends or family may force you to do "fun" things when you're down, things which you wouldn't do if left to your own devices. However, the data of Hammen and Glass (1975) suggest that making the depressed person have fun may not work either.

All in all, the various data on therapeutic self-reward seem sufficiently weak so as to call the notion into question. Examination of the theoretical underpinning for the idea reveals that it rests upon an implicit and largely untested assumption, namely, that affects summate algebraically and so, if you are in a bad mood, you can add some positive affect and this will "cancel" the bad. Though there is precedent for making such an assumption, for example, Solomon and Corbit (1974), other assumptions are possible. Barden et al. (1981), for example, predicted and found evidence for an interactive relationship between consecutive affect-inducing circumstances. Specifically, they were able to show "inoculation" effects whereby preexisting negative affect interfered with the ability of positive affect inducers to produce their "typical" result.

More data is needed before we can safely conclude that rewards are sought as a means of eliminating negative mood. It would seem especially important that future studies be designed so as to rule out potential automatic-process interpretations of mood-behavior relationships. The only example of a study designed with this consideration in mind is that by Manucia et al. (1984). Replication and extension of that work to other self-therapeutic activities is in order. In addition, more confidence that a given behavior reflects self-regulation would be generated if it could be shown that affect subsequently improved. None of the studies which claim to have produced evidence of regulation through self-reward obtained a post-measure of affect.

One behavior that might have been considered under the category of self-reward is alcohol consumption, an activity that many appear to enjoy. However, because of its pharmacological properties, it seemed wise to consider it apart. At an anecdotal level, alcohol is widely mentioned as a way of self-regulating how one feels. Surveys (Parker & Brown, 1982; Rippere, 1977) which ask people how they deal with depressed mood confirm this. Much of the literature on alcohol use has been guided by the "tension reduction hypothesis" (Conger, 1951) which says that people drink to reduce negative feelings or tension (rather than to produce pleasure). The alcohol supposedly would work by directly attacking the foundation of the negative affect rather than by counteracting it with some pleasurable event, a strategy similar to that which underlies relaxation training as a therapy for phobia (Wolpe, 1958).

Some of the most directly relevant data suggesting self-regulation of mood through alcohol use come from a study by Marlatt, Kosturn, and Lang (1975) which, interestingly, has a design that is conceptually identical to that of Cialdini et al. (1973). Marlatt et al. (1975) found that being insulted by a confederate resulted in increased alcohol consumption during a supposedly separate wine-tasting experiment *unless* an opportunity to retaliate by shocking the confederate intervened. Thus, in both experiments, a bad mood induction facilitated an act hypothesized to be remedial of bad mood (helping in Cialdini et al. and alcohol consumption in Marlatt et al.) unless some other mood-improving event intervened. Whereas Cialdini et al. used unexpected money and approval as intervening events, Marlatt et al. used a complex event in which the confederate who had earlier insulted the subject now failed and the subject was permitted to shock him. There is evidence in the literature that either of these components, that is, the failure or the retaliation, could have produced positive affect. Zillman and Cantor (1977) have shown that the mere observation of negative consequences befalling a disliked person produces enjoyment and Hokanson and Edelman (1966) have shown that retaliation toward someone who has attacked you leads to a reduction in blood pressure, presumably reflecting the attenuation of a negative arousal state.

Though the study by Marlatt and colleagues seems to provide strong evidence consistent with the proposition that alcohol is used as a mood regulator, individual differences surely exist in the tendency to do so. Though of a self-report nature, Pearlin and Radabaugh (1976) have provided data confirming this. They used two rating scale items as a measure of "distress-control" drinking. Subjects were asked to indicate their agreement with the statements: "A drink helps me to forget my worries" and "A drink helps cheer me up when I am in a bad mood." Using survey data, Pearlin and Radabaugh found that people who were exposed to economic strain and who experienced increased anxiety as a result, showed stronger tendencies to endorse drinking as a way of controlling distress, but the results were significant only for people who were low in self-esteem and feelings of mastery. This result made good sense to Pearlin and Radabaugh who argued that people who felt generally competent would be more likely to directly confront the problem causing their distress rather than attempting to manage the affective response through drinking.

Further evidence in support of the idea that only certain individuals are predisposed to regulate their moods with alcohol comes from a study by Hull and Young (1983). Subjects in their experiment received success or failure feedback on an intellectual task before participating in what appeared to be a separate "wine-tasting" study. Hull and Young found that failure led to higher levels of alcohol consumption than success, but only among subjects who were high in private self-consciousness as measured by the Self-Consciousness Inventory (Fenigstein, Scheier, & Buss, 1975). Hull and

Young explain this result by suggesting that private self-consciousness, a tendency to be self-aware or introspective, made failure more salient which, in turn, heightened the need for the "self-medication" of drink.

Not only is there evidence that bad mood increases alcohol consumption, at least among some, but there is also data showing that alcohol can be an effective mood management technique in that consumption appears to be followed by a lessening of negative affect. In a recently published meta-analysis, Hull and Bond (1986) found that alcohol reliably improves self-reported mood. Aneshensel and Huba (1983) have applied casual modeling techniques to longitudinal data they collected on the relation between depression and alcohol use. They interpreted their data as suggesting that depressed affect leads to increased alcohol consumption that, in the short term, appeared to be effective in reducing depression somewhat. (However, they note that over the longer term, i.e., a year, increased alcohol use seems to *heighten* depression.) Also relevant are the data reported by Steele, Southwick, and Critchlow (1981). They showed that subjects given alcohol after a standard induced-compliance dissonance manipulation failed to show the typical attitude change effect that was obtained with subjects given no alcohol. To the extent that dissonance can be regarded as a kind of bad mood, a point I take up later, these data also suggest the effectiveness of alcohol as a means of self-regulation.

Though it seems clear that alcohol is sometimes sought for its mood-ameliorating effects, the basis for its effectiveness is still controversial. A relatively provocative explanation has been offered by Hull (1981) who argues that alcohol interferes with the tendency to think self-relevant thoughts. Supportive data have been reported by Hull, Levenson, Young, and Sher (1983). In two separate studies, subjects consumed either alcohol or a placebo beverage after which they were asked to give short speeches concerning their perceptions of their physical appearance. The speeches were coded for the presence of self-focused statements and first-person pronouns; alcohol significantly reduced the number of each. Given that self-relevant thoughts are most likely to be disturbing subsequent to typical bad-mood-inducing events (Strack et al., 1985), interference with such thoughts should provide relief.

If the efficacy of alcohol comes from its ability to direct attention away from a specific disturbing stimulus (i.e., self-relevant thoughts) as the results of Hull et al. (1983) suggest, then it might be appropriate to subsume alcohol consumption under the more general heading of distraction The demonstrated success of distraction as a means of dealing with stimuli that are painful (Leventhal & Everhart, 1979; McCaul & Malott, 1984) or generally unpleasant (e.g., Koriat, Melkman, Averill, & Lazarus, 1972) recommends it as a possible device for managing mood. Moreover, when asked how they deal with depressive affect (Rippere, 1977), people often nominate techniques denoting distraction, for example, "keep busy," or "do something engrossing."

One of the most readily available distractors in our society is television. Pearlin (1959) asked subjects the extent to which they enjoyed "escapist" programs and found that those who scored low on a measure of mastery were most likely to say they liked to watch shows that "help us forget our personal problems and troubles while we watch them" (p. 256). Unfortunately, no clear evidence has yet emerged that *actual choices* of distracting television fare are made by people experiencing negative affect. The most extensive line of research in this general area has been conducted by Zillman and his colleagues (for a review, see Zillman, 1988) and Zillman (1988) does offer a distraction hypothesis. However, none of the research attempts to measure choice between programming that is more or less "distracting" as a function of affective state. The closest we get to such a result is a finding (Bryant & Zillman, 1984) showing that subjects who are bored as a result of having to perform a monotonous motor task for an extended period of time show a strong preference for "exciting" programming over "relaxing" programming whereas subjects who had been stressed by having to answer difficult GRE-type questions under performance pressure did not show such a preference.

Though alcohol and entertainment of various forms may ultimately prove to be an effective way of distracting oneself, the most common means is probably through direct thought control. If one is plagued by distressing thoughts, it may be possible to simply willfully change what one is thinking about and, thus, to terminate the distress. Early evidence suggesting the feasibility of this technique emerged from the literature on delay of gratification. Data gathered by Mischel, Ebbesen, and Zeiss (1972 showed that children who were instructed to think about things which were fun were better able to tolerate a delay of gratification. Mischel and coworkers interpreted their results to mean that the aversive experience of frustrative nonreward encountered during the delay period can be assuaged by the distraction of thinking entertaining thoughts.

However, banishing unwanted negative thoughts through distraction or other means may be more difficult when they are self-relevant because such thoughts appear to be self-perpetuating as indicated by my review of the influence of mood on memory. Worse yet, because of the tendency to think mood-congruent thoughts, depressed individuals who try to distract themselves may be inclined to think other negative thoughts that ultimately link back to and reinforce the original negative thought. Wenzlaff et al. (1988) have corroborated this in a series of studies that show that though depressed college students realize that thinking positive thoughts is more likely to be effective in distracting themselves, when placed in a situation where they are instructed to suppress negative thoughts they are initially successful but over time the thoughts reemerge (as compared with nondepressed controls).

Further research on the role of distraction in alleviating depressive affect is needed to extend these promising beginnings. Especially from a theoretical point of view, distraction would appear to be a most likely means of effective self-regulation. Indeed, considered from the perspective of the cognitive theories (Bower, 1981; Isen, 1984), one could argue that mood is nothing more than a tendency to retrieve a skein of disturbing thoughts. Interruption of this process would, perforce, terminate the mood. Also, if distraction were the primary technique by which bad moods are alleviated, one might expect deficiencies in the ability to distract oneself to be associated with depression as Wenzlaff et al. (1988) have shown. It would be most interesting if it could be demonstrated that this deficiency also exists during "remission" of depressive symptoms as such findings would suggest that the inability to distract oneself might play a causal role in depressive episodes.

Another possible method of mood management is the control of expressive behavior. Evidence to the effect that there are feedback links between expressive behavior and emotional experience has been accumulating in recent years. The most heavily researched link is between feedback from facial behavior and affective experience. The facial feedback hypothesis, derivable either from Differential Emotions Theory (Izard, 1977; Tomkins, 1962) or Self-Perception Theory (Bem, 1967), predicts that emotional experiences will be augmented by highly expressive behavior and diminished by reduced displays. An example of data supporting the facial feedback hypothesis comes from a study by Kleck et al. (1976). These investigators led some subjects to believe that they were being observed while receiving painful electric shocks; other subjects were not led to such a belief. Subjects who thought they were being observed engaged in less facial behavior indicative of pain. As predicted by the facial feedback hypothesis, these subjects reported the shocks to be less painful and, in addition, they were less aroused by the shocks as indicated by skin conductance measures. Laird (1984) has recently reviewed the facial feedback literature and found the data overwhelmingly supportive of the hypothesis (but see Buck, 1984, and Matsumoto, 1987, for a different view as to how compelling these results are).

Though the face is probably the most important component of the expressive system, research by Riskind (1984; Riskind & Gotay, 1982) has shown that feedback from postural adjustments can also influence affective experiences. The most relevant of Riskind's findings is one demonstrating that subjects assigned to adopt a slumped posture report less depressed affect after failure than do subjects assigned to adopt an upright posture. Notice that the direction of this effect is opposite to that found for facial feedback, i.e., with the face, inhibition of expression can control negative affect, whereas with the body, it is the "natural" expressive display that minimizes bad mood.

Though the regulation of expressive behavior may initially be the result of conformity to "display rules" (Ekman & Friesen, 1975), that is, cultural expectations about appropriate expressive behavior, it is possible that individuals might come to recognize the influence they can achieve over their affect by modulating their expressive displays. If so, management of expression could ultimately come to be used in an instrumental fashion to self-regulate the affect itself. Alternatively, it is possible that the effects of expressive behavior on affect are indirect. Expressive displays serve as a cue to others in the environment, signaling the presence of good or bad mood. Riskind (1984) makes this point with regard to slumping, suggesting that it can elicit social support. It may be that activation of a social support network is a highly effective way of dealing with various forms of negative affect (Barrera, 1988).

Finally, in these days of the fitness craze, it is surprising that there is no direct evidence showing that people attempt to manage their moods through some form of exercise. It is clear that regular exercise programs have general effects on mood (Folkins & Sime, 1981) and Thayer (1987a, 1987b) has shown that brisk 10-minute walks have strong beneficial effects on mood. However, it is possible that the feelings of fatigue that often accompany depressed affect may make this particular form of mood management an unlikely option. It is also worth noting that physical exercise, *per se* (as opposed to sports), is probably engaged in by most of its devotees as part of a habitual routine requiring the setting aside of specific times. This would tend to make it unsuitable as a general remedy for bad moods occurring at other times of the day.

Modifying the Meaning or Significance of the Problem. Though arguments rage back and forth over the precise relationships that exist between cognition and affect, there can be little doubt about the influential role cognitive processes sometimes play in modulating emotional reactions. Lazarus (1966, 1975; Lazarus & Folkman, 1984) has been a central figure in advancing the view that individuals can cope with emotion through cognitive maneuvers that alter the meaning of an event, a process that he refers to as cognitive reappraisal.

Good examples of such cognitive means of coping in response to negative mood can be found in the literature on reactions to failure. One example is "downward comparison" which consists of comparing yourself with those who are worse off than you are. For example, if you did badly on a test, it might make you feel better if you focused attention on those who performed even more poorly. By contrast, then, your situation might not seem so bad. Gibbons (1986) has shown that finding out that others are doing worse may help alleviate depression. (See Wills, 1987, for a review of the literature on downward comparison.)

Another possibility that has attracted a good deal of attention is attributional bias. This technique consists of taking personal credit for success but blaming failure on external circumstance. A great deal of evidence now exists documenting this tendency (see Zuckerman, 1979a, for a review). In addition, direct evidence shows that the expected affective consequences ensue; subjects who attribute failure to external causes experience less negative affect than do those who attribute failure to internal causes (McFarland & Ross, 1982). As noted earlier, some now believe that the absence of this particular self-regulatory tactic may be a causal factor in the onset of depression. For example, Sackheim (1983), after reviewing the relevant literature, concluded that:

> At least some types of depression may not simply be associated with but may be a result of the failure to acquire or to use self-deceptive strategies geared to maintaining or enhancing mood. (p. 149)

Though failure is an important potential source of negative affect and, therefore, a fertile ground for the cultivation of self-regulatory cognitive processes, it is well to remember that it is really a special case of an inconsistency or discrepancy between the way we have behaved and the way we expect or want to behave. This more general domain has been the bailiwick of cognitive dissonance, a theory that has probably generated the most diverse examples of self-regulatory cognitive activity. Though it would be inappropriate to go into this literature in detail given its size, a brief discussion as to the propriety of considering dissonance-induced attitude change as an example of the self-regulation of mood seems indicated.

Controversy still exists with respect to the interpretation of this literature (see Cooper & Fazio, 1984, for a recent review), but most social psychologists seem to accept the view that dissonance, which is classified as an aversive arousal or affective state, results from the taking of an action which is inconsistent with one's established views under circumstances where one is committed to an action, the consequences of which are foreseeable, negative, and judged to be the responsibility of self. In these situations, the typical finding is that the individual changes his or her attitude to bring it more into line with the already emitted behavior which, theoretically, should serve to reduce the dissonance.

Attitude change motivated by a discomforting affective state certainly seems to be an example of a cognitive maneuver undertaken in the service of affective self-regulation so the only remaining question is whether or not it is reasonable to think of dissonance as being mood-like. The best argument that it is mood-like is predicated on the fact that the most commonly observed form of dissonance reduction consists of acts of self-deception. For example, in the famous $1 versus $20 experiment (Festinger & Carlsmith, 1959), subjects paid the smaller amount in return for deceiving a waiting subject by telling him that the task he would perform was fun subsequently reported that the boring spool-turning task (that they had themselves already completed) was relatively enjoyable. The dissonance explanation of this result is that the $1 was an insufficient explanation for engaging in a deceitful behavior and so subjects "persuaded" themselves that it was not actually deceitful by changing their assessment of the task.

Students of self-deception, for example, Lazarus and Folkman (1984) and Sackeim (1983), generally hold that self-deception cannot be successfully accomplished if the individual is aware of what he is doing. Thus, when cognitive changes are made, it behooves the individual to either fail to recognize that a change has occurred, a phenomenon which has been demonstrated to be associated with standard dissonance manipulations (Bem &

McConnell, 1970), or to misattribute the change to some more "rational" reason. In either case, it would appear that the state of dissonance must generally go unlabeled, at least when it arises, since labeling near its onset would favor a correct interpretation of its cause and thereby prevent self-deceptive remedies. Completing the argument, recall that in Chapter 2, I suggested that from a conceptual point of view, the principal circumstance responsible for the occurrence of mood as opposed to emotion is a lack of labeling or appraisal of the state when it initially arises.

One implication of the argument that dissonance is typically unlabeled, and, therefore, properly considered mood-like, is that it should be relatively easy to induce subjects to misattribute the feelings produced by dissonance manipulations to causes other than the real one. I consider the fact that such misattribution has been repeatedly demonstrated in connection with dissonance inductions (Drachman & Worchel, 1976; Fazio, Zanna, & Cooper, 1977; Zanna & Cooper, 1974) to be supportive of my argument.

The examples of self-regulatory reinterpretation that I have given to this point all involve mitigation of negative affect resulting from one's own behavior. But obviously, bad mood that arises in other ways might also be susceptible to similar techniques. One illustration involves the negative affect we sometimes experience when observing the suffering of others. It has been argued that a primitive empathetic mechanism exists that causes even young infants to experience distress when exposed to the cries of conspecifics (Sagi & Hoffman, 1975). It is this mechanism, transformed through socialization and cognitive maturation into a tendency to sympathize with distressed others, that is thought to form part of the motivational substrate for altruistic behavior (Hoffman, 1981).

But what happens when we cannot assist those we see suffering? The answer has been supplied by research on the so-called "just world" hypothesis proposed by Lerner (1980). Evidence from this literature indicates that a common response to people whose suffering we cannot remedy is to denigrate them. Lerner accounts for this in cognitive terms: devaluing the sufferer permits one to continue to believe the world is just (which we are motivated to believe) because misfortune befalls those who deserve it. However, an alternative explanation might propose that an altered perception of the victim is motivated by the relief that accompanies it, that is, because we do not experience empathic distress in response to the suffering of those we find unattractive (Zillman & Cantor, 1977), perceiving them in this way can reduce our own negative affect. Clearly, this seemingly plausible rendition of the results could be categorized as an affect-regulating reappraisal.

There are undoubtedly other sorts of similar cognitive "adjustments" that could be adduced here. And, indeed, if my earlier speculation that bad mood interferes with the initiative required to undertake behavioral attempts at mood management is correct, then it would follow that the lion's share of self-regulation of mood is accomplished in this way.

Problem-Directed Action. In addition to mood management and cognitive reappraisal, bad mood may lead to problem-directed action, that is, behavior intended to alter the suspected mood-inducing circumstance. Thus, a mood attributed to an insult might lead to retaliation rather than drinking alcohol or covert denigration of the source or feeling badly after a poor exam outcome might instigate increased effort on that evening's homework rather than attempts at distracting oneself or downward comparison.

Unfortunately, I could find little evidence of this form of self-regulation of mood unless I were to include the self-report data that abounds in the coping with stress literature (e.g., see Folkman & Lazarus, 1988). There, of course, the issue is not whether problem-directed action occurs but rather when and under what circumstances. Problem-oriented action should be relatively more likely in the case of stress than it would with bad mood insofar as people tend to remain focused on the stress-inducing circumstances. With mood, however, the affect may not be detected until well after the instigating event occurred. Such a lag would interfere with the likelihood of problem-directed action for two reasons: first, because delayed detection of the affect makes it less likely that the true cause can be discerned, and second, even when it is, the temporal and (possibly) geographical remoteness of the cause make it relatively unlikely to be incorporated into a solution.

This analysis suggests that problem-directed action would be most likely to occur in response to mood under conditions that favor early detection of mood. And, though the work was designed to demonstrate a somewhat different point, I believe results reported by Carver, Blaney, and Scheier (1979, Experiment 2) are consistent with my argument. Their data implicate "self-focus," that is, the tendency to attend to covert or internal aspects of self (which should favor early discovery of one's own moods), as a key variable in affecting the extent to which subjects in a failure-induced bad mood engage in behavior that I would call problem-directed action.

All subjects were first exposed to a failure experience; they were given very difficult anagrams, thereby guaranteeing poor performance, and were told that previous subjects had done much better. Next, Carver et al, made available an opportunity to perform on a second task which purportedly tapped the same general capability as the first. The main dependent measure was the extent to which subjects persisted on these problems. Among subjects who had some reason to think they could succeed despite their initial failure (positive expectations were created by telling subjects that although the two tasks measured the same general ability, they did so in very different ways and when people did badly on the first, they seemed to do well on the second), self-focus, manipulated through the presence of a mirror, led to more persistence.

I consider persistence in the pursuit of success under these circumstances to be an example of the self-regulation of mood via problem-directed action in that failure-induced negative affect can be eliminated by a second-task success. My interpretation of the data assumes that mirror-induced self-focus makes it more likely that subjects would quickly detect the feelings created by the initial failure. Indeed, Scheier and Carver (1977) have reported data showing that self-focus generally makes affective states, including bad mood, more salient. Detection of the negative feeling state coupled with a positive expectation that one could produce an outcome that would ameliorate it led, I would argue, to self-regulation in the form of problem-directed action.

Affiliation. Of all the means suspected or known to be implicated in the self-regulation of mood, affiliation probably deserves the most attention because of the rather obvious affect-producing potential in our social interactions. And yet there is little data and much of what exists consists of self-reports uncorroborated by observations of actual affiliative behavior. Moreover, the basis for expecting that people in a bad mood would *avoid* others seems to be at least as strong as the basis for expecting affiliation.

The early studies on affiliation by Schachter (1959) certainly seem relevant. The classic paradigm involved frightening subjects with the prospect of undergoing painful electric shock and then offering them the choice to affiliate or not. Findings showed that subjects generally preferred to wait with others rather than alone, especially when the others were purportedly in the same situation, prompting Schachter's well-known observation, "misery doesn't love just any kind of company, it loves only miserable company" (p. 24).

However, subsequent findings provided yet another qualification. It turned out that not all "kinds" of misery loved company. Though results consistently showed that fear increased affiliative tendencies, situations thought to lead to other aversive affective states, for example, poor performance (Cunningham, 1988a; Isen, 1970), the anticipation of a potentially embarrassing experience (Sarnoff & Zimbardo, 1961), and uncertainty-producing pervasive ambiguity (Morris et al., 1976), did quite the contrary, that is, they caused avoidance or reduced interaction with others. Unfortunately, most of the explanations of these findings were *post hoc* and, as interest in this particular research area subsequently waned, there still is no overall account of the findings that I find satisfactory. Similar evidence of an inconsistent relationship between negative affect and affiliative tendencies can be found in self-report studies of coping tendencies. For example, though the most frequently reported means of dealing with depression in Rippere's (1977) interview data was the seeking out of social contact, seeking isolation was also a popular response. Likewise, Folkman and Lazarus (1985) recently found that students who did poorly on a midterm exam reported increased tendencies to isolate themselves from others *and* to seek social support.

Unfortunately, neither Rippere nor Folkman and Lazarus report their data in such a way so as to indicate whether they reflect: (1) ambivalence about affiliating with others, (2) individual differences, with some subjects wanting to affiliate and others not, or (3) differences associated with the relationship one has with the others(s), for example, wanting to be with close friends but avoiding acquaintances. Even if they had, one would need to corroborate such findings with direct observations of behavior.

In retrospect, it is not surprising that negative affect would both promote and inhibit affiliation. The most parsimonious account of this would be that the consequences of social interaction for those in a bad mood are likely to be mixed. The best evidence that social interaction benefits people who are experiencing negative affect comes from the literature that shows the stress-buffering effects of social support (Thoits, 1984). It is commonly assumed that people with more adequate social networks are protected from the adverse effects of stressful life events because of the greater availability of emotional and tangible support. Individuals who have this experience should be motivated to affiliate with members of their social network when distressed.

On the other hand, it is becoming increasingly clear that depressed individuals tend to elicit negative reactions from others (Coyne, 1976a; Gotlib & Robinson, 1982; Hammen & Peters, 1977; Howes & Hokanson, 1979; Howes, Hokanson, Loewenstein, 1985; Strack & Coyne, 1983) and they are aware of their negative impact (Strack & Coyne, 1983), a realization that seems sufficiently punishing to lead to avoidance of others. Even when rejection is unlikely, it could be that avoidance would be preferred because those in neutral or good moods might make one feel worse either by contrast or urging activities that are incompatible with how one currently feels (Hammen & Glass, 1975). Finally, recent evidence (Rook, 1984) suggests that problematic social relationships are a more potent determinant of perceived well-being than supportive ties. If you're not sure of the outcome, perhaps you'd be better off "by your lonesome."

Summary and Conclusions

The literature on the effects of mood on cognitive processes and behavior documents the asymmetry of results found by earlier reviews (Blaney, 1986; Clark & Isen, 1982; Dovidio, 1984; Isen, 1984). The results for positive mood are relatively uniform in showing mood-congruent effects. The memories, perceptions, judgments and behaviors of people who are feeling good reflect their feelings. The world, past, present, and future, seems a better place where one's own success and happiness are the rule, people are nice, cars don't break down, you don't get sick or hit by lightning, and altruistic motives hold rein. Though mood congruence can often be found in the case of bad mood as well, the exceptions are more numerous.

It seems likely that this asymmetry is largely due to the greater tendency of negative moods to undergo the fundamental change from being a ground or context for thought and behavior to the *object* of behavior. Though Isen's argument (e.g., 1984) that positive items are better interconnected in memory than negative ones can explain the asymmetries found in the mood and memory literature, it cannot explain why bad mood leads to increased tendencies to be helpful or self-gratify or even use alcohol. These, and other behavioral effects of bad mood, seem better explained by postulating that moods sometimes generate self-regulatory acts designed to mitigate or eliminate aversive affect.

Unfortunately, though this may be the most appealing way of accounting for the data as a whole, at the level of the individual study it is almost impossible to know whether subjects are electing behaviors based upon their mood-relieving consequences. In large part, this is due to the unsystematic and atheoretical state of the literature. A corrective for this problem would be the adoption of a model describing the way in which a self-regulatory system might work. Such a model has been proposed by Carver and Scheier (1981).

The basic unit in the Carver and Scheier system is a negative feedback loop that functions to reduce any perceived discrepancy between the present state of the organism and some standard or reference value. The system requires three working elements: (1) a perceptual capacity that can assess the current value or state of the organism, (2) a comparator capable of detecting a significant deviation from the standard, and (3) the capability to activate responses that reduce or eliminate any discrepancy discovered by the comparator.

Because this model accords a central role to perceptual processes in instigating self-regulatory action, it fits nicely with my conceptual analysis of mood that suggested it to be a state that can often escape early detection. Such a model also provides a different perspective from that of Clark and Isen (1982) on the application of the automatic-controlled distinction to the regulation of bad mood. Clark and Isen speculated that the factors that might favor the occurrence of automatic over controlled reactions to mood are ones that interfere with the ability to mount a strategic or self-regulatory effort such as fatigue and low expectations of success based upon past failures at self-regulation. Though the Carver and Scheier model also accords an important role to such variables, it raises another possibility, namely, because the model regards perception of a discrepancy as problematic, it suggests the idea that variables that influence the salience of the state would influence whether or not a self-regulatory response would occur.

This model has led Carver and Scheier and their colleagues to propose private self-consciousness or self-focus as a key variable in determining whether self-regulation occurs. And, in fact, a number of studies have been done that tend to support this prediction. I have already discussed the Carver et al. (1979) results under the heading of problem-directed action; they found that self-focus, manipulated through the presence of a mirror, enhanced the effort to succeed among subjects who had previously failed, a finding that can be construed as showing that self-focus can increase the likelihood of action designed to self-regulate mood. Also consistent with this notion are the previously cited results of Hull and Young (1983): failure led to increased alcohol consumption, a behavior that may reflect self-regulation, only among subjects high in private self-consciousness. Other relevant data come from Mullen and Suls (1982) who have shown that the health of persons high in private self-consciousness is not affected by undesirable and uncontrollable life events. They speculate that private self-consciousness mediates the likelihood of noticing psychological and somatic reactions to the events which, in turn, may trigger self-regulatory responses.

Finally, though the data were generated to test a different idea, a study by Reisenzein and Gattinger (1982) is pertinent. Subjects had arousal induced through a period of exercise and were then exposed to a standard bad mood induction, the Velten (1968) procedure. The arousal, when combined with the mood-inducing cognitions associated with the Velten procedure, was effective in producing a bad mood (measured by self-report), unless a mirror was present in the room. One can interpret these data to suggest that self-focused subjects, being more sensitized to the onset of a bad mood, somehow counteracted the mood-inducing cognitions through some form of self-regulation. Notice the similarity of this account to one I gave earlier of the results reported by Schwarz and Clore (1983) wherein I argued that making someone's mood salient will interfere with its ability to influence their evaluative judgments.

In addition to these studies that relate self-focus to self-regulatory behavior, further evidence consistent with the idea that mood salience facilitates efforts at mood repair can be found in the dissonance literature. Wicklund and Brehm (1976) review a number of studies, for example, Brock (1962), Brehm and Wicklund (1970), Carlsmith, Ebbesen, Lepper, Zanna, Joncas, and Abelson (1969), that tested and confirmed the hypothesis, attributed to Festinger (1964), that increased attention to a dissonance-inducing stimulus or the dissonance itself would hasten and/or heighten dissonance-reducing efforts. For example, in a modification of the "forbidden toy" paradigm initially used by Aronson and Carlsmith (1963), Carlsmith et al. (1969) attempted to make the child's (dissonance-inducing) abstinence more salient in two different ways: in one study a janitor entered the room while the child was playing (and abstaining) and asked why the child was not playing with the obviously attractive toy, in the second study, a flashing light was placed directly above the forbidden toy, presumably increasing the child's attention to it. In both cases, salience magnified the dissonance (reducing) effect.

Though these various lines of evidence suggest the utility of attending to affect-inducing stimuli in the sense of being alert to the onset of mood, there are other findings that suggest that such attention can be dysfunctional if it results in dwelling on one's negative affect. Specifically, evidence is accumulating that suggests a positive relationship between the tendency to be introspective or self-focused and chronic levels of negative (Epstein, 1983; Watson & Clark 1984) and depressive (Ingram & Smith, 1984; Smith, Ingram, & Roth, 1985; Pyszczynski & Greenberg, 1987) affect. It is upon this basis that Strack et al. (1985) suggest *avoidance* of self-focus as a way of coping with depressive affect.

Whether focusing on moods promotes self-regulation or exacerbation may well depend upon when, during their time course, they become objects of attention. (See Salovey and Rodin, 1985, who make a similar point.) Moods noted at or near their onset permit better causal attribution thereby allowing the choice of effective remedies (Barden, Garber, Leiman, Ford, & Masters, 1985). However, moods that initially go unnoticed may trigger automatic processes resulting in pessimistic thinking (Johnson & Tverksy, 1983; Mayer & Bremer, 1985), loss of interest in reinforcers (Carson & Adams, 1980), self-defeating patterns of goal setting (Wright & Mischel, 1982), and reduced feelings of control (e.g., Alloy et al., 1981), all of which can insidiously interfere with attempts at self-regulation. Moods that have festered in this way may be less painful if they can be ignored. Indeed, from the point of view of cognitive theories of mood such as those of Isen (1984) and Bower (1981), if one can terminate the associative processes triggered by mood through distraction, the mood itself should disappear. Research on the distraction process (e.g., Wenzlaff et al., 1988) and, more generally, on the topic of thought control (Wegner, 1988) may yield data critical to our understanding of the self-regulation of mood.

Chapter 6

Individual Differences in Mood

Taken as a whole, the evidence reviewed in the previous chapter shows that there is sufficient uniformity in how we respond to mood-inducing events so that nomothetic generalizations are both possible and fruitful. And yet, to the average person, the most noticeable fact about mood is probably how widely individuals vary in their susceptibility to, and expression of, everyday moods. As Wessman (1979) puts it:

> In some individuals . . . affective alternations are conspicuous and dramatic; in others, they seem such slight perturbations that we may wonder exactly what and how much they do feel. Certain people appear to maintain a very persistent emotional character: we find them generally brusque and irritable, always plaintive and sad, frequently tense and apprehensive, or basically zestful and optimistic. These . . . persisting emotional characteristics seem basic features of personality intimately related to the ongoing pattern and quality of individual lives. (p. 73)

Indeed, affective responding differentiates among individuals sufficiently well that Plutchik (1980) has chosen to define a "trait" as a "disposition to react to interpersonal situations with *certain emotional reactions*" (p. 173; italics added).

Though it is intuitively obvious that people differ substantially in terms of their characteristic mood, it is a somewhat more complicated business to identify the fundamental dimensions of mood. For example, even though most would agree that individuals differ in their propensity to be in good and bad moods, the early view that you could characterize individuals in terms of their location on a single bipolar positive versus negative dimension (Underwood & Froming, 1980; Wessman & Ricks, 1966) now appears wrong (e.g., see Costa & McCrae, 1980; Diener, 1984; Warr, Barter, & Brownridge, 1983; Watson & Tellegen, 1985; Zevon & Tellegen, 1982). Rather, the evidence seems to support the idea that these are independent dimensions, at least when measured over time (Diener & Emmons, 1984). Similarly, it has long been assumed that some measure of the tendency to respond strongly would differentiate among individuals (e.g., see Larsen, Diener, & Emmons, 1986; Underwood & Froming, 1980; Wessman & Ricks, 1966) but a great deal of confusion surrounds the effort to measure this dimension, partly because it appears to be correlated with other dimensions such as variability (Larsen, 1987; Underwood & Froming, 1980) and duration (Epstein, 1983; Goplerud & Depue, 1985).

But beyond the normal complications and disagreements one might expect to find in any literature, there are deeper problems. By far the most serious of these is the adoption of a largely unexamined and seemingly dubious assumption, namely, that moods can be adequately measured with a self-report methodology. It is important to evaluate the adequacy of this measurement strategy in light of the conceptual analysis of mood that I have presented. Earlier I showed that mood theorists of very different persuasions generally concur with the view that mood has two manifestations differing in terms of being in or out of focal attention. This makes sense if one conceives of mood as being involved in a self-regulatory system, a point on which there is also consensus. As the discrepancy between the desired or normal state and actual state increases, mood should be more and more likely to cross the awareness threshold, attract attention, and generate self-regulatory behavior.

Which manifestation of mood is measured by self-report methodologies? The answer, almost certainly, is that these methodologies would be more likely to capture those moods that are strong enough to cross the awareness threshold. This is especially so because most studies ask for reports that are retrospective in nature. And yet, more salient moods are not necessarily the best to measure if you wish to characterize the moods of a person. As we saw in Chapter 5, minor moods, though they may not produce a noticeable signal, nonetheless appear to have broad influences on cognition, perception, and behavior and most often the effect appears to be mood-congruent. It seems that it is mood operating in this mode as context or ground that one would wish to measure if one wanted to describe the individual.

This conceptual complication requires a careful and reasoned methodological response. With this reservation in mind, it is time to consider what we have learned to this point by studying self-reported moods.

Dimensions of Mood

In the preceding chapter I found it possible to proceed in my discussion of the effects of mood as if there were basically two kinds: good and bad. On the other hand, when Averill (1975) set out to study the structure of mood he had subjects react to 558 affect terms. And yet, there is no contradiction here. Even though individuals may be able to use a large set of mood terms reliably, it might also be true that the various terms can be shown to reduce to a mood space constructed out of a small set of basic dimensions. Ultimately, the utility of making fine distinctions will rest on the degree to which these are associated with behavioral differentiation.

Though there is little controversy associated with the attempt to identify basic dimensions of self-reported mood, there is disagreement as to how many dimensions there are and how they should be labeled. There appear to be two general types of conclusions reached. Some investigators, for example, Borgatta (1961), Izard (1972), McNair et al. (1971), and Nowlis (1965, 1970), argue that there are at least 5 to 11 factors necessary for an adequate description of the mood space. In general, these multifactorial solutions identify monopolar and discrete mood factors. The set identified by Nowlis (1970) includes aggression, social affection, surgency, elation, sadness, vigor, fatigue, anxiety, concentration, egotism, and skepticism. Alternatively, a number of investigators have come to the conclusion that there are only two or three dimensions required to describe the space and these are generally seen as bipolar in nature, for example, Daly, Lancee, and Polivy (1983), Zevon and Tellegen (1982). Invariably, a "good-bad" dimension is found and accompanied by a dimension related to intensity or arousal.

But even these seemingly disparate conclusions are not necessarily competitive. In an excellent recent review of the literature on self-reported mood, Watson and Tellegen (1985) argue that:

> The situation parallels that in the area of intelligence, in which positing one or more general dimensions is quite consistent with the existence of a larger number of more specific aptitudes. (p. 220)

Watson and Tellegen suggest that the outcomes of studies designed to identify the structure of mood depend more on the aims and analytic strategies chosen by investigators than they do on "nature." More specifically, studies that find multiple discrete mood factors typically use factor analysis; those that argue for two or three bipolar dimensions often employ some sort of scaling analysis. Though there is no necessary correlation between analytic technique and outcome, those who use factor analysis have generally sought to retain as many identifiable factors as the data allowed; those using scaling have sought to clarify primary dimensions in the data (Watson and Tellegen, 1985).

Each of these solutions has potential validity. Multifactorial outcomes retain a degree of articulation that more adequately reflects the phenomenology of mood; phenomenology is a product of focal attention and the very function of focal attention is the production of detailed perceptual and cognitive analysis. On the other hand, remembering the figure-ground distinction and recognizing that focal attention is limited reminds us that many moods may spend only a small part of their existence, if any, in focal attention. If, in fact, moods are most often diffuse, forming the positive or negative ground against which focally-attended-to objects are experienced, then the "data" that are available to questionnaire-induced introspection are largely nominal in nature and this "fact" may be responsible for what is being recovered by scaling solutions.[1] Though each type of solution tells

---

[1]That is not to say, however, that there aren't other possible explanations for the basic structure of affect. It could be that the structure reflects the fundamental evaluative (i.e., good-bad) dimension in language as applied to objects (Osgood, Suci,

us something useful about the structure of affect, most researchers interested in describing individual differences have been satisfied with the coarser level of analysis, perhaps because multifactorial solutions would resist being cast into a manageable typology.

Exactly what dimensions are found in attempts to analyze the basic structure of self-reported affect? The most comprehensive answer may be found in Watson and Tellegen's (1985) review. These authors selected a set of studies that had asked subjects to indicate the degree to which their feelings could be described using various mood terms, e.g., angry, sad, elated, etc. Included were studies by Thayer (1967), Hendrick and Lilly (1970), Borgatta (1961), McNair et al. (1971), Lebo and Nesselroade (1978), Russell and Ridgeway (1983), and Kotsch, Gerbing, and Schwartz (1982), and three analyses with which Watson and Tellegen were involved including the two reported by Zevon and Tellegen (1982) and that reported by Watson, Clark, and Tellegen (1984). The main criteria for inclusion were: (1) the size of the set of mood terms had to be higher than 20, this because a small number of terms may inadequately represent the mood space, and (2) data had to be reported in sufficient detail so as to permit reanalysis. The chosen studies varied in terms of the nature of the rating scale (the number of points and the anchoring terms), and the time period to be rated (subjects might be asked to indicate how they felt "right now" or during the past day or past week).

The specific nature of the reanalysis carried out by Watson and Tellegen depended upon the nature of the data available in the original report. Studies that provided complete orthogonal factor loading matrices or complete oblique factor loading matrices along with intercorrelations among the first-order factors permitted Watson and Tellegen to approximate the original correlation matrix and conduct their own factor analyses. Studies that presented a complete oblique first-order factor intercorrelation matrix and extensive information about the terms that marked each factor permitted a second-order factor analysis employing the first-order factors as variables. In addition to identifying the factors and marker terms for those factors for the various studies, Watson and Tellegen assessed the degree of convergence among the studies by intercorrelating the loadings of factors hypothesized to be convergent. This procedure provides an objective, if rough, determination of the degree of consensus across the various studies.

On the basis of both qualitative and quantitative assessments of the data from these various studies, Watson and Tellegen concluded that the evidence strongly supports the existence of a basic two-dimensional structure of mood. This was most clearly indicated by the fact that principal com-

---

& Tannenbaum, 1957), or perhaps it results from the existence of separate brain structures that underlie positive and negative affect (Sackeim & Weber, 1982). Or, possibly, all such explanations are merely different level accounts of the same phenomenon.

ponents analysis of the data from studies producing more than two factors showed a sudden drop-off in variance accounted for by factors subsequent to the first two. Determination of the major axes in the mood space depends upon the rotation that is applied. Two major alternative possibilities are indicated in Figure 6.1 along with mood terms that were found to best describe the octants that result. Correlations between terms are a function of the number of octants separating them; terms 180° (four octants) apart are highly negatively correlated, those that are 90° apart are independent of each other, and those that are in the same octant are highly positively related.

The axes indicated by dotted lines represent a familiar solution, dating back to Schlosberg's (1952) analysis of the dimensions underlying facial expressions of emotion. These same bipolar dimensions of pleasantness and

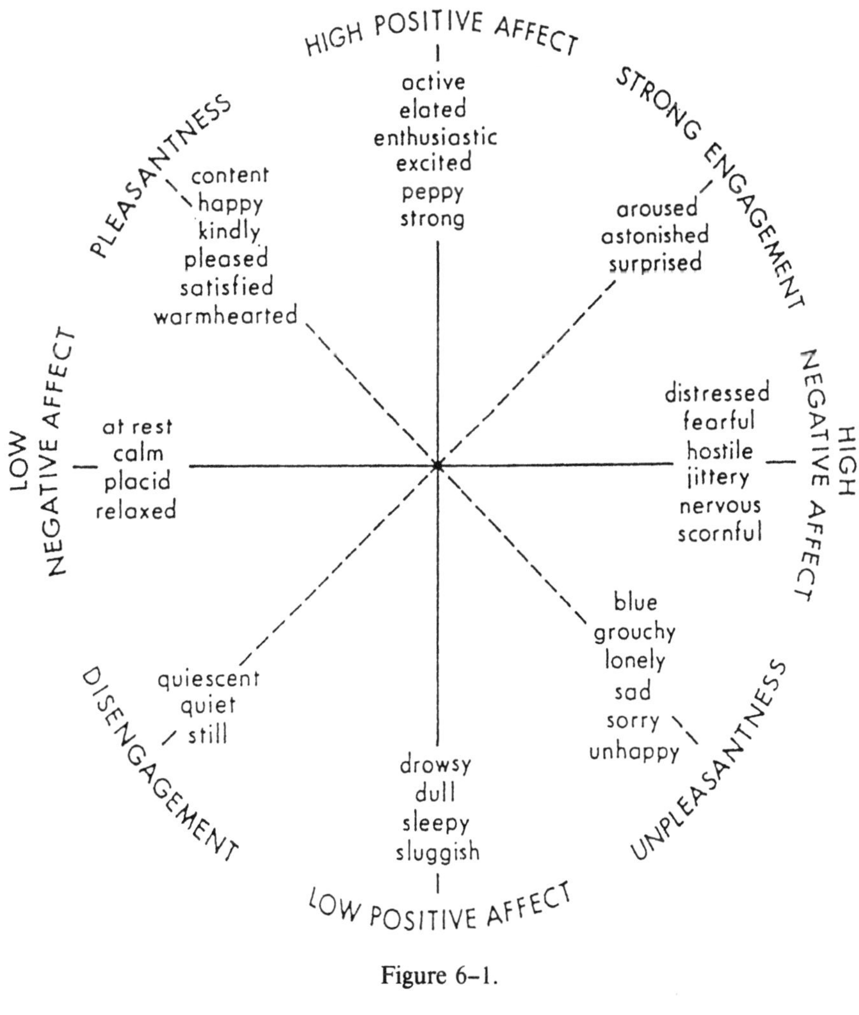

Figure 6–1.

strength or arousal (termed "engagement" by Watson and Tellegen) have often been found in subsequent studies of facial expression (e.g., Abelson & Sermat, 1962) and analyses of vocal emotional expression (e.g., Dittman, 1972), judged similarity of mood words (e.g., Russell, 1980), and semantic differential ratings of mood terms (e.g., Averill, 1975). However, for a variety of reasons Watson and Tellegen prefer to structure the space in terms of the two orthogonal dimensions they refer to as Positive and Negative Affect.[2] One reason is that more of the mood terms used across the various studies tend to cluster about these axes than they do about the alternative set. This is presumably why the Varimax rotation, a rotation that is sensitive to the location of clusters of variables, identified Positive and Negative Affect factors as the first two factors in each of the studies analyzed. Another important reason given by Watson and Tellegen is that various other data, some of which I will discuss later, support the notion that Positive and Negative Affect are the products of separate systems whose action is responsive to different factors.

The Positive Affect factor reflects the extent to which one feels a "zest for life" (Watson & Tellegen, 1985, p. 221); Negative Affect suggests being "upset." These factors have been described as "*descriptively bipolar* but *affectively unipolar*" (Zevon and Tellegen, 1982, p. 112, italics in the original) because:

> only the high end of each dimension represents a state of emotional arousal (or high affect) whereas the low end of each factor is most clearly and strongly defined by terms reflecting a relative absence of affective involvement (Watson & Tellegen, 1985, p. 212).

Because the studies reviewed by Watson and Tellegen vary in terms of the time period about which subjects were to report from "right now" to "today" to "during the past week" (p. 222), their claim about the structure of affect is implicitly a general one, i.e., they do not raise the possibility that the structure of affect may be different at a given moment in time than it is over time. This places them in conflict with Diener and colleagues (Diener, 1984; Diener & Emmons, 1984; Diener & Iran-Nejad, 1986; Diener, Larsen, Levine, & Emmons, 1985) who have been the major proponents of the idea that there is such a difference. Because Diener's work suggests a conclusion diametrically opposed to that of Watson and Tellegen, it will be necessary to examine his data in some detail.

The most direct evidence for the claim that the relation between positive and negative affect varies as a function of time frame comes from a series of studies reported by Diener and Emmons (1984). Using measures of "positive" and "negative" affect based upon a factor analysis, Diener and Em-

[2]It seems unfortunate that Watson and Tellegen selected the terms "positive" and "negative," with their strong implication of oppositeness, to represent two orthogonal dimensions. Nonetheless, to avoid any further confusion, I shall retain their usage.

mons asked various samples of subjects to report their affect at various time intervals (reported as Studies 3, 4, and 5). In the first of these studies, male and female undergraduates filled out the mood reports daily (just before retiring for the night) for 10 consecutive weeks. Undergraduate subjects in another study duplicated this reporting procedure for six consecutive weeks but, in addition, they also completed the form at two random times per day over the six week period. Signals to complete forms at these times were produced by alarm watches set by subjects in the morning. In addition to these moment and daily reports, subjects also completed mood reports for three-week intervals a total of four times. Subjects in the third study were adults recruited through a senior citizen center and a volunteer organization. They filled out the report for 30 consecutive days.

Diener and Emmons found that the correlation between positive and negative affect depended upon the time period being considered. Over a three week period, the correlation was −0.10. Thus, for longer time periods their conclusion is the same as that of Watson and Tellegen (1985), namely, that Positive and Negative Affects are orthogonal. On the other hand, the correlations in the three separate samples for reports covering a day were −0.31, −0.45, and −0.54, and reports asking for feelings at the moment correlated −0.57. (Correlations between terms sharing the same valence did not vary as a function of time frame. Like Watson and Tellegen, Diener and Emmons found that the correlations among similarly valenced terms were high at all reporting intervals.)

From these data, Diener (1984) concluded that there is some suppressive mechanism that tends to prevent the experiencing of positive and negative affects at the same time. The suppression is apparently particularly effective when the affect being experienced is strong. The first sign of this was that Diener & Emmons (1984, Study 3) had also asked their college student subjects to complete the mood measure during times of strong emotion. Positive and negative affect measured at these times showed a strikingly high negative relationship ($r = -0.85$). Subsequently, Diener and Iran-Nejad (1986) confirmed and extended these findings. Using the same scales and instructions similar to those utilized by Diener and Emmons (1984), Diener and Iran-Nejad constructed a frequency count of combinations of positive and negative affect at varying levels of intensity and found that though moderately strong positive and negative affects co-occurred, when intense affects of either valence occurred, affects of the opposite valence were not felt.

Diener and Iran-Nejad (1986) speculate that their findings are consistent with a "mutual exclusion" model of interaction between systems responsible for producing positive and negative affect. More specifically, positive and negative affect might not occur simultaneously at intense levels if some subsystem were necessary to the occurrence of each. The example they give is of smiling and frowning. If facial expressions associated with the positive and negative affects are invariably present when the affects are intensely experienced but not necessarily present when the affects are mild to moderate, then one could not experience intense positive and negative affect at the same time because one cannot smile and frown at the same time. This example is particularly cogent if one accepts the idea that *expression* of emotion, particularly by the face, is critical to the *experience* of emotion (e.g., Ekman, 1984; Izard, 1971).

On the basis of their various results, Diener and colleagues reached two main conclusions: (1) That the relationship between positive and negative affect varies as a function of the time period being considered; the shorter the time period under consideration, the more likely it is that positive and negative affects will be mutually exclusive, and (2) That the relationship between negative and positive affect at any given moment in time varies as a function of the intensity of the affect; the more intense the affect, the more likely it is that opposite affects will be suppressed.

Who is right, Diener and his colleagues or Watson and Tellegen? Though Watson and Tellegen (1985) did not specifically consider the data of Diener and Emmons (1984), they were aware of other data suggesting an inverse relationship between measures of positive and negative affect (e.g., Brenner, 1975; Kammann, Christie, Irwin, & Dixon, 1979). Their explanation of these data was that the measures of positive and negative affect were really of "pleasant" and "unpleasant" affect (see Figure 6.1) which are expected to be inversely related at a given moment in time. Close examination of the development of the Diener and Emmons' measure (Diener & Emmons, 1984, Studies 1 and 3) suggests that their data may indeed be subject to this interpretation.

Diener and Emmons began with a set of 24 emotion terms drawn from lists compiled by Russell (1979, 1980; Russell & Mehrabian, 1977) and Plutchik (1980). Terms were chosen:

> to represent the emotions that might most frequently be related to happiness and unhappiness. Potential items such as *surprised* and *sleepy* were excluded either because of their questionable nature as emotions or because they did not appear to be substantial sources of affect in everyday life. (p. 1108)

Subjects were asked to rate the "extent to which they had felt each of the 24 emotions over the past year" (p. 1108).

Diener and Emmons factor analyzed the results obtained with this set of terms and found two main factors that they label "Pleasant" and "Unpleasant" affect. Diener and Emmons then proceeded to draw four terms (some are composites of what were judged to be synonymous terms as will be seen below) from each factor. The eight were chosen with three criteria in mind: (1) loadings on the appropriate factor had to be high, (2) positive and negative terms were selected so as to have "approximately the same arousal value" (p. 1110), and (3) terms describing affects judged to occur rarely, such as disgust, were eliminated. Finally, "unhappy" was added to the list of negative terms; it had been inadvertently excluded from the factor analytic study but was added because Diener and Emmons believed "it represents the most global level of negative affect" (p. 1110). The resulting measure of positive affect consisted of *happy, joyful, pleased*, and *enjoyment/fun*, and the measure of negative affect was the sum of *depressed/blue, unhappy, frustrated, angry/hostile*, and *worried/anxious.*

An examination of the octant marker terms in Figure 6.1 suggests that the outcome of the various measurement decisions made by Diener and Emmons is that their measures of positive and negative affect are biased toward terms that are low on arousal, an outcome they apparently sought. In fact, Diener (1984, p. 547) has been critical of Bradburn, whose data (1969; Bradburn & Caplovitz, 1965) were the first to strongly suggest the possibility that positive and negative affect might be independent of each other, for using positive terms that too strongly reflect arousal content. But the consequence of this must be a bias toward finding an inverse relationship between "positive" and "negative" affect in that the elimination of terms varying on arousal would tend to produce a one-dimensional factor structure. Though the original factor analysis (Study 1) found orthogonal factors with patterns of factor loadings clearly suggesting independence, it must be remembered that Diener and Emmons made a number of important decisions about which items to include *subsequent to the factor analysis.* It is not at all clear that a factor analysis done on the final scale would find independent factors. In fact, Larsen (1987) reports that when P-technique factor analysis (Cattell, 1973) is applied to daily mood reports using the Diener and Emmons' (1984) affect terms, the majority of subjects show "a powerful bipolar factor . . . that loaded the positive and negative adjectives with fairly equal weights" (p. 1198). Indeed, it is not at all clear what Diener and Emmons would have found using the original set of 24 items had they asked subjects to respond in terms of how they were feeling *at the moment*; remember that the instructions asked subjects to report how much of each affect they had experienced over the past year. In fact, it is hard to think of a more straightforward test of Diener's thesis that the structure of affect depends upon the time frame than to compare the factor analytic results for two such time periods.

My conclusion, then, is that Diener and Emmons (1984) have yet to demonstrate that "positive" and "negative" affects tend to be mutually exclusive at any given moment in time. As a consequence, their more general claim that the relationship between "positive" and "negative" affects depends upon the time frame considered, also remains to be substantiated in my view. The likelihood of such substantiation seems low when one remembers that Watson and Tellegen's (1985) review of the literature can be considered to be an affirmation of Diener and Emmons' null hypothesis in that they claim to find a common structure *across* variations in time frame. Rather, what Diener and Emmons have shown is that "pleasant" and "unpleasant" affects tend to be related inversely at any moment in time and that the relation between *these* affects may vary as a function of time frame.

Exactly why they are independent of each other over relatively long periods of time is an issue that I will take up later in this chapter.

A similar qualification should be attached to the conclusion about the way in which intensity moderates the relationship between opposite affects. Until the results of Diener and Emmons and Diener and Iran-Nejad are replicated using a broader and more representative sample of mood terms, we will not know if their conclusion applies to Positive and Negative affects in addition to Pleasant and Unpleasant affects. However, this conclusion, unlike the one pertaining to the influence of time frame, may well generalize in that the studies reviewed by Watson and Tellegen did not measure feelings at times of "strong emotion" and, therefore, their findings do not tend to preclude these.

Many interesting and important implications flow from the idea that Positive and Negative affects can occur independently of each other. One methodological implication is that because affect is two-dimensional, one-dimensional measurement misses important information. Thus, research that relies upon single bipolar good-bad or happy-sad scales (e.g., Wessman & Ricks, 1966; Eckenrode, 1984) can be misleading.

Clinical implications are also available. More specifically, affective disorders that are mainly characterized by high anxiety could be clearly distinguished from those epitomized by depression in that the former suggest a problem with whatever mechanisms are associated with Negative Affect whereas the latter implicate problems on both dimensions. Data reported by Bouman and Luteijn (1986), and Watson, Clark, and Carey (1988) are consistent with this conclusion.

The most direct implication has to do with the concept of "ambivalence." If affect is structured in terms of a single bipolar dimension, then ambivalence must be conceived of as the result of rapid switching (of attention) back and forth between "opposite" feelings or as a classic approach-avoidance conflict wherein the fluctuation in feelings results from movements (imaginal or real) toward or away from the affect-inducing object. However, within a two-dimensional view, one can experience both "valences" simultaneously as long as the specific affects involved are relatively pure examples of the separate dimensions. An example of this kind of ambivalence is reflected in Lazarus's (e.g., Lazarus & Folkman, 1984) conception of challenge-induced stress:

> A job promotion, for example, is likely to be appraised as holding the potential for gains in knowledge and skills, responsibility, recognition and financial reward. At the same time, it entails the risk of the person being swamped by new demands and not performing as expected. Therefore the promotion is likely to be appraised as both a challenge and a threat. Although threat and challenge appraisals are distinguished from one another by their cognitive component (the judgment of potential harm or loss versus mastery or gain) and their affective component (negative versus positive emotions), *they can occur simultaneously.* (p. 33; italics added)

The assertion that these affects may be simultaneous or compatible is credible from a two-dimensional point of view because the positive affects associated with challenge include eagerness, excitement, and exhilaration whereas the negative feelings associated with threat include fear and anxiety (Lazarus and Folkman, 1984; see also the empirical results reported by Folkman & Lazarus, 1984). Figure 6.1 makes it clear that these specific affects are relatively pure markers of the Positive and Negative dimensions, and, thus, may occur simultaneously.

The added complexity of mood that is inherent in the two-dimensional structure may also help to explain the rather weak evidence reported in Chapter 5 and elsewhere (Morris & Reilly, 1987) in support of the idea that people can mitigate negative affect, especially sadness, by exposing themselves to pleasurable stimuli. The idea that such a strategy should be effective makes sense if there were but one affective (bipolar) dimension of mood. Then, adding pleasure necessarily detracts from pain. But given that depressive affect is a "complex", that is, it results from being high on Negative Affect and being low on Positive Affect, it follows that doing something like getting out and "having fun" may leave the Negative Affect intact even if the Positive Affect dimension is altered. Putting it more concretely, if one can move the depressed person's Positive affect from low to the midpoint by exposing them to activities designed to increase their elation or activity or enthusiasm, the result would be to transform their feelings from those of Unpleasantness to those of Negative affect (see Figure 6.1). Also, the "gain" that is achieved may be more than outweighed by the frustration or helplessness that is engendered by the failure to eliminate the Negative Affect. Perhaps this is why the depressed subjects studied by Hammen and Glass (1975) actually felt worse after being induced to engage in activities they typically enjoyed.

Though acceptance of the two-dimensional structure of affects tells us *which* affects are compatible, it does not tell us *why*. Neither, for the most part, do Watson and Tellegen. The closest they come to explaining the structure is when they note that terms that are 180° apart are "opposite in meaning" (p. 221). This suggests that relationships between terms are dictated by their connotative meanings but this "explanation" begs more questions than it answers and, in addition, again raises doubts about the relationship between what people say about their affect and what they are actually feeling. In view of these complexities, the restraint against speculation exercised by Watson and Tellegen seems wise.

Intensity: A Third Dimension of Momentary Affect?

Though a two-dimensional structure clearly captures the lion's share of the variance in self-reported affect, investigations of the structure of emotion have sometimes identified a third dimension though there has been no consensus as to what it is. One interesting proposal (Daly et al., 1983) is that it is an intensity dimension. Daly et al. (1983) reasoned that certain methodological "habits" may have prevented the earlier discovery of an intensity dimension. Specifically, they suggest that studies of the structure of affect appear to presume that individuals are always experiencing some emotion. This presumption is revealed by the failure to permit subjects the option of indicating a state of neutrality. Were the neutral option made available, one might discover that it anchors an intensity dimension (that would be monopolar in nature). The study they carried out used slides to induce a variety of positive, negative, and neutral affects. Subjects selected from 1 to 3 adjectives from a set of 14 (including "neutral") that best represented how the slide made them feel and, in addition, rated how strongly they felt each of these affective experiences. The data were submitted to multidimensional scaling with the best-fitting solution being three-dimensional.

Daly et al. interpreted the solution as a conical space with the usual dimensions of pleasant-unpleasant and active-passive (similar to the arousal or engagement dimension) creating a circular emotional base and an intensity dimension rising from the base to a peak anchored by "neutral." Daly et al. confirmed the labeling of the third dimension as intensity by correlating the scalar distance of each adjective from neutral with the rated intensity associated with that adjective. The relevant correlations across a series of conceptual replications of this analysis were all strongly positive. The placement of mood terms along the intensity dimension in terms of increasing distance from neutrality were as follows: pleasant, sad, happy, disgusted, tender, and amused.[3]

The three-dimensional solution offered by Daly et al. has a certain face validity to it. In addition, their solution recalls the results of work done with the Semantic Differential (Osgood, Suci, & Tannenbaum, 1957) in that the classic dimensions of Evaluation, Activity, and Potency are very similar to the dimensions found by Daly et al. On the other hand, the ordering of mood terms on the intensity dimension seems counterintuitive in that "tender" and "amused" would seem to be milder affects than "disgusted." Indeed, this finding reveals an important weakness in the data of Daly et al., namely, that they are derived from a small set of possible affects both in terms of the slide inductions and affect terms with the consequence that the results may not be very general. For example, the observed pattern of results could be due to the amusement slides being relatively powerful inducers of their intended affect as compared to the disgust slides rather than

[3]I exclude a subset of the terms used by Daly et al. that fell within the cone, that is, near its core, rather than on its surface. These terms: attentive, bad, nice, disdainful, and angry, are, with the exception of "angry," not regarded as affect terms by Daly et al. Angry, though clearly an affect term, behaved differently in this study than it has in others in terms of its placement in a two-dimensional space. I would speculate this is because none of the slides were designed to produce anger.

amusement being a more intense affect than disgust. Nonetheless, the recognition that people may feel little or no affect and the decision to provide the opportunity to register neutrality are important advances and the procedures employed by Daly et al. deserve to be replicated with a larger set of stimuli and responses.

The idea that an intensity dimension might be necessary to describe the momentary structure of affect is paralleled by an interest in intensity as an individual difference dimension of affective experience over time. A vigorous line of research has been pursued by Larsen and his colleagues (e.g., Diener, Larsen, Levine, & Emmons, 1984; Larsen, Diener & Cropanzano, 1987; Larsen, Diener, & Emmons, 1986; Larsen & Diener, 1987) that purports to show that people can be reliably characterized as strong or weak responders to affect-inducing stimuli. Because the data validating this position consist largely of reports of the amount of affect experienced from *day to day*, I will consider their position in the next section of this chapter which considers affect over time.

Dynamic Dimensions of Mood

The dimensions of affect discussed thus far deal with variation in feelings states considered at a fixed moment in time. Taken together, they permit us to characterize *what kinds* of feeling there are and the degree to which they are compatible or incompatible with each other but the characterization is static and, therefore, incomplete. A full treatment of affective response requires that we consider the dynamic dimensions of moods over time. Considering mood over time enables a description of individual continuities in mood response.

Though a potentially large number of parameters could be investigated, most attention has been directed at three. The questions associated with these parameters are: (1) Are some people habitually in good moods while others are in bad ones?, (2) Do individuals display chronic tendencies to respond at a given level of intensity independent of the quality (i.e., valence) of their moods?, and (3) Do people differ on a dimension of stable versus erratic mood independent of the characteristic intensity with which they respond?

The first (modern) research project that attempted to measure the major dimensions of mood over an extended period of time was that of Wessman and Ricks (1966). These investigators asked 21 Radcliffe women and 17 Harvard men to report their highest, lowest, and average levels of mood every night before retiring for a period of 6 weeks. Overall or "hedonic" level was defined by subjects' reports of their average level of elation-depression (a bipolar scale was used); variability of mood was operationalized in two ways . . . as the standard deviation of the daily mean and the mean daily range (peak minus trough).

Wessman and Ricks concluded that the most general features of mood considered over time are hedonic level and variability and their findings showed these two features or dimensions of affect to be independent of each other. Thus, people could be cast into one of four categories happy-stable, happy-unstable, unhappy-stable, and unhappy-unstable. Though a landmark study, the data presented by Wessman and Ricks suffer because their samples are so small.[4] More specifically, their claim that level and variability are independent amount to accepting the null hypothesis in a low power design. In addition, the relationship between their two measures of variability was weak.

Nonetheless, similar conclusions were reached more recently by Underwood and Froming (1980) based upon a factor analytic investigation of people's self-reported tendencies to be happy versus sad, experience affect weakly versus intensely, and, be variable or stable. Underwood and Froming concluded that characteristic mood responding could be adequately described in terms of "level" (i.e., happy-sad) and "reactivity" (i.e., frequency of mood change). Like Wessman and Ricks (1966), Underwood and Froming "decided to treat happy and sad as endpoints on a continuum, since ... [they knew] of no evidence which argues persuasively for keeping the two aspects separate" (p. 405).

As I indicated earlier, such evidence now exists, at least with respect to attempts to measure positive and negative affect more generally. The first indication that positive and negative affect might be independent of each other was produced by Bradburn (1969; Bradburn & Caplowitz, 1965) who reported survey data from several national samples and showed that positive and negative affect varied independently over time when measured separately with unipolar scales.

Though Bradburn's work has been criticized on various grounds (e.g., see Diener, 1984; Warr et al., 1983), his conclusion that positive and negative affect are independent of each other over time has won broad empirical support (e.g., Andrews & Withey, 1976; Cherlin & Reeder, 1975; Clark & Watson, 1988; Costa & McCrae, 1980; Diener & Emmons, 1984; Emmons & Diener, 1985; Larson, 1987; Warr, 1978; Watson, Clark, & Carey, 1988; Watson & Tellegen, 1985; Zautra & Reich, 1983). No better sign exists of the acceptance of this conclusion than the fact that two recent reviews of self-reported affect have been published, one of which considers the correlates of positive mood (Diener, 1984, also see Argyle, 1987) while the other covers the correlates of negative affect (Watson & Clark, 1984). As we will see later, the correlates of the two are quite different.

[4]Though the sample sizes are quite small for a self-report study such as this, it should be noted that Wessman and Ricks also used an in-depth interview approach to produce case studies that they believed filled in the broad outlines suggested by their more "objective" data. Their sample sizes would be considered reasonably large from a case study point of view.

Though there may be a consensus as to the empirical relationship between positive and negative affect over time, none has emerged in support of a particular explanation for independence. Warr et al. (1983) discussed three different sorts of explanations and introduced data supporting all three. First, Warr et al. proposed that the kind of question one asks will determine whether one finds an inverse relationship or independence. When studies inquire, as did Bradburn's (1969), about the *frequency* of positive and negative feelings over relatively long and ill-defined time periods, "an increment in the number of positive responses has no logical consequence for the number of negative responses" (Warr et al., 1983, p. 645). On the other hand, studies that ask subjects to report *how much of the time* they feel good and bad (e.g., Kammann et al., 1979; Kammann & Flett, 1983) find inverse relationships, perhaps because such questions tend to imply that one is always or typically in a positive or negative state, thereby forcing a reciprocal relationship. Warr et al. demonstrated their point by using Bradburn's terms (with minor refinements) and instructions and replicating his finding of independence but, by changing the instructions so as to inquire about the amount of time, the two scales became highly negatively correlated.

The other two points made by Warr et al. (1983) are more substantive. They argue, in effect, that experiences of positive and negative affect are jointly determined by: (1) the occurrence of desirable and undesirable environmental events, and (2) personal predispositions to be positive and negative. If both positive and negative events and the personality characteristics associated with tendencies to feel good and bad were themselves independent, this would account for the independence of the feeling states over time. Warr et al. substantiated the first idea by using a modified (for college students) version of the Life Events Scale introduced by Dohrenwend, Krasnoff, Askenasy, and Dohrenwend (1978) and correlating the number of desirable and undesirable life events with positive and negative affect as measured by the Bradburn scales. The results showed that positive and negative life events were significantly related to positive and negative affect, respectively (the cross-relationships were not significant), and, confirming their hypothesis, the number of undesirable and desirable events were unrelated.

Their second notion was also supported. Extraversion and Neuroticism, as measured by the Eysenck Personality Questionnaire (Eysenck & Eysenck, 1975), correlated significantly with positive and negative affect, respectively, but the cross-correlations were low and nonsignificant. These findings replicate and extend an earlier report by Costa and McCrae (1980). Moreover, similar results have recently been reported by Emmons and Diener (1985) using the positive and negative affect scales discussed earlier.

A very different approach to explaining the independence of positive and negative affect over time has been taken by Diener and his colleagues. As noted earlier, Diener and Emmons (1984) found that when subjects were asked to report *how much* positive and negative affect they had experienced over 3 week periods of time (four such reports were made), the correlation between the two was a nonsignificant −0.10, a finding that Diener and Emmons regarded as a corroboration of the findings of Bradburn (1969). But, Diener et al. (1985) point out that this result must be reconciled with theory (e.g., Brenner, 1975) and data (e.g., Kammann et al., 1979) suggesting inverse relationships.

Their proposed reconciliation begins by noting that positive and negative affect "are unlikely to occur within the same person at the same time" (p. 1254), an assertion that is based upon the inverse relationship Diener and Emmons (1984) found between positive and negative affect measured at given moments in time (a finding that I have discussed extensively earlier in this chapter). Diener et al. deduce from this that the more time one feels positive the less they will feel negative, a deduction that has been confirmed by Kammann and colleagues (1979; Kammann & Flett, 1983) and Warr et al. (1983). According to Diener et al. (1985), the reason why this inverse relationship does not produce a negative correlation between average levels of positive and negative affect is because average levels result from the combination of two components: intensity and frequency:

> If the intensity and frequency dimensions are relatively independent across persons, a great deal of confusion can be resolved. Specifically, both a strong positive correlation between the intensity of positive and negative affect and a strong negative correlation between the frequency of positive and negative affect would tend to cancel each other out over time.... The result is that overall mean levels of the two types of affect will tend to be uncorrelated, because mean levels of affect result from the independent contribution of frequency and intensity. (p. 1255)

Diener et al. tested their hypotheses by deriving measures of "frequency" and "intensity" for the same subjects whose data were reported in Diener and Emmons (1984; Studies 3, 4, and 5). In general, their findings, reported as Studies 1, 2, and 3, demonstrated that: (1) average daily positive and negative intensities are highly correlated, (2) the correlations between intensity (positive and negative combined) and frequency were not significant, and (3) though the correlations between mean "positive" and mean "negative" affect were nonsignificant, when intensity was partialed out, the correlations became strongly inverse. Diener et al. (1985) conclude that intensity and frequency combine in an additive way to form mean levels of affect.

Examination of the operational definitions of intensity and frequency, however, reveals some conceptual confusion and compromises the conclusions drawn by Diener et al. (1985). *Frequency* was defined, oddly, as the proportion of days that an individual was predominantly positive as indicated by their average positive affect score being higher than their negative score for that day. *Intensity* was defined as the "strength with which subjects experienced their dominant affect" and was computed by taking the mean positive affect score on those days that were predominantly positive and the mean negative score on days that were predominantly negative. This is a curious operationalization of the strength of affective experience. Recall that the questionnaire used by Diener et al. (1985) asks subjects to report *how much* they had experienced of the four positive and five negative affects. Logically, the answer to such a question would seem to depend upon three potentially separable variables: (1) the incidence or frequency with which one experienced positive and negative affects, (2) the duration of these experiences, and (3) the intensity of them. Thus, when a subject reports a great deal of negative affect on a given day, we would not be able to discern whether this is because he was beset by many problems (where one possibly predisposes others) versus a problem that persists or a problem that is acutely upsetting.

Though this problem with the "intensity" measure weakens the explanation Diener et al. (1985) offer for the independence of positive and negative affect, some confidence is restored by other findings reported by Diener et al. (1985; Study 2) and Hedges, Jandorf, and Stone (1985) showing that the amount of positive and negative affect reported by subjects at the end of the day is highly correlated with reports of peak mood obtained during the day (Hedges et al., 1985) as well as with reports of mood made in response to alarm watch prompts and times of emotion (Diener et al., 1985; Study 2). These findings are reassuring because momentary indications of the amount of affect felt would not seem likely to reflect incidence and duration parameters and, therefore, are better measures of intensity.

Whatever one makes of this particular account as to why positive and negative affect are independent of each other over time, it should not detract from the solid evidence in support of independence itself. Moreover, it should be noted that independence of positive and negative affects over time is found even when the positive and negative affects are inversely related over short intervals as Diener and Emmons (1984) have shown. The implication of independence is that insofar as tendencies to be positive and negative are concerned, a minimally satisfactory description of individuals requires separate assessments of each dimension. Thus, some individuals apparently experience a relatively great amount of mood of both sorts; some feel little of either, some would be relatively high on positive affects, and others would tend toward dysphoria.

The second variable that has been well-studied is intensity. Do individuals differ in the characteristic strength with which they experience affect? Wessman and Ricks (1966) asked their subjects to report their "peaks" and "troughs," i.e., their daily highs and lows. Such data would seem ideally suited as indices of the intensity of affective response but Wessman and Ricks were more interested in their joint contribution as a measure of within-day variability (i.e., range). Perhaps they ignored intensity as a dimension of affective responding because their data failed to suggest that such a dimension existed; the correlations between mean peak and mean trough were low in both their male and female samples, −0.14 and −0.07, respectively. However, the data that have accumulated in the decade of the

80's uniformly support the existence of a disposition to respond with a characteristic degree of intensity to affect-producing events. Two strategies have been pursued: some investigators correlate subjects' self-reported responses to positive and negative events whereas others have attempted to create inventories that measure the disposition. I will briefly review these in order.

Four studies have followed in the Wessman and Ricks tradition of correlating positive and negative reactions. DeLongis et al. (1982) created scales designed to measure the occurrence of minor life events that they referred to as "hassles" and "uplifts." DeLongis et al. reported that the intensity ratings for the two kinds of events were positive correlated. Monroe, Imhoff, Wise, and Harris (1983) found much the same in a study that also looked at the impact of life events. Epstein (1983) had his 30 college student subjects report about their strongest affective experience each day for 28 consecutive days. Averaging across the various positive and negative affects, he found that there was a highly significant correlation of +0.58 between the most intense of each. Finally, Diener et al. (1985) showed that the amount of positive and negative affect experienced on days that, respectively, were predominantly positive or negative was correlated +0.70 in each (*sic*!) of three separate samples (Studies 1, 2, and 3, respectively). In addition, intercorrelations between day-end reports and momentary reports were similarly high and correlations between the extremity of responding on individual positive and negative affect terms averaged +0.41. Importantly, Diener et al. (1985) carefully ruled out a variety of self-report artifact explanations. For example, subjects were also asked to generate verbal descriptions of their emotional experiences and these were rated by independent judges. Subjects whose negative affects were rated as intense by judges were also rated as having relatively intense positive affects.

Two groups of investigators have attempted to develop inventories to measure the intensity of affective responding. Underwood and Froming (1980) assembled a 34-item self-report questionnaire designed to ascertain perceptions of one's own general level of mood, frequency of mood change, and intensity of reaction to mood-inducing events. Factor analysis showed that intensity of mood and frequency of mood change resided together in a factor Underwood and Froming named Reactivity. They suggested that more reactive individuals:

> are likely to experience mood changes more frequently than less intense reactors because there are a greater number of events capable of producing such changes. According to this view, separate factors for frequency and intensity do not emerge because these two characteristics are intrinsically correlated. (p. 407)

More recently, Larsen and Diener (1987) have agreed that intensity and variability covary though they maintain that they are logically separable. This intimate, part-whole connection between parameters of strength and variability is a problem that has beset attempts to reach separate conclusions about each, at least until recently (Larsen, 1987).

The other instrument for studying affective intensity is called the Affect Intensity Measure (AIM). It is a 40-item questionnaire developed by Larsen (1984) that asks subjects to indicate on a six-point scale (anchored by "never" and "always") the extent to which their characteristic emotional responses are intense or mild. Positively-keyed examples are "When I'm happy I bubble over with energy" and "Sad movies deeply touch me"; negatively-keyed items include "The memories I like the most are of those times when I felt content and peaceful rather than zestful and enthusiastic", and "When I get angry it's easy for me to still be rational and not overreact." The scale appears to have adequate psychometric properties (Larsen & Diener, 1987).

In a recent pair of studies, Larsen et al. (1986) have shown that AIM predicts how individuals respond to everyday affect-eliciting events as well as standardized event descriptions presented in the laboratory. Not only did differences appear in reactions obtained in both laboratory and field settings, but the results were found to hold across objectively defined (i.e., judge-rated) intensities ranging from "low" to "extreme" as well as across positive and negative affects. Further validation of the scale derives from data showing that AIM scores are correlated .50 with parental reports of emotional intensity (Larsen & Diener, 1985) and .41 with peer reports (Larsen and Diener, 1987). Finally, Larsen and Diener (1987) note that AIM scores are positively correlated with average daily affective intensity (using the Diener et al., 1985 measure) in three separate samples with r's ranging from .49 to .61.

Convincing as all these results seem in terms of establishing that individuals can be reliably differentiated with regard to the intensity of their affective responding, I have a reservation above and beyond my concern that the question as to how much affect is experienced over the course of a day is not a very clean measure of intensity. It is that Larsen and Diener and their colleagues may have done no more than "reinvent the wheel." By this, I mean to refer back to Watson and Tellegen's (1985) argument that the data from many studies establishes a basic two-dimensional structure for self-reported affect. Though Watson and Tellegen prefer to interpret the space in terms of the dimensions of Positive and Negative affect, they acknowledge the alternative possibility which involves a happy-unhappy dimension and a dimension they refer to as engagement but which is often described as an arousal dimension. Recall that in constructing their measures of affect, Diener and Emmons (1984) systematically excluded terms that anchor this arousal dimension. Thus, their measure basically captures the happy-unhappy dimension as they had intended. Therefore, when Diener et al. (1985) attempted to derive a measure of intensity from the extremity of responding, they may have been detecting nothing other than the arousal dimension that they had previously banished.

How might this have happened? Consider the possibility that a given individual typically experiences positive affect in forms infused with arousal, e.g., excitement or eagerness or enthusiasm. How might such a person cope with the rather restricted response alternatives offered by Diener and Emmons, i.e., happy, pleased, joyful, and enjoyment/fun? It does not seem unlikely that they would use the high intensity end of the scale to express their feelings. Indeed, Diener et al. (1985) note themselves that an "arousal dimension may be congruent with our intensity dimension" (p. 1263) and in their recent review of the literature on affect intensity, Larsen and Diener (1987) describe the differences between the subjective well-being states of high and low intensity types as qualitatively different, i.e., when feeling positive, high intensity types experience "exuberance, animated joyfulness, and zestful enthusiasm" whereas low intensity types feel "contentment, easygoing composure, serenity, and tranquil calmness" (p. 27). Reference to Figure 6.1 makes it clear how very close Larsen and Diener (1987) are to more traditional analyses of affect in terms of the importance of an arousal dimension.

A third major dimension of affective experience is variability which I would define as the speed or frequency with which mood changes. As noted earlier, Wessman and Ricks (1966), relying on data from daily mood reports, argued that it was one of the two basic dimensions of mood with which one could differentiate individuals; Underwood and Froming (1980), using a self-report survey of mood reactions, agreed. But both sets of investigators found variability to be associated with the intensity of an individual's reactions to mood-inducing events. In the case of Underwood and Froming, this association was indicated by the fact that items meant to capture intensity and variability of responding loaded on the same factor. As for Wessman and Ricks, the association was intrinsic in that their two operational definitions of variability . . . the standard deviation of the daily mean and the mean daily range, were based on the extremity of responding. Other investigators interested in variability of mood have also used the within-subjects standard deviation or variance as their measure (e.g., Cattell, 1973; Clum & Clum, 1973; Depue et al., 1981; Eckenrode, 1984; Folstein, DePaulo, & Trepp, 1982; Gorman & Wessman, 1974; Johnson & Larson, 1982; Larson, 1983; Larson, Csikzentmihalyi, & Graef, 1980; Linville, 1982; Stallone, Huba, Lawlor & Fieve, 1973; Tobacyk, 1981; Wessman, 1979).

The obvious problem, then, is that such measures are confounded insofar as they reflect both the frequency and extremity of change. What is needed is a measure that is sensitive only to the speed or frequency of change. The solution appears to lie in a technique called *spectral analysis* (Jenkins & Watts, 1968; Gottman, 1981). Spectral analysis is applied to time series data, decomposing it into a specified number of periodic functions. As with regression analysis, the object is to account for variance by fitting a model but unlike regression, spectral analysis fits a non-linear model based on sine-cosine waves. Many waves, differing in period length, amplitude, and phase, are fit to the data with the output of the analysis indicating the amount of variance accounted for by each periodic component.

This technique has recently been applied to two data sets containing daily mood reports (Eastwood, Whitton, Kramer, and Peter, 1985; Larsen, 1987). Eastwood et al. (1985) had 34 normal controls and 30 outpatients who had been diagnosed as affectively disordered (25 bipolar and 5 unipolar) complete a brief questionnaire every morning upon arising for 14 months. Included was an item that asked subjects to rate their mood from "saddest" to "happiest" on a 9-point scale. The data were examined for the presence of "peaks" of amplitude for periods ranging from 3 to 128 days with a peak considered as significant if its:

> 95% confidence limit did not include the expected value for gaussian noise and if the same peak was significant in power spectra on both the first and second halves of the time series and in the spectrum of the complete series. (p. 296)

Eastwood et al. found that patients had significantly more mood cycles than did healthy controls and also found the amplitudes to be significantly greater in the disordered group. However, there were no differences in the period and distribution of cycle length. For all subjects, their most significant cycles were skewed toward "seasonal" lengths (85 to 128 days).

Larsen (1987) used the daily mood rating form generated by Diener and Emmons (1984), and had subjects complete it each evening for 56 (Study 1) or 84 days (Study 2). A single daily mood score was generated for each subject by subtracting the average of the negative affect ratings from the average of the positive ones and these data were exposed to spectral analysis. Larsen (1987) arbitrarily broke period lengths into categories labeled fast (periodic components of less than 3 days in length), medium (periodic components of 3 to 5 days in length), and slow (periodic components of 5 to 28 days in length). Like Eastwood et al. (1985), Larsen found that more cycling was associated with longer periods although it should be noted that Eastwood et al. had a much larger range of cycle lengths to study.

Larsen's prime purpose, however, was to determine whether the degree of variance accounted for by his three categories of spectra could be demonstrated to have predictable relationships with variables that should be related to mood variability. Two such variables were employed. First, in Study 1 and Study 2, Larsen examined the degree to which one's score on the AIM was associated with the amount of variance accounted for by slow, medium, and fast period lengths. In both cases, the results indicated that high AIM subjects had more variance associated with more rapidly changing mood frequencies than did low AIM subjects. Larsen had predicted these effects on the grounds that the AIM is designed to capture extreme positive and negative responses. Consequently, a person who scores high "is likely to be emotionally variable, vacillating between strong positive and negative emotions" (p. 1198). Secondly, Larsen was able to get 85% of the parents

(N = 65) of subjects in Study 2 to fill out the AIM for their children. Creating extreme AIM groups by taking subjects from the lower and upper ends of the parent-reported mood-reactivity distribution, Larsen once again found that for the high parent-reported AIM group, variance in daily moods was associated with more rapid shifts of affect. A final validating note: In Study 2, Larsen calculated the amount of variance accounted for by periodic components of each length and then compared males and females. The only significant sex difference was for the 28 day length, a finding that Larsen associates with the effect of the menstrual cycle (see Chapter 4).

The spectral analysis technique seems promising as a relatively pure measure of mood variability in that both of these efforts found it to be sensibly related to individual differences. Somewhat disappointing is the decision by both investigators to use what amounts to bipolar measurement of mood. Though Larsen used unipolar scales that separately measured positive and negative affect, his decision to subtract the mean of one set from that of the other obscures possible differences between them. Because I remain persuaded by Watson and Tellegen (1985) that there are two orthogonal dimensions of self-reported affect, it seems a mistake to calculate a difference score as a daily index. Rather, if there are separate mechanisms underlying Positive and Negative affective responses as the mounting evidence continues to suggest, then it could be the case that how variable these affects are might also be independent.

More troublesome is the unexamined assumption that a day-to-day mood measure adequately captures the individual's tendencies to be variable. As noted by Hedges et al. (1985), moods are commonly understood to be relatively transient phenomena, rarely lasting as long as a day. Because the data on the typical duration of event-induced moods (see below) suggests this is true, the periodicities uncovered by Larsen (1987) and Eastwood et al. (1985) may reflect differences in the changeability of peoples' internal (i.e., biological) and external environments rather than the sort of ups and downs we normally associate with "moody" (i.e., variable) persons.

The empirical literature on mood duration tends to suggest their brevity. Experimental studies (Frost & Green, 1982; Isen et al., 1976; Isen & Gorglione, 1983; Mayer, Mamberg, & Volanth, 1988) find the effects of various mood inductions (carried out in both laboratory and field settings) to be gone within 30 minutes although in these cases, the presence of mood was indexed by its ability to influence a mood-related behavior rather than by self-report.

Generally,[5] studies of mood responses to naturally occurring life events also show that they come and go within the day. Stone and Neale (1984)

[5]The exceptions to these findings come from studies using disordered individuals. Zevon and Rounds (1985) have reported that people who score high on measures of psychological distress do show evidence of moods that carry over across days and

asked for negative life-event and mood reports over a long time period, hoping to identify periods where only one such event occurred in the midst of a string of generally uneventful days so that they could quasi-experimentally look at mood "before" and "after" the event. The events included such problems as arguments with coworkers or one's spouse, illness within the family or among friends, etc. Their findings indicated that though mood clearly deteriorated relative to normal on the day of the event, there was no detectable dysphoria on the day after the event occurred. Similarly, Verbrugge (1985) analyzed data obtained from 589 adults who kept diaries for at least one week. Included were measures of mood and major life events. Her findings showed that if one controlled for the occurrence of negative events on target days, the influence on mood of negative events on days preceding target days was minimal. Finally, in a study looking at *within-day* disappearance of mood, Larson et al. (1980), using autocorrelation techniques, found that extreme mood states were undetectable after 3 hours among adults and 2 hours later among adolescents.

The implication of these data for students of affective variability is that moods must be measured more frequently than once a day if one wishes to capture the full extent of their fluctuation. Indeed, it would seem that there is a good chance that within-day and across-day variability are unrelated in normal samples. I conclude this from the fact that though Wessman and Ricks (1966) found that they were (weakly) positively related, their relatedness may have been due to the influence that intensity of responding had on both measures; partialling out intensity might well leave no relationship at all.

Studying the ways in which moods change in response to events, especially over smaller time periods, would also have the salutory effect of broadening the set of parameters that are seen as potentially responsible for variable versus stable mood. For example, Larsen's approach to mood variability is to tie it to a single parameter: the volatility of one's response to affect-inducing events.[6] This is apparent in his decision to validate spectral analysis by using the AIM which was designed as a measure of the extremity of

---

Goplerud and Depue (1985) have found that individuals classified as subsyndromally bipolar and depressed (i.e., cyclothymic and dysthymic) recover more slowly than normals from negative life events. In fact, DeLongis, Folkman, and Lazarus (1988) have recently reported data showing a next-day mood rebound effect among normals; for a very large majority of their subjects, the more stressful a given day was (defined in terms of the number of "hassles" they experienced), the *better* their mood on the following day.

[6]However, Larsen also speculates that the disposition to be variable may not be associated with a sensitivity to external events alone leading to the idea that the source of variability could be largely endogenous in nature. Consistent with this possibility, spontaneous endogenous variability due to dysregulation of neurotransmitter processes has been theorized to be the source of the affective disorders (Siever & Davis, 1985).

affective responding. This is tantamount to dismissing the insight involved in recognizing that extremity of responding and frequency or speed of change over time are conceptually distinct. If mood variability is defined as the speed or frequency of mood change, then rapidly moving toward extremes of positive and negative affect is literally only half of the story. A complete measure of affective fluctuation must also capture the *rate of return*; highly variable people would be those whose affect frequently and/or rapidly intensifies *and* deintensifies. Also relevant would be differences in *inertial tendencies*. That is, it is already known that moods tend to persist in the sense that they provide resistance against induction by opposite-valenced events (Barden et al., 1981). Those with stronger inertial tendencies would, perforce, be less changeable.

Part of the confusion both here and in some of the earlier literature I reviewed on both mood intensity and mood valence may be due to a failure to begin with a consideration of the fundamental nature of mood itself. Researchers interested in individual differences in mood appear to have implicitly adopted a number of assumptions about mood states, namely that they are continuous and accessible by introspection. Although these assumptions are consistent with the idea that mood is a general indicator of well-being and serves a function in self-regulation, and encouraged by the ease with which one can find receptive respondents willing to evaluate their internal states, they are at odds with an alternative view of mood that is event-based and presumes that we are not always aware of feelings that have been aroused (e.g., Clark & Isen, 1982; Zajonc, 1980). From this perspective, what is interesting about people is the way their moods differ in response to environmental and/or endogenous occurrences.

Viewed in this latter way, moods are events or states (rather than continuous indicators) that can be described in terms of various parameters such as rise time, peak intensity, duration, rate of decay, imperviousness to subsequent mood-relevant occurrences, etc. These parameters could be related to characteristics of individuals such as excitatory and inhibitory processes at both neurophysiological and psychological levels and attentional processes (see Derryberry & Rothbart, 1988, who specify a similar set of variables as worthy of study in examining individual differences in temperament). Complicating matters, some of these parameters and individual differences may ultimately need to be separately estimated for positive and negative affect given the likelihood that good and bad feelings are mediated by different neurophysiological and psychological systems.

But, as should be evident by now, it is my opinion that both sets of assumptions about mood are correct. The two views of mood are not mutually exclusive although at any given moment in time, mood is in one mode or the other–in or out of focal attention. Of critical significance for the study of individual differences, the "behavior" of the mood may depend importantly on the degree to which it becomes the focus of conscious attention (see Chapter 5). Therefore, the need to extend beyond the methodology of directed introspection and self-report is more important than simply providing a means of validating self-report measures;[7] it is necessary because more behaviorally-oriented measurement may be the only effective means of assessing mood in its mode as ground or context.

In conclusion, my review of the data on the temporal dynamics of mood suggests individuals may differ on up to four fundamental dimensions. First, the degree to which desirable and undesirable affects occur over time seems orthogonal so that persons must be separately characterized in terms of their capacities for positive and negative mood. This has been shown to be true of the reported *frequency* of occurrence of these affects (Bradburn, 1969; Bradburn & Caplowitz, 1965; Larson, 1987; Warr et al., 1983) and for reports of *how much* of the affects are reported over time (Diener & Emmons, 1984; Zevon & Tellegen, 1982); it has even been shown to be true when the measured affects are inversely related in terms of their momentary structure (Diener & Emmons, 1984).

The situation is much more ambiguous for the other two postulated dimensions of affect: intensity and variability. First, it is not yet clear whether an intensity dimension of responding exists that is different from the classically posited arousal dimension. As noted earlier, it is possible that people who regularly report stronger affect when given that option would also report qualitatively different affects, for example, excitement rather than happiness, if offered that opportunity. In this connection, it is interesting to note that the explanation offered by Larsen and Diener (1987) for individual differences in the intensity of responding is in terms of arousal needs and regulation.

Even if strength of responding is ultimately shown to be at least partly independent of the type or quality of affect experienced, it appears to be related to variability of affective responding (Underwood & Froming, 1980; Larsen, 1987), forming a variable that has been termed Reactivity (Underwood & Froming, 1980). It is too early to tell whether sufficiently different correlates of intensity and variability will be found so as to justify their separate existence.

Finally, the relationships between measures of intensity and/or variability and the propensities to experience desirable and undesirable affects are quite confusing at this point. Underwood and Froming (1980) found that more reactive individuals reported that they were typically less happy, Derryberry and Rothbart (1988) have data showing that subjects who report high levels

---

[7]In fact, there are two studies suggesting some degree of consistency between mood reflected in self-reports and behavior. Stone (1981; Stone & Neale, 1984) asked the wife of each of his subjects to fill out daily mood forms describing her husband's moods and found that these reports reflected the day's events in much the same way that the husband's mood reports did. Such data are less than totally convincing about the validity of the mood reports, however, because the report of the wife may reflect the husband's self-report to her more than any behavioral indicator.

of peripheral reactivity claim to experience more negative emotions, and Depue et al. (1981) found that individuals who scored high on the General Behavior Inventory, a measure of cyclothymic tendencies, had a mean "trough" that was lower than that of low scorers on the GBI. But Wessman and Ricks (1966) did not find a significant association between day-to-day variability and elation-depression and Diener et al. (1985) actually found a positive relationship between an overall intensity measure and the proportion of days that were judged predominantly positive.

Making sense of these findings is difficult because of the variation from study to study in terms of the operational definition of variables. More important, though, than settling upon common measurement procedures is the need, discussed above, to carefully examine the assumptions about mood that underlie measurement decisions. If mood exists in fundamentally different forms, measurement must reflect this or be doomed to create, rather than dispel, confusion. At a minimum, however, research on intensity and variability of mood must begin to move away from self-reports toward nonverbal measures.

Correlates of the Tendency to Experience Positive Affect

There is a rather large literature dealing with subjective well-being and general happiness (See Diener, 1984, and Argyle, 1987, for recent reviews.). However, because many early attempts to measure these constructs used global bipolar scales (see Wilson, 1967, for a review), their correlates reflected the combination of what we now know to be the independent components of positive and negative affect.

Beginning with the work of Bradburn (1969; Bradburn & Caplowitz, 1965), researchers have been moving slowly toward the use of monopolar scales designed to measure positive and negative affect separately. The results of this body of work (Beiser, 1974; Cherlin & Reeder, 1975; Clark & Watson, 1988; Costa & McCrae, 1980; Diener & Emmons, 1984, Study 4; Emmons & Diener, 1985; Moriwaki, 1974; Warr et al., 1983) are quite consistent in showing that the tendency to report relatively large amounts of positive affect is associated with measures of Extraversion, especially the sociability component (see Emmons & Diener, 1985), as well as related variables such as the frequency of contact with friends and relatives, making new acquaintances, and involvement in social organizations.

Because measures of extroversion are thought to have relatively high heritability quotients (Eysenck, 1956), these findings avoid some of the ambiguity as to the direction of causation that is normally associated with such correlations. Also suggestive of the influence of sociability on positive affect is a panel study carried out by Headey and Wearing (1986) as described in Argyle (1987). These researchers found that extraversion predisposed more favorable life events which led to a high level of positive well-being. In addition to creating more positive affect by increasing the likelihood of good times, the tendency to be sociable might also increase the magnitude of positive experiences when they occur by way of social facilitation effects (Zajonc, 1965). If the presence of others heightens general arousal, then positive affects experienced in the presence of others would seem more intense (Schachter & Singer, 1962). It is also possible that a predisposition to be happy might also increase the likelihood of affiliative behavior. As was noted in Chapter 5, though no studies have directly established that good mood increases the likelihood of interacting with others, there is evidence that good mood increases the perceived attractiveness of potential social partners (e.g., Gouaux, 1971).

Correlates of the Tendency to Experience Negative Affect

Whereas good mood is associated with measures of sociability, Costa and McCrae (1980), Warr et al. (1983), and Emmons and Diener (1985) have shown bad mood to be correlated with Neuroticism or Emotionality as measured by the Eysenck Personality Inventory (Eysenck & Eysenck, 1968) or its successor, the Eysenck Personality Questionnaire (Eysenck & Eysenck, 1975).

Watson and Clark (1984) have recently proposed a broader construct than that of the Eysencks'. They refer to their construct as Negative Affectivity (NA) and base their claims of breadth on the very high intercorrelations they found to exist among established measures of the tendency to experience such diverse negative states as "nervousness, tension, worry . . . anger, scorn, revulsion, guilt, self-dissatisfaction, a sense of rejection, and, to some extent, sadness" (p. 465). The specific measures include the Taylor Manifest Anxiety Scale (Taylor, 1953), the Repression-Sensitization Scale (Byrne, 1961), the Eysenck Personality Inventory Neuroticism Scale (Eysenck & Eysenck, 1968) and others. (Also see Gotlib, 1984, who more or less simultaneously published very similar results.)

Watson and Clark (1984) review the relationship between NA (as measured by these various scales) and (1) measures of self-concept, (2) measures of transient mood, (3) indications of adjustment problems and pathology, and (4) cognitive and behavioral processes that might be responsible for NA status. The average correlation between measures of NA and negative self-descriptions in the studies reviewed by Watson and Clark was 0.46. They regard this evidence to be sufficiently compelling so as to include feelings of self-dissatisfaction as part of the NA construct. Emmons and Diener (1985) also found that their measure of self-esteem (Soares & Soares, 1965) was significantly correlated with their daily measure of negative mood (but not positive mood). Nonetheless, the decision to treat negative self-concept as part of the NA construct rather than a correlate of it seems odd in the sense that the self-concept consists of a set of judgments rather than feelings.

As for transient mood, Watson and Clark reviewed a large number of studies that employed some dispositional measure of NA and they concluded that the "data confirm our contention that high-NA subjects report more distress across a wide variety of situations, both stress and nonstress" (p. 475). The existence of differences in nonstress situations is important in that it suggests that high NA reflects more than the tendency to respond more strongly to negative events; people high on NA are *chronically* distressed.

Of all the forms of distress associated with high NA, none is better documented than that associated with health problems. Dysphoric individuals have more psychosomatic complaints, health problems, and psychophysiological disorders (Beiser, 1974; Clark & Watson, 1988; Harding, 1982; Watson & Pennebaker, 1989) and trait measures of NA have been shown (Costa & McCrae, 1985) to be highly correlated with total scores on the Cornell Medical Index, a measure of physical complaints.

In addition to the relation of NA to self-reported distress, peers and clinicians rate high-NA individuals as more distressed and dysphoric. Moreover, in comparison to normal groups, various psychiatric patient categories score higher on NA though the results were much more convincing for patients diagnosed as neurotic as opposed to those deemed psychotic, having character disorders, or being substance abusers. Watson and Clark argue that these results "support our contention that NA primarily represents subjective differences in mood and self-concept rather than objective differences in actual adjustment" (p. 480).

Finally, Watson and Clark (1984) review a variety of studies that led them to conclude that high-NA individuals "willingly acknowledge and even exaggerate failure experiences and accept negative information about themselves more easily than low-NA subjects" (p. 482). This tendency to dwell on the negative side of things has increasingly been implicated as a factor in the likelihood of depressive reactions. For example, Nolen-Hoeksema (1987) has recently reviewed the rather large literature on sex differences in unipolar depression and concludes that the greater vulnerability of females may be due to their self-reported tendency to focus on their bad moods and ruminate as compared to the typical male response which is active and distractive.

These self-report data have been corroborated in a series of studies reported by Ingram, Cruet, Johnson, and Wisnicki (1988). These investigators showed that manipulations of self-awareness, that is, seeing one's image on a mirror or a television monitor, caused female subjects to become more self-focused and experience heightened negative affect whereas males became somewhat less self-focused in these situations. They speculated that these tendencies may serve to insulate males from the experience of depression while making it more likely in females.

Most striking, however, are the results of Pyszczynski and Greenberg (1985, 1986) who have shown that the tendency of depressives to focus on self is associated with task outcomes in such a way so as to maintain their rather negative view of themselves. The "normal" pattern would be to prefer self-focus after success rather than after failure because self-focus has been shown to intensify an ongoing affective state (Scheier & Carver, 1977). Such results were obtained by Pyszczynski and Greenberg (1985). But, subjects scoring as mildly to moderately depressed on the Beck Depression Inventory showed a reversed pattern, avoiding self-focus more (as indexed by the amount of time spent in front of a mirror) after success than after failure or a no-outcome control experience (Pyszczynski & Greenberg, 1986). Pyszczynski and Greenberg (1986) speculate that the avoidance of self-focus after success may serve to maintain a negative self-image to which high Beck scorers have become accustomed and may even function to provide a sense of stability and security.

If preserving a negative view of self were of value to subclinically depressed individuals, as these results suggest, one would expect to observe a pattern of attributions about task outcomes that functioned to achieve that end. And, in fact, there is no better established correlate of depressive tendencies than attributional style. In a recent meta-analytic review, Sweeney et al. (1986) considered over 100 studies involving nearly 15,000 subjects and found that depression, measured in a variety of ways, was reliably associated with several attributional tendencies. The strongest tendency was for depressed individuals to attribute negative events to internal, stable, and global causes; bad events are due to aspects of self, not to others or circumstances, the aspects are relatively enduring and they are general, such as intelligence. A complementary set of attributions occurred when the outcomes were positive, that is, depressives regarded the causes of these events to be external, unstable, and specific. This is exactly the pattern of attributions that was predicted by the reformulation (Abramson et al., 1978) of Seligman's (1975) theory of helplessness, a theory that Seligman uses to explain depression.

Though the correlation between attributional style and depressive tendencies is clear, the explanation of this finding is in dispute (e.g., compare Peterson & Seligman, 1984, with Coyne & Gotlib, 1983). A recent statement of the reformulated theory of helplessness (Peterson & Seligman, 1984) subscribes to what Brewin (1985) has called the "vulnerability" model. This model, more generally referred to as a diathesis-stress model (e.g., see Abramson, Alloy, & Metalsky, 1988), supposes that individuals have characteristic ways of explaining negative events. Vulnerability to depression is conferred by an attributional style wherein bad events are inferred to be the result of internal, stable, and global causes. According to Brewin (1985), to adequately test this model one would have to first measure attributional style, introduce a bad event, determine that attributions about the event are in line with those predicted by the attributional style measure, and show that attributional style predicts depression after the event has occurred. A study has recently appeared that has all of these characteristics but which fails to find support for the vulnerability model. Follette and Jacobson (1987) measured attributional style using the Expanded Attributional Style Questionnaire (EASQ) (Peterson & Seligman, 1984) and found that though attributional style was associated with the attribution about the specific negative event (an exam outcome equal to or less than that which the students had indicated would make them unhappy), the EASQ score did not predict post-outcome depression as measured by the Mood Affect Adjective Check List Today Form (Zuckerman & Lubin, 1965). Still, one clearly negative result is hardly enough to have a major impact. We need many more careful tests of this theory following the prescriptions set out by Brewin (1985) and expanded upon by Abramson et al. (1988) and Alloy, Hartlage, and Abramson (1988).

The literature on the correlates of the tendency to experience negative moods yields a picture of a highly stable system designed to maintain itself over time. In fact, Costa and McCrae (1980) have shown that the correlation between a trait measure of NA and a state measure of negative mood collected some 10 years later was 0.39.

Correlates of Reactivity

Because the most common indices of mood variability, the standard deviation or variance associated with a mean over days and the mean daily range (i.e., peak minus trough), confound the intensity of reaction with speed of change in reaction, any correlate of variability calculated in this way could, in fact, be associated with intensity, variability (defined as the speed with which moods change), or both. Indeed, Larsen and Diener (1987) report that their AIM correlates 0.41 and 0.39 (both p s < 0.01) with the standard deviations of their daily positive and negative affect scores and, of course, we have already seen that AIM classification is related to the speed of mood change as estimated by spectral analysis (Larsen, 1987). Consequently, it seems sensible to review the correlates of intensity and variability together under the heading of *reactivity*, a term used by both Underwood and Froming (1980) and by Larsen (1987). It is to be hoped, however, that the demonstrations by Eastwood et al. (1985) and Larsen (1987) of a viable measure of speed of change of mood that is unconfounded with intensity will foster a careful consideration of the differences between the two.

The first systematic evidence of the correlates of Reactivity came from the seminal work of Wessman and Ricks (1966). These investigators administered a large number of personality inventories and intensive interviews to male and female college students in addition to collecting daily mood reports from them. They found that mood variability was associated with measures of affective complexity and openness to emotion. The former, which was a significant correlate only for males, was operationalized as the number of factors (explaining 10% or more of the common variance) that resulted from factor analyses conducted on 6 weeks' worth of daily scores from 16 different rating scales of feelings such as harmony versus anger, tranquility versus anxiety, energy versus fatigue. The smaller the number of factors, the more accurate it is to say that an individual's feelings varied together rather than being independent of each other. Males whose affects varied independently of each other had less fluctuating mood on the elation-depression dimension. The relationship with openness to emotion is suggested by the strong negative relationship between variability and tendencies to repress and deny as measured by the MMPI R scale. Wessman and Ricks also claim that a large number of other variables derived from clinical ratings and a Rorschach analysis support the same conclusion.

Both of these correlates have found indirect support in subsequent work with seemingly related variables. For example, Linville (1985) reports two studies in which measures of self-complexity were found to be associated with measures of reactivity. In Study 1, male subjects were given a set of traits and asked to sort the ones descriptive of themselves into groups that they thought belonged together. Those subjects whose self-representation was complex in the sense that their groupings were more numerous and distinct reacted less strongly to manipulated success and failure experiences. In Study 2, female subjects engaged in a similar sorting task but here the stimuli were roles rather than traits. Complexity of role sort was negatively related to variability in daily mood over a 2-week period ($r = -0.36$, $p < 0.02$).

Linville's hypothesis is that complexity prevents spill-over from occurring when positive or negative life-experiences occur. Thus, the affect that is induced is literally contained by the many boundaries that make for a highly differentiated self. Linville (1987) has further corroborated this hypothesis by showing that self-complexity serves as a buffer against the impact of negative life events, reducing the likelihood that depression and physical symptoms would result. In addition to the support deriving from her own data and that of Wessman and Ricks, Linville's notions are consistent with Bower's (1981) spreading activation theory of mood.

Wessman and Rick's (1966) other claimed correlate of variability–openness to emotion–tends to be supported by findings obtained by Larsen (1984) as reported in Larsen and Diener (1987). Larsen (1984) developed a checklist of 28 typical activities for college students and asked his subjects to indicate their activity patterns for 14 days. Each of the activities had been previously scaled in terms of how much affect it would normally induce. Larsen derived an "emotion-provoking activity" score for each subject by counting the number of activities they engaged in which ranked in the upper quartile and subtracting the reported number of activities that were in the bottom quartile. This score correlated 0.42 ($p < 0.01$) with AIM scores. These findings go beyond those of Wessman and Ricks because they suggest that not only are individuals high in Reactivity open to affect, they actively seek it out. On the other hand, Larsen et al. (1986) found that AIM scores were uncorrelated with scores on Sensation Seeking (Zuckerman,

1979b). Thus, it is not thrilling or risky activities that individuals high on Reactivity seek, merely those everyday activities that are relatively arousing, for example, sexual activity, attending sports events, going to a party.

Activity choice data suggest a broader interpretation of the Reactivity construct. Whereas previously cited data suggest only that individuals differ in the typical intensity of responding to affect-inducing events, these findings suggest that individuals high in Reactivity can be characterized as being *motivated* to experience more affect in their daily lives. Also consistent with this notion are findings reported by Jolly (1986) who showed that high AIM scorers' social worlds had more independent units, that is, their friends were more likely to not know each other than low AIM scorers' friends, and Emmons (1986) who showed that high AIM scorers had more current life goals that were independent of each other than low AIM scorers. Each of these findings can be interpreted in terms of having a greater variety of activities. If variety is the "spice of life," one might argue that high AIM scorers are seeking a spicier, more exciting daily life.

Such a life style does have its costs, however. Individuals high in Reactivity describe themselves as being generally more distressed (Underwood & Froming, 1980), they report more physical symptoms and poorer health (Larsen & Diener, 1987), and Linville (1987) has shown that a correlate of Reactivity, namely a relatively undifferentiated self-image, is associated with being more depressed by negative life-events. Though Wessman and Ricks (1966) tried to suggest that Reactive persons may have their low points compensated for by their peaks, there may be an asymmetry between positive and negative affects that punishes the extreme responder. One possibility is that relatively extreme movement in a negative direction may stimulate more attributional and other explanatory cognitive activity than would a comparable positive experience. Consistent with this idea, Epstein (1983) has reported that intense responders find thoughts about negative events recur over longer periods of time than is true for positive events (also see Goodhart, 1985).

On the other hand, other findings suggest that there is no penalty associated with volatile affective reactions. Both Wessman and Ricks (1966) and Diener and his colleagues (Diener et al., 1985) found that Reactivity and valence were independent of each other and Larsen and Diener (1987) showed that AIM scores were uncorrelated with a large number of measures of psychological well-being. Hopefully, these conflicting results can be resolved as measurement of these mood dimensions improves.

Summary and Conclusions

Though the affective lives of individuals seem incredibly complex and rich (Wessman and Ricks, 1966), the evidence I reviewed in this chapter suggests that they can be successfully submitted to dimensional analysis that, in turn, allows an orderly search for individual differences associated with these dimensions of mood response. But progress in this general area has been stymied by an interrelated set of conceptual and methodological problems. Mood has been uncritically assumed to be adequately measured by self-reports using instruments that are validated by other self reports. Though I admit to the bias of an experimentalist, I can still freely say that I am shocked that there is no evidence as yet to show that individuals who claim to be typically positive, negative, intense versus mild, and erratic versus stable have been shown to respond in these ways under carefully controlled conditions.

Clearly, it is time to bridge the gap that separates the freestanding literature on the individual differences in mood with the largely experimental literature that considers the effects of mood on cognition, perception, and behavior (see Chapter 5 for reviews). As we gain knowledge about mood inductions and their influence on various behaviors, it becomes increasingly possible to use the latter as surrogate measures of mood (see Chapter 3 for a discussion of possible measures). Just as clinicians have found that various behavioral symptoms are reliably associated with depressed and manic states, personologists could measure characteristic affective responses through careful observational procedures. An added bonus of this approach is the opportunity to measure repeatedly, at time intervals of the investigator's choosing, without worrying either about reactivity or the possibility that one's data reflects the extensive knowledge people have about affect (e.g., see Shaver, Schwartz, Kirson, & O'Connor, 1987) rather than actual subjective feelings.

I do not intend to advocate discontinuing the long and fruitful tradition of studying psychological processes via introspection. As I noted in Chapter 3, self-reported moods are inherently valid with cooperative and truthful subjects. But, such reports are clearly valid only for mood in its manifestation as figure. Thus, we know (with confidence) little about individual differences in mood as context and virtually nothing about the important dynamic whereby mood moves in and out of attention.

Not only have personologists maintained too great a distance from their nomothetically-inclined colleagues in experimental psychology, but it also might be said that they have avoided considering the implications of their work for an understanding of affect that is so negative, positive, intense, or variable, as to be considered of clinical significance. And, in a complementary (but hardly compl*i*mentary!) way, clinical researchers have been at least as likely to ignore the literature on individual differences in "normal" affect as well as the experimental literature on mood.

The most striking example of the lack of dialogue surrounding the natural boundaries that separate these disciplines is the lack of any careful consideration of what has been referred to as the "continuity hypothesis." This hypothesis presumes that "depressed mood in otherwise normal persons is quantitatively but not qualitatively different than the depression found in hospitalized patients" (Coyne, 1986, p. 3). Cast in this way, the hypothesis takes no position as to whether normal and pathological moods are primarily due to psychological versus biological causes. However, because everyday moods are implicitly assumed to be the result of psychological processes, the continuity hypothesis has come to be associated with the rather rich array of theories that have proposed a psychological etiology for major affective disorders, principally of the unipolar variety. The next chapter is devoted to a consideration of the viability of this hypothesis.

Chapter 7

The Continuity Hypothesis

The idea that everyday good and bad moods might differ from clinically significant depression and mania only in terms of degree rather than kind suggests that these states are on continua such that intensification of normal processes can produce disorder. This view, sometimes referred to as the continuity hypothesis (e.g., see Beck, 1967; Blatt et al., 1976; Coyne, 1986; Depue et al., 1981; Eastwood et al., 1985; Gotlib, 1984), is a controversial one that has tended to divide clinicians and researchers into two camps. Opposed to the continuity hypothesis are those who take a biomedical orientation toward affective disorder, regarding it as a disease traceable to abnormal neurophysiological and biochemical processes (e.g., Whybrow & Mendels, 1969; Siever & Davis, 1985). In support of the hypothesis, one finds an uneasy alliance of behaviorally, cognitively, and psychoanalytically oriented psychologists and psychiatrists who believe that psychological processes and vulnerabilities are sufficient to explain clinically significant depression. At stake are the implications of the continuity hypothesis: that we can learn more about the nature of affective disorder through "analog" research, that is, by studying the moods of "normal" individuals, and that psychological therapies can be effective remedies, especially to the extent that they are based on evidence about ways to successfully eliminate everyday bad moods.

The case against the continuity hypothesis rests on three bodies of literature. First there is the rather extensive evidence of neurobiological abnormality in cases of affective disorder (see Chapter 4 for a review). Such evidence is consistent with the idea that affective disorders can be directly caused by neurobiological dysfunction or that the dysfunction operates as a vulnerability in a diathesis-stress model of disorder. Second, the treatment of choice, especially for affective disorders of a more profound sort, is medication. The effectiveness of drugs is also consistent with a biological etiology. Finally, evidence of a possible genetic basis for affective disorder is strengthening; disorders with an hereditary basis are generally seen as biologically based.

It is beyond the scope of this book to consider these three realms of evidence beyond the treatment provided in Chapter 4. The interested reader can consult reviews provided by Beardslee, Bemporad, Keller, & Klerman (1983), Paykel (1982), Whybrow et al. (1984), and Willner (1985). Despite this evidence, consideration of the case for psychological causation of affective disorder makes sense because though the three areas of evidence are consistent with biological etiology, none is good evidence *against* psychological causation. Neurochemical and physiological abnormality could simply reflect systemic breakdown in response to psychologically-based stress. Disproving this would require prospective studies showing that such abnormalities are precursors of disorder. Drugs may be effective because they are capable of altering affect and thereby interfering with the disorder once it reaches its apparently autonomous or stable state but that stable state may have been reached as the result of psychological processes. Finally, though vulnerability may be conferred by heredity, psychological causes would still be sought unless one opted for a strong form of reductionism.

My plan for this chapter is to assess the viability of the continuity hypothesis. There are two main steps in that process. First, if affective disorders are like everyday moods but stronger, exactly how do moods intensify to the point where dysfunction occurs? I will begin by describing the surprisingly diverse array of theories that attempt to answer this question by proposing a particular psychological process gone awry. All of these theories try to explain the emergence of clinically significant depression. Affective disorders characterized by the presence of both depressed and manic episodes, referred to as cyclothymia and bipolar disorder in the current nomenclature, have not attracted much attention from theorists who rely upon psychological accounts. This is probably because the stronger evidence of heritability for such disorders (Depue et al., 1981) is often taken as suggesting a biological cause. Nonetheless, after considering the case for the continuity hypothesis as it relates to depressive disorder I will consider the possibility of continuity between normal mood swings and cyclothymia and bipolar disorder.

I will not try to indicate which of the many psychological theories is best supported by the evidence. Such an effort would be futile insofar as very few attempts have been made to test between the different theories. Rather, researchers have thus far preferred to look for evidence consistent with a given view and thereby establish its viability. Moreover, the explanations offered by the various theories are not necessarily mutually exclusive. Each tends to focus on one of the prominent symptoms associated with depression, such as, a negative self-image, dysphoric mood, or reduced efforts to procure pleasure, generally interposing it in the form of a vulnerability or latent tendency between certain environmental events and other prominent symptoms. It is possible, however, that some or all of these psychological processes are locked together in a mutually reinforcing system that can be activated through any "member" process. If so, attempts to integrate the various theories will be more successful than efforts to test between them. Hyland (1987) and Pyszczynski and Greenberg (1987) have recently attempted to integrate psychological-process theories and I will review their proposals below. Whybrow et al. (1984) have made the heroic effort to integrate biological and psychological processes (see Chapter 4) into a single model. Time will tell whether the field is ready for such complex models or whether, as suggested by Coyne (1986), simpler single-process accounts should continue to be tested and refined.

Each of the theories is a specific realization of its more abstract parent, the continuity hypothesis. How should one assess this hypothesis? Because the continuity hypothesis asserts that everyday moods and affective disorders are fundamentally the same, it can be evaluated in whatever ways are appropriate for determining that two entities are of a kind. The most obvious test involves matching the entities in terms of their distinctive features which, in this case, consists of the "symptoms" associated with each state. I will depend upon the most widely accepted classification of affective disorders, the *Diagnostic and Statistical Manual* (1987) (DSM-III-R) of the American Psychiatric Association, for determining the symptoms of affective disorder and then attempt to indicate the degree to which the correlates of everyday mood match.

Theories of Depression

In previous chapters (especially Chapters 3, 5, and 6) I have described processes that are triggered in normal people by bad moods and that have the capacity to make them even worse. For example, I reviewed a great deal of evidence showing that people who are in a bad mood often demonstrate bias in memory such that negative items are more likely to be retrieved. This effect has been found most consistently for recollections that are self-relevant. Furthermore, it is clear that remembering negative things about self is, in itself, an inducer of negative mood. Thus, one could easily imagine a vicious cycle due to (1) selective memory effects. Similar vicious cycles might arise in connection with the effect of mood on (2) self-focused attention, (3) perceptions of control, (4) evaluative judgments, especially of self, (5) expectations and perceptions of the reinforcement value of everyday activities, and (6) social behavior. In addition to vicious cycling resulting from mutually reinforcing effects of mood and each of the above-mentioned categories of mood-related processes and behaviors, vicious cycling might also proceed *across* these categories. Hyland (1987) argues that direct causal relationships among the various deficits associated with depressive disorders can help explain the relatively uniform psychological symptomatology that is characteristic of them (Miller, 1975).

Each of these positive feedback loops is implicated in one or more theories of depression. For the convenience of exposition, I have grouped the theories into *psychoanalytic, loss of control, cognitive, behavioral, social-interactive,* and *self-regulatory failure* categories but, as will soon be evident, many of the theories readily cross these arbitrary boundaries to account for the diverse symptomatology associated with affective disorders.

Psychoanalytic Theories of Depression. The classic psychoanalytic formulations of Freud (1986) and Abraham (1986) view depression as a complex reaction to loss. Major losses in life typically lead to mourning and grief but in the case of depression, grief goes overboard. Freud thought that pathological responding to loss was due to an overstrong superego that punished the individual with guilt over the loss. The result was "an extraordinary diminution of his self-regard, an impoverishment of his ego on a grand scale" (Freud, 1986, p. 51). The historical antecedent to such a response was supposedly loss or disturbance of an important relationship during early childhood that generates anger (toward the loved one) that the superego turns inward.

Freud's account of depression is a good one with which to begin because it is a prototypical example of how a theory is founded on the continuity hypothesis. The theory begins by noting the similarity between the etiology and symptoms of the "normal" state of mourning and the "pathological" state of depression:

> The correlation of melancholia and mourning seems justified by the general picture of the two conditions.... The distinguishing mental features of melancholia are a profoundly painful dejection, cessation of interest in the outside world, loss of the capacity to love, inhibition of all activity, and a lowering of the self-regarding feelings.... The disturbance of self-regard is absent in mourning; but otherwise the features are the same.... Moreover, the exciting causes due to environmental influences are, so far as we can discern them at all, the same for both conditions. (Freud, 1986, pps. 48–49)

Because both the normal and pathological states were said to result from an event we all encounter, namely loss, especially of a loved one, it became necessary to postulate the vulnerability that permitted some persons to become disordered while others coped. Freud's solution was to find the one nonoverlapping symptom in the cases he considered, namely, the disturbance of self-regard, and build his theory upon that. He was further encouraged in this direction because the differentiating symptom was the only one that did not seem an understandable, that is, rational (to him), consequence of the loss of a loved one.

Freud's discussion of depression seems surprisingly current in certain respects. For example, he acknowledged that depression came in different clinical forms and suspected that some had "somatic" bases. Anticipating the current controversy (see Chapter 5) as to the degree to which depressives' negative self-images are distorted or accurate, Freud wondered whether the self-reproach of the melancholic might not be justified by the facts:

> When in his heightened self-criticism he describes himself as petty, egoistic, dishonest, lacking in independence, one whose sole aim has been to hide the weaknesses of his own nature, it may be, so far as we know, that he has come pretty near to understanding himself; we only wonder why a man has to be ill before he can be accessible to truth of this kind. (Freud, 1986, p. 51)

Freud offered his ideas about the origin of depression in a rather tentative way, thereby inviting different views. Best known of the variants proposed by other psychodynamicists is that of Bibring (1953). Like Freud, he was impressed with the negativity of the self-image among the clinically depressed. Bibring concluded that this was due to the ego's recognition that it was helpless in regard to its most important aspirations which were:

> (1) the wish to be worthy, to be loved, to be appreciated, not to be inferior or unworthy; (2) the wish to be strong, superior, great, secure, not to be weak and insecure; and (3) the wish to be good, to be loving, not to be aggressive, hateful and destructive. (p. 27)

Once again, one is struck by the similarity of Bibring's views to a number of more modern accounts ranging from those that emphasize the loss of control (see Seligman, 1975), to those that propose that depressives are plagued by unrealistically high standards for self (see Weiner & White, 1982).

The rich texture of psychodynamic accounts continues to attract adherents (see Blatt, 1974), but as has so often been the case, the theory resists being rendered into testable hypotheses (Akiskal & McKinney, 1975; Coyne, 1986) and when it is, the results have not been encouraging (Crook & Elliot, 1980).

Loss of Control Theories of Depression. One of the most provocative theories of depression has been Seligman's "learned helplessness" theory (1975) that holds that generalized expectations of uncontrollability are sufficient to produce depression. One reason why the learned helplessness theory generated so much controversy was its brash dependence upon analog research with dogs and rats, and later with college students.

What attracted Seligman's attention was the similarity between some symptoms of clinical depression and the reactions of laboratory animals and college sophomores to noncontingent outcomes (uncontrollable shock for the animals and unsolvable problems for the sophomores), most especially a reduced tendency to initiate instrumental responding and an inability to learn when presented with a change in contingency. In his research with humans, Seligman (Miller and Seligman, 1973) was also able to show that noncontingent outcomes on laboratory tasks produced the negative cognitive set, for example, a tendency to attribute outcomes to luck that were actually the result of skilled actions by the actor, which Beck (1967) considers to be a key symptom of depressive disorders.

Ultimately, the theory was abandoned because it could not explain much of the data generated with human subjects (see Costello, 1978, for a review). Two main problems emerged. First, it became apparent to Seligman and his colleagues that a viable theory must address the tendency of subjects to try to make sense of the situation they were in through the processes of causal attribution. This recognition led to various revisions (see below). Second, and more damning of the studies spawned by the theory than of the theory itself, were data produced by Frankel and Snyder (1978) which implied that the standard noncontingent laboratory outcome, namely failure, was not producing passivity at all but, rather, a strategic attempt to protect self-esteem and self-image from further failure by trying less hard, that is, "sham" passivity. (See also Buchwald, Coyne, & Cole, 1978, for a similar argument.) These data suggest that the standard "helplessness" treatment, when used with unselected human lab subjects, does not produce effects similar to those observed in animal studies and actual clinical cases.

Cognitive Theories of Depression. During the last 20 years, cognitive theories of depression, especially those of Beck (1967, 1976; Kovacs & Beck, 1978) and the reformulated attributional versions (Abramson et al., 1978; Abramson et al., 1989) of learned helplessness theory (Seligman, 1975) have undoubtedly stimulated the greatest amount of interest and research. These theories and other related formulations, e.g., Ingram (1984), Olinger, Kuiper, and Shaw (1987), take the position that the way in which an individual thinks about and construes life events is responsible for the motivational, affective, and behavioral symptoms of depression. (An excellent review of theory and data implicating cognitive processes in depression has recently been provided by Alloy, 1988.)

Beck believes that unfavorable life experiences such as the loss of a parent or chronic peer group failure tend to produce a vulnerability so that when some stressful experience occurs, the individual tends to think about it in ways that are "depressogenic." Specifically, depression-prone individuals are subject to tendencies to think about self, circumstances, and the future in negative ways. They develop negative schemata that guide their explanations for their current situation and prevent them from changing their views when evidence inconsistent with their beliefs arises.

The reformulated version of learned helplessness theory (Abramson et al., 1978; Peterson & Seligman, 1984) focuses on one part of the cognitive machinery Beck held responsible for depression, namely, the way in which individuals explain or understand the events that occur in their lives. Critical events are those that signal loss of control, that is, where outcomes, especially important ones, do not appear to be contingent on one's behavior. As noted in Chapter 6, the theory argues that people vulnerable to depression are those whose attributions about the inability to exercise control are internal, global, and stable. This pattern of attributions results in self-blame that is generalized to broad areas of functioning, and is seen as chronic, thereby perpetuating the expectation that important outcomes cannot be controlled.

The success of these theories in generating research and novel therapeutic approaches is clear. Though there is little dispute that negative cognitions are associated with clinically significant depression, doubt remains as to their causal significance. (For reviews see Abramson et al., 1988; Alloy et al., 1988; Alloy & Abramson, 1988; Brewin, 1985; Coyne & Gotlib, 1983, 1986; Miller & Poretti, 1988; and Sweeney et al., 1986.)

Behavioral Theories of Depression. The key feature of behavioral theories of depression (Ferster, 1973; Lewinsohn, 1974) is their focus on a reduced rate of (contingent) positive reinforcement. According to Lewinsohn (1974), this low rate of reinforcement constitutes an extinction procedure that explains the low rate of various behaviors observed in depressed individuals. In addition, the low rate of reinforcement is presumed to be an unconditioned stimulus producing depressive symptoms such as dysphoria and fatigue. As extinction proceeds, a vicious cycle of even lower activity rates, further reduced reinforcement, and exacerbated symptoms occurs.

According to Lewinsohn, the rate of reinforcement for any given individual is a function of (1) the number of events that individual finds potentially reinforcing, that is, people who find few things in life to be gratifying are likely to encounter fewer reinforcements, (2) the number of potentially reinforcing events that are available in the person's environment, and (3) the ability to enact whatever skilled behaviors lead to reinforcement in his environment. Because so many of the important reinforcements we obtain in life are socially mediated, social losses through divorce, dislocation, death, and the lack of social skills receive particular attention from Lewinsohn (1974; Youngren & Lewinsohn, 1980). The modal picture of the onset of depression deriving from this theory is that of an individual who is heavily invested in one other person, a spouse or parent or child, who then loses that individual. The sudden sharp decrease in the availability of reinforcements coupled with the absence of substitutable alternative relationships and the inability to form new ones because of social ineptitude, combine to yield a gloomy prognosis. This picture is quite consistent with descriptive clinical accounts (Brown & Harris, 1978) of the psychosocial origins of depression.

In recent years, Lewinsohn has moved away from his earlier reliance upon a functional or behavioral approach to a more eclectic stance that considers the importance of cognitive and attentional (Lewinsohn, Hoberman, Teri, & Hautzinger, 1985) processes. A similar eclecticism marks the self-control (of reinforcement) model of depression offered by Rehm (1977). Inspired by the work of Kanfer (e.g., Kanfer & Karoly, 1972), this model assumes that stable functioning requires that an individual regulate his own behavior so that it is somewhat independent of controlling stimuli in the environment. The processes involved include *self-monitoring*, that is, attending to one's behavior and its antecedents and consequences, *self-evaluation*, that is, interpreting one's behavior and comparing it to an internal standard, and *self-reinforcement*, that is providing oneself with material reinforcers and praise (or blame). When one or more of these processes operates in a faulty way, symptoms of depression may result, especially when some interruption is experienced in the "normal" flow of environmental reinforcers. For example, selectively attending to negative performances, attributing negative performances to self, overly high standards, and stinginess toward self, have all been shown to be characteristic of depressed persons. The chief advantage of the self-control model is that its specificity lends itself to the development of theraputic interventions that appear to be somewhat successful (Rehm, 1982).

The pragmatism of this generation of reinforcement theorists preserves their presence on the scene but sometimes at the cost of careful theoretical statement and test. Nonetheless, it is to be hoped that careful attention to the role of reinforcement will not fade from the scene. Though a reduced rate of reinforcement is suspected by many to be a consequence rather than a primary cause of depression, it derives importance, even in this subsidiary role, because it seems particularly well-suited to account for the autonomy of clinically significant depression once it arises.

Social-Interactive Models of Depression. Advocates of the importance of social and interactional processes in the etiology of depression, such as, Brown and Harris (1978), Billings and Moos (1982), and Coyne (1976b), believe that the key to understanding whether individuals succumb to affective disorders after stressful life events lies in the sort of social behaviors they enact and the nature of their social support networks.

The most highly elaborated view is that of Coyne (1976a, 1976b, Coyne, Kessler, Tal, Turnbull, Wortman, & Greden, 1987, Strack & Coyne, 1983). He argues that negative life events cause people to experience dysphoric moods and seek social support and reassurance. The problem is that people in a bad mood make generally unpleasant company. Expressions of depressed affect and disclosures marked by self-devaluation and hopelessness have been shown to lead to negative evaluations and rejection (Gurtman, 1987). Demands for support may strain ongoing relationships, viciously creating the need for even more support and reassurance (e.g., see Pearlin and Schooler, 1978). Friends, relatives, and coworkers may find such interactions aversive (as may therapists!; see Cohen, Baker, Cohen, Fromm-Reichmann, & Weigert, 1954) but be unwilling to directly express their annoyance for fear of making matters worse. And yet, evidence shows that the depressed person is aware of how undesirable others find them as interaction partners (Strack & Coyne, 1983). It is easy to see how such a scenario, multiplied over occasions and significant others, could significantly exacerbate the original bad mood into something much more serious.

And yet, it is also clear that one of the most potent protections against the development of depression in response to stressful life events is the existence of a strong social support network (Billings & Moos, 1982; Oatley & Bolton, 1985) and, especially, the presence of a close, confiding relationship (Brown & Harris, 1978). Such findings underline the importance of conducting fine-grained analyses of the interactions between dysphoric individuals and their interaction partners both together and with others to determine the specific conditions responsible for amelioration versus intensification. One likely candidate would appear to be the way in which the need for support becomes known. As noted above, support that one must ask for, verbally or nonverbally, may be viewed as counterfeit and generate negative feelings in the recipient above and beyond that associated with his need (Fisher, Nadler, & Whitcher-Alagna, 1982). Thus, the combination of a person who is reluctant to request support along with an individual who is sensitive to the indication that it is needed may produce the most favorable outcome.

Self-Regulatory Failure Theories of Depression. The last theories I will consider regard depressive disorders to be the result of either the absence or dysfunction of self-regulatory processes that "normally" facilitate adjustment to, and recovery from, events capable of producing depressive affect. These theories arise out of the fertile soil provided by general cybernetic models of purposive behavior (e.g., Powers, 1973a, 1973b), and especially their application to self-regulation in the form of what has been termed *control theory* (Carver & Scheier, 1981).

As noted in Chapter 5, the basic unit in control theory is the negative feedback loop. Each such loop has a standard or reference criterion corresponding to an individual's goal. Goals are assumed to be hierarchically arranged with higher level goals, referred to as *principle* level goals, governing lower or *program* level goals. Principle level goals include valued end-states such as freedom or happiness and ideal characteristics of self, for example, being honest, responsible, or hard-working; program level goals are those specific outcomes that are seen as leading to or supporting principle level goals. Periodically or especially as the result of environmental events such as goal-related outcomes, progress toward achieving or maintaining goals is assessed, that is, perceptual input is gathered and compared to the reference criterion. The discrepancy between the two, sometimes referred to as *error*, functions to generate behavior designed to reduce the disparity. The degree of vigor associated with this reaction is a function of *error sensitivity* (Hyland, 1987) which refers to the amplification of the signal produced by error. Sensitivity is, in part, a function of the salience of the goal.

One way of connecting such a system to mood is to suppose, as have Duval and Wicklund (1972) and Pyszczynski and Greenberg (1987), that error triggers negative affect or mood which, because it is aversive, motivates error- (and mood-) reducing behavior.[1] Notice that such a cue-motivator function is exactly the role early mood theorists, for example, Nowlis, Jacobsen, and Pribram (see Chapter 1), cast for the construct.

[1]However, Carver and Scheier (1981) do not employ mood in this way. Rather, they suppose that negative affect arises only to the extent that the individual perceives a low likelihood of being able to reduce the perceived discrepancy between the reference criterion and the existing state of affairs. Although there are some data consistent with this assumption (Carver et al., 1979; Steenbarger & Aderman, 1979), the issue is far from settled at this point (see the discussion in Pyszczynski & Greenberg, 1987).

The most obvious way to eliminate error and error-induced bad mood is to act upon the environment in such a way that perceptual input is altered in the direction of the criterion but other possibilities exist: one may alter one's perception of the environment, one may reduce one's sensitivity to the discrepancy, or one may change the reference criterion. It is worth mentioning that a way of coping that would be relatively ineffective according to control theory is to take steps to attenuate the affect itself, that is, emotion-focused coping (see Chapter 5). Even if one were successful in temporarily doing so, because the error would be unaffected, the system would eventually retrigger.

Hyland (1987) has proposed a control theory interpretation of depression. According to this view:

> Prolonged discrepancy between reference criterion and perceptual input in a control loop characterized by high error sensitivity ... is a sufficient condition for depression. (p. 111)

Though we are all subject to short-term discrepancies, which Hyland refers to as *transient mismatches*, people vulnerable to depression are those who do not avail themselves of the self-regulatory possibilities suggested by control theory and described above, namely, change of perceptual input, change in error sensitivity, and change in reference criterion.[2] The result is that the discrepancy remains.

Hyland regards his theory to be an integration of previous theories of depression that implicate the inability to achieve a given goal as playing a central role in the development of the disorder. Specific examples would be learned helplessness theory where the goal is to perceive oneself to be in control of important outcomes, psychoanalytic theories such as those of Freud and Bibring that focus on an unsatisfactory level of self-esteem, and behavioral theories that emphasize an inadequate rate of reinforcements.

The most relevant evidence for evaluating the theory would come from studies comparing depressives and normals in their use of the self-protective mechanisms described above. Most supportive are the accumulated data suggesting that depressives evaluate themselves realistically as compared with normals who display egotistic biases such as the "illusion of control" (see Alloy & Abramson, 1988 and Miller & Poretti, 1988 for reviews of this evidence). Such bias amounts to a change in the perceptual input. Also consistent with the theory are the data of Pyszczynski and Greenberg (1985, 1986) that I reviewed in Chapter 6. These researchers showed that normals avoided self-focus more after failure than after success (Pyszczynski & Greenberg, 1985) whereas depressed individuals showed the opposite pat-

---

[2]Hyland (1987) does not mention the possibility of changing to a different instrumental behavior, that is, problem-focused coping, as a way of dealing with transient mismatch. It may be that he is implicitly assuming that the goal in question has become (is perceived to be) unattainable.

tern (Pyszczynski & Greenberg, 1986). Self-focusing increases error sensitivity by making discrepancies between accomplishments and goals more salient, therefore, these data suggest that normals reduce error sensitivity if it is painful but depressed individuals not only fail to employ this self-protective device, they actually move in the opposite direction.

It is too early to tell how much attention Hyland's effort will receive. Its chief advantage is the well-established conceptual and empirical framework supplied by control theory whose proponents are vigorously pushing its application to clinical problems (e.g., Carver & Scheier, 1982, 1986). In addition, the theory stands to profit from parallel developments in the study of coping processes associated with stress (e.g., see Lazarus & Folkman, 1984).

Another recently proposed theory of self-regulatory failure is that of Pyszczynski and Greenberg (1987). Like Hyland, Pyszczynski and Greenberg employ the general framework provided by control theory, merging it with an emphasis on the role of self-awareness (Duval & Wicklund, 1972; Wicklund, 1975) or self-focused attention (Carver & Scheier, 1981).

Within control theory, self-focused attention leads to the comparison of standards to existing levels of accomplishment, thereby functioning to maintain the individual's pursuit of important goals. When the goal is reached, the control loop is exited and self-focused attention ceases. Alternatively, when instrumental behaviors are not producing satisfactory progress toward the goal, an assessment is made of the likelihood that the gap can be narrowed. If the assessment is optimistic, further efforts ensue, if pessimistic, the individual is expected to withdraw effort and experience negative affect but in either case, the state of self-focused attention is temporary and ends with satisfactory discrepancy reduction or disengagement.

The theory of depression offered by Pyszczynski and Greenberg originates in the observations already noted in Chapters 5 and 6 showing that depressed individuals are highly and chronically self-focused during depressive episodes, for example, Smith and Greenberg (1981), Ingram and Smith (1984), Ingram, Lumry, Cruet, and Sieber (1987). They go on to propose that under some circumstances, one can become stuck in a state of self-focused attention, unable to disengage from an unattainable goal. It is this condition that leads toward the widening spiral of symptomatology that defines depression.

Problems begin with what Pyszczynski and Greenberg (1987) call an "irreducible discrepancy" (p. 126). Normally such unattainable goals are dealt with by abandoning them or through the pursuit of substitute goals. Alternatively, protective cognitive mechanisms of the sort discussed by Hyland (1987) might be employed, such as, minimizing the importance of the goal. But in some cases, most often when what is lost is of central importance to the person, the result may be fruitless persistence, that is, one is unable to exit the loop.

The inability to exit the loop means that self-focus persists, maintaining awareness of the discrepancy and the negative affect that accompanies it.

Like a snowball rolling downhill, the process gains momentum. Because the self-focus persists, self-blame is more likely, a conclusion that follows from evidence showing that causal attributions are attracted to salient stimuli (for example, Taylor & Fiske, 1978), here, the self. And, self-blame for failure increases the amount of anguish experienced (McFarland & Ross, 1982).

> The mounting self-criticism, negative affect, and self-blame begin to push the individual's self-image in a negative direction. To the extent that the individual's self-image was highly dependent on the lost object, the stability of his or her self-schema is likely to be undermined. The loss of stability in the self-image, coupled with the other consequences of self-regulatory perseveration, make a shift to a negative self-image quite likely. (Pyszczynski & Greenberg, 1987, p. 127)

Now preoccupied with disturbing thoughts, cognitive functioning is compromised (Miller, 1975) and the individual is more likely to experience failure in other realms of his life, attributing these in like fashion to self. At some point, the need for reassurance may build to the point where one's social relationships are compromised as well (Coyne, 1976b).

The final stroke according to Pyszczynski and Greenberg is the development of the *depressive self-focusing style* discussed above. Though the depressed individual is now highly and chronically self-focused with respect to his shortcomings, should a positive outcome occur, self-focus is actively avoided (Greenberg & Pyszczynski, 1986; Pyszczynski & Greenberg, 1986):

> [B]ecause positive outcomes may be viewed as distractions that interfere with efforts to work out problems, self-focus may be avoided when positive outcomes occur. After a significant loss, people do not want to be temporarily cheered up; rather, they want their problems to be resolved. In addition, dwelling on positive outcomes might suggest cause for optimism, which would provide the possibility of further disappointment and disillusionment. (p. 127)

The Pyszczynski and Greenberg approach is distinctive in that it does not directly implicate some characteristic of the person as the source of vulnerability to depression. Rather, it is the nature of the loss or failure that accounts for disorder. Though they attribute an important role to the depressive self-focusing style, Pyszczynski and Greenberg clearly state that this is a consequence of experiencing a loss that can neither be restored nor abandoned. The closest they come to indicating a basis for depression in personality is when they suggest that those who succumb may be too heavily dependent upon some other person as a source of self-worth.

This theory is impressive in its specification of the linkages among the various psychological symptoms and it profits from the rather large experimental and individual difference literatures on the effects of self-awareness. Indeed, Pyszczynski and Greenberg are not alone in advancing theories of depression that depend on the perturbation of self-attentional processes (e.g., see Kanfer & Hagerman, 1981; Lewinsohn et al., 1985; Kuhl & Helle, 1986), although their theory is more ambitious than the others. Moreover, the idea that perseverating self-focus is responsible for worsening also fits well with the view that persistently mulling over one's problems may be a risk factor for depression (Nolen-Hoeksema, 1987). Finally, the notion that a self-regulatory loop is running amok, continually producing an error message, can nicely account for the state markers referred to as *automatic thoughts* (Beck, 1976; Hollon & Kendall, 1980; Hollon, Kendall, & Lumry, 1986; Beck, Brown, Steer, Eidelson, & Riskind, 1987) and *ruminative thinking* (Nelson & Mazure, 1985). These intrusive and repetitive stream-of-consciousness thoughts, such as "I'm a loser" and "Nothing ever works out for me," sound like output from such a loop.

To these virtues, I would add the observation that accounts of disordered mood that focus on attentional processes fit most comfortably within the comprehensive figure-ground treatment of mood I am trying to advance in this monograph. Attentional processes are our way of dealing with a complex and demanding world where multiple tasks must be accomplished in an orderly way. Focal attention represents a high effort, high resolution processing reserved for those goals that are momentarily of greatest significance. Mood is the signal that operates in this system to attract focal attention. But signalling systems can go awry, especially when one cannot "turn off" the signal. In such a case, the signal itself becomes punishing in much the way an alarm clock that cannot be turned off might. Not only is the persistent signal punishing but, in addition, until it can be eliminated it interferes with one's ability to sequence other goals through focal attention in that the mood itself becomes the priority concern.

Psychological Theories of Depression: A Modest Conclusion

I trust I have fulfilled any expectation I might have created by describing psychological theories of depression as "surprisingly diverse." The existence of such a richly varied set of accounts is undoubtedly a product of the fact that depression presents in the form of a syndrome or set of symptoms, some of which offer possible insights into etiology. Most of the theories reviewed above originated in a theorist being attracted to a particular psychological symptom that was proposed as the proximal psychological event in a diathesis-stress model of depression.

Each of the theories can claim some empirical support with the result that recent theoretical efforts, for example, Hyland (1987) and Pyszczynski and Greenberg (1987), look to integrate the various processes proposed by prior theorists into their more complex models. Unfortunately, the sort of studies that must be done to effectively assess the comparative ability of the various theories to account for the development of depressive disorders, namely prospective studies with at risk populations, have not been attempted. Instead, analog studies that examine the validity of single theorized links have been the rule. Thus, I am forced to agree with Coyne (1986) who observed that "the ascension of one theory over another is more often a conceptual than an empirical matter" (p. 422). Conceptual appeal seems to rise and fade with the times. It would appear that theories within a particular category temporarily dominate the scene as part of a broader *Zeitgeist* only to give way to theories from some other category; the cognitive theories that dominated from the mid 1970s through the mid 1980s may now give way to the self-regulatory theories that have recently been proposed.

Though the empirical literature relating to theories of depression is disappointing to those who hope to find a single best etiology, it does provide broad support for the continuity hypothesis in the sense that many studies exist documenting a possible path whereby initially "normal" levels of mood might worsen until a disordered state is reached. But even here, longitudinal studies, especially ones that antedate initial depressive episodes are needed though it must be acknowledged that such studies are enormously costly and time-consuming.

Matching Symptoms of Depression With Correlates of Everyday Mood

The next step in evaluating the continuity hypothesis is to determine the degree to which the broad domain of symptoms recognized as characteristic of depressive disorders can be matched with the effects associated with everyday levels of bad mood. Though the continuity hypothesis was originally proposed because of the similarity between the *feeling state* associated with the universal human experience of depression and that reported by individuals judged to have a depressive *disorder*, the expanding literature on the effects of normal bad moods now permits an assessment of the degree of *syndromal similarity* between the two states. This exercise is particularly important in that clinicians use the presence of a cluster of symptoms as one way of distinguishing between normal mood swings and pathological affect (Whybrow et al., 1984). For example, in discussing the symptoms of mania, Tyrer and Shopsin (1982) note that "The diagnosis of mania is not synonymous with euphoria and elation. The term mania refers to a *syndrome*" (p. 14, italics added).

Diagnosis of depressive disorders is difficult because the most prominent symptom, dysphoric mood, that is, feeling depressed, irritable, and worried, can be found when no pathology exists and also in connection with other kinds of pathology such as alcoholism (see Robins & Guze, 1972, for a longer list). Consequently, a great deal of effort has been expended on assembling the sets of symptoms and other markers that characterize and distinguish between depressive and other affective disorders.

The most generally accepted classification scheme is the *Diagnostic and Statistical Manual* (*DSM-III-R, 1987*, being the current version) produced by the American Psychiatric Association. It breaks affective disorders down into two main categories:[3] *major affective illness*, including bipolar disorder and major (unipolar) depression, and *other specific disorders*, including cyclothymia and dysthymia. Because cyclothymia and dysthymia present with symptoms that are less severe but similar to those associated with bipolar and major unipolar disorder, it is tempting to interpose them between the major disorders and everyday mood fluctuations in an expanded continuity hypothesis. I will attempt to evaluate that possibility after considering the simpler version of the continuity hypothesis that deals only with "everyday" depression and major depressive disorder.

As noted in Chapter 4, the two most common hallmarks of major depressive disorder are dysphoric affect and the loss of interest or pleasure (anhedonia) in almost all usual activities and pastimes. Other symptoms that contribute to the diagnosis are: (1) significant weight loss or weight gain or decrease or increase in appetite, (2) insomnia or hypersomnia, (3) psychomotor agitation or retardation, (4) fatigue or loss of energy, (5) feelings of worthlessness or excessive or inappropriate guilt, (6) diminished ability to think or concentrate, or indecisiveness, (7) recurrent thoughts of death or suicide.

Some cases of major depression are especially severe and labeled as major depressive disorder with melancholia. These cases are described as *autonomous* in the sense that they resist psychosocial intervention, leaving drugs and electroconvulsive shock as treatments of choice. The symptoms associated with melancholia are: (1) loss of interest or pleasure in all, or almost all activities, (2) lack of reactivity to usually pleasurable stimuli, (3) depression regularly worse in the morning, (4) early morning awakening, (5) psychomotor retardation or agitation, and (6) significant anorexia or weight loss. Matching melancholic symptomatology with everyday depression is a sterner test for the continuity hypothesis in that it has a larger proportion of vegetative or somatic (as opposed to psychological) signs than does major depression without melancholia.

Matched "Symptoms" of Everyday Depressed Mood

(1) *Affect.* Though it was the similarity of the subjective feelings associated with everyday depression to those associated with clinical episodes that originally encouraged the continuity hypothesis, it is still possible that careful evaluation would show the affects to be qualitatively different. Whybrow et al. (1984), for example, contrast ordinary "transient depressive mood" with the clinical variety by suggesting that the former is more akin to anxiety while the latter is also marked by anhedonia, that is, the inability to experience pleasure.

[3] A third category, *atypical affective disorder*, has also been recognized.

This observation translates readily into the two-factor structure of mood identified by Watson and Tellegen (1985) that was discussed in Chapter 6. Within that scheme, the distinction made by Whybrow et al. is equivalent to saying that everyday dysphoria consists of simply being high on the negative affect dimension whereas the affective state of a person suffering from major unipolar disorder is a combination of being high on the negative affect dimension and low on the positive affect dimension (see Figure 6.1) Data recently reported by Bouman and Luteijn (1986) are consistent with this characterization of the affective state of major depressives. As compared to a group of psychiatric controls, they scored higher on a measure of state anxiety *and* lower on measures of the frequency and enjoyability of pleasant events.

However, contrary to the suggestion of Whybrow et al. (1984), available evidence suggests that "normal" subjects induced to experience dysphoric affect also show a reduced capacity to experience pleasure, thereby supporting the continuity hypothesis. The first such indication came from data reported by Carson and Adams (1980). These investigators manipulated depression using the Velten procedure and found that this led to reduced ratings of the enjoyability of everyday events using the same measure employed by Bouman and Luteijn (1986), namely the Pleasant Events Schedule of MacPhillamy and Lewinsohn (1971). Though these data are relatively weak in that they derive from self-reports gathered in a setting where demand characteristics are high, converging evidence comes from a study by Barden et al. (1981) that does not suffer from these problems. Using child subjects, Barden et al. found that typical behavioral consequences of good and bad mood inductions did not appear among subjects who were first exposed to an oppositely-valenced affect induction. They interpreted these results to mean that when consecutive affect-inducing events occur, the first "innoculates" against the second. This conclusion is compatible with the idea that dysphoric mood interferes with the ability of positive events to engender a positive affective response. Finally, the results of Diener and Emmons (1984) and Diener and Iran-Nejad (1986) that were discussed in Chapter 6 also show that experiences of enjoyment and happiness are incompatible with those of depression in normal subjects, especially if the depression is strongly felt.

The combined data of Barden et al. (1981), Bouman and Luteijn (1986), Carson and Adams (1980), Diener and Emmons (1984) and Diener and Iran-Nejad (1986) provide clear support for the continuity hypothesis insofar as comparisons of the affective states of clinically depressed versus normally "blue" subjects is concerned. Though major unipolar depression may be associated with a far more profound deficit than is displayed by normals as far as the capability to experience pleasure is concerned, it appears that a form of anhedonia is present in both cases.

The other affective marker of clinically significant depression (of the melancholic variety) that one might wish to compare to the experiences of normals is that the feeling of depression is worse in the morning.[4] Assessment of the continuity hypothesis with regard to this symptom requires comparison data indicating typical diurnal patterns of affect among normal subjects who are undergoing some sort of stress. Two studies (Robbins & Tanck, 1987; Thayer, 1987b, Study 1[5]) have recently reported such results.

Thayer (1987b, Study 1) asked his subjects, six females and two males who were undergoing a bothersome personal problem of somewhat longstanding duration (e.g., a painful marital separation, an unyielding weight problem, severe parental discord), to record their mood on five separate occasions each day: immediately upon arising, 11 AM, 4 PM, just before sleep, and after a rapid 10-minute walk at any chosen time of day (the time of day varied across subjects but for any given subject the walk was to be the same time each day) but at least 1.5 hours away from any other rating occasion. Moods were measured using the Short Form Activation-Deactivation Adjective Check List (Thayer, 1967) which produces two scores: one for "energetic arousal" measured by the adjectives "energetic," "lively," "active," "vigorous," and "full of pep," and one for "tense arousal" measured by the adjectives "tense," "clutched-up," "fearful," "jittery," and "intense." Notice that these sets of terms correspond well with what Watson and Tellegen (1985) claim to be measures of Positive and Negative affect though they do not directly measure "depressed" affect. Subjects were required to select 10 days out of a 3- to 4-week experimental period for recording, choosing days that were as much alike as possible in terms of previous night's sleep, time of awakening, and anticipated daily activities. Analysis of variance revealed that tense arousal (negative affect) did not vary significantly as a function of time of completion but the effect of time of day (including the occasion of exercise as one level) was highly significant for energetic arousal (positive affect). Subjects reported the lowest energetic arousal on waking and before sleep and the highest energetic arousal during late morning and after waking.

Robbins and Tanck (1987) asked 105 undergraduates to complete a daily diary for 10 days. At the end of each day, subjects were asked to indicate whether or not they had been depressed at any time during the day and, if so, to indicate which of eight patterns of diurnal variability best fit their experience that day. The patterns included: most morning-least afternoon, most morning-least evening, most afternoon-least morning, most afternoon-least evening, most evening-least morning, most evening-least afternoon,

[4]It is not clear whether this means that the low point of the day occurs in the morning or whether, on average, dysphoric affect is worst during the morning as compared with the afternoon and evening. As will become evident when I compare (below) results reported by Thayer (1987b) and Robbins and Tanck (1987), this is a troublesome ambiguity.

[5]Thayer (1987b, Study 2) also reports data on mood variation within days but because 11 AM and 4 PM were the only times used they permit only the most limited of pictures of diurnal patterning.

same all day long. Ninety-five subjects reported feeling depressed on at least 1 day during the 10-day period. The most frequent pattern showed depression lowest in the morning and highest in the evening, least likely was depression that was worst in the morning and least in the afternoon; diurnal variation was the rule with only 16% of all instances being described as "the same all day long." The authors concluded that, contrary to the continuity hypothesis, the diurnal pattern of mild depression is opposite to that which is associated with melancholic depression.

Various features of these studies prevent firm conclusions about the continuity hypothesis.[6] The main problem with the data reported by Thayer is that he measured "tense" and "energetic" arousal rather than depressive affect. Though the analysis of Watson and Tellegen (1985) and the data of Bouman and Luteijn (1986) show that depressed affect is associated with high Negative affect scores and low scores on Positive affect, it is not clear how to directly derive an index of depression from these scores. Perhaps a better indication of depressive affect are ratings Thayer asked subjects to make (on each rating occasion) of how serious and unsolvable their particular problem (remember that each subject had some ongoing problem) seemed to be; because optimism-pessimism is clearly a correlate of depressed affect we might substitute one measure for the other. A one-way analysis of variance with measurement occasion as the independent variable was marginally significant with problems seeming most solvable in the late morning and after a walk. No particular time was associated with problems seeming worst for all subjects, but Thayer does report that personal worst times (when problems seem least solvable) are those when energetic arousal is rated lowest and tense arousal highest. Of the eight subjects, this occasion is on awakening for three, 4 PM for two, and before sleep for three.

There are a number of problems with the Robbins and Tanck data but the most serious is the inappropriateness of the majority of their sample for purposes of testing the continuity hypothesis. The Robbins and Tanck sample, unlike the Thayer sample, was not selected for any sort of ongoing problem. Rather, the data they report on diurnal patterns of depressed affect presumably reflect mostly within-day variations among those individuals who experience some "garden variety" negative life event, the effect of which appears to be felt entirely during a given day with no carryover to the next (Stone & Neale, 1984). From a general methodological point of view, (normal) subjects with ongoing problems would seem the more appropriate sample to compare with cases of major unipolar disorder[7] in that depressive

[6]In fairness it should be noted that Thayer did not intend to shed light on that particular hypothesis whereas Robbins and Tanck did.

[7]This same point is valid for all tests of the continuity hypothesis. Consequently, there are very few such valid tests as the majority of data come from laboratory studies with normal subjects where depressed affect is temporarily induced. However, it seems reasonable to assume that if one can obtain similar "symptoms" with such

episodes must last for at least 2 weeks before a diagnosis can be confirmed and, in this sense, their problems might also be described as "ongoing." Holding chronicity of problem constant gives vicious cycling processes an equal opportunity to produce symptomatology in either group. Chronicity of stress also seems especially important in the case of this particular symptom of mood being worse in the morning because, by definition, ongoing problems would be there as soon as one awoke in the morning. From a design standpoint this is important as it "protects" the (average) morning rating from cases that are irrelevant as far as this symptom is concerned, namely those cases where the depressed affect results from an event occurring later in the day.

In view of this argument, it is interesting to note that Robbins and Tanck (1987) identified a subgroup (34%) of their sample who had at least one day of depression they described as "the same all day." Compared with subjects who reported diurnal variation in their depressive affect, this subgroup reported that (1) their affect was more intense, (2) they experienced more physical symptoms, (3) they were depressed more days, and (4) they derived less pleasure from their social relationships. Furthermore, examination of the explanations subjects offered for these relatively recurrent, intense, anhedonic, and diurnally stable episodes of depressed affect showed them most often to be associated with "lingering" problems, for example, school difficulties, relationship woes, or general feelings of malaise pertaining to school or relationships. Given the logic discussed above, I would consider this subset of subjects to be a more appropriate sample for purposes of evaluating the continuity hypothesis and more nearly equivalent to the sample employed by Thayer (1987b, Study 1).

The continuity hypothesis emerges with little support but at least escapes the damage claimed by Robbins and Tanck (1987). If I am right in arguing that the majority of the subjects used by Robbins and Tanck are inappropriate for purposes of evaluating the continuity hypothesis, then the most harmful argument they can make is that unlike victims of melancholic depression whose mood is worse in the morning, subjects with lingering problems perceive their depressive mood to be stable throughout the day. However, Thayer's data showing substantial morning variation in energy levels among individuals with ongoing problems suggests that similar subjects (those with lingering problems) in the Robbin's and Tanck study might have had trouble making the judgments asked of them. If morning moods are highly variable, one might be disinclined to characterize them in terms of average level. Or, to put it more precisely, high variability should dis-

---

treatments, the continuity hypothesis is supported. It is only when there is a failure to find support for the continuity hypothesis that one might invoke this point and argue that subjects with ongoing problems must be studied. Though this seems to offer an "unfair" advantage to the continuity hypothesis, it is not clear what to do about the situation.

courage the making of distinctions and encourage the null judgment of "same all day." I conclude that this description of diurnal patterning may be concealing the fact that one's lowest single point occurred in the morning. And remember that this was established to be the case for three of Thayer's eight subjects if ratings of problem seriousness can be substituted for self-reports of depression.

(2) *Increased or decreased appetite and weight loss or weight gain.* Because everyday moods are typically brief, there are no data on weight change. However, the evidence from studies looking at the relationship of mood to eating and self-reported appetite are consistent with the continuity hypothesis. Studies by Ruderman (1983) and Mehrabian and Riccioni (1986) suggest that negative mood states can either increase or decrease appetite among normals. Ruderman (1983) found that food consumption by obese individuals was inversely related to how anxious they were. Mehrabian and Riccioni (1986) asked their subjects to report the way in which their eating was affected by depressive affects (loneliness, unhappiness, boredom, sadness, and depression) versus "distressed" affects (pained, humiliated, puzzled, unsafe, embarrassed). Consistent with Ruderman's results, Mehrabian and Riccioni report that distressed affects, which seem closely related to anxiety, are perceived to interfere with appetite and eating whereas the depressive affects are associated with increased hunger and food consumption, especially among subjects who report experiencing uncontrollable urges to eat. Finally, Frost et al. (1982) manipulated depressed versus neutral mood using the Velten procedure and found that subjects who characteristically fluctuate a good deal in weight ate more freely available food after the depression induction; no such effects were found among subjects with stable weights. These results closely match the self-report data obtained by Mehrabian and Riccioni (1986).

(3) *Sleep disturbance.* The belief that distressing life circumstances lead to depressive affect and interfere with normal sleep (and dreams) is so widespread and generally accepted that the assertion of a relationship is sometimes made without bothering to offer evidence, for example, see Whybrow et al. (1984, p. 16). Though weak evidence of a negative life event-sleep disturbance relationship does exist (Cernovsky, 1984), it is based on retrospective self-reports. A self-report methodology is particularly suspect when there is reason to believe that subjects have expectations about the relationship between the variables being measured (Nisbett & Wilson, 1977), and that is clearly the case with respect to mood and sleep (Wilson et al., 1982). What we need are data on the mood-sleep relationship where the sleep data are objective in nature.

Such data have been reported by Berry and Webb (1983, 1985). These researchers examined the relation between self-reported mood states in normal middle-aged volunteer subjects and sleep variables measured objectively in a sleep laboratory. Unfortunately, the data from these two studies are not analyzed in an optimal way and, in addition, the results of the two studies appear to be somewhat contradictory.

In the initial study, healthy male and female subjects spent four nights in the sleep laboratory but mood reports were apparently gathered only on the second evening and thus only one set of prior mood-subsequent sleep correlations are available.[8] Given that there are 90 such correlations (5 mood variables × 18 sleep variables) and that the degree of intercorrelation within each class of variables is not reported, any given significant result would not mean much unless it could be shown to replicate across days (that could not be ascertained in this study). The one clear outcome was that there were substantially more significant correlations among females than males, a result that Berry and Webb attribute to greater sensitivity of females to state variables. One intriguing result in the female data was that the more depressed they were on retiring, the lower the latency to their first REM period. Latency to first REM period has been suggested as a marker of depressive disease (Kupfer, 1977).

In an attempt to follow up on these results, Berry and Webb (1985) replicated and extended their original study using 25 middle-aged females judged to be normal and healthy. On this occasion, they collected mood reports on the last three of the four nights that subjects spent in the sleep lab. Increasing the number of mood measurements permitted the data to be examined for results that replicated across days, increasing confidence that they were more than chance results. Only 1 of the 144 (18 sleep variables × 8 mood variables, 3 having been added to the original 5) possible relationships between mood and subsequent sleep was significant (*alpha* had been set at 0.01) on more than one occasion . . . cheerfulness was negatively related to latency to first REM period on the second and third days of the study. Notice that this finding is a substantive reversal of the depression-REM latency relationship reported by Berry and Webb (1983) if one assumes that being depressed and being cheerful are negatively correlated. The only evidence of replicability of results *across* the two data sets is in the relationship between anxiety and disturbed sleep. In the initial data set, high anxiety before retiring was associated with frequent and long periods of awakening during sleep (among females). In the second data set, anxiety was associated with low sleep efficiency, that is, the percent of bedtime that was sleep, but this association was significant on only one of three possible occasions. Berry and Webb (1985) conclude that:

> This limited covariation between mood and sleep variables is consistent with the notion of sleep as a predominately biologically determined be-

---

[8]Correlations between Night 1 sleep variables and mood reports collected on Night 2 were also reported. More numerous significant correlations were found in the sleep-mood direction, but these are not relevant to the present discussion.

havior which is, in normal subjects, largely buffered from the effects of day-to-day mood variations. (p. 1727)

My own view of the Berry and Webb data is that a clearer picture might have emerged had the authors taken a factor analytic approach to their results. It is also worth noting that Berry and Webb (1985) found a large number of significant relationships involving latency to first REM period though only the cheerfulness result replicated across days. In view of the report by Hauri (1983) showing that latency to first REM period clusters with variables indicative of disturbed sleep, more research would seem necessary before rejecting the possibility that mood influences sleep among normals. Finally, it is possible that sleep disturbances are not found among normals except when undergoing negative life events. With only 25 subjects recording across three days, the likelihood is that very few such events were captured.

As for hypersomnia, little is known about it in normals and none of the available data permit an examination of the degree to which it is produced by depressed affect. However, it is interesting that oversleeping, considered as an independent variable, has been related to self-reports of heightened depressive affect and fatigue and impaired cognitive functioning (Globus, 1969) and that these subjective reports have been corroborated by sleep laboratory data (Taub, 1980) showing that when extended amounts of ad lib sleep are permitted (resulting in an augmentation of 2.1 hours over normal sleep time), various kinds of performance decrements and heightened feelings of sleepiness can be observed on arising as compared to control nights. Such findings suggest that when (and if) hypersomnia is produced by depression, it can participate in yet another vicious cycle.

Finally, early-morning (at least 2 hours before normal) awakening, a symptom of melancholic depression, has not been specifically examined among normals or normals exposed to ongoing problems.

(4) *Psychomotor agitation or retardation.* Evidence consistent with the continuity hypothesis can be found for this symptom but only for retardation. Such evidence comes from correlational studies (Johnson, 1937; Mayer & Bremer, 1985) and studies that manipulated mood (e.g., Hale & Strickland, 1976; Natale, 1977; Velten, 1968). Findings show that more depressed mood is associated with less spontaneous verbalization (Johnson, 1937; Velten, 1968), slower speech rate (Mayer & Bremer, 1985; Natale, 1977). slower writing speed (Hale & Strickland, 1976; Velten, 1968), and slower time to complete a letter cancellation task (Mayer & Bremer, 1985).

The failure to find evidence for psychomotor agitation may be due to the fact that in none of the studies reported above is there any evidence of elevated levels of anxious affect that is known to be present in clinically depressed individuals (Bouman & Luteijn, 1986). Perhaps it is only when anxious affect predominates that one will find agitation. (Recall that a depression/anxiety distinction proved important in predicting the relation between affect and eating behavior.) The studies that manipulated affect used the Velten procedure that is designed to mimic the effects of pure depressive affect. Velten presumed that one such effect was psychomotor retardation and included a number of statements in his procedure suggesting the lack of energy and general sluggishness.[9] Of the studies that measured existing affect, Johnson (1937) relied upon a simple euphoria-depression rating but Mayer and Bremer (1985) used multiple adjectives and did do a factor analysis. The correlations that I reported above were between measures of psychomotor speed and a bipolar factor that Mayer and Bremer described as pleasant arousal versus unpleasant tiredness with the latter end anchored by the terms "discontent," "inactive," and "blue." The other principal factor they identified was anchored at its negative end by the terms "fearful" and "stirred up," which sounds more like anxiety. However, scores on this factor showed very small and generally uninterpretable relationships with the various performance measures.

(5) *Fatigue or loss of energy.* There would appear to be little need to document that a relationship exists between feelings of fatigue and depression in normal individuals. Though a lack of energy can be conceptually distinguished from the feeling and thought processes that define what it means to be depressed, few have tried to maintain the distinction. Indeed, the most common manipulation of depressed affect, the Velten procedure (1968), uses statements that focus equally upon mood, thought, and physical energy levels.

(6) *Feelings of worthlessness, self-reproach, or inappropriate guilt.* Though these are certainly stronger terms than one typically finds in the literature relating depressed mood to self-evaluative responses, they surely do not differ in kind. Sad mood induced in the laboratory clearly results in more negative self-evaluative responses (e.g., Salovey, 1987; Wright & Mischel, 1982).

(7) *Diminished ability to think clearly or concentrate or indecisiveness.* The literature relevant to this symptom is small and inconclusive. Some of the studies mentioned above under the category of psychomotor retardation could be reinterpreted as evidence suggesting the inability to concentrate. For example, Mayer and Bremer (1985) report that mood correlates with performance on a task where subjects are required to read through columns of letters as quickly as possible and cancel every instance of a particular letter. (The psychomotor interpretation seems a bit stronger in that mood was similarly correlated when *all* letters were to be cancelled, a task that

---

[9]Indeed, one might argue on these grounds that the Velten effects on psychomotor retardation might be direct effects not requiring the postulation of affective mediation.

seems to require little in the way of concentration.) Another example would be the finding of Natale (1977) showing that manipulated depressed affect resulted in a slower speech rate during an interview; clearly this result could reflect either psychomotor or thought processes or both.

For the few studies where cognitive processes are more clearly tapped, the results are inconsistent. Johnson (1937) asked elated and depressed subjects to say which of five pairs of weights were heavier (pair members were always equally heavy) and found that decisions were made much more slowly by depressed subjects. However, no neutral mood comparisons were reported and so it is hard to known whether the effect is associated with elation, depression, or both. Isen, Daubman, and Nowicki (1987) induced positive and negative affect using humorous and depressing films and measured creativity using Duncker's (1945) candle task and the Remote Associates Test (Mednick, Mednick, & Mednick, 1964). These investigators found that as compared with control subjects, Positive Affect facilitated creative performance but Negative-Affect subjects did not differ from controls. Finally, Ellis et al. (1985) found that subjects who had been made depressed using the Velten procedure were less able to retrieve target words that had been embedded in a set of unrelated sentences but mood had no such effect on retrieval when integrated story materials were used. Ellis and his colleagues believe these results are consistent with a resource allocation theory of mood effects on memory (see Ellis & Ashbrook, 1988) that supposes that relatively demanding encoding tasks would be more likely to be interfered with by mood because the processing resources required to accomplish the task must be shared with those allocated to mood-related processing. Notice that such a theory could also be tested by holding task requirements constant and manipulating the degree to which mood-related processing demands were high assuming we knew how to manipulate the latter. Indeed, Ellis (1985) argues that the failure to obtain mood effects on overall recall in data reported by Hasher et al. (1985) might be partially due to the mildness of the mood state. (Hasher et al. simply measured existing mood rather than manipulating it.)

The resource allocation model is useful in that it directs us to be concerned about the degree to which the task and the mood occupy processing capacity. It is this latter mediating variable that, together with interference thresholds, enable predictions to be made as to whether or not performance decrements will occur in any given situation. Unfortunately, the model cannot be readily used to explain why Johnson (1937) found that mood interfered with decision-making but Isen et al. (1987) could detect no effect of bad mood on creativity because in neither case do we have any way of estimating the demands associated with either the mood or the task. In fact, the effect observed by Johnson (1937) might not reflect processing problems at all. Slow decision times might just as easily be due to low confidence deriving from the loss of self-esteem that is associated with depressed affect. Clearly, more careful parametric work must be done to test the resource allocation model. However, the few supportive results that it has generated thus far (Ellis et al., 1984; Ellis et al., 1985) are quite consistent with the continuity hypothesis.

(8) *Recurrent thoughts of death, suicidal ideation, wishes to be dead, or suicide attempt.* I am unaware of evidence of these kinds of thoughts among normals subjects. Obtaining such evidence might be difficult when one considers the stigma associated with suicide. Nonetheless, when stripped of its religious, moral, legal, and social significance, suicide is only an extreme form of giving up and there certainly is plenty of evidence suggesting that conditions that normally produce depressed affect, for example, failure and loss, lead to defeatism and a breakdown of coping (Seligman, 1975).

In summary, though the amount of evidence for the various symptoms ranges from paltry to nonexistent, the preponderance of evidence favors the continuity hypothesis for five of the eight symptoms, namely: affect, appetite, psychomotor effects, negative feelings about self, and diminished ability to think. For two symptoms, feelings of fatigue and suicidal ideation, there is no evidence. Only in the case of sleep disturbance is the evidence mildly nonsupportive but even there one can find some support in the relation between anxiety and time or percentage time awake at night. Moreover, as noted earlier, the appropriate "normal" sample to which one should be comparing clinically depressed individuals is one experiencing some sort of ongoing problem. Such was not the case for the Berry and Webb (1983, 1985) subjects and so their data do not do great damage to the continuity hypothesis.

An Extended Continuity Hypothesis: The Case of Dysthymia

As mentioned earlier, dysthymia, literally "ill-humored," is included in *DSM-III-R* under the category "Other Specific Disorders." This diagnosis replaces what in previous years had been referred to as neurotic depression. According to Akiskal (1983), the characteristics of dysthymia that set it apart from major unipolar disorder are: (1) chronicity–dysphoria is persistent or intermittent rather than episodic, (2) affective intensity–depressed affect is less intense than that which is observed in major depression, and (3) onset is either "insidious," that is, there is no precipitating life event, or follows a major depressive episode.

It is the subsyndromal intensity associated with dysthymia that might initially encourage the belief that this is a disorder occupying an intermediary position on the hypothetical continuum I am considering. Also consistent with an extended continuity hypothesis are the widely cited data gathered by Akiskal, Bitar, Puzanitan, Rosenthal, and Walker (1978). These investigators undertook a prospective study of a sample of 100 persons who had been diagnosed as being neurotically depressed and found that over a 3- to 4-year period, 36% developed major melancholic episodes. As noted by Akiskal (1983), these data suggest that "minor depressions often form the substrate from which major affective episodes arise." (p. 14)

However, the extension of the continuity hypothesis to dysthymia seems inconsistent with the two other characteristics mentioned above, namely time course and the conditions surrounding onset. If there were a "mild" version of clinically significant depression, intermediate between normal bad mood and major unipolar disorder, one would expect the condition to be episodic, like the other two, with the length of the episodes intermediate. Moreover, if the continuity hypothesis were validly applied, one would also expect all three sorts of dysphoria to be associated with a triggering event.

Further complicating the attempt to assess the relationship between dysthymia and other forms of affective disorder is recent evidence reviewed by Akiskal (1983) suggesting that there are four distinct subtypes of chronic depression with only one being a truly subsyndromal affective disorder. Disorders masquerading as such include: (1) primary depressions with residual chronicity, that is, the patient does not fully recover from a major episode, (2) chronic secondary dysphorias where affective symptoms are associated with nonaffective physical and/or "mental" disorders that run a chronic course, (3) character-spectrum disorders where the depressive affect seems secondary to a syndrome of personality characteristics described as "dependent," "histrionic," and "sociopathic." Only in the case of what Akiskal refers to as "subaffective dysthymic disorders" does one find a set of pharmacologic response, REM latency, family history, and other factors suggesting that one is dealing with the same problem that is encountered in major unipolar disorder. However, even in this case nasty loose ends assail the conclusion, namely Akiskal (1983) is unable to account for the differences in onset and time course between these two disorders and, in addition, patients with subaffective dysthymia display "distinct bipolar tendencies" such as brief hypomanic switches activated by tricyclic challenge. Even so, the careful attempt to systematically distinguish among this large and important category of disorders is likely to yield fruit a bit further down the path as research evidence continues to accumulate.

Extending the Continuity Hypothesis to Bipolar Disorder and Cyclothymia

Major affective disorders are of two main sorts: major unipolar disorders and bipolar disorders. Bipolar disorder, referred to in years past as manic-depressive psychosis, differs from unipolar depression in that patients experience at least one manic episode[10] in addition to major depressive epi-

---

[10]Actually, this is only true of disorders referred to as Bipolar I. *DSM-III-R* also acknowledges the presence of related, probably transitional disorders referred to as Bipolar II and Bipolar III. These disorders only require brief hypomanic periods for diagnosis rather than a full-blown manic episode.

sodes. Though bipolar patients appear to differ from unipolar ones in a number of ways, for example, in terms of family history and pharmacologic responsiveness (Depue & Monroe, 1978), no consensually accepted agreement exists as to symptomatic differences between the depressive episodes associated with each disorder. That is why one cannot be sure whether an individual is bipolar until a manic episode occurs. According to DSM-III-R (American Psychiatric Association, 1987), the symptoms associated with a manic episode are: (1) abnormally and persistently elevated, expansive, or irritable mood; (2) increase in goal-directed activity or psychomotor agitation; (3) more talkative than usual; (4) flight of ideas or the subjective experience that thoughts are racing; (5) inflated self-esteem or grandiosity; (6) decreased need for sleep; (7) distractability; (8) excessive involvement in pleasurable activities that have a high potential for painful consequences.

Cyclothymia is regarded as an attenuated form of bipolar disorder displaying similar (but subsyndromal) symptomatology, family history, and drug response (Akiskal, Djenderedjian, Rosenthal, & Khani, 1977; Depue et al., 1981).

Applying the continuity hypothesis to these disorders is a more complicated business than was the case with major unipolar disorder. In the case of unipolar disorder, one is trying to explain the emergence of a relatively stable (univalent) *state*. Because the state is univalent, it makes sense to try to understand its occurrence in terms of a triggering life-event or the interaction of a life-event and some predisposing vulnerability. But with bipolar disorder, one starts with the initially more difficult job of explaining the emergence of *two* states: depression and mania. Given that these states are psychological "opposites" (see Chapter 6) and that psychologically opposite states would not be expected to result from the same type of life-event, it would seem to follow that one cannot explain bipolar disorders by appealing to a vulnerability to a single kind of event.

Perhaps this is why psychological theories of bipolar disorders are so scarce. Indeed, the only such account to be cited with any regularity entails the view, generally attributed to Melanie Klein, that whereas the depressive episode may result from a triggering event (plus any vulnerability to the event that is needed to explain the intensity of reaction), the mania is, instead, a response to the depression, in the form of a defense against it, rather than an "over-response" to some euphoria-inducing event. But such an account would seem to predict an invariant sequence of episodes in a depression-mania order whereas the evidence suggests that individual episodes of one or the other are quite common (Depue et al., 1981). Moreover, Goodwin and Jamison (1984) report that at least 50% of cases present initially with a manic episode. The lack of systematic sequencing of episodes across cases suggests that there is some degree of independence involved, that is, not all episodes can be explained as a consequence of an earlier episode.

If prior depressive episodes do not account for subsequent manic episodes, two general explanations remain. First, it may be that the proximal causes of episodes are abnormal endogenous processes of a biochemical or neurophysiological sort. Onset could be associated with diverse triggers including other illness, drug use, maturational changes, etc. Though a life event might conceivably play a role, it would be a nonspecific one, that is, it might act as a general stressor or arousal producer. Under circumstances such as these, correlated psychological processes (especially appraisal) might arise as the *consequence* of registration of abnormal endogenous processes. Indeed, a possible endogenous etiology seems the optimum situation in which to apply the arousal-plus-label theory of emotion (Schachter & Singer, 1962) to affective disorder. Whatever the real source of the arousal, one would expect afflicted individuals to try to make sense of their affective experiences by attributing them to surrounding life events. One bit of evidence consistent with this analysis has been reported by Ambelas (1979) who reviewed case notes obtained upon admission for 67 psychiatric patients diagnosed as bipolars looking for the presence of life events. In positive instances, that is, cases where a life event was found, a rather high percentage (50%) were initial episodes of the disorder. One would predict that initial episodes would be more likely to stimulate mention of life events in that the ensuing diagnosis (of affective illness) would thereafter be viewed as a sufficient "cause" of later episodes.

Though I am unaware of attempts to employ Schachter and Singer's theory to explain aspects of mania, some researchers only seem a step away. Jacobs and Silverstone (1986), for example, have recently introduced a dextroamphetamine-induced arousal model of mania. Their research, administering dextroamphetamine or placebo and looking for symptomatology matching that associated with mania, lacks only the deceptions employed by Schachter and Singer (1962).

The other general explanation of the manic and depressive episodes of a person with bipolar disorder or cyclothymia results from an extension of the continuity hypothesis. One might argue that vulnerable individuals would be those who suffer from a tendency to overrespond to hedonically-relevant events regardless of their valence (see Chapter 6 for a review of the literature on individual differences in the intensity of affective responding in normal populations). According to this view, one would expect to find that precipitating life events occurred prior to the onset of episodes. Moreover, one would expect the initial affect, i.e., depression, elation, or irritation, to be predictable from the nature of the life event.

An evaluation of the continuity hypothesis with respect to bipolar affective disorder would require at least two kinds of evidence. First, we need to know about the relationship of life events to episodes and, as was the case in assessing the application of the continuity hypothesis to unipolar depression, we need to determine whether the syndrome of symptoms defining manic episodes differ only quantitatively from the elation or irritation associated with everyday events.

The evidence on the relationship of life events to the onset of episodes in bipolars is not extensive but all of the available studies (Ambelas, 1979; Bidzinska, 1984; Dunner, Patrick, & Fieve, 1979; Hall, Dunner, Zeller, & Fieve, 1978; Kennedy, Thompson, Stancer, Roy, & Persad, 1983; Leff, Fischer, & Bertelsen, 1976; Patrick, Dunner, & Fieve, 1978) find an association.[11] Given the consensus that bipolar disorder is more endogenously-based than unipolar disorder, it is interesting to note that Bidzinska (1984) and Patrick et al. (1978) found no difference between these two diagnostic categories in the likelihood that a stressful life event would precede an episode.

Though most of these studies make efforts to compare life-event reports of bipolars with some sort of control subjects, they suffer in general because the reports are retrospective. In the single exception, Hall et al. (1977) administered a life events questionnaire to bipolar patients during monthly interviews. This allowed a prospective examination of the role of such events as possible precipitants of manic or depressive episodes as indicated by independent ratings of mood produced by a nurse rating team or the attending physician. Hall et al. found that as compared with patients who remained euthymic or became depressed, patients who became manic reported significantly more life events in the employment area (most notably "problems with superiors") during the interview preceding symptom onset. Other investigators, e.g. Kennedy et al. (1983), have also obtained findings implicating the workplace.

The major weakness in this literature from the point of view of the continuity hypothesis is that little attention has been paid to the possibility that positive life events may be related to the onset of manic episodes. Generally, the life event interviews used in these studies underrepresent such events and when they are included it is because they are judged to be possible stressors. Nonetheless, Leff et al. (1976) noted that the events preceding manic episodes were "mixed in character, some being what would generally be labeled 'pleasant' and others 'unpleasant' " (p. 435) and Ambelas (1979) found that of the 14 cases where life events preceded a manic episode, two were positive (marriage of daughter and wife became pregnant). Unfortunately, the studies generally fail to report whether the presenting manic affect was elated, irritated or mixed. All in all, the results regarding the relationship

[11]This is especially notable when one considers the serious methological difficulties facing anyone wishing to do such research. Because individuals are rather difficult to interview during a manic episode, one is generally forced to rely upon post-episode retrospective interviews with newly medicated patients (e.g., Leff et al., 1976; Patrick et al., 1978) or rely upon admitting case notes produced by psychiatrists whose "deeply rooted ideas as to the genetic and biochemical etiology of mania militate against . . . asking the relevant questions" (Ambelas, 1979, p. 19).

between *type* of inducing event and *type* of affective episode must be regarded as inconclusive though it seems reasonably clear that events are involved in instigating episodes in bipolar patients.

Pursuing the continuity hypothesis by matching the syndrome of manic symptoms to correlates of everyday elation fares somewhat better, largely because many of the studies already reviewed while considering the continuity hypothesis in the case of unipolar depression included measurements and/or manipulations of elation as well as of depression. Once again, I will list the symptoms, briefly indicating evidence for or against continuity.

(1) *Abnormally and persistently elevated, expansive, or irritable mood.* The main question here is whether high levels of euphoria in normal individuals are associated with heightened irritability as in the clinical condition. According to DSM-III-R (American Psychiatric Association, 1987), the irritation "may be most apparent when the person is thwarted" (p. 215). I am unaware of studies in which elated normals are frustrated and have had their irritability compared with that of non-elated normals. Consequently, nothing can be concluded with respect to the similarity of the affective responses of normally versus abnormally elated individuals.

(2) *Increase in goal-directed activity or psychomotor agitation.* Whether increased psychomotor activity reflects "agitation" is a subjective judgment. Available studies of elated normal individuals have measured increases in psychomotor activity without characterizing them in this way. The studies in question are the same ones that were discussed earlier in connection with unipolar depression and changes in psychomotor activity. Mayer and Bremer (1985) measured existing mood on a one-time basis and found it to be correlated with behaviors suggesting psychomotor activation such as counting, letter search, and letter cancellation. However, because their mood measure was bipolar and did not measure positive and negative affect independently, one cannot tell whether the correlations are due to elation, depression, or both. Data collected by Johnson (1937) are also mute on this point because Johnson only analyzed the difference in psychomotor activation between days of elation and days of depression (i.e., there was no "neutral" days comparison). However, studies by Hale and Strickland (1976) and Natale (1977) are not subject to this limitation. These investigators manipulated elated, depressed, and neutral mood using variations of the Velten procedure and found that speed of speech onset, articulation rates, digit-symbol substitution, writing speed, and graphic expansiveness were all significant for the elation vs. neutral comparison but not for the depression-neutral comparison. These data clearly suggest that increases in general activity are associated with everyday levels of elated mood.

As for goal-directed activity, Wessman and Ricks (1966) reported that their chronically happy male subjects were involved in a larger number of goals. Similarly, Emmons and Diener (1986) found that end-of-day mood diary reports of positive affect were correlated with self-reports indicating that one felt involved in seeking important goals. It is interesting to note that this relationship was independent of perceptions of goal *attainment* making it somewhat less likely that the correlation reflects the alternative causal direction, i.e., happiness being the *result* of goal-directed activity rather than its cause. However it seems likely that happiness and goal-directed activity are reciprocally related. Klinger (1977), for example, views positive affect as feedback indicating the general perception that one is making progress towards important life goals. That the affect might function as a reinforcement and instigate new striving could hardly be limited to victims of affective disorder.

(3) *More talkative than usual.* The results from the work of Natale (1977) mentioned above are consistent with this symptom. More directly pertinent, though subject to the limitation mentioned above, Johnson (1937) found very large differences in spontaneous vocalizations (the ratio being over 1.5 to 1) when comparing days where subjects reported being depressed versus those when they were relatively elated. Given that these vocalization counts (consisting of all the queries and remarks they made while being given a variety of behavioral measures) were obtained covertly, it seems unlikely that they would have resulted from any sort of demand characteristics.

(4) *Flight of ideas or subjective experience that thoughts are racing.* Given the subjective nature of this symptom, it is not surprising that few relevant data can be found in the literature on the correlates of everyday mood. However, the work of Alice Isen and her associates (Isen et al., 1985; Isen et al., 1987) is seemingly consistent with what one would predict from the continuity hypothesis. Using a variety of different types of positive affect manipulations, Isen et al. (1985) showed that subjects in a good mood produce more unusual associations to words, whereas Isen et al. (1987) found performance on standard tests of creativity to be facilitated. Isen argues that these data support the notion that positive affect increases the likelihood of perceiving relatedness among stimuli, a tendency that has been asserted to be the essence of creativity. Enhanced perceptions of relatedness are, in turn, supposedly due to the fact that good mood primes positive material in memory and positive material is more extensive and diverse than other material (Boucher & Osgood, 1969). If thought networks accessed during good moods are more densely packed, the subjective outcome could easily be one of ideas flying or racing. However, Isen's explanation seems to suppose that the perception of speed is due to cognitive objects being closer together rather than faster transit time. Regardless of how these data are ultimately explained, they do seem consistent with the manic symptom.

In addition, it seems worth noting that although *DSM-III-R* does not propose that manic episodes be diagnosed based upon evidence of heightened creativity, a number of researchers, most notably Andreasen (e.g., Andreasen & Powers, 1975), have found evidence suggesting that creative artists and manic-depressives perform similarly on tests of thought processes. More recently, Holden (1987) has offered a preliminary review of evidence suggesting that such artists, especially writers and poets, show a much heightened degree of susceptibility to affective disorder. The most compelling findings, however, come from a study published by Richards, Kinney, Lunde, Benet, and Merzel (1988). These investigators used the complementary procedure of selecting subjects based upon psychiatric diagnosis and evaluating their overall creative accomplishments. Their results indicated that the combined index group of manic-depressives, cyclothymes, and first-degree relatives of the bipolar subjects were significantly higher in lifetime creative activity than a control group. The parallels are quite intriguing here.

(5) *Inflated self-esteem (grandiosity, which may be delusional).* In three direct tests, Kavanagh and Bower (1985), Wright and Mischel (1982) and Salovey (1987) reported that positive mood, induced by asking subjects to recall or imagine a positive incident, led to heightened feelings of self-esteem or self-efficacy just as the recall of negative incidents led to temporarily reduced self-evaluations. Wright and Mischel were able to further demonstrate that the effect of the mood manipulation persisted so that subsequent to task performance and a manipulated success or failure experience, elation condition subjects still rated their general abilities higher than did subjects who had had a neutral mood induction.

(6) *Decreased need for sleep.* The data here are weak and inconclusive. Though early self-report data suggested that sleep suffers more from euphoric mood than depressed mood (Hersey, 1932), the objective data on measures of sleep efficiency collected by Berry and Webb (1983, 1985) show it to be uncorrelated with measures of positive mood. The only sleep variable that was reliably correlated with euphoria was latency to first REM period but the interpretation of this result is clouded because Berry and Webb (1985) found that the night-to-night correlations of the mood scales were quite high (median $r = 0.66$), suggesting that the Lorr, Daston, and Smith (1967) mood measure they used may be tapping traits more than states.

(7) *Distractibility, i.e., attention too easily drawn to unimportant or irrelevant external stimuli.* I am unaware of data that directly bear on the degree to which everyday euphoria is associated with distractibility. One might certainly predict such effects based upon the evidence reviewed above (Isen et al., 1985; Isen et al., 1987) showing that good mood seems to increase the availability of remote and unusual associations. To the extent that the task calls for these as it often does in the case of creative problem-solving, they may facilitate performance, but if the task is simple and depends upon focused attention, performance may suffer from the presence of extraneous cognitive activity.

(8) *Excessive involvement in activities that have a high potential for painful consequences which is not recognized, e.g., buying sprees, sexual indiscretions, foolish business investments, reckless driving.* The most relevant data here would appear to be those relating good mood to measures of risk-taking. In an initial study, Isen and Patrick (1983) found that affect inter-

acted with the degree of risk involved in a gambling situation with positive affect subjects gambling more than controls when the odds were good (83% chance of winning) but less when the odds were bad (17% chance of winning).

In light of these and other relevant data (i.e., Isen & Geva, 1987; Isen et al., 1988; Johnson & Tversky, 1983), Isen has concluded that positive affect creates a "cautious optimism" that influences behavior in risk-taking situations. The optimism reflects a tendency to attach high probabilities to desirable events and low probabilities to undesirable ones when in a good mood (Johnson & Tversky, 1983); the caution is associated with an apparent change in subjective utilities that is associated with a good mood, namely, the negative utilities of losses are greater (Isen et al., 1988), perhaps because losing when in a good mood not only deprives one of the lost resource but deflates the good mood as well. At first glance, these data seem inconsistent with the continuity hypothesis in that the behavior of manics hardly seems to suggest cautious optimism. However, one might conceivably argue that the very high levels of euphoria associated with mania cause a *complete* discounting of the possibility of the negative alternative in which case the supposedly heightened negative utilities would fail to come into play.

In summary, the evidence for syndromal similarity of everyday elation and manic excitement is good. When combined with the evidence suggesting a role for psychosocial events in the precipitation of episodes, the continuity hypothesis fares surprisingly well when one considers that it is generally disregarded in the case of bipolar disorder, e.g., see Whybrow et al. (1984).

The most exciting possibility for obtaining more definitive data on the way in which affect-inducing events might be involved in the etiology of manic and depressive episodes in bipolar individuals grows out of the work being done by Depue and his colleagues with the General Behavior Inventory (e.g., Depue, Kleiman, Davis, Hutchinson, & Krauss, 1985; Depue, Krauss, Spoont, & Arbisi, 1989; Depue et al., 1981; Goplerud & Depue, 1985; Klein, Depue, & Slater, 1986). The GBI is a self-report inventory predicated on the assumption that individuals predisposed to bipolar disorder ought to differ from those not so predisposed in terms of the "core behaviors" associated with the disorder. That is, predisposed individuals are expected to be more likely to premorbidly (and intermorbidly) experience behavior tendencies symptomatic of manic and depressive episodes. More than that, however, Depue et al. (1981) argue that separation of cases from non-cases requires careful attention to "non-behavioral" dimensions of intensity, duration, frequency, and rapidity of reaction. The insistence on measuring these non-behavioral or parametric features of the core behaviors reflects Depue's contention that subsyndromal and fully syndromal reactions are continuous, differing in strength rather than quality.

In five separate validation studies, Depue et al. (1981) were able to show that the GBI does a reasonably good job of picking individuals who are at risk for bipolar disorder. For example, in Study 4, Depue et al. compared the family histories of cases and non-cases as identified by the GBI and found that 53% of cases had at least one first-degree relative afflicted with one of the varieties of bipolar disorder recognized by *DSM-III* as compared to 15% of the noncases.

In the most interesting of the validation studies in terms of its relevance to the continuity hypothesis, Depue et al. (1981; Study 5) compared reports of daily mood by cases and noncases over a 28-day period using a questionnaire called the Inventory for Behavioral Variation. The first 18 items on the IBV asked subjects to report the degree to which they were very high or low in terms of a variety of bipolar scales drawn from the research of Wessman and Ricks (1966), for example, confidence versus self-doubt, elation versus depression, sociability versus withdrawal. Factor analysis revealed a single major factor, basically good versus bad mood, and so subjects received a single score that was the sum of their responses to these 18 items. Analyses comparing cases and noncases found the following differences in means and variances: 1) Across days, cases reported a lower "trough" than noncases; 2) Across days, cases report a larger peak-to-trough range then noncases; 3) Across days, cases have a significantly greater variance associated with their daily average, their daily range, their daily peak, and their daily trough. Depue et al. (1981) added eight additional questions that resulted in the following differences between cases and noncases: 1) Cases reported a greater frequency of within day mood and energy changes; 2) Cases reported generally poorer health and more physical symptoms than noncases; the variance of physical symptoms was also higher for cases; 3) The variance associated with daily sleep reports was greater for cases than for noncases.

The results of this study are important because they give a more fine-grained picture of the day-to-day lives of subsyndromal individuals and, more specifically, provide an indication of features that are episodic versus chronic. Chronic features, namely those variables that show a mean difference between cases and noncases but no difference in variance, are especially interesting in that they suggest stable markers that might be involved in creating a vulnerability to the instigation of episodes. The only variable that behaved that way in the study was the frequency of within-day mood and energy changes.

Of critical significance to a proper evaluation of the continuity hypothesis is the degree to which these daily "ups and downs" are associated with affect-inducing events as opposed to alternative possibilities such as more volatile circadian rhythm effects (e.g., see Wehr, 1984, for a discussion of possible connections between bipolar disorder and circadian and other biological rhythms), or greater levels of random output or "noise" from affect-relevant neurophysiological systems of cases (e.g., see Siever & Davis, 1985). If the relatively large within-day fluctuations of the cyclothymes are, themselves, responses to events then it would be tempting to suppose that the vulnerabilities—biological, psychological, or both—that are responsible for amplifying these everyday mood reactions are also capable, in concert with a life-event of relatively great significance, of instigating an episode of clinical proportions. This sort of account would assume psychological mediation because life events of this sort are presumed to always engage such processes. However, if the large daily swings can be shown to be independent of life-events it would be possible to argue that this process is necessarily endogenously-based and does not require the participation of any psychological processes except registration of the resulting feelings. In fact, even registration of feelings would not necessarily occur in that people may deny affect in the absence of events they have learned to identify as emotion-inducing. Recall (see Chapter 4) that dysphoric mood need not be present in order to diagnose depressive episodes as these can be identified on the basis of other symptoms.

The idea that exacerbation of chronically erratic output of affect-relevant systems is the culprit in promoting manic and depressive episodes has been advanced by Siever and Davis (1985). Their theory assumes that the failure of homeostatic mechanisms that normally control neurotransmitter activity is the root of the problem (Also see Goplerud & Depue, 1985, for a similar argument). In support, Siever and Davis (1985) cite data published by Demet, Halaris, and Gwirtsman (1982) showing that plasma-obtained 3-methoxy-4-hydroxy-phenylglycol (MHGP), a catecholamine metabolite, fluctuated more in depressed patients than in controls over a 24-hour period. But, such results are ambiguous because the patients are clearly stressed and so the greater fluctuation could as easily be the *result* of psychological variability as its cause. Somewhat more persuasive are the data of Depue et al. (1985). These investigators repeatedly sampled serum-free cortisol over a 3-hour laboratory period from cyclothymes and normals who were selected using the GBI in concert with clinical interviews. They found a significantly greater intraindividual variance across the entire session among the cyclothymes. Even here though, it could be argued that the fluctuation was in response to stress in that all subjects first experienced venipuncture and, after a 1-hour rest period, were exposed to a silent math task described as "tedious but not difficult" (Depue et al., 1985, p. 176).

An important link in the attempt to tie such endogenous fluctuation to the within-day mood variability results reported by Depue et al. (1981) is forged by data recently collected in my own laboratory (Morris, Kelley, & Napps, 1989). Using a revised GBI scoring procedure (Depue et al., 1989) that enables identification of subjects who are dysthymic and cyclothymic, we selected subjects from these two categories and a stratified sample of normals taken from the non-case region. Mood was repeatedly measured over a 40-minute laboratory period using a deception. All subjects were told that we were interested in subliminal perception, especially of emotion-inducing stimuli. They were informed that we would display such stimuli using a tachistoscope. Though they would be unaware of having "seen" a stimulus, we told them that careful introspection of their feelings might reveal a correspondence between what they were feeling and the nature of the stimulus. In fact, no emotion-inducing stimuli were used and, of course, subjects only saw flashes of light. Given that the situation was literally "uneventful," we assumed that variability in mood reports would reflect the sort of endogenous fluctuations hypothesized by Siever and Davis (1985). The results were quite consistent with the predictions derived by extrapolation from Siever and Davis; dysthymic and cyclothymic subjects had significantly higher intraindividual variance associated with reports of the intensity of their feelings than normals.

What, if anything, do these data suggest about the etiology of a disordered episode, either of mania or depression? One possibility is that this chronic fluctuation can be precipitated by endogenous or exogenous stressors into swings of much greater amplitude. One could argue, as have Goplerud and Depue (1985), that the chronically disinhibited process moves even further out of control until it achieves a relatively autonomous disordered state. Notice that such an account can completely bypass psychological-process explanation if one assumes, as do Goplerud and Depue, that the disinhibited processes directly produce the neurophysiological and behavioral symptoms that we associate with the disorder.

For my own part, I think it unlikely that we will be able to account for the syndromes associated with mania and depression by appealing solely to biology. Human beings do not necessarily respond in reflexive fashion simply because the stimuli are endogenous. Though the receptor mechanisms may be different, *we may construct or construe the meaning of apparent biological reactions as much as we would external events.* An understanding of the way in which such psychological processes intertwine with poorly regulated biological ones will finally tie together the strands that have, thus far, remained separated by disciplinary lines.

A Final Comment

Reading the literature on major unipolar depression and bipolar disorder yields two very different impressions as far as perceptions of the viability of the continuity hypothesis are concerned. In the case of major unipolar disorder, researchers on each side of the issue appear to have backed away from the more contentious attitudes of the past. Few would claim that there is no room for the ideas of the other side . . . the pie is big enough for everybody to share; there is so much depression and etiology is acknowledged to be diverse. This "truce" appears to rely upon an acceptance by both sides of an endogenous-reactive partition (Andreasen, 1982).

According to this partition, reactive depressions would supposedly result from the occurrence of a depression-inducing life event such as the loss of a loved one, possibly in combination with a pre-existing psychological vulnerability to such events, e.g., low self-esteem, or a concurrent source of vulnerability, e.g., an ineffective or non-existent social support network. On the other hand, endogenous depressions, expected to yield a diagnosis of melancholia, would be viewed either as having a "spontaneous" onset, i.e., no precipitating life-event need occur, or would be seen as a consequence of a diathesis-stress process in which a defect of a biological sort would be triggered by a stressor which could either be biological, e.g., an illness, or psychological, i.e., a stressful life event. The life-event trigger in this case, however, would not necessarily be a depression-inducing event in that the diathesis-stress explanation does not involve a *magnification of the specific affective state induced by the event* as is true in the case of reactive depression as explained by psychological theories. Rather, the idea behind a diathesis-stress model is that the vulnerability leaves the individual more precariously balanced so that a stressor can more easily produce dysfunction and pathology of a neurophysiological sort which is the proximal cause of symptoms.

Although the endogenous-reactive partition appears to create a neatly patrolled demilitarized zone sanctioned by the DSM in the form of the distinction between melancholia and non-melancholic major depression, the available facts are not cooperating. As was pointed out in Chapter 4, the search for spontaneous onsets of melancholia has been frustrating. Reviewers of the literature (Brown & Harris, 1978; Monroe & Peterman, 1988; Paykel, 1982) have not found that the occurrence of life events differentiates among different sub-types of depression. In addition, a general diathesis-stress model of depressive disorder is inconsistent with the findings of Brown and Harris (1978) which show that a *particular type of life event*, namely the threat or actual occurrence of loss, typically precedes depression. Findings such as these suggest that negotiated settlements of territory may be less useful than efforts to integrate, e.g. see Whybrow et al. (1984) and the intriguing attempt of Healy and Williams (1988) who offer a model of depressive pathogenesis involving reciprocal influences of circadian dysrhythmia and cognitive vulnerability.

Matters are very different insofar as bipolar disorder is concerned. That is the "turf" of psychiatry. The degree to which their hegemony is respected is suggested by the fact that Larsen (1987), who is examining individual differences in the tendency to experience rapidly changing or variable affect . . . arguably the principal symptom that sets bipolars apart from other sorts of affective disorders . . . never mentions the potential relevance of his work to that disorder. A further indication of a lack of interest in possible psychological mediation of the disorder is apparent in conclusions expressed by Whybrow et al. (1984). Noting that there have been few studies examining psychosocial instigation of manic or hypomanic episodes, they suggest that studies "seeking specific precipitants . . . may not be asking a question critical to a better understanding of the disorder" (p. 191). They go on to point out that "the best known precipitants of hypomania *per se* (and, to a lesser extent, of mania) are drugs and physiological procedures" (p. 191) that are instituted as countermeasures against depression. The clear evidence of "pharmacological switching" coupled with the belief that bipolar individuals "rarely" convert from a euthymic (i.e., normal mood) to a hypomanic state (no reference is offered in support of this observation) lead Whybrow et al. (1984) to conclude that:

> the relationship between melancholia and mania is physiologically determined and psychosocial factors play little if any specific role in "selecting" the manic syndrome. (p. 191)

I remain unpersuaded by these arguments. The reason why drugs are the "best-known" precipitants of hypomania is because we are in a better position to observe the drug-hypomania conversion. Affectively disordered individuals are more likely to seek help or to be referred during a depressive phase than they are during a hypomanic phase and drugs are likely to be the treatment of choice. The fact that these drugs often cause the depression to convert to hypomania does not mean that hypomanic episodes do not result from psychosocial events. The latter conclusion must depend upon careful studies of the very sort Whybrow et al. (1984) discourage. Unfortunately, subsequent to diagnosis, it is very difficult to study the relationship between life-events and mania or hypomania both because of the likelihood of the use of drugs and the psychological impact associated with the diagnosis, itself. The emergence of the GBI may solve this problem in that it permits one to identify individuals at risk, many of whom are not on drugs and have not been diagnosed.

In the final analysis, the continuity hypothesis is no more than a framework that specifies what data are relevant to an understanding of affective disorders. Narrowly conceived, the continuity hypothesis encourages a more serious consideration of the role of positive feedback loops, that is, vicious cycling, in the exacerbation of mood states that are initially caused by psychosocial events. Such loops, capable of propagating across cognitive, perceptual, motivational, and interpersonal domains (Hyland, 1987), could hypothetically cause an exacerbation of mood sufficient to produce dysfunction. More broadly, the continuity hypothesis is indifferent to arguments over endogenous versus exogenous factors. In its simplest form it asserts only that everyday mood states and clinically significant episodes are understandable in terms of the same processes and precipitants. Thus, those who take it seriously should be as interested in how circadian variations in cortisol influence the mood of normal individuals as they are in the attributions of bipolars about their interpersonal difficulties. At the moment, neither sort of question is being actively pursued.

Postscript

In his commentary on the papers on affect and cognition provided for the Seventeenth Annual Carnegie Symposium on Cognition, Simon (1982) noted that as he read from one paper to the next, he was reminded of "the traditional blind men, now touching one part of the elephant, now another" (p. 334). In spite of the considerable expansion of the empirical literature on mood since the early 1980s, the overall coherence of the research has not improved. Indeed, I am led to conclude that those groping at the pachyderm must be deaf as well since they appear to be unaware that there are others working at their sides.

Why has research on the causes, consequences, and correlates of mood proceeded on such divergent paths? I believe there are two interrelated explanations, the first having to do with terminology and the second with the lack of an overall theoretical framework to guide research. Simon (1982) also felt that terminological problems were hindering research on affect. He argued that scientific advance requires that we "construct and adhere to a vocabulary that makes the necessary distinctions in a consistent way" (p. 334). Simon went on to propose a mood-emotion distinction that rests on the urgency of the precipitating event and which, in most respects, is like that offered by Isen (e.g., Clark & Isen, 1982). Emotion is instigated in situations requiring action where interruption of ongoing activity occurs and redirection of attention is necessary. Mood is associated with events that create more "diffuse and subtle" levels of arousal that do not interrupt but, rather, operate as a context that influences cognitive processes.

Simon believed that most researchers interested in affect would accept this distinction. I would disagree. But even if they did, they must also *adhere* to the distinction in terms of their choice of operationalizations in research. That was not the case in the research Simon was commenting upon, nor is it the case now. For example, there are no attempts of which I am aware to demonstrate some parametric relationship between the significance of an affect-inducing event and its ability to interrupt an ongoing focus of attention. Similarly, I know of no systematic evidence to show that events that interrupt fail to provide the context effects that are supposedly associated only with non-interruptive occurrences.[1] Finally, it is hard to see how the

[1]However, the results of Schwarz and Clore (1983) come close. As noted in Chapter 5, they showed that making mood-inducing stimuli salient *eliminated* their char-

process distinctions that Simon and others offer to distinguish between mood and emotion constructs can be adequately assessed by self-report methodologies that require interruption by their very nature. This is the root problem in creating bridges between idiographic and nomothetic approaches to mood, a problem discussed in Chapter 6.

I believe that the lack of consistency between theoretical construct and operational definition is a symptom of the more fundamental need to restore a broader theoretical perspective to the literature on mood. Such a perspective was made available by mood theorists such as Nowlis (1965, 1970) and Jacobsen (1957) who saw mood as having an important *function*. Though they disagreed on specifics, each believed that mood was an integral part of the system whereby people were able to control or self-regulate their psychological states.

And yet, in spite of the early consensus on this point, the empirical literature on mood has moved away from a focus on self-regulation toward the issue of the relationship between mood and cognition (Clark & Fiske, 1982; Isen, 1984, 1987; Blaney, 1986) and, curiously, to the connection between mood and helping (Dovidio, 1984; Carlson et al., 1988). How did this happen? Playing historian, I would suggest a *Zeitgeist* explanation. In the early 1970s, Alice Isen started producing the first studies in what would become a long and productive line of research on mood. The earliest results (Isen, 1970; Isen & Levin, 1972) found a positive relationship between good mood and helping. Because of the ascendance of cognitive approaches in social psychology during the 1970s, it is not surprising that Isen would turn in that direction (Isen, 1975; Isen et al., 1978) seeking an explanation for the good mood-helping relationship. The specific hypothesis that emerged, namely that positive affect serves as a retrieval cue for other positive material in memory, dovetailed with similar ideas being promulgated by Bower (1981); both theoretical positions derived support from the expanding clinical literature suggesting that mood might be playing a role in the generally negative outlook held by depressed individuals.

Though the connection between mood and self-regulation took a backseat to the more topical concerns of mood congruent memory, perception, and behavior, it did not completely disappear from the scene. Although most studies found congruence, a consistent minority failed or, even more telling, found mood-incongruent results (see Chapter 5), forcing Isen (Clark & Isen, 1982; Isen, 1984, 1985) to revive the self-regulatory link with the ideas of mood maintenance and mood repair. Nonetheless, mood incongruent results were the exceptions rather than the rule and reviewers of the mood literature (Blaney, 1986; Morris & Reilly, 1987) were unimpressed with the

acteristic (context) effect on judgments. Thus, it can be argued that when attention is directed toward affective processes, they lose their ability to influence. Obviously, it is important to demonstrate similar effects on other behaviors that have previously been shown to be influenced by mood.

data offered in support of these hypothetical processes. But the most telling blow against a thorough-going self-regulatory account of mood was the increasingly widespread view that mood congruence played an important role in the *worsening* of bad mood, even to the point of being responsible for clinically significant depression (See Chapter 7). Given this circumstance, maintaining a functional analysis of mood appeared to make as much sense as having the foxes guard the chickens.

However, abandoning functional analyses of mood may be premature. As noted by Blaney (1986), though evidence of mood congruence is easy to come by, clear demonstrations of a full cycle wherein mood produces a mood congruent effect that then intensifies the mood do not exist. And, even if such cycles could be shown, they would have to be reconciled with findings showing that the moods of normal subjects, whether induced by laboratory mood manipulations or real life-events are typically quite brief (see Chapter 6). So, even if it is eventually discovered that moods do spiral up or down for some brief period of time after a mood-inducing event, they must return toward normal soon thereafter. From this point of view, the problem with mood research is that single measurements are made of a process that is dynamic and that should be measured repeatedly over time (Blaney, 1986; Salovey & Rodin, 1985). Hopefully, the subliminal-perception paradigm (Morris et al., 1989) discussed in Chapter 7 or other new methodologies will permit such repeated measurements to be made without producing the reactivity that would normally accompany them.

But whether or not mood congruent memory and perception can be shown to produce intensification over the short term, mood congruence must, itself, be explained. Is mood congruence the result of automatic memory processes and, if so, what role might these hypothetical mnemonic processes play in a self-regulatory system? Even though there is a great deal of evidence consistent with the idea that mood congruence results from memory processes, Blaney (1986) has suggested a variety of alternative explanations for mood-congruence effects that assume that a motivational process is responsible. And, in some of these explanations, mood-congruent memory is a byproduct of a hypothetical self-regulatory process. For example, Blaney suggests that superior recall of negative material by dysphoric individuals may be the result of attention being directed at negative items so as to rebut them, and he cites findings of Wyer and Frey (1983) in support. Subjects were "incidentally" given arguments favoring and opposing the validity of a test upon which they then proceeded to do well or poorly. Failure subjects remembered more arguments in favor of the validity of the test than did success subjects, a finding that Blaney considers mood-congruent, but they also disparaged the test more than success subjects. Though it is difficult to deny *post hoc* motivational interpretations of this sort in the case of any given study, the principle of parsimony suggests that mood-congruent memory is a superior explanation for the literature as a whole.

If memory is mood congruent, does this tell us more about memory or mood? That is, is mood-congruent memory a consequence of the way in which memory is organized or is it because mood influences cognitive processes in ways that are consistent with its role in a self-regulatory system? Answering this question requires separate consideration of good and bad moods because within a self-regulatory system, the two kinds of moods have very different implications. As for bad moods, they indicate that some deficit has been detected ... that some standard has not been met. The mood-emotion distinction described above assumes that the events that generate bad mood are relatively less significant than those that instigate emotion. This permits attention to remain focused on whatever agenda had been in place before the occurrence of the mood-inducing event. However, if the mood is to serve its cue[2] function, it must remain active until the limited supply of focal attention becomes available to address the precipitating circumstance. Automatic cognitive processes may serve this function. That is, they may extend the life of the feeling state by acting as a reverberating circuit. One could even argue that such a process permits a rudimentary assessment of the importance of the problem. Setbacks in areas that have not previously posed significant problems for a person might "reverberate" less because there would be few associative links. This would permit rapid decay with the result that the individual would probably never even realize that a mood had existed. But if the negative event were related to goals where problems had been frequently encountered, the richer associative links might "automatically" maintain or even exacerbate the mood. Consistent with this analysis, my review of the literature on mood-congruent memory in Chapter 5 showed that the effects were stronger when the material to be retrieved was self-relevant; presumably self-relevant areas are ones with more associative links. Such an analysis could also explain the phenomenon of intruding automatic thoughts (Hollon & Kendall, 1980) as being due to the periodic eruption into awareness of an ongoing associative process that is feeding upon the large supply of negative memories possessed by people with depressive tendencies.

What about good mood? Systems that are self-regulatory are readily applied to deficit situations in that it is the detection of a nonoptimal circumstance that triggers the system. However, there is a place for good mood in

[2]To speak of a cue function implies that mood accomplishes its purpose by attracting attention. But, I also agree with Nowlis (Nowlis & Nowlis, 1956) who thought that moods that were out of focal attention could directly predispose behavior. This aspect of mood is revealed in the phrase "in the mood to . . . ." Without knowing why, we sometimes feel that certain activities should either be approached or avoided. Responses prompted in this way bear a resemblance to what Simon refers to as "weak methods" for dealing with a situation. This term, drawn from the literature on artificial intelligence, denotes programs (of action) that can be enacted with minimal information, and are widely applicable if somewhat inefficient.

such a system, namely, as a cue indicating that a satisfactory situation exists or has been restored.

Is mood congruent memory in the case of positive affect explicable in terms of automatic cognitive processes as was the case with bad mood? Because good moods are enjoyable, even to the point of generating a hypothetical mood maintenance process (Isen, 1984, 1987), it seems likely that at least some of the findings demonstrating congruence are the result of strategic (rather than automatic) cognitive processes. For example, "rehearsal" of one's successes would seem to be reinforcing and a process that would occupy focal attention. Such rehearsal should increase the likelihood that a study designed to detect mood-congruent memory would find it. The possibility that mood congruence might contribute to lengthening a good mood is not inconsistent with the participation of mood in a self-regulatory system although is not a clearly useful feature of such a system either.

But the more critical question is whether the view that good mood is a cue to a satisfactory state of affairs can explain the accumulated data on mood and prosocial responding and cognitive processes, much of which has been interpreted as evidence of the influence of mood on memory and other cognitive processes (see Isen, 1987, for a review of this literature). Though this is not the place to offer an extended answer to that question, especially because more research is what is needed, in general terms I think the literature is consistent with such an idea. Most compatible are the results showing people in good moods to be more helpful, friendly, and positive in their perception of others. People who are in good moods are that way because some (manipulated) event has made them feel relatively competent, advantaged, secure, and/or content. Such "feelings" have been independently (i.e., outside of the mood literature) shown to lead to a general positive orientation; feelings of competence have been shown to be related to helping (Latane & Darley, 1970), feelings of advantage produce helping due to equity considerations (e.g., see Rosenhan et al., 1981), and given that insecurity seems to produce negativity (Amabile & Glazebrook, 1981), it does not seem farfetched to assume the obverse. Also consistent with this interpretation of the effect of good mood are the findings showing that people are more likely to reward themselves (Mischel et al., 1968) and do as they please (Isen & Simmonds, 1978; Forest et al., 1979) as both of these consequences seem reasonably likely reactions after having met some standard.

The literature on good mood and cognitive processes other than memory includes demonstrations that positive affect increases: (1) the likelihood that subjects would solve problems intuitively rather than attempting a more difficult algorithmic solution (Isen, Means, Patrick, & Nowicki, 1982), (2) the erroneous use of simple heuristics to solve problems (Isen et al., 1982), (3) the speed with which subjects make decisions among hypothetical choices (Isen et al., 1982), and (4) creative solutions to problems (Isen et al., 1987). Isen (1987) argues resourcefully that all those results and more can be explained by assuming that positive affect influences various cognitive processes but she has admitted that they are also compatible with the idea that good mood produces a "sense of relaxation (and) freedom from tension" (p. 239). Sometimes such a sense would promote good performance, for example, when nondominant responses are required as in creative problem-solving, but on other occasions it might lead to less diligence causing performance to deteriorate. This sense-of-well-being explanation is exactly what would be generated from a self-regulatory position.

Thus, I would argue that the very large literature reviewed in Chapter 5 is generally consistent with the idea that moods can be viewed as cues in a self-regulatory system. Further evidence of the durability and widespread applicability of this idea is indicated by its emergence as a new focus for theories of affective disorder. As noted in Chapter 7, though cognitive theories of depression must still be considered the dominant approach among those who regard affective disorders to be the product of psychological (rather than neurophysiological) processes, two recent attempts to integrate psychological approaches have recently appeared (Hyland, 1987; Pyszczynski & Greenberg, 1987) and both of these proposals independently arrived at the conclusion that self-regulatory failure is the proximal circumstance in clinically significant depressive reactions.

Adding further credibility to self-regulatory failure approaches to affective disorder is the recent and completely independent development of neurophysiological models that also emphasize dysfunction in systems thought to be homeostatic or inhibitory with respect to affect (Goplerud & Depue, 1985; Siever & Davis, 1985). These more or less concurrent theoretical developments appear to offer a unique opportunity to bridge the gulf between biology and psychology and restore a connection between theory and research on mood in its normal and abnormal manifestations.

The possibility that experimental and clinical approaches to mood may move toward common ground as they come to recognize their shared interest in the way human beings self-regulate makes me optimistic about the possibility of significant advances in the near term. I am less enthusiastic about the direction in the two other major literatures reviewed in this book. As far as the role played by endogenous processes in everyday mood, it is hard to find much interest except as a control in studies of abnormality. I presume that this is due to the implicit beliefs that: (1) normal moods are event produced whereas, (2) abnormal moods are often unrelated to events. However, as evidence accumulates showing mood variation among normals that is tied to diurnal (Thayer, 1987; Robbins & Tanck, 1987) and infradian rhythms (Eastwood et al., 1985; Larsen, 1987), some reassessment is bound to take place. One interesting question regarding these endogenous neurophysiological processes is whether they are directly activated by stimuli such as the amount of available sunlight or partly psychologically mediated, for example, winter depression being the result of being denied warm sunny days and associated outdoor activities. If psychological mediation can be shown, such phenomena would be more readily compatible with a self-regulatory point of view. Progress in this area is likely to depend upon the degree to which interest is maintained in phenomena such as seasonal affective disorder and premenstrual syndrome as research on these conditions will require normal comparison groups.

I am most pessimistic about the direction being taken in the literature on individual differences in mood. This is partly due to the overreliance upon self-reports. Not only does this raise serious validity questions but it keeps significant distance from research in the other areas where the dependent measures are principally behavioral. And yet, in spite of these deficiencies, at least from my point of view, it is a lively research area. I suspect that the breakthrough will occur here in response to the success I anticipate in merging experimental and clinical approaches to mood. This will quite naturally produce an inclination to examine individual differences in self-regulatory mechanisms as a way of approaching the sources of vulnerability to a disordered state.

The belief that there are cycles in science, or, more generally, in the history of ideas, and that we periodically return to old notions in some slightly modified guise is a cliche and perhaps nothing other than a way for the old guard to protect itself against the militant rejection of their views by members of the new wave. And yet, it seems that in the three decades that have passed since Nowlis (Nowlis & Nowlis, 1956) and Jacobsen (1957) first argued that moods should be understood as a functioning part of a system whereby we self-regulate ourselves, we have done exactly that. Though we may have come full circle, we have hardly returned to where we began. As I survey where we have been, where we are, and where we seem to be headed, my mood is one of excitement and anticipation . . . the consequence of my perception that things are going very well indeed.

References

Abelson, R.P., & Sermat, V. (1962). Multidimensional scaling of facial expression. *Journal of Experimental Psychology, 63*, 546–554.

Abplanalp, J.M., Livingston, L., Rose, R.M., & Sandwisch, D. (1977). Cortisol and growth hormone responses to psychological stress during the menstrual cycle. *Psychosomatic Medicine, 39*, 158–177.

Abraham, K. (1986). Notes on the psychoanalytic investigation and treatment of manic-depressive insanity and allied conditions. In J.C. Coyne (Ed.), *Essential papers on depression* (pp. 31–47). New York: New York University Press. (Original work published in 1911).

Abramson, L.Y., Alloy, L.B., & Metalsky, G.I. (1988). The cognitive diathesis—stress theories of depression: Toward an adequate evaluation of the theories' validities. In L.B. Alloy (Ed.), *Cognitive processes in depression* (pp. 3–30). New York: Guilford.

Abramson, L.Y., Metalsky, G.I., & Alloy, L.B. (1989). Hopelessness depression: A theory-based subtype of depression. *Psychological Review, 96*, 358–372.

Abramson, L.Y., Seligman, M.E.P., & Teasdale, J. (1978). Learned helplessness in humans: Critique and reformulation. *Journal of Abnormal Psychology, 87*, 49–74.

Affonso, D.D., & Domino, G. (1984). Postpartum depression: A review. *Birth, 11*, 231–235.

Akiskal, H.S. (1983). Dysthymic disorder: Psychopathology of proposed chronic depressive subtypes. *American Journal of Psychiatry, 140*, 11–20.

Akiskal, H.S., Bitar, A.H., Puzantian, V.R., Rosenthal, T.L., & Walker, P.W. (1978). The nosological status of neurotic depression: A prospective three-to-four year follow-up examination in light of the primary-secondary and unipolar-bipolar dichotomies. *Archives of General Psychiatry, 34*, 756–766.

Akiskal, H.S., Djenderedjian, A.H., Rosenthal, R.H., & Khani, M. (1977). Cyclothymic disorder: Validating criteria for inclusion in the bipolar affective group. *American Journal of Psychiatry, 134*, 1227–1233.

Akiskal, H.S., & McKinney, W.T. (1973). Depressive disorders: Toward a unified hypothesis. *Science, 182*, 20–28.

Akiskal, H.S., & McKinney, W.T. (1975). Overview of recent research in depression: Integration of ten conceptual models into a comprehensive clinical frame. *Archives of General Psychiatry, 32*, 285–305.

Alloy, L.B. (1988). *Cognitive processes in depression.* New York: Guilford.

Alloy, L.B., & Abramson, L.Y. (1979). Judgments of continency in depressed and nondepressed students: Sadder but wiser? *Journal of Experimental Psychology: General, 108*, 441–485.

Alloy, L.B., & Abramson, L.Y. (1988). Depressive realism: Four theoretical perspectives. In L.B. Alloy (Ed.), *Cognitive processes in depression* (pp. 223–265). New York: Guilford.

Alloy, L.B., Abramson, L.Y., & Viscusi, D. (1981). Induced mood and the illusion of control. *Journal of Personality and Social Psychology, 41*, 1129–1140.

Alloy, L.B., Hartlage, S., & Abramson, L.Y. (1988). Testing the cognitive diathesis–stress theories of depression: Issues of research design, conceptualization, and assessment. In L.B. Alloy (Ed.), *Cognitive processes in depression* (pp. 31–73). New York: Guilford.

Amabile, T.M., & Glazebrook, A.H. (1981). A negativity bias in interpersonal evaluation. *Journal of Experimental Social Psychology, 18*, 1–22.

Ambelas, A. (1979). Psychologically stressful events in the precipitation of manic episodes. *British Journal of Psychiatry, 135*, 15–21.

American Psychiatric Association. (1987). *Diagnostic and statistical manual of mental disorders (3rd edition revised).* Washington, D.C.: American Psychiatric Association.

Amir, S., Brown, Z.W., & Amit, A. (1980). The role of endorphins in stress: Evidence and speculations. *Neuroscience and Biobehavioral Review, 4*, 77–86.

Anderson, J.R., & Bower, G.H. (1973). *Human associative memory.* Washington, D.C.: Winston.

Andreasen, N.C. (1982). Concepts, diagnosis, and classifications. In E.S. Paykel (Ed.), *Handbook of affective disorders* (pps. 24–44). New York: Guilford.

Andreasen, N.C., & Powers, P.S. (1975). Creativity and psychosis. *Archives of General Psychiatry, 32*, 70–73.

Andrews, F.M., & Withey, S.B. (1976). *Social indicators of well-being: America's perception of life quality.* New York: Plenum.

Aneshensel, C.S., & Huba, G.J. (1983). Depression, alcohol use, and smoking over one year: A four-wave longitudinal causal model. *Journal of Abnormal Psychology, 92*, 119–133.

Argyle, M. (1987). *The psychology of happiness.* London & New York: Methuen.

Arizmendi, T.G., & Affonso, D.D. (1984). Research on psychosocial functions and postpartum depression: A critique. *Birth, 11*, 237–240.

Aronson, E., & Carlsmith, J.M. (1963). Effect of severity of threat on the valuation of forbidden behavior. *Journal of Abnormal and Social Psychology, 66*, 584–588.

Arora, R.C., Kregel, L., & Meltzer, H.Y. (1984). Seasonal variation of serotonin uptake in normal controls and depressed patients. *Biological Psychiatry, 19*, 795–804.

Ashby, C.R., Carr, L.A., Cook, C.L., Steptoe, M.M., & Franks, D.D. (1988). Alteration of platelet serotonergic mechanisms and monoamine oxidase activity in premenstrual syndrome. *Biological Psychiatry, 24*, 225–233.

AuBuchon, P.G., & Calhoun, K.S. (1985). Menstrual cycle symptomatology: The role of social expectancy and experimental demand characteristics. *Psychosomatic Medicine, 47*, 35–45.

Averill, J.R. (1975). A semantic atlas of emotional concepts. *JSAS Catalog of Selected Documents in Psychology, 5*, 330.

Bäckström, T., Sanders, D., Leask, R., Davidson, D., Warner, P., & Bancroft, J. (1983). Mood, sexuality, hormones, and the menstrual cycle. II. Hormone levels and their relationship to premenstrual syndrome. *Psychosomatic medicine, 45*, 503–507.

Ballenger, J.C., Post, R.M., Jimerson, D.C., Lake, C.R., & Zuckerman, M. (1984). Neurobiological correlates of depression and anxiety in normal individuals. In R.M. Post & J.C. Ballenger (Eds.), *Neurobiology of Mood Disorders* (pp. 481–501). Baltimore, MD: Williams & Wilkins.

Bancroft, J., & Bäckström, T. (1985). Premenstrual syndrome. *Clinical Endocrinology, 22*, 313–336.

Bandura, A. (1977). *Social learning theory.* Englewood Cliffs, NJ: Prentice-Hall.

Barden, R.C., Garber, J., Duncan, S.W., & Masters, J.C. (1981). Cumulative effects of induced affective states in children: Accentuation, inoculation, and remediation. *Journal of Personality and Social Psychology, 40*, 750–760.

Barden, R.C., Garber, J., Leiman, B., Ford, M.E., & Masters, J.C. (1985). Factors governing the effective remediation of negative affect and its cognitive and behavioral consequences. *Journal of Personality and Social Psychology, 49*, 1040–1053.

Baron, R.A. (1987). Effects of negative ions on interpersonal attraction. *Journal of Personality and Social Psychology, 52*, 547–553.

Baron, R.A., Russell, G.W., & Arms, R.L. (1985). Negative ions and behavior: Impact on mood, memory, and aggression among Type A and Type B persons. *Journal of Personality and Social Psychology, 48*, 746–754.

Barrerra, M.J. (1988). Models of social support and life stress. In L.H. Cohen (Ed.), *Life events and psychological functioning* (pp. 211–236). Beverly Hills, CA: Sage.

Bartlett, J.C., Burleson, G., & Santrock, J.W. (1982). Emotional mood and memory in young children. *Journal of Experimental Child Psychology, 34*, 59–76.

Bartlett, J.C., & Santrock, J.W. (1977). Affect-dependent episodic memory in young children. *Child Development, 50*, 513–518.

Baumann, D.J., Cialdini, R., & Kenrick, D. (1981). Altruism as hedonism: Helping and self-gratification as equivalent processes. *Journal of Personality and Social Psychology, 40*, 1039–1046.

Baumgardner, A.H., & Arkin, R.M. (1988). Affective state mediates causal attributions for success and failure. *Motivation and Emotion, 12*, 99–111.

Beardslee, W.R., Bemporad, J., Keller, M.B., & Klerman, G.L. (1983). Children of parents with major affective disorder: A review. *American Journal of Psychiatry, 140*, 825–832.

Beck, A.T. (1967). *Depression: Clinical, experimental and theoretical aspects.* New York: Hoeber.

Beck, A.T. (1976). *Cognitive therapy and the emotional disorders.* New York: International Universities Press.

Beck, A.T., Brown, G., Steer, R.A., Eidelson, J.I., & Riskind, J.H. (1987). Differentiating anxiety and depression: A test of the cognitive content-specificity hypothesis. *Journal of Abnormal Psychology, 96*, 179–183.

Beck, A.T., Ward, C.H., Mendelsohn, M., Mock, J., & Erbaugh, J. (1961). An inventory for measuring depression. *Archives of General Psychiatry, 4*, 561–571.

Beck-Friss, J., von Rosen, D., Kjellman, B.F., Ljunggren, J., & Wetterberg, L. (1984). Melatonin in relation to body measures, sex, age, season, and the use of drugs in patients with major affective disorder and healthy subjects. *Psychoneuroendocrinology, 9*, 261–267.

Beiser, M. (1974). Components and correlates of mental well-being. *Journal of Health and Social Behavior, 15*, 320–327.

Bell, P.A. (1978). Affective state, attraction and affiliation. *Personality and Social Psychology Bulletin, 4*, 616–619.

Belmaker, R.H., Murphy, D.L., Wyatt, R.J., & Loriaux, L. (1974). Human platelet monoamine oxidase changes during the menstrual cycle. *Archives of General Psychiatry, 31*, 553–556.

Bem, D.J. (1965). An experimental analysis of self-persuasion. *Journal of Experimental Social Psychology, 1*, 199–218.

Bem, D.J. (1967). Self-perception: An alternative interpretation of cognitive dissonance phenomena. *Psychological Review, 74*, 183–200.

Bem, D.J., & McConnell, H.K. (1970). Testing the self-perception explanation of dissonance phenomena: On the salience of premanipulation attitudes. *Journal of Personality and Social Psychology, 14*, 23–31.

Berkowitz, L. (1987). Mood, self-awareness, and willingness to help. *Journal of Personality and Social Psychology, 52*, 721–729.

Berkowitz, L., Lepinski, J.P., & Angulo, E.J. (1969). Awareness of own anger level and subsequent aggression. *Journal of Personality and Social Psychology, 11*, 293–300.

Berkowitz, L., & Troccoli, B.T. (1986). An examination of the assumptions in the demand characteristics thesis: With special reference to the Velten Mood Induction Procedure. *Motivation and Emotion, 10*, 337–350.

Bernsted, L. Luggin, R., & Peterson, B. (1984). Psychosocial considerations of the premenstrual syndrome. *Acta Psychiatrica Scandanavica, 69*, 455–460.

Berry, D.T.R., & Webb, W.B. (1983). State measures and sleep stages. *Psychological Reports, 52*, 807–812.

Berry, D.T.R., & Webb, W.B. (1985). Mood and sleep in aging women. *Journal of Personality and Social Psychology, 49*, 1724–1727.

Berscheid, E. (1983). Emotion. In H.H. Kelley, E. Berscheid, A. Christensen, J.H. Harvey, T.L., Houston, G. Levinger, & E. McClintock (Eds.), *Close relationships* (pp. 110–168). New York: W.H. Freeman.

Bibring, E. (1953). The mechanism of depression. In P. Greenacre (Ed.), *Affective disorders* (pp. 13–48). New York: International Universities Press.

Bidzinska, E. (1984). Stress factors in affective diseases. *British Journal of Psychiatry, 144*, 161–166.

Biglan, A., & Craker, D. (1982). Effects of pleasant activities manipulation on depression. *Journal of Consulting and Clinical Psychology, 50*, 436–438.

Billings, A.G., & Moos, R.N. (1982). Psychosocial theory and research on depression: An integrative framework and review. *Clinical Psychology Review, 2*, 213–237.

Blaney, P.H. (1986). Affect and memory: A review. *Psychological Bulletin, 99*, 229–246.

Blatt, S.J. (1974). Levels of object representation in anaclitic and introjective depression. *Psychoanalytic Study of the Child, 29*, 107–157.

Blatt, S.J., D'Afflitti, J.P., & Quinlan, D.M. (1976). Experience of depression in normal young adults. *Journal of Abnormal Psychology, 85*, 383–389.

Borgatta, E.I. (1961). Mood, personality, and interaction. *Journal of General Psychology, 64*, 105–137.

Boucher, J., & Osgood, C.E. (1969). The Pollyanna hypothesis. *Journal of Verbal Learning and Verbal Behavior, 8*, 1–8.

Bouman, T.K., & Luteijn, F. (1986). Relations between the Pleasant Events Schedule, depression, and other aspects of psychopathology. *Journal of Abnormal Psychology, 95*, 373–377.

Bousfield, W.A. (1950). The relationship between mood and the production of affectively toned associates. *Journal of General Psychology, 42*, 67–85.

Bower, G.H. (1981). Mood and memory. *American Psychologist, 36*, 129–148.

Bower, G.H., & Cohen, P.R. (1982). Emotional influences in memory and thinking: Data and theory. In M.S. Clark, & S.T. Fiske (Eds.), *Affect and cognition: The Seventeenth Annual Carnegie Symposium on Cognition* (pp. 291–331). Hillsdale, NJ: Erlbaum.

Bower, G.H., Gilligan, S.G., & Monteiro, K.P. (1981). Selectivity and learning caused by affective states. *Journal of Experimental Psychology: General, 110*, 451–473.

Bower, G.H., & Mayer, J.D. (1985). Failure to replicate mood-dependent retrieval. *Bulletin of the Psychonomic Society, 23*, 39–42.

Bower, G.H., Monteiro, K.P., & Gilligan, S.G. (1978). Emotional mood as a context for learning and recall. *Journal of Verbal Learning and Verbal Behavior, 17*, 573–587.

Bradburn, N.M. (1969). *The structure of psychological well-being*. Chicago: Aldine.

Bradburn, N.M., & Caplovitz, D. (1965). *Reports on happiness*. Chicago: Aldine.

Bradley, B., & Mathews, A. (1983). Negative self-schemata in clinical depression. *British Journal of Clinical Psychology, 22*, 173–181.

Brehm, J.W., & Wicklund, R.A. (1970). Regret and dissonance reduction as a function of postdecision salience of dissonant information. *Journal of Personality and Social Psychology, 14*, 1–7.

Brenner, B. (1975). Enjoyment as a preventive of depressive affect. *Journal of Community Psychology, 3*, 346–357.

Breslow, R., Kocsis, J., & Belkin, B. (1981). Contribution of the depressive perspective to memory function in depression. *American Journal of Psychiatry, 138*, 227–230.

Brewer, D., Doughtie, E.B., & Lubin, B. (1980). Induction of mood and mood shift. *Journal of Clinical Psychology, 36*, 215–226.

Brewin, C.R. (1985). Depression and causal attributions: What is their relation? *Psychological Bulletin, 98*, 297–309.

Brock, T.C. (1962). Cognitive restructuring and attitude change. *Journal of Abnormal and Social Psychology, 64*, 264–271.

Brown, G.W., & Harris, T. (1978). *Social origins of depression: A study of psychiatric disorder in women.* New York: Free Press.

Brown, J.D., & Taylor, S.E. (1986). Affect and the processing of personal information: Evidence for mood-activated self-schemata. *Journal of Experimental Social Psychology, 22*, 436–452.

Bruner, J.S., & Postman, L. (1947). Emotional selectivity in perception and reaction. *Journal of Personality, 16*, 69–77.

Bryant, J., & Zillman, D. (1984). Using television to alleviate boredom and stress: Selective exposure as a function of induced excitational states. *Journal of Broadcasting, 28*, 1–20.

Buchwald, A.M. (1977). Depressive mood and estimates of reinforcement frequency. *Journal of Abnormal Psychology, 86*, 443–446.

Buchwald, A.M., Coyne, J.C., & Cole, C.S. (1978). A critical evaluation of the learned helplessness model. *Journal of Abnormal Psychology, 87*, 180–193.

Buchwald, A.M., Strack, S., & Coyne, J.C. (1981). Demand characteristics and the Velten Mood Induction Procedure. *Journal of Consulting and Clinical Psychology, 49*, 478–479.

Buck, R. (1984). *The communication of emotion.* New York: Guilford.

Byck, R. (1976). Peptide transmitters: A unifying hypothesis for euphoria, respiration, sleep and the action of lithium. *Lancet, 2*, 72–73.

Byrne, D. (1961). The Repression-Sensitization Scale: Rationale, reliability, and validity. *Journal of Personality, 29*, 334–349.

Byrne, D. (1971). *The attraction paradigm.* New York: Academic Press.

Byrne, D., & Nelson, D. (1965). Attraction as a linear function of proportion of positive reinforcements. *Journal of Personality and Social Psychology, 1*, 659–663.

Caccioppo, J.T., Petty, R.E., Losch, M.E., & Kim, H.S. (1986). Electromyographic activity over facial muscle regions can differentiate the valence and intensity of affective reactions. *Journal of Personality and Social Psychology, 50*, 260–268.

Cantor, J.R., Bryant, J., & Zillman, D. (1974). Enhancement of humor appreciation by transferred excitation. *Journal of Personality and Social Psychology, 30*, 812–821.

Cantor, J.R., & Zillman, D. (1973). The effect of affective state and emotional arousal on music appreciation. *Journal of General Psychology, 89*, 97–108.

Cantor, J.R., Zillman, D., & Bryant, J. (1975). Enhancement of experienced sexual arousal in response to erotic stimuli through misattribution of unrelated residual excitation. *Journal of Personality and Social Psychology, 32*, 69–75.

Carlsmith, J.M., Ebbesen, E.E., Lepper, M.R., Zanna, M.P., Joncas, A.J., & Abelson, R.P. (1969). Dissonance reduction following forced attention to the dissonance. *Proceedings of the 77th Annual Convention of the American Psychological Association, 4*, 321–322.

Carlson, M., Charlin, V., & Miller, N. (1988). Positive mood and helping behavior: A test of six hypotheses. *Journal of Personality and Social Psychology, 55*, 211–229.

Carlson, M., & Miller, N. (1987). Explanation of the relation between negative mood and helping. *Psychological Bulletin, 102*, 91–108.

Carroll, B.J., Feinberg, M., Greden, J.F., Tarika, J., Albala, A.A., Haskett, R.I., McI. James, N., Kronfol, Z., Lohr, N., Steiner, M., deVigne, J.P., & Young, E. (1981). A specific laboratory test for the diagnosis of melancholia. *Archives of General Psychiatry, 38*, 15–22.

Carson, T.P., & Adams, H.E. (1980). Activity valence as a function of mood change. *Journal of Abnormal Psychology, 89*, 368–377.

Carver, C.S., Blaney, P.H., & Scheier, M.F. (1979). Reassertion and giving up: The interactive role of self-directed attention and outcome expectancy. *Journal of Personality and Social Psychology, 37*, 1859–1870.

Carver, C.S., & Scheier, M.F. (1981). *Attention and self-regulation: A control-theory approach to human behavior.* New York: Springer-Verlag.

Carver, C.S., & Scheier, M.F. (1982). Control theory: A useful conceptual framework for personality-social, clinical, and health psychology. *Psychological Bulletin, 92*, 111–135.

Carver, C.S., & Scheier, M.F. (1986). Functional and dysfunctional responses to anxiety: The interaction between expectancies and self-focused attention. In R. Schwarzer (Ed.), *Self-related cognitions in anxiety and motivation* (pp. 111–141). Hillsdale, NJ: Erlbaum.

Cattell, R.B. (1973). *Personality and mood by questionnaire.* San Francisco: Jossey-Bass.

Cernovsky, Z.Z. (1984). Life stress measures and reported frequency of sleep disorders. *Perceptual and Motor Skills, 58*, 39–49.

Charney, D.S., & Heninger, G.R. (1986). Alpha-adrenergic and opiate receptor blockade. *Archives of General Psychiatry, 43*, 1037–1041.

Charry, J.M., & Hawkinshire, F.B.W. (1981). Effects of atmospheric electricity on some substrates of disordered social behavior. *Journal of Personality and Social Psychology, 41*, 185–197.

Cherlin, A., & Reeder, L.G. (1975). The dimensions of psychological well-being: A critical review. *Sociological Methods and Research, 4*, 189–214.

Choung, C.J., Coulam, C.B., Bergstralh, E.J., O'Fallon, W.M., & Steinmetz, G.F. (1988). Clinical trial of naltrexone in premenstrual syndrome. *Obstetrics and Gynecology, 72*, 332–336.

Choung, C.J., Coulam, C.B., Kao, P.C., Bergstralh, E.J., & Go, V.L. (1985). Neuropeptide levels in premenstrual syndrome. *Fertility and Sterility, 44*, 760–765.

Cialdini, R.B., Baumann, D.J., & Kenrick, D.T. (1981). Insights from sadness: A three step model of the development of altruism as hedonism. *Developmental Review, 1*, 207–223.

Cialdini, R.B., Darby, B., & Vincent, J. (1973). Transgression and altruism: A case for hedonism. *Journal of Experimental Social Psychology, 9*, 502–516.

Cialdini, R.B., & Kenrick, D.T. (1976). Altruism as hedonism: A social developmental perspective on the relationship of negative mood state and helping. *Journal of Personality and Social Psychology, 34*, 907–914.

Cialdini, R.B., Schaller, M., Houlihan, D., Arps, K., Fultz, J., & Beaman, A.L. (1987). Empathy-based helping: Is it selflessly or selfishly motivated? *Journal of Personality and Social Psychology, 52*, 749–758.

Clark, D.M., & Teasdale, J.D. (1982). Diurnal variation in clinical depression and accessibility of memories of positive and negative experiences. *Journal of Abnormal Psychology, 91*, 87–95.

Clark, D.M., & Teasdale, J.D. (1985). Constraints on the effects of mood on memory. *Journal of Personality and Social Psychology, 48*, 1595–1608.

Clark, D.M., Teasdale, J.D., Broadbent, D.E., & Martin, M. (1983). Effect of mood on lexical decisions. *Bulletin of the Psychonomic Society, 21*, 175–178.

Clark, L.A., & Watson, D. (1988). Mood and the mundane: Relations between daily life events and self-reported mood. *Journal of Personality and Social Psychology, 54*, 296-308.

Clark, M.S., & Fiske, S.T. (1982). *Affect and cognition: The Seventeenth Annual Carnegie Symposium on Cognition.* Hillsdale, NJ: Erlbaum.

Clark, M.S., & Isen, A.M. (1982). Toward understanding the relationship between feeling states and social behavior. In A.H. Hastorf, & A.M. Isen (Eds.), *Cognitive social psychology* (pp. 73–108). New York: Elsevier.

Claustrat, B., Chazot, G., Brun, J., Jordan, I., & Sassolas, G. (1984). A chronobiological study of melatonin and cortisol secretion in depressed subjects: Plasma melatonin, a biochemical marker for depression. *Biological Psychiatry, 19*, 1215–1228.

Clum, G.A, & Clum, J. (1973). Mood variability and defense mechanism preference. *Psychological Reports, 32*, 910.

Cohen, J. (1977). *Statistical Power Analysis for the Behavioral Sciences.* Orlando, FL: Academic Press.

Cohen, M.B., Baker, G., Cohen, R.A., Fromm-Reichmann, F., & Weigert, E.V. (1954). An intensive study of twelve cases of manic-depressive psychosis. *Psychiatry, 17*, 103–137.

Cohen, M.R., & Pickar, D. (1981). Pharmacological challenges to the endogenous opiod system in affective illness. *Journal of Clinical Psychopharmacology, 1*, 223–231.

Colby, C.Z., Lanzetta, J.T., & Kleck, R.E. (1977). Effects of the expression of pain on autonomic and pain tolerance responses to subject-controlled pain. *Psychophysiology, 14*, 537-540.

Cole, J.O. (1964). Therapeutic efficacy of antidepressive drugs. *Journal of the American Medical Association, 1*, 448–462.

Coleman, R.E. (1975). Manipulation of self-esteem as a determinant of mood of elated and depressed women. *Journal of Abnormal Psychology, 84*, 693–700.

Colt, E.W.D., Wardlaw, S.L., & Frantz, A.G. (1981). The effect of running on plasma beta-endorphin. *Life Sciences, 28*, 1637–1640.

Conger, J.J. (1951). The effects of alcohol on conflict behavior in the albino rat. *Quarterly Journal of Studies on Alcohol, 12*, 1–29.

Cooper, J., & Fazio, R.H. (1984). A new look at dissonance theory. In L. Berkowitz (Ed.), *Advances in experimental social psychology* (pp. 229–266, Vol. 17). New York: Academic Press.

Coppen, A.J., & Shaw, D.M. (1963). Mineral metabolism in melancholia. *British Medical Journal, 2*, 1439–1444.

Coppen, A.J., Shaw, D.M., Malleson, A., & Costain, R. (1966). Mineral metabolism in mania. *British Medical Journal, 1*, 71–75.

Coppen, A., Whybrow, P.C., Noguera, R., Maggs, R., & Prange, A.J. (1972). The comparative antidepressant value of L-tryptophan and imipramine with and without attempted potentiation by liothyronine. *Archives of General Psychiatry, 26*, 234–241.

Costa, P.T., & McCrae, R.R. (1980). Influence of extraversion and neuroticism on subjective well-being: Happy and unhappy people. *Journal of Personality and Social Psychology, 38*, 668–678.

Costa, P.T., & McCrae, R.R. (1985). Hypochondriasis, neuroticism, and aging: When are somatic complaints unfounded? *American Psychologist, 40*, 19–28.

Costello, C.G. (1978). A critical review of Seligman's laboratory experiments on learned helplessness and depression in humans. *Journal of Abnormal Psychology, 87*, 21–31.

Coyne, J.C. (1976a). Depression and the response of others. *Journal of Abnormal Psychology, 85*, 186–193.

Coyne, J.C. (1976b). Toward an interactional description of depression. *Psychiatry, 39*, 28–40.

Coyne, J.C. (1986). *Essential papers on depression*. New York: New York University Press.

Coyne, J.C., & Gotlib, I.H. (1983). The role of cognition in depression: A critical appraisal. *Psychological Bulletin, 94*, 472–505.

Coyne, J.C., & Gotlib, I.H. (1986). Studying the role of cognition in depression: Well-trodden paths and cul-de-sacs. *Cognitive Therapy and Research, 7*, 695–705.

Coyne, J.C., Kessler, R.C., Tal, M., Turnbull, J., Wortman, C.B., & Greden, J.F. (1987). Living with a depressed person. *Journal of Consulting and Clinical Psychology, 55*, 347–352.

Craighead, W.E., Hickey, K.S., & DeMonbreun, B.G. (1979). Distortion of perception and recall of neutral feedback in depression. *Cognitive Therapy and Research, 3*, 291–298.

Cramer, P. (1968). *Word association*. New York: Academic Press.

Crook, T., Eliot, J. (1980). Parental death during childhood and adult depression: A critical review of the literature. *Psychological Bulletin, 87*, 252–259.

Cunningham, M.R. (1979). Weather, mood, and helping behavior: quasi-experiments with the sunshine samaritan. *Journal of Personality and Social Psychology, 37*, 1947–1956.

Cunningham, M.R. (1988a). Does happiness mean friendliness? Induced mood and heterosexual self-disclosure. *Personality and Social Psychology Bulletin, 14*, 283–297.

Cunningham, M.R. (1988b). What do you do when you're happy or blue? Mood, expectancies and behavioral interest. *Motivation and Emotion, 12*, 309–332.

Cunningham, M.R., Steinberg, J., & Grev, R. (1980). Wanting to and having to help: Separate motivations for positive mood and guilt-induced helping. *Journal of Personality and Social Psychology, 38*, 181–192.

Daly, E.M., Lancee, W.J., & Polivy, J. (1983). A conical model for the taxonomy of emotional experience. *Journal of Personality and Social Psychology, 45*, 443–457.

Darwin, C. (1872). *The expression of the emotions in man and animals*. London: John Murray.

Davis, J.M., Koslow, S.H., Gibbons, R.D., Maas, J.W., Bowden, C.L., Casper, R., Hanin, I., Javaid, J.I., Chang, S.S., & Stokes, P.E. (1988). Cerebrospinal fluid and urinary biogenic amines in depressed patients and healthy controls. *Archives of General Psychiatry, 45*, 705–717.

Dawson, M.E., & Schell, A.M. (1982). Electrodermal responses to attended and nonattended significant stimuli during dichotic listening. *Journal of Experimental Psychology: Human Perception and Performance, 8*, 315–324.

DeJong, R., Rubinow, D.R., Roy-Byrne, P., Hoban, M.C., Grover, G.N., & Post, R.M. (1985). Premenstrual mood disorder and psychiatric illness. *American Journal of Psychiatry, 142*, 1359–1361.

DeLeon-Jones, F.A., Steinberg, J., Dekirmejian, H., & Garner, D. (1978). MHPG excretion during the menstrual cycle of women. *Communications in Psychopharmacology, 2*, 267–274.

DeLongis, A., Coyne, J.C., Dakof, G., Folkman, S., & Lazarus, R.S. (1982). Relationship of daily hassles, uplifts and major life events to health status. *Health Psychology, 1*, 119–136.

DeLongis, A., Folkman, S., & Lazarus, R.S. (1988). The impact of daily stress on health and mood: Psychological and social resources as mediators. *Journal of Personality and Social Psychology, 54*, 486–495.

DeMet, E.M., Halaris, A.E., & Gwirtsman, H.E. (1982). Effects of desipramine on diurnal rhythms of plasma 3-methoxy-4-hydroxyphenylglycol (MHPG) in depressed patients. *Psychopharmacological Bulletin, 18*, 221–223.

DeMonbreun, B.G., & Craighead, W.E. (1977). Distortion of perception and recall of positive and neutral feedback in depression. *Cognitive Therapy and Research, 1*, 311–329.

Dennard, D.O., & Hokarson, J.E. (1986). Performance on two cognitive tasks by dysphoric and nondysphoric students. *Cognitive Therapy and Research, 10*, 377–386.

Depue, R.A. (1979). *The psychobiology of the depressive disorders: Implications for the effects of stress.* New York: Academic Press.

Depue, R.A. (1987). *General Behavior Inventory.* University of Minnesota, Department of Psychology, Minneapolis, MN.

Depue, R.A., Kleiman, R.M., Davis, P., Hutchinson, M., & Krauss, S.P. (1985). The behavioral high-risk paradigm and bipolar affective disorder, VIII: Serum free cortisol in nonpatient cyclothymic subjects selected by the General Behavior Inventory. *American Journal of Psychiatry, 142*, 175–181.

Depue, R.A., Krauss, S., Spoont, M.R., & Arbisi, P. (1989). General Behavior Inventory identification of unipolar and bipolar affective conditions in a nonclinical university population. *Journal of Abnormal Psychology, 98*, 117–126.

Depue, R.A., & Monroe, S.M. (1978). The unipolar-bipolar distinction in the depressive disorders. *Psychological Bulletin, 85*, 1001–1030.

Depue, R.A., Monroe, S.M., & Shackman, S.L. (1979). The psychobiology of human disease: Implications for conceptualizing the depressive disorders. In R.A. Depue (Ed.), *The psychobiology of the depressive disorders: Implications for the effects of stress* (pp. 3–20). New York: Academic Press.

Depue, R.A., Slater, J.F., Wolfstetter-Kausch, H., Klein, D., Goplerud, E., & Farr, D. (1981). A behavioral paradigm for identifying persons at risk for bipolar depressive disorder: A conceptual framework and five validation studies. *Journal of Abnormal Psychology Monograph, 90*, 381–437.

Dermer, M., Cohen, S.J., Jacobsen, E., & Anderson, E.A. (1979). Evaluative judgments of aspects of life as a function of vicarious exposure to hedonic extremes. *Journal of Personality and Social Psychology, 37*, 247–260.

Derry, P., & Kuiper, N. (1981). Schematic processing and self-reference in clinical depression. *Journal of Abnormal Psychology, 90*, 286–297.

Derryberry, D. (1988). Emotional influences on evaluative judgments: Roles of arousal, attention, and spreading activation. *Motivation and Emotion, 12*, 23–54.

Derryberry D., & Rothbart, M.K. (1988). Arousal, affect, and attention as components of temperament. *Journal of Personality and Social Psychology, 55*, 958–966.

Diener, E. (1984). Subjective well-being. *Psychological Bulletin, 95*, 542–575.

Diener, E., & Emmons, R.A. (1984). The independence of positive and negative affect. *Journal of Personality and Social Psychology, 47*, 1105–1117.

Diener E., & Iran-Nejad, A. (1986). The relationship in experience between different types of affect. *Journal of Personality and Social Psychology, 50*, 1131–1138.

Diener, E., Larsen, R.J., Levine, S., & Emmons, R.A. (1985). Intensity and frequency: The underlying dimensions of positive and negative affect. *Journal of Personality and Social Psychology, 48*, 1253–1265.

Dittman, A.T. (1972). *Interpersonal messages of emotion.* New York: Springer.

Dobson, K.S., & Shaw, B.F. (1981). The effects of self-correction on cognitive distortions in depression. *Cognitive Therapy and Research, 5*, 391–403.

Dohrenwend, B.S., & Dohrenwend, B.P. (1974). *Stressful life events: Their nature and effects.* New York: Wiley.

Dohrenwend, B.S., Krasnoff, L., Askenasy, A.R., & Dohrenwend, B.P. (1978). Exemplification of a method for scaling life events: The PERI life events scale. *Journal of Health and Social Behavior, 19*, 205–229.

Dovidio, J.F. (1984). Helping behavior and altruism: An empirical and conceptual overview. In L. Berkowitz (Ed.), *Advances in experimental social psychology* (Vol. 17, pp. 362–427). New York: Academic Press.

Dovidio, J.F., & Morris, W.N. (1975). Effects of stress and commonality of fate on helping behavior. *Journal of Personality and Social Psychology, 31*, 145–149.

Drachman, D., & Worchel, S. (1976). Misattribution of dissonance arousal as a means of dissonance reduction. *Sociometry, 39*, 53–59.

Dunbar, G.C., & Lishman, W.A. (1984). Depression, recognition-memory and hedonic tone: A signal detection analysis. *British Journal of Psychiatry, 144*, 376–382.

Duncker, K. (1945). On problem solving. *Psychological Monographs, 58*, (5, Whole No. 270).

Dunner, D.L., Patrick, V., & Fieve, R.R. (1979). Life events at the onset of bipolar affective illness. *American Journal of Psychiatry, 136*, 508–511.

Duval, S., & Wicklund, R. (1972). *A theory of objective self-awareness.* New York: Academic Press.

Eastwood, M.R., Whitton, J.L., Kramer, P.M., & Peter, A.M. (1985). Infradian rhythms: A comparison of affective disorders and normal persons. *Archives of General Psychiatry, 42*, 295–299.

Eckenrode, J. (1984). Impact of chronic and acute stressors on daily reports of mood. *Journal of Personality and Social Psychology, 46*, 907–918.

Ehlers, C.L., Frank, E., & Kupfer, D.J. (1988). Social zeitgebers and biological rhythms. *Archives of General Psychiatry, 45*, 948–952.

Ehrlichman, H., & Halpern, J.N. (1988). Affect and memory: Effects of pleasant and unpleasant odors on retrieval of happy and unhappy memories. *Journal of Personality and Social Psychology, 55*, 769–779.

Eich, J.E. (1980). The cue-dependent nature of state-dependent retrieval. *Memory and Cognition, 8*, 157–173.

Ekman, P. (1984). Expression and the nature of emotion. In K.R. Scherer, & P. Ekman (Eds.), *Approaches to emotion* (pp. 319–344). Hillsdale, NJ: Erlbaum.

Ekman, P., & Friesen, W.V. (1975). *Unmasking the face.* Englewood Cliffs, NJ: Prentice-Hall.

Ellis, H.C. (1985). On the importance of mood intensity and encoding demands in memory: Commentary on Hasher, Rose, Zacks, Sanft, and Doren. *Journal of Experimental Psychology: General, 114*, 392–395.

Ellis, H.C., Thomas, R.L., McFarland, A.D., & Lane, J.W. (1985). Emotional mood states and retrieval in episodic memory. *Journal of Experimental Psychology: Learning, Memory, and Cognition, 11*, 363–370.

Ellis, H.C., Thomas, R.L., & Rodriguez, I.A. (1984). Emotional mood states and memory: Elaborative encoding, semantic processing, and cognitive effort. *Journal of Experimental Psychology: Learning, Memory, and Cognition, 10*, 470–482.

Ellis, H.C., & Ashbrook, P.W. (1988). Resource allocation model of the effects of depressed mood states on memory. In K. Fiedler, & J.P. Forgas (Eds.), *Affect, cognition and social behavior* (pp. 25–43). Toronto: Hogrefe.

Emmons, R.A. (1986). *Personal strivings: Toward a theory of personality and subjective well-being.* Unpublished doctoral dissertation, University of Illinois at Champaign.

Emmons, R.A., & Diener, E. (1985). Personality correlates of subjective well-being. *Personality and Social Psychology Bulletin, 11*, 89–97.

Emmons, R.A., & Diener, E. (1986). A goal-affect analysis of everyday situational choices. *Journal of Research in Personality, 20*, 309–326.

Epstein, S. (1983). A research paradigm for the study of personality and emotions. In M.M. Page (Ed.), *Personality—Current theory and research: 1982 Nebraska symposium on motivation* (pp. 91–154). Lincoln: University of Nebraska Press.

Ewert, O. (1970). The attitudinal character of emotion. In M. Arnold (Ed.), *Feelings and emotions* (pp. 233–240). New York: Academic Press.

Extein, I., Pottash, A.L.C., Gold, M.S., & Cowdry, R.W. (1984). Changes in TSH responses to TRH in affective illness. In R.M. Post and J.C. Ballenger (Eds.), *Neurobiology of Affective Disorders* (pp. 297–310). Baltimore, MD: Williams & Wilkins.

Eysenck, H.J. (1956). The inheritance of extraversion-introversion. *Acta Psychologica, 12*, 95–110.

Eysenck, H.J., & Eysenck, S.B.G. (1968). *Manual of the Eysenck personality inventory*. San Diego: Education and Industrial Testing Service.

Eysenck, H.J., & Eysenck, S.B.G. (1975). *Manual of the Eysenck Personality Questionnaire*. London: Hodder and Stoughton.

Fazio, R.H., Zanna, M.P., & Cooper, J. (1977). Dissonance and self-perception: An integrative view of each theory's proper domain of application. *Journal of Experimental Social Psychology, 13*, 464–479.

Feinberg, M., & Carroll, B.J. (1984). Biological "markers" for endogenous depression: Effect of age, severity of illness, weight loss, and polarity. *Archives of General Psychiatry, 41*, 1080–1085.

Feldmacher-Reiss, E.E. (1958). The application of triiodothyronine to the treatment of mental disorders. *Journal of Nervous and Mental Disease, 127*, 540–548.

Fenigstein, A., Scheier, M.F., & Buss, A.H., (1975). Public and private self-consciousness: Assessment and theory. *Journal of Consulting and Clinical Psychology, 43*, 522–527.

Ferster, C. (1973). A functional analysis of depression. *American Psychologist, 28*, 857–870.

Feshbach, S., & Feshbach, N. (1963). Influence of the stimulus object upon the complementary and supplementary projection of fear. *Journal of Abnormal and Social Psychology, 66*, 498–502.

Feshbach, S., & Singer, R.D. (1957). The effects of fear arousal and suppression fear upon social perception. *Journal of Abnormal and Social Psychology, 55*, 283–288.

Feski, A., Harris, B., Walker, R.F., Riad-Fahney, D., Newcombe, R.G. (1984). "Maternity blues" and hormone levels in saliva. *Journal of Affective Disorders, 6*, 351–355.

Festinger, L. (1974). *Conflict, decision, and dissonance*. Stanford: Stanford University Press.

Festinger, L., & Carlsmith, J.M. (1959). Cognitive consequences of forced compliance. *Journal of Abnormal and Social Psychology, 58*, 203–211.

Fibiger, W., Singer, G., Miller, A.J., Armstrong, S., & Datar, M. (1984). Cortisol and catecholamine changes as functions of time-of-day and self-reported mood. *Neuroscience and Biobehavioral Reviews, 8*, 523–530.

Finkel, C.B., Glass, C.R., & Merluzzi, T.V. (1982). Differential discrimination of self-referent statements by depressives and nondepressives. *Cognitive Therapy and Research, 6*, 173–183.

Fisher, J.D., Nadler, A., & Whitcher-Alagna, S. (1982). Recipient reactions to aid. *Psychological Bulletin, 91*, 27–54.

Fogarty, S.L., & Hemsley, D.R. (1983). Depression and the accessibility of memories. *British Journal of Psychiatry, 142*, 232–237.

Folkins, C.H., & Sime, W.E. (1981). Physical fitness training and mental health. *American Psychologist, 36*, 373–389.

Folkman, S., & Lazarus, R.S. (1985). If it changes it must be process: Study of emotion and coping during the three stages of a college examination. *Journal of Personality and Social Psychology, 48*, 150–170.

Folkman, S., & Lazarus, R.S. (1988). Coping as a mediator of emotion. *Journal of Personality and Social Psychology, 54*, 466–475.

Folkman, S., Lazarus, R.S., Dunkel-Schetter, C., DeLongis, A., & Gruen, R. (1986). The dynamics of a stressful encounter: Cognitive appraisal, coping, and encounter outcomes. *Journal of Personality and Social Psychology, 50*, 992–1003.

Follette, V.M., & Jacobson, N.S. (1987). Importance of attributions as a predictor of how people cope with failure. *Journal of Personality and Social Psychology, 52*, 1205–1211.

Folstein, M.F., DePaulo, J.R., & Trepp, K. (1982). Unusual mood stability in patients taking lithium. *British Journal of Psychiatry, 140*, 188–191.

Forest, D., Clark, M.S., Mills, J., & Isen, A.M. (1979). Helping as a function of feeling state and nature of the helping behavior. *Motivation and Emotion, 3*, 161–169.

Forgas, J.P., & Bower, G.H. (1987). Mood effects on person perception judgments. *Journal of Personality and Social Psychology, 53*, 53–60.

Forgas, J.P., Bower, G.H., & Krantz, S.E. (1984). The influence of mood on perception of social interactions. *Journal of Experimental Social Psychology, 20*, 497–513.

Forgas, J.P., & Moylan, S. (1987). After the movies: Transient mood and social judgments. *Personality and Social Psychology Bulletin, 13*, 467–477.

Frankel, A., & Snyder, M.L. (1978). Poor performance following unsolvable problems: Learned helplessness or egotism? *Journal of Personality and Social Psychology, 36*, 1415–1423.

Freud, S. (1927). *The ego and the id.* London: Hogarth.

Freud, S. (1986). Mourning and melancholia. In J.C. Coyne (Ed.), *Essential papers on depression* (pp. 48–63). New York: New York University Press. (Original work published in 1917).

Frey, A.H. (1961). Human behavior and atmospheric ions. *Psychological Review, 68*, 225–228.

Fried, R., & Berkowitz, L. (1979). Music hath charms . . . and can influence helpfulness. *Journal of Applied Social Psychology, 9*, 199–208.

Fries, E.D. (1954). Mental depression in hypertensive patients treated for long periods with large doses of reserpine. *New England Journal of Medicine, 251*, 1006–1008.

Frith, C.D., Stevens, M., Johnstone, E.C., Deakin, J.F.W., Lawler, P., & Crow, J. (1983). Effects of ECT and depression on various aspects of memory. *British Journal of Psychiatry, 142*, 610–617.

Frost, R.O., Goolkasian, G.A., Ely, R.J., & Blanchard, F.A. (1982), Depression, restraint, and eating behavior. *Behaviour Research and Therapy, 20*, 113–121.

Frost, R.O., & Green, M.L. (1982). Velten mood induction procedure effects: Duration and post-experimental removal. *Personality and Social Psychology Bulletin, 8*, 341–347.

Fuchs, C.Z., & Rehm, L.P. (1977). A self-control behavior therapy program for depression. *Journal of Consulting and Clinical Psychology, 45*, 206–215.

Gage, D.F., & Safer, M.A. (1985). Hemisphere differences in the mood state-dependent effect for recognition of emotional faces. *Journal of Experimental Psychology: Learning, Memory, and Cognition, 11*, 752–763.

Garfinkel, P.E., Warsh, J.J., & Stancer, H.C. (1979). Depression: New evidence in support of biological differentiation. *American Journal of Psychiatry, 136*, 535–539.

Gazzaniga, M.S. (1985). *The social brain: Discovering the networks of the mind.* New York: Basic Books.

Gerner, R.H., & Bunney, W.E. (1986). Biological hypothesis of affective disorder. In S. Arieti (Ed.), *Handbook of Psychiatry, Vol. 8: Biological Psychiatry* (pp. 265–301). NY: Basic Books.

Gerner, R.H., Catlin, D.H., Gorelick, D.A., Hui, K., & Lui, C.H. (1980). Beta-endorphin: Intravenous infusion causes behavioral change. *Archives of General Psychiatry, 37*, 642–647.

Gerrig, R.J., & Bower, G.H. (1982). Emotional influences on word recognition. *Bulletin of the Psychonomic Society, 19,* 197–200.

Giannini, A.J., Price, W.A., & Loiselle, R.H. (1984). Beta-endorphin withdrawal: A possible cause of premenstrual tension syndrome. *International Journal of Psychophysiology, 1,* 341–343.

Gibbons, F.X. (1986). Social comparison and depression: Company's effect on misery. *Journal of Personality and Social Psychology, 51,* 140–148.

Gibbons, R.D., & Davis, J.M. (1986). Consistent evidence for a biological subtype of depression characterized by low CSF monoamine levels. *Acta Psychiatrica Scandanavica, 74,* 8–12.

Gilligan, S.G., & Bower, G.H. (1984). Cognitive consequences of emotional arousal. In C.E. Izard, J. Kagan, & R.B. Zajonc (Eds.), *Emotions, cognition, and behavior* (pp. 547–588). New York: Cambridge University Press.

Gillin, J.C., Duncan, W., Pettigrew, K.D., Frankel, B.L., & Snyder, F. (1979). Successful separation of depressed, normal, and insomniac patients by EEG sleep data. *Archives of General Psychiatry, 36,* 85–90.

Gillin, J.C., Sitaram, M., Wehr, T., Duncan, W., Post, R., Murphy, D.L., Mendelson, W.B., Wyatt, R.J., & Bunney, W.E. (1984). Sleep and affective illness. In R.M. Post & J.C. Ballenger (Eds.), *Neurobiology of mood disorders* (pp. 157–189). Baltimore, MD: Williams & Wilkins.

Globus, G.G. (1969). A syndrome associated with sleeping late. *Psychosomatic Medicine, 31,* 528–535.

Gold, M.S., Pottash, A.L.C., & Extein, I. (1981). Hypothyroidism and depression: Evidence from complete thyroid function evaluation. *Journal of the American Medical Association, 25,* 1919–1922.

Goldstein, I.B. (1965). The relationship of muscle tension and autonomic activity to psychiatric disorders. *Psychosomatic Medicine, 27,* 39–52.

Goodhart, D.E. (1985). Some psychological effects associated with positive and negative thinking about stressful event outcomes: Was Pollyanna right? *Journal of Personality and Social Psychology, 48,* 216–232.

Goodwin, F.K., & Jamison, K.R. (1984). The natural course of manic-depressive illness. In R.M. Post, & J.C. Ballenger (Eds.), *Neurobiology of mood disorders* (pp. 20–37). Baltimore: Williams & Wilkins.

Goplerud, E., & Depue, R.A. (1985). Behavioral response to naturally occurring stress in cyclothymia and dysthymia. *Journal of Abnormal Psychology, 94,* 128–139.

Gorman, B.S., & Wessman, A.E. (1974). The relationship of cognitive styles and moods. *Journal of Clinical Psychology, 30,* 18–25.

Gotlib, I.H. (1983). Perception and recall of interpersonal feedback: Negative bias in depression. *Cognitive Therapy and Research, 7,* 399–412.

Gotlib, I.H. (1984). Depression and general psychopathology in university students. *Journal of Abnormal Psychology, 93,* 19–30.

Gotlib, I.H., & McCann, C.D. (1984). Construct accessibility and depression: An examination of cognitive and affective factors. *Journal of Personality and Social Psychology, 47,* 427–439.

Gotlib, I.H., & Robinson, L.A. (1982). Responses to depressed individuals: Discrepancies between self-report and observer-rated behavior. *Journal of Abnormal Psychology, 91,* 231–240.

Gottman, J.M. (1981). *Time series analysis: A comprehensive introduction for social scientists.* Cambridge, England: Cambridge University Press.

Gouaux, C. (1971). Induced affective states and interpersonal attraction. *Journal of Personality and Social Psychology, 20,* 37–43.

Greenberg, J., & Pyszczynski, T. (1986). Persistent high self-focus after failure and low self-focus after success: The depressive self-focusing style. *Journal of Personality and Social Psychology, 50,* 1039–1044.

Greenspan, K., Schildkraut, J.J., Gordon, E.K., Baer, L., Aronoff, M.S., & Durell, J. (1970). Catecholamine metabolism in affective disorders, III: MHPG and other catecholamine metabolites in patients treated with lithium carbonate. *Journal of Psychiatry Research, 7*, 171–183.

Griest, J., & Griest, T. (1979). *Antidepressant treatment.* Baltimore, MD: Williams & Wilkins.

Griffitt, W., & Veitch, R. (1971). Hot and crowded: Influences of population density and temperature on interpersonal affective behavior. *Journal of Personality and Social Psychology, 11*, 92–98.

Gurtman, M.B. (1987). Depressive affect and disclosures as factors in interpersonal rejection. *Cognitive Therapy and Research, 11*, 89–99.

Haier, R.J., Quaid, K., & Mills, J.S.C. (1981). Naloxone alters pain perception after jogging. *Psychiatry Research 5*, 231–232.

Halbreich, U., Alt, I.H., & Paul, L. (1988). Premenstrual changes: Impaired hormonal homeostasis. *Endocrinology and Metabolism Clinics of North America, 17*, 173–194.

Halbreich, U., Asnis, G.M., Shindledecker, M.A., Zumoff, B., & Nathan, S. (1985a). Cortisol secretion in endogenous depression: II. Time-related functions. *Archives of General Psychiatry, 42*, 909–914.

Halbreich, U., Asnis, G.M., Shindledecker, M.A., Zumoff, B., & Nathan, S. (1985b). Cortisol secretion in endogenous depression: I. Basal plasma levels. *Archives of General Psychiatry, 42*, 904–908.

Halbreich, U., Assael, M., Bendavid, M., & Borsten, R. (1976). Serum prolactin in women with premenstrual syndrome. *Lancet, 2*, 654–656.

Halbreich, U., & Endicott, J. (1985). Methodological issues in studies of premenstrual changes. *Psychoneuroendocrinology, 10*, 15–32.

Halbreich, U., Endicott, J., Goldstein, S., & Nee, J. (1986). Premenstrual changes and changes in gonadal hormones. *Acta Psychiatrica Scandanavica, 74*, 576–586.

Hale, W.H., & Strickland, B.R. (1976). Induction of mood states and their effect on cognitive and social behaviors. *Journal of Consulting and Clinical Psychology, 44*, 155.

Hall, K.S., Dunner, D.L., Zeller, G., & Fieve, R.R. (1977). Bipolar illness: A prospective study of life events. *Comprehensive Psychiatry, 18*, 497–502.

Hamilton, J.A., Aloi, J., Mucciardi, B., & Murphy, D.L. (1983). Human plasma beta-endorphin through the menstrual cycle. *Psychopharmacology Bulletin, 19*, 586–587.

Hammarbäck, S., & Bäckström, T. (1988). Induced anovulation as a treatment of premenstrual tension syndrome. *Acta Obstetrica Gynecologica Scandanavica, 67*, 159–166.

Hammen, C.L., & Glass, D.R.J. (1975). Depression, activity, and evaluation of reinforcement. *Journal of Abnormal Psychology, 84*, 718–721.

Hammen, CL, Miklowitz, D.J., & Dyck, D.G. (1986). Stability and severe parameters of depressive self-schema responding. *Journal of Social and Clinical Psychology, 4*, 23–45.

Hammen, C.L., & Peters, S.D. (1977). Differential responses to male and female depressive relations. *Journal of Consulting and Clinical Psychology, 45*, 994–1001.

Hammen, C., & Zupan, B.A. (1984). Self-schemas, depression, and the processing of personal information in children. *Journal of Experimental Child Psychology, 37*, 598–608.

Handley, S.L., Dunn, T.L., Waldron, G., & Baker, J.M. (1980). Tryptophan, cortisol, and puerperal mood. *British Journal of Psychiatry, 136*, 498–506.

Harada, J. (1983). The effects of positive and negative experiences on helping behavior. *Japanese Psychological Research 25*, 47–51.

Harding, S.D. (1982). Psychological well-being in Great Britain: An evaluation of the Bradburn Affect Balance Scale. *Personality and Individual Differences, 3*, 167-175.

Harris, M.B. (1977). Effects of altruism on mood. *Journal of Social Psychology, 102*, 197-208.

Hasher, L., Rose, K.C., Zacks, R.T., Sanft, H., & Doren, B. (1985). Mood, recall, and selectivity in normal college students. *Journal of Experimental Psychology: General, 114*, 104-118.

Haskett, R.I., Steiner, M., & Carroll, B.J. (1984). A psychoendocrine study of premenstrual tension syndrome. *Journal of Affective Disorders, 6*, 191-199.

Hauri, P. (1983). A cluster analysis of insomnia. *Sleep, 6*, 326-388.

Hawkins, W.L., French, L.C., Crawford, B.D., & Enzle, M.E. (1988). Depressed affect and time perception. *Journal of Abnormal Psychology, 97*, 275-280.

Headey, B., & Wearing, A. (1986). *Chains of well-being, chains of ill-being*. International Sociological Association Conference, New Delhi.

Healy, D., & Williams, J.M.G. (1988). Dysrhythmia, dysphoria, and depression: The interaction of learned helplessness and circadian dysrhythmia in the pathogenesis of depression. *Psychological Bulletin, 103*, 163-178.

Hebb, D.O. (1949). *The organization of behavior*. New York: Wiley.

Hedges, S.M., Jandorf, L, & Stone, A.A. (1985). Meaning of daily mood assessments. *Journal of Personality and Social Psychology, 48*, 428-434.

Hellekson, C.J., Kline, J.A., & Rosenthal, N.E. (1986). Phototherapy for seasonal affective disorder in Alaska. *American Journal of Psychiatry, 143*, 1035-1037.

Helson, H. (1964). *Adaptation level theory: An experimental and systematic approach to behavior*. New York: Harper & Row.

Hendrick, C., & Lilly, R.S. (1970). The structure of mood: A comparison between sleep deprivation and normal wakefulness conditions. *Journal of Personality, 38*, 453-465.

Hersey, R.B. (1932). *Worker's emotions in the shop and home*. Philadelphia: University of Pennsylvania Press.

Hoffman, M.L. (1981). Is altruism part of human nature? *Journal of Personality and Social Psychology, 40*, 121-137.

Hokanson, J.E., & Edelman, R. (1966). Effects of three social responses on vascular processes. *Journal of Personality and Social Psychology, 3*, 442-447.

Holden, C. (1987). Creativity and the troubled mind. *Psychology Today, 21*(4), 9-10.

Hollon, S.D., & Kendall, P.C. (1980). Cognitive self-statements in depression: Development of an automatic thoughts questionnaire. *Cognitive Therapy and Research, 4*, 383-395.

Hollon, S.D., Kendall, P.C., & Lumry, A. (1986). Specificity of depressotypic cognitions in clinical depression. *Journal of Abnormal Psychology, 95*, 52-59.

Holloway, S., Tucker, L., & Hornstein, H.A. (1977). The effects of social and nonsocial information on interpersonal behavior of males: The news makes news. *Journal of Personality and Social Psychology, 35*, 514-522.

Holmes, T.H., & Rahe, R.H. (1967). The Social Readjustment Rating Scale. *Journal of Psychosomatic Research, 11*, 213-218.

Hopkins, J., Marcus, M., & Campbell, S.D. (1984). Postpartum depression: A critical review. *Psychological Bulletin, 95*, 498-515.

Hornberger, R.H. (1960). The projective effects of fear and sexual arousal on the rating of pictures. *Journal of Clinical Psychology, 16*, 328-331.

Horrobin, D.F. (1973). *Prolactin: Physiology, pharmacology, and clinical significance*. Lancaster, England: MTP Press.

Horrobin, D.F. (1983). The role of essential fatty acids and prostaglandins in the premenstrual syndrome. *Journal of Reproductive Medicine, 28*, 465-468.

Howarth, E., & Hoffman, M.S. (1984). A multidimensional approach to the relationship between mood and weather. *British Journal of Psychology, 75*, 15–23.

Howes, M.J., & Hokanson, J.E. (1979). Conversational and social responses to depressive interpersonal behavior. *Journal of Abnormal Psychology, 88*, 625–634.

Howes, M.J., Hokanson, J.E., & Loewenstein, D.A. (1985). Induction of depressive affect after prolonged exposure to a mildly depressed individual. *Journal of Personality and Social Psychology, 49*, 1110–1113.

Hull, J.G. (1981). A self-awareness model of the causes and effects of alcohol consumption. *Journal of Abnormal Psychology, 90*, 586–600.

Hull, J.G., & Bond, C.F.J. (1986). Social and behavioral consequences of alcohol consumption and expectancy: A meta-analysis. *Psychological Bulletin, 99*, 347–360.

Hull, J.G., Levenson, R.W., Young, R.D., & Sher, K.J. (1983). The self-awareness reducing effects of alcohol consumption. *Journal of Personality and Social Psychology, 44*, 461–473.

Hull, J.G., & Young R.D. (1983). Self-consciousness, self-esteem, and success-failure as determinants of alcohol consumption in male social drinkers. *Journal of Personality and Social Psychology, 44*, 1097–1109.

Hyland, M.E. (1987). Control theory interpretation of psychological mechanisms of depression: Comparison and integration of several theories. *Psychological Bulletin, 102*, 109–121.

Ingram, R.E. (1984). Toward an information-processing analysis of depression. *Cognitive Therapy and Research, 8*, 443–478.

Ingram, R.E., Cruet, D., Johnson, B.R., & Wisnicki, K.S. (1988). Self-focused attention, gender, gender role, and vulnerability to negative affect. *Journal of Personality and Social Psychology, 55*, 967–978.

Ingram, R.E., Lumry, A.E., Cruet, D., & Sieber, W. (1987). Attentional processes in depressive disorders. *Cognitive Therapy and Research, 11*, 351–360.

Ingram, R.E., & Smith, T.W. (1984). Depression and internal versus external focus of attention. *Cognitive Therapy and Research, 8*, 139–151.

Ingram, R.E., Smith T.W., & Brehm, S.S. (1983). Depression and information processing: Self-schemata and the encoding of self-referent information. *Journal of Personality and Social Psychology, 45*, 412–420.

Isaacs, G., Stainer, D.S., Sensky, T.E., Moor, S., & Thompson, C. (1988). Phototherapy and its mechanisms of action in seasonal affective disorder. *Journal of Affective Disorders, 14*, 13–19.

Isen, A.M. (1970). Success, failure, attention and reaction to others: The warm glow of success. *Journal of Personality and Social Psychology, 15*, 294–301.

Isen, A.M. (1975). Positive affect, accessibility of cognitions and helping. Paper presented as part of the symposium, "Directions in theory on helping behavior" (J. Piliavin, Chair). Eastern Psychological Association Convention, New York.

Isen, A.M. (1984). Toward understanding the role of affect in cognition. In R.S. Wyer, & T.K. Srull (Eds.), *Handbook of social cognition* (pp. 179–236). Hillsdale, NJ: Erlbaum.

Isen, A.M. (1985). Asymmetry of happiness and sadness in effects on memory in normal college students: Comment on Hasher, Rose, Zacks, Sanft, and Doren. *Journal of Experimental Psychology: General, 114*, 388–391.

Isen, A.M. (1987). Positive affect, cognitive processes, and social behavior. In L. Berkowitz (Ed.), *Advances in experimental social psychology* (Vol. 20, pp. 203–253). New York: Academic Press.

Isen, A.M., Clark, M.S., & Schwartz, M.F. (1976). Duration of the effect of good mood on helping: Footprints on the sands of time. *Journal of Personality and Social Psychology, 34*, 385–393.

Isen, A.M., & Daubman, K.A. (1984). The influence of affect on categorization. *Journal of Personality and Social Psychology, 47*, 1206–1217.
Isen, A.M., Daubman, K.A., & Nowicki, G.P. (1987). Positive affect facilitates creative problem solving. *Journal of Personality and Social Psychology, 52*, 1122–1131.
Isen, A.M., & Geva, N. (1987). The influence of positive affect on acceptable level of risk and thoughts about losing: The person with a large canoe has a large worry. *Organizational Behavior and Human Decision Processes, 39*, 145–154.
Isen, A.M., & Gorgoglione, J.M. (1983). Some specific effects of four affect-induction procedures. *Personality and Social Psychology Bulletin, 9*, 136–143.
Isen, A.M. Johnson, M.M.S., Mertz, E., & Robinson, G. (1985). The influence of positive affect on the unusualness of word association. *Journal of Personality and Social Psychology, 48*, 1413–1426.
Isen, A.M., & Levin, P.F. (1972). The effect of feeling good on helping: Cookies and kindness. *Journal of Personality and Social Psychology, 34*, 384–388.
Isen, A.M., & Means, B. (1983). The influence of positive affect on decision-making strategy. *Social Cognition, 2*, 18–31.
Isen, A.M., Means, B., Patrick, R,. & Nowicki, G. (1982). Some factors influencing decision-making strategy and risk taking. In M.S. Clark, & S.T. Fiske (Eds.), *Affect and cognition: The seventeenth annual Carnegie Symposium on Cognition* (pp. 243-262). Hillsdale, NJ: Erlbaum.
Isen, A.M., Nygren, T.E., & Ashby, F.G. (1988). Influence of positive affect on the subjective utility of gains and losses: It is just not worth the risk. *Journal of Personality and Social Psychology, 55*, 710–717.
Isen, A.M., & Patrick, R. (1983). The effect of positive feelings on risk-taking: When the chips are down. *Organizational Behavior and Human Performance, 31*, 194–202.
Isen, A.M., & Shalker, T.E. (1982). The influence of mood state on evaluation of positive, neutral, and negative stimuli: When you "accentuate the positive" do you "eliminate the negative"? *Social Psychology Quarterly, 45*, 58–63.
Isen, A.M., Shalker, T.E., Clark, M.S., & Karp, L. (1978). Positive affect, accessibility of material in memory, and behavior: A cognitive loop? *Journal of Personality and Social Psychology, 36*, 1–12.
Isen, A.M., & Simmonds, S.F. (1978). The effect of feeling good on a helping task that is incompatible with good mood. *Social Psychology, 41*, 346–349.
Izard, C.E. (1971). *The face of emotion.* New York: Appleton-Century-Crofts.
Izard, C.E. (1972). *Patterns of emotions: A new analysis of anxiety and depression.* New York: Academic Press.
Izard, C.E. (1977). *Human emotions.* New York and London: Plenum.
Izard, C.E., Wehmer, G.M., Livsey, W., & Jennings, J.R. (1965). Affect, awareness, and performance. In S.S. Tomkins, & C.E. Izard (Eds.), *Affect, cognition and personality* (pp. 2–41). New York: Springer.
Jackson, S.W. (1986). *Melancholia and Depression.* New Haven: Yale University Press.
Jacobs, D,. & Silverstone, T. (1986). Dextroamphetamine-induced arousal in human subjects as a model for mania. *Psychological Medicine, 16*, 323–329.
Jacobsen, E. (1957). Normal and pathological moods: Their nature and functions. In R.S. Eisler, A.F. Freud, H. Hartman, & E. Kris (Eds.), *The psychoanalytic study of the child* (pp. 73–113). New York: International University Press.
Jacobsen, F.M., Sack, D.A., Wehr, T.A., Rogers, S., & Rosenthal, N.E. (1987). Neuroendocrine response to 5-hydroxytryptophan in seasonal affective disorder. *Archives of General Psychiatry, 44*, 1086–1091.
James, S.P., Wehr, D.A., Sack, P.A., Parry, B.L., & Rosenthal, N.E. (1985). Treatment of seasonal affective disorder with light in the evening. *British Journal of Psychiatry, 147*, 424–428.

Janal, M.N., Colt, E.W.D., Clark, W.C., & Glusman, M. (1984). Pain sensitivity, mood, and plasma endocrine levels in man following long-distance running: Effects of naloxone. *Pain, 19*, 13–25.

Jenkins, G.M., & Watts, D.G. (1968). *Spectral analysis and its applications.* San Francisco: Holden-Day.

Johnson, W.B. (1937). Euphoric and depressed moods in normal subjects. *Character and Personality, 6*, 79–98.

Johnson, C., & Larson, R. (1982). Bulimia: An analysis of moods and behavior. *Psychosomatic Medicine, 44*, 341–351.

Johnson, J.E., Petzel, T.P., Hartney, L.M., & Morgan, L.M. (1983). Recall and importance ratings of completed and uncompleted tasks as a function of depression. *Cognitive Therapy and Research, 7*, 51–56.

Johnson, E.J., & Tversky, A. (1983). Affect, generalization, and the perception of risk. *Journal of Personality and Social Psychology, 45*, 20–31.

Jolly, A. (1986, May). *Social environments and emotional experience.* Paper presented at the meeting of the Midwestern Psychological Association, Chicago.

Josephson, A.M., & MacKenzie, T.B. (1979). Appearance of manic psychosis following rapid normalization of hypothyroidism. *American Journal of Psychiatry, 136*, 846–847.

Judd, L.L., Janowsky, D.S., Segal, D.S., & Huey, L.Y. (1980). Naloxone-induced behavioral and physiological effects in normal and manic subjects. *Archives of General Psychiatry, 37*, 583–586.

Kagan, J. (1984). The idea of emotion in human development. In C.E. Izard, J. Kagan, & R.B. Zajonc (Eds.), *Emotions, cognition, and behavior* (pp. 38–72). New York: Cambridge University Press.

Kammann, R., Christie, D., Irwin, R., & Dixon, G. (1979). Properties of an inventory to measure happiness (and psychological health). *New Zealand Psychologist, 8*, 1–9.

Kammann, R., & Flett, R. (1983). Affectometer 2: A scale to measure current level of general happiness. *Australian Journal of Psychology, 35*, 257–265.

Kanfer, F.H., & Hagerman, S. (1981). The role of self-regulation. In L.P. Rehm (Ed.), *Behavior therapy for depression: Present status and future directions* (pp. 143–180). New York: Academic Press.

Kanfer, F.H., & Karoly, P. (1972). Self-control: A behavioristic excursion into the lion's den. *Behavior Therapy, 2*, 398–416.

Kanfer, F.H., & Karoly, P. (1982). The psychology of self-management: Abiding issues and tentative directions. In F.H. Kanfer, & P. Karoly (Eds.), *Self-management and behavior change* (pp. 571–599). New York: Pergamon.

Katkin, E.S. (1985). Blood, sweat, and tears: Individual differences in automatic self-perception. *Psychophysiology, 22*, 125–137.

Kavanagh, D.J., & Bower, G.H. (1985). Mood and self-efficacy: Impact of joy and sadness on perceived capabilities. *Cognitive Therapy and Research, 9*, 507–525.

Kenealy, P.M. (1986). The Velten Mood Induction Procedure: A methodological review. *Motivation and Emotion, 10*, 315–335.

Kennedy, S., Thompson, R., Stancer, H.C., Roy, A., & Persad, E. (1983). Life events precipitation mania. *British Journal of Psychiatry, 142*, 398–403.

Kenrick, D.T., Baumann, D.J., & Cialdini, R.B. (1979). A step in the socialization of altruism as hedonism: Effects of negative mood on children's generosity under public and private conditions. *Journal of Personality and Social Psychology, 36*, 747–755.

Kleck, R.E., Vaughan, R.C., Cartwright-Smith, J., Vaughan, K.B., Colby, C.Z., & Lanzetta, J.T. (1976). Effects of being observed on expressive, subjective, and physiological responses to painful stimuli. *Journal of Personality and Social Psychology, 34*, 1211–1218.

Klein, D.N., Depue, R.A., & Slater, J.F. (1986). Inventory identification of cyclothymia. *Archives of General Psychiatry, 43*, 441–445.

Klein, D.N., Taylor, E.B., Dickstein, S., & Harding, K. (1988). Primary early-onset dysthymia: Comparison with primary nonbipolar nonchronic major depression on demographic, clinical, familial, personality, and socioenvironmental characteristics and short-term outcome. *Journal of Abnormal Psychology, 97*, 387–398.

Klerman, G.L., & Hirshfeld, R.M.A. (1979). Treatment of depression in the elderly. *Geriatrics, 34*, 51.

Klinger, E. (1977). *Meaning and void: Inner experience and the incentives in people's lives.* Minneapolis: University of Minnesota Press.

Koriat, A., Melkman, R., Averill, J.R., & Lazarus, R.S. (1972). The self-control of emotional reactions to a stressful film. *Journal of Personality, 40*, 601–619.

Kotsch, W.E., Gerbing, D.W., & Schwartz, L.E. (1982). The construct validity of the Differential Emotions Scale as adapted for children and adolescents. In C.E. Izard (Ed.), *Measuring emotions in infants and children* (pp. 251–278). New York: Cambridge University Press.

Kovacs, M., & Beck, A.T. (1978). Maladaptive cognitive structures in depression. *American Journal of Psychiatry, 135*, 525–533.

Krauthamer, C., & Klerman, G.L. (1978). Secondary mania: Manic syndromes associated with antecedent physical illness or drugs. *Archives of General Psychiatry, 35*, 1333–1339.

Kripke, D.F. (1981). Photoperiodic mechanisms for depression and its treatment. In C. Perris, G. Struwe, & B. Jansson (Eds.), *Biological Psychiatry, 1981* (pp. 1248–1252). Amsterdam: Elsevier.

Kripke, D.F., Risch, S.C., & Janowsky, D.S. (1983). Lighting up depression. *Psychopharmacology Bulletin, 19*, 526–530.

Kuevi, V., Causon, R., Dixson, A.F., Everand, D.M., Hall, J.M., Hale, D., Whitehead, S.A., Wilson, C.A., & Wise, J.C.M. (1983). Plasma amine and hormone changes in postpartum blues. *Clinical Endocrinology, 19*, 39–46.

Kuhar, M.J., Pert, C.B., & Snyder, S.H. (1973). Regional distribution of opiate receptor binding in monkey and human brains. *Nature, 245*, 447–450.

Kuhl, J., & Helle, P. (1986). Motivational and volitional determinants of depression: The degenerated intention hypothesis. *Journal of Abnormal Psychology, 95*, 247–251.

Kuiper, N.A., & Derry, P.A. (1982). Depressed and nondepressed content self-reference in mild depressives. *Journal of Personality, 50*, 67–79.

Kuiper, N.A., Olinger, L.J., MacDonald, M.R., & Shaw, B.F. (1985). Self-schema processing of depressed and nondepressed content: The effects of vulnerability to depression. *Social Cognition, 3*, 77–93.

Kunst-Wilson, W.R., & Zajonc, R.B. (1980). Affective discrimination of stimuli that cannot be recognized. *Science, 207*, 557–558.

Kupfer, D. (1977). REM latency: A psychobiologic marker for primary depressive disease. *Biological Psychiatry, 11*, 159–174.

Kupfer, D.J., & Foster, F.G. (1972). Intervals between onset of sleep and rapid-eye-movement sleep as an indicator of depression. *Lancet, 2*, 684–686.

Laird, J.D. (1974). Self-attribution of emotion: The effects of expressive behavior on the quality of emotional experience. *Journal of Personality and Social Psychology, 29*, 475–486.

Laird, J.D. (1984). The real role of facial response in the experience of emotion. A reply to Tourangeau & Ellsworth and others. *Journal of Personality and Social Psychology, 47*, 909–917.

Laird, J.D., & Crosby, M. (1974). Individual differences in self-attribution of emotion. In H. London, & R.E. Nisbett (Eds.), *Thought and feeling: Cognitive alteration of feeling states* (pp. 44–59). Chicago: Aldine.

Laird, J.D., Wagener, J.J., Halal, M., & Szegda, M. (1982). Remembering what you feel: Effects of emotion on memory. *Journal of Personality and Social Psychology, 42*, 646–657.

Lanzetta, J.T., Cartwright-Smith, J., & Kleck, R.E. (1976). The effects of nonverbal dissimulation on emotional experience and autonomic arousal. *Journal of Personality and Social Psychology, 33*, 354–370.

Larsen, R.J. (1984). Theory and measurement of affect intensity as an individual difference characteristic. *Dissertation Abstracts International, 5*, 2297B (University Microfilms No. 84–22112).

Larsen, R.J. (1987). The stability of mood variability: A spectral analytic approach to daily mood assessments. *Journal of Personality and Social Psychology, 52*, 1195–1204.

Larsen, R.J., & Diener, E. (1985). A multitrait-multimethod examination of affect structure: Hedonic level and emotional intensity. *Personality and individual differences, 6*, 631–636.

Larsen, R.J., & Diener, E. (1987). Affect intensity as an individual difference characteristic: A review. *Journal of Research in Personality, 21*, 1–39.

Larsen, R.J., Diener, E., & Cropanzano, R.S. (1987). Cognitive operations associated with individual differences in affect intensity. *Journal of Personality and Social Psychology, 53*, 767–774.

Larsen, R.J., Diener, E., & Emmons, R.A. (1986). Affect intensity and reactions to daily life events. *Journal of Personality and Social Psychology, 51*, 803–814.

Larson, R.W. (1983). Adolescents' daily experience with family and friends: Contrasting opportunity systems. *Journal of Marriage and the Family, 45*, 739–750.

Larson, R.W. (1987). On the independence of positive and negative affect within hour-to-hour experience. *Motivation and Emotion, 11*, 145–156.

Larson, R.W., Csikzentmihalyi, M., & Graef, R. (1980). Mood variability and the psychosocial adjustment of adolescents. *Journal of Youth and Adolescence, 9*, 469–489.

Latane, B., & Darley, J.M. (1970). *The unresponsive bystander: Why doesn't he help?*. New York: Appleton-Century-Crofts.

Lazarus, R.S. (1966). *Psychological stress and the coping process.* New York: McGraw-Hill.

Lazarus, R.S. (1975). The self-regulation of emotion. In L. Levi (Ed.), *Emotions–Their parameters and measurement* (pp. 46–67). New York: Raven Press.

Lazarus, R.S. (1982). Thoughts on the relations between emotion and cognition. *American Psychologist, 37*, 1019–1024.

Lazarus, R.S. (1984a). On the primacy of cognition. *American Psychologist, 39*, 124–129.

Lazarus, R.S. (1984b). Puzzles in the study of daily hassles. *Journal of Behavioral Medicine, 7*, 375–389.

Lazarus, R.S., & Folkman, S. (1984) *Stress, appraisal, and coping.* New York: Springer.

Lazarus, R.S., & McCleary, R.A. (1951). Autonomic discrimination without awareness: A study of subception. *Psychological Review, 58*, 113–122.

Lebo, M.A., & Nesselroade, J.R. (1978). Intraindividual differences dimensions of mood change during pregnancy identified in five P-technique factor analyses. *Journal of Research in Personality, 12*, 205–224.

Leff, J.P., Fischer, M., & Bertelsen, A. (1976). A cross-national epidemiological study of mania. *British Journal of Psychiatry, 129*, 428–437.

Leff, M.J., Roatch, J.F., & Bunney, E.E. (1970) Environmental factors preceding the onset of severe depressions. *Psychiatry, 33*, 293–311.

Leight, K.A., & Ellis, H.C. (1981). Emotional mood states, strategies, and state-dependency in memory. *Journal of Verbal Learning and Verbal Behavior, 20*, 251–275.

Lerner, M.J. (1980). *The belief in a just world: A fundamental delusion.* New York: Plenum.
Leventhal, H. (1980). Toward a comprehensive theory of emotion. In L. Berkowitz (Ed.), *Advances in experimental social psychology,* (Vol. 13, pp. 139-207). New York: Academic Press.
Leventhal, H., & Everhart, D. (1979). Emotion, pain, and physical illness. In C.E. Izard (Ed.), *Emotions in personality and psychopathology* (pp. 263–299). New York: Plenum.
Levy, A.B., & Stern, S.L. (1987). DST and TRH stimulating test in mood disorder subtypes. *American Journal of Psychiatry, 144,* 472–475.
Lewinsohn, P.M. (1974). A behavioral approach to depression. In R.J. Friedman, & M.M. Katz (Eds.), *The psychology of depression: Contemporary theory and research.* (pp. 157–185). New York: Wiley.
Lewinsohn, P.M., & Graf, M. (1973). Pleasant activities and depression. *Journal of Consulting and Clinical Psychology, 41,* 261-268.
Lewinsohn, P.M., Hoberman, H., Teri, L., & Hautzinger, M. (1985). An integrative theory of depression. In S. Reiss, & R. Bootzin (Eds.), *Theoretical issues in behavior therapy* (pp. 331-359). New York: Academic Press.
Lewinsohn, P.M., & Libet, J. (1972). Pleasant events, activity schedules and depression. *Journal of Abnormal Psychology, 79,* 291–295.
Lewy, A.J. (1984). Human melatonin secretion (II): A marker for the circadian system and the effects of light. In R.M. Post & J.C. Ballenger (Eds.), *Neurobiology of mood disorders* (pp. 215–226). Baltimore, MD: Williams & Wilkins.
Lewy, A.J., Nurnberger, J.I., Wehr, T.A., Pack, D., Becker, L.E., Powell, R., & Newsome, D.A. (1985). Supersensitivity to light: Possible trait marker for manic depressive illness. *American Journal of Psychiatry, 142,* 725–727.
Lewy, A.J., Sack, R.A., & Singer, C.L. (1984). Assessment and treatment of chronobiologic disorders using plasma melatonin levels and bright light exposure: The clock-gate model and the phase-response curve. *Psychopharmacology Bulletin, 20,* 561–565.
Lewy, A.J., Sack, R.A., & Singer, C.L. (1985). Treating phase-typed chronobiologic sleep and mood disorders using appropriately-timed bright artificial light. *Psychopharmacology Bulletin, 21,* 368–372.
Lewy, A.J., & Stern, S.L. (1987). DST and TRH stimulating test in mood disorder subtypes. *American Journal of Psychiatry, 144,* 472–475.
Lewy, A.J., Wehr, T.A., Goodwin, F.K., Newsome, D.A., & Markey, S.P. (1980). Light suppresses melatonin secretion in humans. *Science, 210,* 1267–1269.
Lewy, A.J., Wehr, T.A., Goodwin, F.K., Newsome, D.A., & Rosenthal, N.E. (1981). Manic-depressive patients may be super-sensitive to light. *Lancet, 1,* 383–384.
Lieberman, H.R., Waldhauser, F., Garfield, G., Lynch, H.J., & Wurtman, R.J. (1984). Effects of melatonin on human mood and performance. *Brain Research, 323,* 201–207.
Lindstrom, L.H., Widerlov, E., Gunne, A., Wahlstrom, A., & Terenius, L. (1978). Endorphins in human cerebrospinal fluid: Clinical correlations in some psychotic states. *Acta Psychiatrica Scandinavica, 57,* 153–164.
Linville, P.W. (1982). Affective consequences of complexity regarding the self and others. In M.S. Clark, & S. Fiske (Eds.), *Affect and cognition: Seventeenth Annual Symposium on Cognition* (pp. 79–109). Hillsdale, NJ: Erlbaum.
Linville, P.W. (1985). Self-complexity and affective extremity: Don't put all of your eggs in one cognitive basket. *Social Cognition, 3,* 94–120.
Linville, P.W. (1987). Self-complexity as a cognitive buffer against stress-related illness and depression. *Journal of Personality and Social Psychology, 52,* 663–676.
Lishman, W.A. (1972). Selective factors in memory: Affective disorder. *Psychological Medicine, 2,* 248–253.

Lloyd, G.G., & Lishman, W.A. (1975). Effect of depression on the speed of recall of pleasant and unpleasant experiences. *Psychological Medicine, 5*, 173–180.

Logue, C.M., & Moos, R.H. (1986). Perimenstrual symptoms: Prevalence and risk factors. *Psychomatic Medicine, 48*, 388–414.

Lorr, M., Daston, P., & Smith, I. (1967). An analysis of mood states. *Educational and Psychological Measurement, 27*, 89–96.

Lubin, B. (1965). Adjective checklists for the measurement of depression. *Archives of General Psychiatry, 17*, 57–62.

Maas, J.W. (1975). Biogenic amines and depression: Biochemical and pharmacological separation of two types of depression. *Archives of General Psychiatry, 35*, 1333–1339.

Maas, J.W., Koslow, S.H., Davis, J., Katz, M., Frazer, A., Bowden, C.L., Berman, N., Gibbons, R., Stokes, P., & Landis, D.H. (1987). Catecholamine metabolism and disposition in healthy and depressed subjects. *Archives of General Psychiatry, 44*, 337–344.

MacPhillamy, D., & Lewinsohn, P.M. (1971). *Pleasant events schedule.* University of Oregon, Eugene.

MacPhillamy, D.J., & Lewinsohn, P.M. (1974). Depression as a function of levels of desired and obtained pleasure. *Journal of Abnormal Psychology, 83*, 651–657.

Madden, J., Akil, H., Patrick, R., & Barchas, J. (1977). Stress-induced parallel changes in central opioid levels and pain responsiveness in the rat. *Nature, 265*, 358–360.

Maddocks, S., Hahn, P., Moller, F., & Reid, R.L. (1986). A double-blind placebo-controlled trial of progesterone vaginal suppositories in the treatment of premenstrual syndrome. *American Journal of Obstetrics and Gynecology, 154*, 573–581.

Madigan, R.J., & Bollenbach, A.K. (1982). Effects of induced mood on retrieval of personal episodic and semantic memories. *Psychological Reports, 50*, 147–157.

Mandler, G. (1975). *Mind and emotion.* New York: Wiley.

Mandler, G. (1984). *Mind and body.* New York: Norton.

Manstead, A.S.R., Wagner, H.L., & MacDonald, C.J. (1983). A contrast effect in judgments of own emotional state. *Motivation and Emotion, 7*, 279–290.

Manucia, G.K., Baumann, D.J., & Cialdini, R.B. (1984). Mood influences on helping: Direct effects or side effects? *Journal of Personality and Social Psychology, 46*, 357–364.

Markoff, R.A., Ryan, P., & Young, T. (1982). Endorphins and mood changes in long-distance running. *Medicine and Science in Sports and Exercise, 14*, 11–15.

Marlatt, G.A., Kosturn, C.F., & Lang, A.R. (1975). Provocation to anger and opportunity for retaliation as determinants of alcohol consumption in social drinkers. *Journal of Abnormal Psychology, 84*, 652–659.

Marshall, G.D., & Zimbardo, P.G. (1979). Affective consequences of inadequately explained arousal. *Journal of Personality and Social Psychology, 37*, 970–988.

Martin, D., Abramson, L.Y., & Alloy, L.B. (1984). The illusion of control for self and others in depressed and nondepressed college students. *Journal of Personality and Social Psychology, 46*, 125–136.

Maslach, C. (1979). Negative emotional biasing of unexplained arousal. *Journal of Personality and Social Psychology, 37*, 953–969.

Masters, J.C., & Furman, W. (1976). Effects of affect states on noncontingent outcome expectancies and beliefs in internal or external control. *Developmental Psychology, 12*, 481–482.

Mathews, A., & Bradley, B. (1983). Mood and the self-reference bias in recall. *Behavior Research and Therapy, 21*, 233–239.

Matlin, M.W., & Stang, D. (1979). *The Pollyanna Principle: Selectivity in language, memory and thought.* Cambridge, MA: Shenkman.

Matsumoto, D. (1987). The role of facial response in the experience of emotion: More methodological problems and a meta-analysis. *Journal of Personality and Social Psychology, 52*, 769–774.
Mauro, R. (1988). Opponent processes in human emotions? An experimental investigation of hedonic contrast and affective interactions. *Motivation and Emotion, 12*, 333–352.
Mayer, J.D., & Bower, G.H. (1985). Naturally occurring mood and learning: Comment on Hasher, Zacks, Rose, Sanft, and Doren. *Journal of Experimental Psychology: General, 114*, 396–403.
Mayer, J.D., & Bremer, D. (1985). Assessing mood with affect-sensitive tasks. *Journal of Personality Assessment, 49*, 95–99.
Mayer, J.D., Mamberg, M.H., & Volanth, A.J. (1988). Cognitive domains of the mood system. *Journal of Personality, 56*, 453–486.
Mayer, J.D., & Volanth, A. (1985). Cognitive involvement in the mood response system. *Motivation and Emotion, 9*, 261–275.
Mayo, P.R. (1983). Personality traits and the retrieval of positive and negative memories. *Personality and Individual Differences, 4*, 465–471.
McCaul, K.D., & Malott, J.M. (1984). Distraction and coping with pain. *Psychological Bulletin, 95*, 516–533.
McDowall, J. (1984). Recall of pleasant and unpleasant words in depressed subjects. *Journal of Abnormal Psychology, 93*, 401–407.
McFarland, C., & Ross, M. (1982). The impact of causal attributions on affective reactions to success and failure. *Journal of Personality and Social Psychology, 43*, 937–946.
McLean, P. (1976). Depression as a specific response to stress. In I.G. Sarason, & C.D. Spielberger (Eds.), *Stress and anxiety* (Vol. 3, pp. 297–323). Washington, D.C.: Hemisphere.
McMillen, D.L., Sanders, D.Y., & Solomon, G.S. (1977). Self-esteem, attentiveness, and helping behavior. *Personality and Social Psychology Bulletin, 3*, 257–261.
McNair, D.M., Lorr, M., & Droppleman, L.F. (1971). *Manual: Profile of mood states.* San Diego: Educational and Industrial Testing Service.
Mecklenbräuker, S., & Hager, W. (1984). Effects of mood on memory: Experimental tests of mood-state-dependent retrieval hypothesis and of a mood-congruity hypothesis. *Psychological Research, 46*, 355–376.
Mednick, M.T., Mednick, S.A., & Mednick, E.V. (1964). Incubation of creative performance and specific associative priming. *Journal of Abnormal and Social Psychology, 69*, 84–88.
Mehrabian, A., & Riccioni, M. (1986). Measures of eating-related characteristics for the general population: Relationships with temperament. *Journal of Personality Assessment, 50*, 610–629.
Miller, D.T., & Moretti, M.M. (1988). The causal attributions of depressives: Self-serving or self-disserving? In L.B. Alloy (Ed.), *Cognitive processes in depression* (pp. 266–286). New York: Guilford.
Miller, W.R. (1975). Psychological deficits in depression. *Psychological Bulletin, 82*, 238–260.
Miller, W.R., & Seligman, M.E.P. (1973). Depression and the perception of reinforcement. *Journal of Abnormal Psychology, 82*, 62–73.
Mischel, W. (1973). Toward a cognitive social learning reconceptualization of personality. *Psychological Review, 80*, 252–283.
Mischel W., Coates, B., & Raskoff, A. (1968). Effects of success and failure on self-gratification. *Journal of Personality and Social Psychology, 10*, 381–390.
Mischel, W., Ebbesen, E.E., & Zeiss, A.M. (1972). Cognitive and attentional mechanisms in delay of gratification. *Journal of Personality and Social Psychology, 27*, 204–218.

Mischel, W., Ebbesen, E., & Zeiss, A. (1973). Selective attention to the self: Situational and dispositional determinants. *Journal of Personality and Social Psychology, 27*, 204–218.

Mischel, W., Ebbesen, E.B., & Zeiss, A.M. (1976). Determinants of selective memory about the self. *Journal of Consulting and Clinical Psychology, 44*, 92–103.

Monroe, S.M., Imhoff, D.F., Wise, B.D., & Harris, J.E. (1983). Prediction of psychological symptoms under high-risk psychosocial circumstances: Life events, social support, and symptom specificity. *Journal of Abnormal Psychology, 92*, 338–350.

Monroe, S.M., & Peterman, A.M. (1988). Life stress and psychopathology. In L.H. Cohen (Ed.), *Life events and psychological functioning: Theoretical and methodological issues* (pp. 31–63). Beverly Hills: Sage.

Moore, R.Y. (1973). Retinohypothalamic projection in mammals: A comparative study. *Brain Research, 49*, 403–409.

Moore, B.S., Clyburn, A., & Underwood, B. (1976). The role of affect in the delay of gratification. *Child Development, 47*, 237–276.

Moore, B.S., Underwood, B., & Rosenhan, D.L. (1973). Affect and altruism. *Developmental Psychology, 8*, 99–104.

Moriwaki, S.Y. (1974). The Affect Balance Scale: A validity study with aged samples. *Journal of Gerontology, 29*, 73–78.

Morris, W.N., Kelley, S.T., & Napps, S.E. (1989). *A behavioral test of a dysregulation hypothesis of affective disorders*, Manuscript submitted for publication.

Morris, W.N., & Reilly, N.P. (1987). Toward the self-regulation of mood: Theory and research. *Motivation and Emotion, 11*, 215–249.

Morris, W.N., Reilly, N.P., & Englis, B.E. (1984). *[Self-reports about the relationship between mood and activity in a college population]*. Unpublished raw data.

Morris, W.N., Worchel, S., Bois, J.L., Pearson, J.A., Rountree, C.A., Samaha, G.M., Wachtler, J., & Wright, S.L. (1976). Collective coping with stress: Group reactions to fear, anxiety, and ambiguity. *Journal of Personality and Social Psychology, 33*, 674–679.

Muecher, H., & Ungeheuer, H. (1961). Meterologic influences on reaction time, flicker-fusion frequency, job accidents, and medical treatment. *Perceptual and Motor Skills, 12*, 163–168.

Mullen, B., & Suls, J. (1982). "Know thyself": Stressful life changes and the ameliorative effect of private self-consciousness. *Journal of Experimental Social Psychology, 18*, 43–55.

Munday, M., Brush, M.G., & Taylor, R.W. (1981). Correlations between progesterone, estradiol, and aldosterone levels in the premenstrual syndrome. *Clinical Endocrinology, 14*, 1-9.

Murphy, D.L., Belmaker, R.H., Buchshaum, M., Martin, N.F., Ciaranello, R., & Wyatt, R.J. (1977). Biogenic amine-related enzymes and personality variations in normals. *Psychological Medicine, 7*, 149–157.

Muse, K.N., Cetel, N.S., Futterman, L.A., & Yen, S.S.C. (1984). The premenstrual syndrome: Effects of medical ovariectomy. *New England Journal of Medicine, 311*, 1345–1349.

Nagata, D.K., & Trierweiler, S.J. (1988). Exploring the effects of mood checklist pretesting on experimental mood induction procedures. *Personality and Social Psychology Bulletin, 14*, 125–135.

Nasby, W., & Yando, R. (1982). Selective encoding and retrieval of affectively valent information: Two cognitive consequences of children's mood states. *Journal of Personality and Social Psychology, 43*, 1244–1253.

Natale, M. (1977). Effects of induced elation-depression on speech in the initial interview. *Journal of Consulting and Clinical Psychology, 45*, 45–52.

Natale, M., & Bolan, R. (1980). The effect of Velten's mood-induction procedure for depression on hand movement and head-down posture. *Motivation and Emotion, 4*, 323–333.
Natale, M., & Hantas, M. (1982). Effect of temporary mood states on selective memory about the self. *Journal of Personality and Social Psychology, 42*, 927–934.
Neale, J.M., Hooley, J.M., Jandorf, L., & Stone, A.A. (1987). Daily life events and mood. In C.R. Snyder, & C.E. Ford (Eds.), *Coping with negative life events: Clinical and social psychological perspectives* (pp. 161–189). New York: Plenum.
Nelson, R.E., & Craighead, W.E. (1977). Selective recall of positive and negative feedback, self-control behaviors, and depression. *Journal of Abnormal Psychology, 86*, 379–388.
Nelson, J.C., & Mazure, C. (1985). Ruminative thinking: A distinctive sign of melancholia. *Journal of Affective Disorders, 9*, 41–46.
Nisbett, R.E., & Ross, L. (1980). *Human inference: Strategies and shortcomings.* Englewood Cliffs, NJ: Prentice-Hall.
Nisbett, R.E., & Wilson, T.D. (1977). Telling more than we can know: Verbal reports on mental processes. *Psychological Review, 84*, 231–259.
Nolen-Hoeksema, S. (1987). Sex differences in unipolar depression: Evidence and theory. *Psychological Bulletin, 101*, 259–282.
Nott, P.N., Franklin, M., Armitage, C., & Gelder, M.G. (1976). Hormonal change and mood in the puerperium. *British Journal of Psychiatry, 128*, 279–283.
Nowlis, V. (1965). Research with the mood adjective checklist. In S.S. Tomkins, & C.E. Izard (Eds.), *Affect, cognition and personality* (pp. 352–389). New York, NY: Springer.
Nowlis, V. (1970). Mood: Behavior and experience. In M. Arnold (Ed.), *Feelings and emotions.* (pp. 261–277). New York: Academic Press.
Nowlis, V., & Nowlis, H.H. (1956). The description and analysis of mood. *Annals of the New York Academy of Sciences, 65*, 345–355.
Oatley, K., & Bolton, W. (1985). A social-cognitive theory of depression in reaction to life events. *Psychological Review, 92*, 372–388.
O'Brien, P.M.S., Selby, C., & Symonds, E.M. (1980). Progesterone, fluid, and electrolytes in premenstrual syndrome. *British Medical Journal, 1*, 1161–1163.
Olinger, L.J., Kuiper, N.A., & Shaw, B.F. (1987). Dysfunctional attitudes and stressful life events: An interactive model of depression. *Cognitive Therapy and Research 11*, 25–40.
Orne, M.T. (1962). On the social psychology of the psychological experiment: With particular reference to demand characteristics and their implications. *American Psychologist, 17*, 776–783.
Osgood, C.E., Suci, G.J., & Tannenbaum, P.H. (1957). *The measurement of meaning.* Urbana: University of Illinois Press.
Pancheri, P., DeMartino, V., Spiombi, G., Biondi, M., & Mosticone, S. (1979). Life stress events and state-trait anxiety in psychiatric and psychosomatic patients. In C.D. Spielberger, & I.G. Sarason (Eds.), *Stress and anxiety* (Vol. 6, pp. 169–197). Washington, D.C.: Hemisphere.
Parker, E.S,. Birnbaum, I.M., & Noble, E.P. (1976). Alcohol and memory: Storage and state-dependency. *Journal of Verbal Learning and Verbal Behavior, 15*, 691–702.
Parker, G.B., & Brown, L.B. (1982). Coping behaviors that mediate between life events and depression. *Archives of General Psychiatry, 39*, 1386–1391.
Patrick, V., Dunner, D.L., & Fieve, R.R. (1978). Life events and primary affective illness. *Acta Psychiatrica Scandinavica, 58*, 48–55.
Paulson, G.W., & Gottlieb, G. (1961). A longitudinal study of the electroencephalographic arousal response in depressed patients. *Journal of Nervous and Mental Disease, 133*, 524–528.

Paykel, E.S. (1982). *Handbook of affective disorders.* New York: Guilford.
Pearlin, L.I. (1959). Social and personal stress and escape television viewing. *Public Opinion Quarterly, 23,* 255–259.
Pearlin, L.I., & Radabaugh, C.W. (1976). Economic strains and the coping functions of alcohol. *American Journal of Sociology, 82,* 652–663.
Pearlin, L.I., & Schooler, C. (1978). The structure of coping. *Journal of Health and Social Behavior, 19,* 2–21.
Pepper, G.M., & Krieger, D.T. (1984). Hypotholamic-pituitary-adrenal abnormalities in depression: Their possible relation to central mechanisms regulating ACTH release. In R.M. Post & J.C. Ballenger (Eds.), *Neurobiology of Mood Disorders* (pp. 245–270). Baltimore, MD: Williams & Wilkins.
Peters, R., & McGee, R. (1982). Cigarette smoking and state-dependent memory. *Psychopharmacology, 76,* 232–235.
Peterson, C., & Seligman, M.E.P. (1984). Causal explanations as a risk factor for depression: Theory and evidence. *Psychological Review, 91,* 347–374.
Petty, R.E., & Cacioppo, J.T. (1981). *Attitudes and persuasion: Classic and contemporary approaches.* Dubuque, IA: Wm. C. Brown.
Pickar, D., Cohen, M.R., Naber, D., & Cohen, R.M. (1982). Clinical studies of the endogenous opiod system. *Biological Psychiatry, 17,* 1243–1276.
Pickar, D., Vartanian, F., Bunney, W.E., Maier, H.P., Gastpar, M.T., Prakash, R., Sethi, B.B., Lideman, R., Belyaev, B., Tsutsulkovskaja, M.V.A., Jungkunz, A., Nedopil, N., Verhoeven, W. & van Praag, H. (1982). Short-term naloxone administration in schizophrenic and manic subjects: A World Health Organization collaborative study. *Archives of General Psychiatry, 39,* 313–319.
Pietromonaco, P.R., & Markus, H. (1985). The nature of negative thoughts in depression. *Journal of Personality and Social Psychology, 48,* 799–807.
Pitt, B. (1973). Maternity blues. *British Journal of Psychiatry, 122,* 431–433.
Plutchik, R. (1980). *Emotion: A psychoevolutionary synthesis.* New York: Harper & Row.
Polivy, J., & Doyle, C. (1980). Laboratory induction of mood states through reading self-referential statements: Affective changes or demand characteristics? *Journal of Abnormal Psychology, 89,* 286–290.
Posner, M.I., & Snyder, C.R.R. (1975). Attention and cognitive control. In R.L. Solso (Ed.), *Information processing and cognition: The Loyola symposium.* (pp. 55–85). Hillsdale, NJ: Lawrence Erlbaum Associates.
Post, R.D., Lobitz, W.C., & Gasparikova-Krasnec, M. (1980). The utilization of positive and negative feedback in the self-evaluation responses of depressed and nondepressed psychiatric patients. *Journal of Nervous and Mental Disease, 168,* 481–486.
Post, R.M., Pickar, D., Ballenger, J.C., Naber, D., & Rubinow, D.R. (1984). Endogenous opiates in cerebrospinal fluid: Relationship to mood and anxiety. In R.M. Post & J.C. Ballenger (Eds.), *Neurobiology of Mood Disorders* (pp. 356–368). Baltimore, MD: Williams & Wilkins.
Post, R.M., Rubinow, D.R., & Ballenger, J.C. (1984). Conditioning, sensitization, and kindling: Implications for the course of affective illness. In R.M. Post & J.C. Ballenger (Eds.), *Neurobiology of Mood Disorders* (pp. 432–466). Baltimore, MD: Williams & Wilkins.
Postman, L., & Brown, D.R. (1952). The perceptual consequences of success and failure. *Journal of Abnormal and Social Psychology, 47,* 213–221.
Potter, W.Z., & Linnoila, M. (1989). Biochemical classifications of diagnostic subgroups and D-Type scores. *Archives of General Psychiatry, 46,* 269–271.
Powers, W.T. (1973a). Feedback: Beyond behaviorism. *Science, 179,* 351–356.
Powers, W.T. (1973b). *Behavior: The control of perception.* Chicago: Aldine.

Prange A. (1964). The pharmacology and biochemistry of depression. *Diseases of the Nervous System, 25*, 217–221.

Prange, A.J., Wilson, I.C., Rabon, A.M., & Lipton, M.A. (1969). Enhancement of imipramine antidepressant activity by thyroid hormone. *American Journal of Psychiatry, 126*, 39–51.

Prange, A.J., Wilson, I.C., Lara, P.P., Alltop, L., & Breese, G. (1972). Effects of thyrotropin-releasing hormone in depression. *Lancet, 2*, 999–1002.

Pribram, K.H. (1970). Feelings as monitors. In M. Arnold (Ed.), *Feelings and emotions* (pp. 41–53). New York: Academic Press.

Procidano, M.E., & Heller, K. (1983). Measures of perceived social support from friends and from family: Three validation studies. *American Journal of Community Psychology, 11*, 1–24.

Pyszczynski, T., & Greenberg, J. (1985). Depression and preference for self-focusing stimuli after success and failure. *Journal of Personality and Social Psychology, 49*, 1066–1075.

Pyszczynski, T., & Greenberg, J. (1986). Evidence for a depressive self-focusing style. *Journal of Research in Personality, 20*, 95–106.

Pyszczynski, T., & Greenberg, J. (1987). Self-regulatory perseveration and the depressive self-focusing style: A self-awareness theory of reactive depression. *Psychological Bulletin, 102*, 122–138.

Ranieri, D.J., & Zeiss, A.M. (1984). Induction of depressed mood: A test of opponent-process theory. *Journal of Personality and Social Psychology, 47*, 1413–1421.

Rehm, L.P. (1977). A self-control model of depression. *Behavior Therapy, 8*, 787–804.

Rehm, L.P. (1978). Mood, pleasant events, and unpleasant events: Two pilot studies. *Journal of Clinical and Consulting Psychology, 46*, 854–859.

Rehm, L.P. (1982). Self-management in depression. In P. Karoly, & F.H. Kanfer (Eds.), *Self management and behavior change: From theory to practice* (pp. 522–567). New York: Pergamon.

Rehm, L.P., & Plakosh, P. (1975). Preference for immediate reinforcement in depression. *Journal of Behavior Therapy and Experimental Psychiatry, 6*, 101–103.

Reich, J.W., & Zautra, A.J. (1981). Life events and personal causation: Some relationships with distress and satisfaction. *Journal of Personality and Social Psychology, 41*, 1002–1012.

Reich, J.W., & Zautra, A.J. (1988). Direct and stress-moderating effects of positive life experiences. In L.H. Cohen (Ed.), *Life events and psychological functioning: Theoretical and methodological issues* (pp. 149–180). Beverly Hills: Sage.

Reid, R.L. (1985). Premenstrual syndrome. *Current Problems in Obstetrics, Gynecology, and Fertility, 8(2)*, 1–57.

Reid, R.L., & Yen, S.S.C. (1981). Premenstrual syndrome. *American Journal of Obstetrics and Gynecology, 139*, 85–104.

Reilly, N.P. (1985). *The problems of perception and regulation in the relationship between activities and mood.* Unpublished doctoral dissertation, Dartmouth College, Hanover, NH.

Reisenzein, R. (1983). The Schachter theory of emotion: Two decades later. *Psychological Bulletin, 94*, 239–264.

Reisenzein, R., & Gattinger, E. (1982). Salience of arousal as a mediator of misattribution of transferred excitation. *Motivation and Emotion, 6*, 315–328.

Rholes, W.S., Riskind, J.H., & Lane, J.W. (1987). Emotional states and memory biases: Effects of cognitive priming and mood. *Journal of Personality and Social Psychology, 52*, 91–99.

Richards, R., Kinney, D.K., Lunde, I., Benet, M., & Merzel, A.P.C. (1988). Creativity in manic-depressives, cyclothymes, their normal relatives, and control subjects. *Journal of Abnormal Psychology, 97*, 281–288.

Richelson, E., & Pfennig, M. (1984). Blockade by antidepressants and related compounds of biogenic amine uptake into rat brain synaptosomes: Most antidepressants selectively block norepinephrine uptake. *European Journal of Pharmacology, 104*, 277–286.

Rippere, V. (1977). "What's the thing to do when you're feeling depressed?" A pilot study. *Behavior Research and Therapy, 15*, 185–191.

Riskind, J.H. (1983). Nonverbal expressions and the accessibility of life experience memories: A congruency hypothesis. *Social Cognition, 2*, 62–86.

Riskind, J.H. (1984). They stoop to conquer: Guiding and self-regulatory functions of physical posture after success and failure. *Journal of Personality and Social Psychology, 47*, 479–493.

Riskind, J.H., & Gotay, C.C. (1982). Physical posture: Could it have regulatory or feedback effects upon emotion and motivation? *Motivation and Emotion, 6*, 273–296.

Riskind, J.H., Rholes, W.S., & Eggers, J. (1982). The Velten Mood Induction Procedures: Effects on mood and memory. *Journal of Consulting and Clinical Psychology, 50*, 146–147.

Ritchie, R.G. (1986). Momentary affect and attention allocation. *Motivation and Emotion, 10*, 387–395.

Robbins, P.R., & Tanck, R.H. (1987). A study of diurnal patterns of depressed mood. *Motivation and Emotion, 11*, 37–49.

Robins, E., & Guze, S.B. (1972). Classification of affective disorders: The primary-secondary, the endogenous-reactive, and the neurotic-psychotic concepts. In T.A. Williams, D.M. Katz, & J.A. Shield (Eds.), *Recent advances in the psychobiology of depressive illnesses* (pp. 283–292.). Washington, D.C.: U.S. Government Printing Offices.

Rogers, M., Miller, N., Mayer, S., & Duval, S. (1982). Personal responsibility and salience of the request for help: Determinants of the relation between negative affect and helping behavior. *Journal of Personality and Social Psychology, 43*, 956–970.

Rook, K.S. (1984). The negative side of social interaction: Impact on psychological well-being. *Journal of Personality and Social Psychology, 46*, 1097–1108.

Rosenhan, D.L., Salovey, P., & Hargis, K. (1981). The joys of helping: Focus of attention mediates the impact of positive affect on altruism. *Journal of Personality and Social Psychology, 40*, 899–905.

Rosenhan, D.L., Underwood, B., & Moore, B.S. (1974). Affect moderates self-gratification and altruism. *Journal of Personality and Social Psychology, 30*, 546–552.

Rosenthal, N.E., Sack, D.A., Carpenter, C.J., Parry, B.L., Mendelson, W.B., & Wehr, T.A. (1985). Antidepressant effects of light in seasonal affective disorder. *American Journal of Psychiatry, 142*, 163–170.

Rosenthal, N.E., Sack, D.A., Gillin, J.C., Lewy, A.J., Goodwin, F.K., Davenport, Y., Mueller, P.S., Newsome, D.A., & Wehr, T.A. (1984). Seasonal affective disorder. *Archives General Psychiatry, 41*, 72–80.

Rosenthal, R. (1966). *Experimenter effects in behavioral research.* New York: Appleton-Century-Crofts.

Roth, D., & Rehm, L.P. (1980). Relationships among self-monitoring processes, memory, and depression. *Cognitive Therapy and Research, 4*, 149–157.

Roy-Byrne, P.P., Rubinow, D.R., Hoban, M.C., Grover, G.N., & Blank, D. (1987). TSH and prolactin responses to TRH in patients with premenstrual syndrome. *American Journal of Psychiatry, 144*, 480–484.

Rubin, E. (1915). *Synsoplevede figurer.* Copenhagen: Gyldendalska.

Rubin, E. (1921). *Visuell wahrgenommene figuren.* Copenhagen: Gyldendalska.

Rubinow, D.R., & Roy-Byrne, P. (1984). Premenstrual syndromes: Overview from a methodological perspective. *American Journal of Psychiatry, 141*, 163–172.

Rubinow, D.R., Roy-Byrne, P., Hoban, M.C., Gold, P.W., & Post, R.M. (1984). Prospective assessment of menstrually related mood disorders. *American Journal of Psychiatry, 141*, 684–686.

Ruble, D. (1977). Premenstrual symptoms: A reinterpretation. *Science, 197*, 291–292.

Ruckmick, C.A. (1936). *The psychology of feeling and emotion.* London and New York: McGraw-Hill.

Ruderman, A.J. (1983). Obesity, anxiety, and food consumption. *Addictive Behaviors, 8*, 235–242.

Ruehlman, L.S., West, S.G., & Pasahow, R.J. (1985). Depression and evaluative schemata. *Journal of Personality, 53*, 46–92.

Russell, J.A. (1979). Affective space is bipolar. *Journal of Personality and Social Psychology, 37*, 345–355.

Russell, J.A. (1980). A circumplex model of affect. *Journal of Personality and Social Psychology, 39*, 1161–1178.

Russell, J.A., & Mehrabian, A. (1977). Evidence for a three-factor theory of emotions. *Journal of Research in Personality, 11*, 273–294.

Russell, J.A., & Ridgeway, D. (1983). Dimensions underlying children's emotion concepts. *Developmental Psychology, 19*, 795–804.

Russell, J.A., & Woudzia, L. (1986). Affective judgments, common sense, and Zajonc's thesis of independence. *Motivation and Emotion, 10*, 169–184.

Ryle, G. (1949). *The concept of mind.* London: Hutchinson.

Sachar, E.J., Frantz, A., Altman, N., & Sassin, J. (1973). Growth hormone and prolactin in unipolar and bipolar depressed patients: Responses to hypoglycemia and L-dopa. *American Journal of Psychiatry, 130*, 1362–1367.

Sachar, E.J., Hellman, L., Fukushima, D.K., & Gallagher, T.F. (1970). Cortisol production in depressive illness. *Archives of General Psychiatry, 23*, 289–298.

Sackeim, H.A. (1983). Self-deception, self-esteem, and depression: The adaptive value of lying to oneself. In G. Schwartz, & D. Shapiro (Eds.), *Empirical studies of psychoanalytic theory* (pp. 101–157). Hillsdale, NJ: Erlbaum.

Sackeim, H.A., & Weber, S.L. (1982). Functional brain asymmetry in the regulation of emotion: Implication for bodily manifestations of stress. In L. Goldberger, & S. Breznitz (Eds.), *Handbook of stress: Theoretical and clinical aspects* (pp. 183–199). New York: Free Press.

Sagi, A., & Hoffman, M.L. (1976). Empathic distress in newborns. *Developmental Psychology, 12*, 175–176.

Salovey, P. (1987, August). *Mood, focus of attention, and self-relevant thought.* Paper presented at the annual meeting of the American Psychological Association, New York, NY.

Salovey, P., & Rodin, J. (1985). Cognitions about the self. In P. Shaver (Ed.), *Self, situations, and social behavior: Review of personality and social psychology* (Vol. 6, pp. 143–166). Beverly Hills: Sage.

Sandvik, E., Diener, E., & Larsen, R.J. (1985). The opponent process theory and affective reactions. *Motivation and Emotion, 9*, 407–418.

Sarason, I.G., & Sarason, B.S. (1984). *Abnormal Psychology* (4th edition). Englewood Cliffs, NJ: Prentice-Hall.

Sarnoff, I., & Zimbardo, P.G. (1961). Social behavior in stressful situations. *Journal of Abnormal and Social Psychology, 62*, 356–363.

Schachter, S. (1959). *The psychology of affiliation.* Stanford: Stanford University Press.

Schachter, S., & Singer, J.E. (1962). Cognitive, social, and psychological determinants of emotional state. *Psychological Review, 69*, 379–399.

Schaller, M., & Cialdini, R.B. (1988). The economics of empathic helping: Support for a mood management motive. *Journal of Experimental Social Psychology, 24*, 163–181.

Schare, M.L., Lisman, S.A., & Spear, N.E. (1984). The effects of mood variation on state-dependent retention. *Cognitive Therapy and Research, 8*, 387–408.

Schatzberg, A.F., Orsulak, P.J., Rosenbaum, A.H., Maruta, T., Kruger, E.R., Cole, J.O., & Schildkraut, J.J. (1982). Toward a biochemical classification of depressive disorders, IV: Heterogeneity of unipolar depressions. *American Journal of Psychiatry, 139*, 471–475.

Schatzberg, A.F., Samson, J.A., Bloomingdale, K.L., Orsulak, P.J., Gerson, B., Kizuka, P.P., Cole, J.O., & Schildkraut, J.J. (1989). Toward a biochemical classification of depressive disorders, V. Urinary catecholamines, their metabolites, and D-type scores in subgroups of depressive disorders. *Archives of General Psychiatry, 46*, 260–268.

Scheier, M.F., & Carver, C.S. (1977). Self-focused attention and the experience of emotion: Attraction, repulsion, elation, and depression. *Journal of Personality and Social Psychology, 35*, 625–636.

Schiffenbauer, A. (1974). Effect of observer's emotional state on judgments of the emotional state of others. *Journal of Personality and Social Psychology, 30*, 31–35.

Schildkraut, J.J. (1965). The catecholamine hypothesis of affective disorders: A review of supporting evidence. *American Journal of Psychiatry, 122*, 509–522.

Schildkraut, J.J. (1973). Norepinephrine metabolites as biochemical criteria for classifying depressive disorders and predicting responses to treatment: preliminary findings. *American Journal of Psychiatry, 130*, 696–699.

Schildkraut, J.J., Klerman, G.L., Hammond, R., & Friend, D.G. (1964). Excretion of 3-methoxy-4-hydroxymandelic acid (VMA) in depressed patients treated with anti-depressant drugs. *Journal of Psychiatry Research, 2*, 257–266.

Schilgen, B., & Tolle, R. (1980). Partial sleep deprivation as therapy for depression. *Archives of General Psychiatry, 37*, 267–271.

Schlenker, B.R. (1980). *Impression management: The self-concept, social identity, and interpersonal relations.* Monterey, CA: Wadsworth.

Schlosberg, H. (1952). The description of facial expressions in terms of two dimensions. *Journal of Experimental Psychology, 44*, 229–237.

Schumer, I. (1983). *Abnormal Psychology.* Lexington, MA: Heath.

Schnurr, P.P. (in press). Measuring amount of symptom change in the diagnosis of premenstrual syndrome. *Psychological Assessment: A Journal of Consulting and Clinical Psychology.*

Schnurr, P.P. (1988). Some correlates of prospectively-defined premenstrual syndrome. *American Journal of Psychiatry, 145*, 491–494.

Schwartz, G.E., Fair, P.L., Salt, P., Mandel, M.K., & Klerman, G.L. (1976). Facial muscle patterning to affective imagery in depressed and non-depressed subjects. *Science, 192*, 489–491.

Schwartz, N., & Clore, G.L. (1983). Moods, misattribution, and judgments of well-being: Informative and directive functions of affective states. *Journal of Personality and Social Psychology, 45*, 513–523.

Schwartz, N., & Clore, G.L. (1988). How do I feel about it? The informative function of affective states. In K. Fiedler, & J.P. Forgas (Eds.), *Affect, cognition and social behavior* (pp. 44–62). Toronto: Hogrefe.

Schwarz, J.C., & Pollack, P.R. (1977). Affect and delay of gratification. *Journal of Research in Personality, 11*, 147–164.

Seamon, J.G., Brody, N., & Kauff, D.M. (1983a). Affective discrimination of stimuli that are not recognized: Effects of shadowing, masking, and cerebral laterality. *Journal of Experimental Psychology: Learning, Memory, and Cognition, 9*, 544–555.

Seamon, J.G., Brody, N., & Kauff, D.M. (1983b). Affective discrimination of stimuli that are not recognized: II. Effect of delay between study and test. *Bulletin of the Psychonomic Society, 21*, 187–189.

Seeman, G., & Schwarz, J.C. (1974). Affective state and preference for immediate versus delayed reward. *Journal of Research in Personality, 7*, 384–394.

Seligman, M.E.P. (1975). *Helplessness: On depression, development, and death.* San Francisco: Freeman.

Shagass, C., & Schwartz, M. (1966). Cerebral cortical reactivity in psychotic depressions. *Archives of General Psychiatry, 6*, 235–242.

Shaver, P., & Klinnert, M. (1982). Schachter's theories of affiliation and emotion: Implications for developmental research. In L. Wheeler (Ed.), *Review of personality and social psychology* (Vol. 3, pp. 37–72). Beverly Hills: Sage.

Shaver, P., Schwartz, J., Kirson, D., & O'Connor, C. (1987). Emotion knowledge: Further exploration of a prototype approach. *Journal of Personality and Social Psychology, 52*, 1061–1086.

Shaw, D.M. (1966). Mineral metabolism, mania, and melancholia. *British Medical Journal, 2*, 262–267.

Siegel, J.M., Johnson, J.H., & Sarason, I.G. (1979). Mood states and the reporting of life changes. *Journal of Psychosomatic Research, 23*, 103–108.

Siever, L.J., & Davis, K.L. (1985). Overview: Toward a dysregulation hypothesis of depression. *American Journal of Psychiatry, 142*, 1017–1031.

Simon, H.A. (1982). Comments. In M.S. Clark, & S.T. Fiske (Eds.), *Affect and cognition: The Seventeenth Annual Carnegie Symposium on Cognition* (pp. 333–342). Hillsdale, NJ: Erlbaum.

Skelton, J.A., & Pennebaker, J.W. (1982). The psychology of physical symptoms and sensations. In G.S. Sanders, & J. Suls (Eds.), *Social psychology of health and illness* (pp. 99–128). Hillsdale, NJ: Erlbaum.

Skinner, B.F. (1953). *Science and human behavior.* New York: Macmillan.

Slife, B.D., Miura, S., Thompson, L.W., Shapiro, J.L,. & Gallagher, D. (1984). Differential recall as a function of mood disorder in clinically depressed patients: Between- and within-subject differences. *Journal of Abnormal Psychology, 93*, 391–400.

Small, S.A. (1986). The effect of mood on word recognition. *Bulletin of the Psychonomic Society, 24*, 453–455.

Smith, T.W., & Greenberg, J. (1981). Depression and self-focused attention. *Motivation and Emotion, 5*, 323–331.

Smith, T.W., Ingram, R.E., & Roth, D.L. (1985). Self-focused attention and depression: Self-evaluation, affect, and life stress. *Motivation and Emotion, 9*, 381–389.

Snyder, M., & White, P. (1982). Moods and memories: Elation, depression, and the remembering of the events of one's life. *Journal of Personality, 50*, 149–167.

Soares, A.T., & Soares, L.M. (1965). *Self-perception inventory.* Trumbull, CT: ALSO Corporation.

Solomon, R.L. (1980). The opponent-process theory of acquired motivation: The costs of pleasure and the benefits of pain. *American Psychologist, 35*, 691–712.

Solomon, R.L., & Corbit, J.D. (1974). An opponent-process theory of motivation: I. Temporal dynamics of affect. *Psychological Review, 81*, 119–145.

Stallone, F., Huba G.J., Lawlor, W.G., & Fieve, R.R. (1973). Longitudinal studies of diurnal variation in depression: A sample of 643 patient days. *British Journal of Psychiatry, 123*, 311–318.

Steele, C.M., Southwick, L.L., & Critchlow, B. (1981). Dissonance and alcohol: Drinking your troubles away. *Journal of Personality and Social Psychology, 41*, 832–846.

Steenbarger, B.N., & Aderman, D. (1979). Objective self-awareness as a nonaversive state: Effects of anticipating discrepancy reduction. *Journal of Personality, 47*, 330–334.

Stein, G., Milton, F., Bebbington, P., Wood, K., & Coppen, A. (1976). Relationship between mood and total plasma tryptophan in postpartum women. *British Medical Journal, 2*, 457.

Steiner, M. (1979). Psychobiology of mental disorders associated with child bearing. *Acta Psychiatrica Scandinavica, 60*, 449–464.

Steiner, M., Haskett, R.F., Carroll, B.J., Hays, S.E., & Rubin, R.T. (1984). Circadian hormone secretory profiles in women with severe premenstrual tension syndrome. *British Journal of Obstetrics and Gynecology, 91*, 466–471.

Steiner, M., & Haskett, R.F., Osman, J.N., Starkman, M.N., Peterson, E., Metski, R., & Carroll, B.J. (1983). The treatment of severe premenstrual dsyphoria with bromocriptine. *Journal of Psychosomatic Obstetrics and Gynecology, 2(4)*, 223–227.

Stone, A.A. (1981). The association between perceptions of daily experiences and self- and spouse-rated mood. *Journal of Research in Personality, 15*, 510–522.

Stone, A.A., Hedges, S.M., Neale, J.M., & Satin, M.S. (1985). Prospective and cross-sectional mood reports offer no evidence of a "Blue Monday" phenomenon. *Journal of Personality and Social Psychology, 49*, 129–134.

Stone, A.A., & Neale, J.M. (1984). Effects of severe daily events on mood. *Journal of Personality and Social Psychology, 46*, 137–144.

Strack, S., Blaney, P.H., Ganellen, R.J., & Coyne, J.C. (1985). Pessimistic self-preoccupation, performance deficits, and depression. *Journal of Personality and Social Psychology, 49*, 1076–1085.

Strack, S., & Coyne, J.C. (1983). Social disconfirmation of dysphoria: Shared and private reactions to depression. *Journal of Personality and Social Psychology, 44*, 798–806.

Strickland, B.R., Hale, W.D., & Anderson, L.K. (1975). Effect of induced mood states on activity and self-reported affect. *Journal of Consulting and Clinical Psychology, 43*, 587.

Strom-Olsen, R., & Weil-Malherbe, H. (1958). Hormonal changes in manic-depressive psychosis with particular reference to the excretion of catecholamines in urine. *Journal of Mental Science, 104*, 696–704.

Sulman, F.G., Levy, D., Levy, A., Pfeifer, Y., Superstine, E., & Tal, E. (1974). Ionometry of hot, dry desert winds (sharav) and application of ionizing treatment to weather-sensitive patients. *International Journal of Biometeorology, 18*, 313–318.

Swade, C., & Coppen, A. (1980). Seasonal variations in biochemical factors related to depressive illness. *Journal of Affective Disorders, 2*, 249–255.

Sweeney, P.D., Anderson, K., & Bailey, S. (1986). Attributional style in depression: A meta-analytic review. *Journal of Personality and Social Psychology, 50*, 974–991.

Tam, W.Y.K., Chan , M.Y., & Lee, P.H.K. (1985). The menstrual cycle and platelet 5-HT uptake. *Psychosomatic Medicine, 47*, 352–362.

Tassinary, L.G., Orr, S.P., Wolford, G.W., Napps, S.E., & Lanzetta, J.T. (1984). The role of awareness in affective information processing: An exploration of the Zajonc hypothesis. *Bulletin of the Psychonomic Society, 22*, 489–492.

Taub, J.M. (1980). Effects of ad lib extended-delay sleep on sensorimotor performance, memory and sleepiness in the young adult. *Physiology and Behavior, 25*, 77–87.

Taylor, D.L., Matthew, R.J., Ho, B.T., & Weinman, M.L. (1984). Serotonin levels and platelet uptake during premenstrual tension. *Neuropsychobiology, 12*, 16–18.

Taylor, J.A. (1953). A personality scale of manifest anxiety. *Journal of Abnormal and Social Psychology, 48*, 285–290.

Taylor, J.M. (1979). Plasma progesterone, oestradiol 17 beta, and premenstrual symptoms. *Acta Psychiatrica Scandanavica, 60*, 76–86.

Taylor, S.E., & Fiske, S.T. (1978). Salience, attention and attribution: Top of the head phenomena. In L. Berkowitz (Ed.), *Advances in experimental social psychology* (Vol. 10, pp. 250–288). New York: Academic Press.

Teasdale, J.D. (1983). Negative thinking in depression: Cause, effect or reciprocal relationship. *Advances in Behavioral Research and Therapy, 5*, 3–25.

Teasdale, J.D., & Fogarty, S.J. (1979). Differential effects of induced mood on retrieval of pleasant and unpleasant events from episodic memory. *Journal of Abnormal Psychology, 88*, 248–257.

Teasdale, J.D., & Russell, M.L. (1983). Differential effects of induced mood on the recall of positive, negative and neutral words. *British Journal of Clinical Psychology, 22*, 163–171.

Teasdale, J.D., & Spencer, P. (1984). Induced mood and estimates of past success. *British Journal of Clinical Psychology, 23*, 149–150.

Teasdale, J.D., & Taylor, R. (1981). Induced mood and accessibility of memories: An effect of mood state or of induction procedure? *British Journal of Clinical Psychology, 20*, 39–48.

Teasdale, J.D., Taylor, R., & Fogarty, S.J. (1980). Effects of induced elation-depression on the accessibility of memories of happy and unhappy experiences. *Behaviour Research and Therapy, 18*, 339–346.

Terenius, L., Wahlstrom, A., & Agren, H. (1977). Nalaxone (Narcan) treatment in depression: Clinical observations and effects on CSF endorphins and monoamine metabolites. *Psychopharmacology, 54*, 31–33.

Thayer, R.E. (1967). Measurement of activation through self-report. *Psychological Reports, 20*, 663–678.

Thayer, R.E. (1987a). Energy, tiredness, and tension effects of a sugar snack versus moderate exercise. *Journal of Personality and Social Psychology, 52*, 119–125.

Thayer, R.E. (1987b). Problem perception, optimism, and related states as a function of time of day (diurnal rhythm) and moderate exercise: Two arousal systems in interaction. *Motivation and Emotion, 11*, 19–36.

Thayer, S. (1980a). The effect of facial expression sequence upon judgments of emotion. *Journal of Social Psychology, 111*, 305–306.

Thayer, S. (1980b). The effect of expression sequence and expressor identity on judgments of the intensity of facial expression. *Journal of Nonverbal Behavior, 5*, 71–79.

Thibaut, J.W., & Kelley, H.H. (1959). *The social psychology of groups*. New York: Wiley,

Thoits, P.A. (1984). Coping, social support, and psychological outcomes: The central role of emotion. In P. Shaver (Ed.), *Review of personality and social psychology* (Vol. 5, pp. 219–238). Beverly Hills: Sage.

Thompson, K.C., & Hendrie, H.C. (1972). Environmental stress in primary depressive illness. *Archives of General Psychiatry, 26*, 130–132.

Thompson, W., Cowan, C., & Rosenhan, D. (1980). Focus of attention mediates the impact of negative affect on altruism. *Journal of Personality and Social Psychology, 38*, 291–300.

Titchener, E.B. (1909). *Lectures on the experimental psychology of the thought-processes*. New York: MacMillan.

Tobacyk, J. (1981). Personality differentiation, effectiveness of personality integration, and mood in female college students. *Journal of Personality and Social Psychology, 41*, 348–356.

Tomkins, S.S. (1962). *Affect, imagery, consciousness*. New York: Springer.

Tomkins, S.S. (1979). Script theory: Differential magnification of affects. In H.E.J. Howe, & R.A. Dienstbier (Eds.), *Nebraska Symposium on Motivation* (pp. 201–236). Lincoln: University of Nebraska Press.

Tomkins, S.S. (1981). The quest for primary motives: Biography and autobiography of an idea. *Journal of Personality and Social Psychology, 41*, 306–329.

Tourangeau, R., & Ellsworth, P.C. (1979). The role of facial response in the experience of emotion. *Journal of Personality and Social Psychology, 37*, 1519–1531.

Treadway, C.R., Kane, I.J., Jarrahi-Zadeh, A., & Lipton, M.A. (1969). A Psychoendocrine study of pregnancy and puerperium. *American Journal of Psychiatry, 125*, 1380–1386.

Tuomisto, J., & Tukiainen, E. (1976). Decreased uptake of 5-hydroxytryptamine in blood platelets from depressed patients. *Nature, 262*, 596–598.

Tyrer, S., & Shopsin, B. (1982). Symptoms and assessment of mania. In E.S. Paykel (Ed.), *Handbook of affective disorders* (pp. 13–23). New York: Guilford.

Underwood, B., & Froming, W.J. (1980). The mood survey: A personality measure of happy and sad moods. *Journal of Personality Assessment, 44*, 404–414.

Underwood, B., Froming, W.J., & Moore, B.S. (1977). Mood, attention, and altruism: A search for mediating variables. *Developmental Psychology, 5*, 541–542.

Underwood, B., Moore, B.S., & Rosenhan, D.L. (1973). Affect and self-gratification. *Developmental Psychology, 8*, 209–214.

Veitch, R., & Griffitt, W. (1976). Good news—Bad news: Affective and interpersonal effects. *Journal of Applied Social Psychology, 6*, 69–75.

Velten, E.J. (1968). A laboratory task for induction of mood states. *Behaviour Research and Therapy, 6*, 473–482.

Verbrugge, L.M. (1985). Triggers of symptoms and health care. *Social Science and Medicine, 20*, 855–876.

Vrbicky, K.W., Baumstark, J.S., Wells, I.C., Hilgers, T.W., Rable, W.T., & Elias, C.J. (1982). Evidence for the involvement of beta-endorphin in the human menstrual cycle. *Fertility & Sterility, 38*, 701–704.

Warr, P. (1978). A study of psychological well-being. *British Journal of Psychology, 69*, 111–121.

Warr, P., Barter, J., & Brownbridge, G. (1983). On the independence of negative and positive affect. *Journal of Personality and Social Psychology, 44*, 644–651.

Watson, D. (1988). Intraindividual and interindividual analyses of positive and negative affect: Their relation to health complaints, perceived stress, and daily activities. *Journal of Personality and Social Psychology, 54*, 1020–1030.

Watson, D., & Clark, L.A. (1984). Negative affectivity: The disposition to experience aversive emotional states. *Psychological Bulletin, 96*, 465–490.

Watson, D., Clark, L.A., & Carey, G. (1988). Positive and negative affectivity and their relation to anxiety and depressive disorders. *Journal of Abnormal Psychology, 97*, 346–353.

Watson, D., Clark, L.A., & Tellegen, A. (1984). Cross-cultural convergence in the structure of mood: A Japanese replication and a comparison with U.S. findings. *Journal of Personality and Social Psychology, 47*, 127–144.

Watson, D., & Pennebaker, J.W. (1989). Health complaints, stress, and distress: Exploring the central role of Negative Affectivity. *Psychological Review, 96*, 234–254.

Watson, D., & Tellegen, A. (1985). Toward a consensual structure of mood. *Psychological Bulletin, 98*, 219–235.

Wegner, D.M. (1988). Stress and mental control. In S. Fisher, & J. Reason (Eds.), *Handbook of life stress, cognition, and health* (pp. 685–699). New York: Wiley.

Weherenberg, W.B., Wardlaw, S.L., Frantz, A.G., & Ferin, M. (1982). Beta-endorphin in hypophyseal portal blood: Variations throughout the menstrual cycle. *Endocrinology, 111*, 879–882.

Wehr, T.A. (1984). Biological rhythms and manic depressive illness. In R.M. Post, & J.C. Ballenger (Eds.), *Neurobiology of mood disorders* (pp. 190–206). Baltimore: Williams & Wilkins.

Wehr, T.A., & Goodwin, F.K. (1981). Biological rhythms and psychiatry. In S. Arieti & H.K.H. Brodie (Eds.), *American Handbook of Psychiatry, 2nd Edition, 7*, 46–74.

Wehr, T.A. & Goodwin, F.K. (1987). Do antidepressants cause mania? *Psychopharmacology Bulletin, 23*, 61–65.
Wehr, T.A., Goodwin, F.K., Wirz-Justice, A., Craig, C., & Breitmeier, J. (1982). Forty-eight hour sleep-wake cycles in manic-depressive illness: Naturalistic observations and sleep deprivation experiments. *Archives of General Psychiatry, 39*, 559–565.
Wehr, T.A., Jacobson, F.M., Sack, D.A., Arendt, J., Tamarkin, L., & Rosenthal, N.R. (1986). Phototherapy of seasonal affective disorder. *Archives of General Psychiatry, 43*, 870–875.
Wehr, T.A., Sack, D.A., & Rosenthal, N.E. Seasonal affective disorder with summer depression and winter hypomania. *American Journal of Psychiatry, 144*, 1602–1603.
Wehr, T. A., Skwerer, R.G., Jacobsen, F.M., Sack, D.A., & Roscnthal, N.E. (1987). Eye versus skin phototherapy of seasonal affective disorder. *American Journal of Psychiatry, 144*, 753–757.
Wehr, T.A., & Wirz-Justice, A. (1982). Circadian rhythm mechanisms in affective illness and in antidepressant drug action. *Pharmacopsychiatria, 15*, 30–38.
Weiner, M.B., & White, M.T. (1982). Depression as the search for the lost self. *Psychotherapy, 19*, 491–499.
Weingartner, H., Miller, H., & Murphy, D.L. (1977). Mood-state-dependent retrieval of verbal associations. *Journal of Abnormal Psychology, 86*, 276–284.
Weissman, M.M., & Klerman, G.L. (1977). Sex differences in the epidemiology of depression. *Archives of General Psychiatry, 34*, 98–111.
Wener, A.E., & Rehm, L.P. (1975). Depressive affect: A test of behavioral hypothesis. *Journal of Abnormal Psychology, 84*, 221–227.
Wenzlaff, R.M., Wegner, D.M., & Roper, D.W. (1988). Depression and mental control: The resurgence of unwanted negative thoughts. *Journal of Personality and Social Psychology, 55*, 882–892.
Wertheim, E.H., & Schwarz, J.C. (1983). Depression, guilt, and self-management of pleasant and unpleasant events. *Journal of Personality and Social Psychology, 45*, 884–889.
Wessman, A.E. (1979). Moods: Their personal dynamics and significance. In C.E. Izard (Ed.), *Emotions in personality and psychopathology* (pp. 73–102). New York: Plenum.
Wessman, A.E., & Ricks, D.F. (1966). *Mood and personality*. New York: Holt, Rinehart & Winston.
Wetzler, S. (1985). Mood state-dependent retrieval: A failure to replicate. *Psychological Reports, 56*, 759–765.
Weyant, J. (1978). Effects of mood states, cost, and benefits on helping. *Journal of Personality and Social Psychology, 35*, 1169–1176.
Whybrow, P.C., Akiskal, H.S., & McKinney, W.T.J. (1984). *Mood disorders: Toward a new psychology*. New York: Plenum.
Whybrow, P.C., & Mendels, J. (1969). Toward a biology of depression: Some suggestions from neurophysiology. *American Journal of Psychiatry, 125*, 45–54.
Whybrow, P.C., & Prange, A.J. (1981). A hypothesis of thyroid-catecholamine-receptor interaction. *Archives of General Psychiatry, 38*, 106–113.
Wicklund, R. (1975). Objective self-awareness. In L. Berkowitz (Ed.), *Advances in experimental social psychology* (Vol. 8, pp. 233–275). New York: Academic Press.
Wicklund, R.A., & Brehm, J.W. (1976). *Perspectives on cognitive dissonance*. Hillsdale, NJ: Erlbaum.
Williams, J.M.G., & Broadbent, K. (1986). Autobiographical memory in suicide attempters. *Journal of Abnormal Psychology, 95*, 144–149.
Willner, P. (1985). *Depression: A psychobiological synthesis*. New York: Wiley-Interscience.

Wills, T.A. (1987). Downward comparison as a coping mechanism. In C.R. Snyder, & C.E. Ford (Eds.), *Coping with negative life events* (pp. 243–268). New York: Plenum.

Wilson, W. (1967). Correlates of avowed happiness. *Psychological Bulletin, 67*, 294–306.

Wilson, W.R. (1979). Feeling more than we can know: Exposure effects without learning. *Journal of Personality and Social Psychology, 37*, 811–821.

Wilson, T.D. (1985). Strangers to ourselves: The origins of accuracy of beliefs about one's own mental states. In J.H. Harvey, & G. Weary (Eds.), *Attribution in contemporary society* (pp. 9–36). New York: Academic Press.

Wilson, T.D., Laser, P., & Stone, J. (1982). Judging the predictors of one's own mood: Accuracy and the use of shared theories. *Journal of Experimental Social Psychology, 18*, 537–556.

Winton, W.M. (1986). The role of facial response in self-reports of emotion: A critique of Laird. *Journal of Personality and Social Psychology, 50*, 808–812.

Wofford, J.C. (1966). Negative ionization: An investigation of behavioral effects. *Journal of Experimental Psychology, 71*, 608–611.

Wolpe, J. (1958). *Psychotherapy by reciprocal inhibition.* Stanford: Stanford University Press.

Woodworth, R.S., & Schlosberg, H. (1954). *Experimental psychology.* New York: Holt, Rinehart, & Winston.

Wright, J., & Mischel, W. (1982). Influence of affect on cognitive social learning person variables. *Journal of Personality and Social Psychology, 43*, 901–914.

Wyer, R.S.J., & Frey, D. (1983). The effects of feedback about self and others on the recall and judgments of feedback-relevant information. *Journal of Experimental Social Psychology, 19*, 540–559.

Wyer, R.S.J., & Srull, T.K. (1986). Human cognition in its social context. *Psychological Review, 93*, 322–359.

Yalom, I.D., Lunde, D.T., Moos, R.H., & Hamburg, D.A. (1968). "Postpartum blues" syndrome: A description and related variables. *Archives of General Psychiatry, 18*, 16–27.

Youngren, M.A., & Lewinsohn, P.M. (1980). The functional relation between depression and problematic interpersonal behavior. *Journal of Abnormal Psychology, 89*, 333–341.

Zajonc, R.B. (1965). Social facilitation. *Science, 149*, 269–274.

Zajonc, R.B. (1980). Feeling and thinking: Preferences need no inferences. *American Psychologist, 35*, 151–175.

Zajonc, R.B. (1984). On the primacy of affect. *American Psychologist, 39*, 117–123.

Zanna, M.P., & Cooper, J. (1974). Dissonance and the pill: An attribution approach to studying the arousal properties of dissonance. *Journal of Personality and Social Psychology, 29*, 703–709.

Zautra, A.J., Guarnaccia, C.A., Reich, J.W., & Dohrenwend, B.P. (1988). The contribution of small events to stress and distress. In L.H. Cohen (Ed.), *Life events and psychological functioning: Theoretical and methodological issues* (pp. 123–148). Beverly Hills: Sage.

Zautra, A.J., & Reich, J.W. (1983). Life events and perceptions of life quality: Developments in a two factor approach. *Journal of Community Psychology, 11*, 121–132.

Zeiss, A.M., Lewinsohn, P.M., & Munoz, R.F. (1979). Nonspecific improvement effects in depressives using interpersonal skills training, pleasant activity schedules, or cognitive training. *Journal of Consulting and Clinical Psychology, 47*, 427–439.

Zevon, M.A., & Rounds, J.B. (1985, August). *Intraindividual mood and its relation to personality: Time-series analyses.* Paper presented at the 93rd annual convention of the American Psychological Association, Los Angeles.

Zevon, M.A., & Tellegen, A. (1982). The structure of mood change: An idiographic/nomothetic analysis. *Journal of Personality and Social Psychology, 43*, 111–122.
Zillman, D. (1978). Attribution and misattribution of excitatory reactions. In J.H. Harvey, W. Ickes, & R.F. Kidd (Eds.), *New directions in attribution research* (pp. 335–368). Hillsdale, NJ: Erlbaum.
Zillman, D. (1988). Mood management: Using entertainment to full advantage. In L. Donohew, H.E. Sypher, & E.T. Higgins (Eds.), *Communication, social cognition, and affect* (pp. 147–171). Hillsdale, NJ: Erlbaum.
Zillman, D., & Bryant, J. (1974). The effect of residual excitation on the emotional response to provocation and delayed aggressive behavior. *Journal of Personality and Social Psychology, 30*, 782–791.
Zillman, D., & Cantor, R.J. (1977). Affective responses to the emotion of a protagonist. *Journal of Experimental Social Psychology, 13*, 155–165.
Zillman, D., Johnson, R.C., & Day, K.D. (1974). Attribution of apparent arousal and proficiency of recovery from sympathetic activation affecting excitation transfer to aggressive behavior. *Journal of Experimental Social Psychology, 10*, 503–515.
Zillman, D., Katcher, A.H., & Milavsky, B. (1972). Excitation transfer from physical exercise to subsequent aggressive behavior. *Journal of Experimental Social Psychology, 8*, 247–259.
Zuckerman, M. (1979a). Attribution of success and failure revisisted, or: The motivational bias is alive and well in attribution theory. *Journal of Personality, 47*, 245–287.
Zuckerman, M. (1979b). *Sensation seeking: Beyond the optimal level of arousal.* Hillsdale, NJ: Erlbaum.
Zuckerman, M., Klorman, R., Larrance, D.T., & Spiegel, N.H. (1981). Facial, autonomic, and subjective components of emotion: The facial feedback hypothesis versus the externalizer-internalizer distinction. *Journal of Personality and Social Psychology, 41*, 929–944.
Zuckerman, M., & Lubin, B. (1965). *Manual for the Multiple Affect Adjective Check List.* San Diego: Educational and Industrial Testing Service.
Zuckerman, M., Lubin, B., Vogel, L., & Valerius, E. (1964). Measurement of experimentally induced affects. *Journal of Consulting Psychology, 28*, 418–425.
Zuroff, D.C. (1980). Distortions of memory in depressed, formerly depressed, and never depressed college students. *Psychological Reports, 46*, 415–425.
Zuroff, D.C., Colussy, S.A., & Wielgus, M.S. (1983). Selective memory and depression: A cautionary note concerning response bias. *Cognitive Therapy and Research, 7*, 223–232.

Author Index

Subject Index

Springer Series in Social Psychology
Recent Titles

Entrapment in Escalating Conflicts: A Social Psychological Analysis
Joel Brockner/Jeffrey Z. Rubin

The Attribution of Blame:
Causality, Responsibility, and Blameworthiness
Kelly G. Shaver

Language and Social Situations
Joseph P. Forgas (Editor)

Power, Dominance, and Nonverbal Behavior
Steve L. Ellyson/John F. Dovidio (Editors)

Changing Conceptions of Crowd Mind and Behavior
Carl F. Graumann/Serge Moscovici (Editors)

Changing Conceptions of Leadership
Carl F. Graumann/Serge Moscovici (Editors)

Friendship and Social Interaction
Valerian J. Derlega/Barbara A. Winstead (Editors)

An Attributional Theory of Motivation and Emotion
Bernard Weiner

Public Self and Private Self
Roy F. Baumeister (Editor)

Social Psychology and Dysfunctional Behavior:
Origins, Diagnosis, and Treatment
Mark R. Leary/Rowland S. Miller

Communication and Persuasion:
Central and Peripheral Routes to Attitude Change
Richard E. Petty/John T. Cacioppo

Theories of Group Behavior
Brian Mullen/George R. Goethals (Editors)

Changing Conceptions of Conspiracy
Carl F. Graumann/Serge Moscovici (Editors)

Controversial Issues in Social Research Methods
Jerald Greenberg/Robert G. Folger

The Social Psychology of Intergroup Conflict
Wolfgang Stroebe/Arie W. Kruglanski/Daniel Bar-Tal/Miles Hewstone (Editors)

The Social Psychology of Facial Appearance
Ray Bull/Nichola Rumsey

Attitudes and Behavioral Decisions
Arnold Upmeyer (Editor)

Springer Series in Social Psychology
Recent Titles

Intuitive Judgments of Change
Linda Silka

Stereotyping and Prejudice:
Changing Conceptions
Daniel Bar-Tal/Carl F. Graumann/Arie W. Kruglanski/
Wolfgang Stroebe (Editors)

Mood: The Frame of Mind
William N. Morris

Group Beliefs: A Conception for Analyzing
Group Structure, Processes, and Behavior
Daniel Bar-Tal

The Social Psychology of Intergroup and
International Conflict Resolution
Ron Fisher

MIX
Papier aus verantwortungsvollen Quellen
Paper from responsible sources
FSC® C105338

If you have any concerns about our products,
you can contact us on
ProductSafety@springernature.com

In case Publisher is established outside the EU,
the EU authorized representative is:
Springer Nature Customer Service Center GmbH
Europaplatz 3, 69115 Heidelberg, Germany

Printed by Libri Plureos GmbH
in Hamburg, Germany